Internet Dreams

Internet Dreams
Archetypes, Myths, and Metaphors

Mark Stefik

The MIT Press
Cambridge, Massachusetts
London, England

This book was set in Sabon by Asco Trade Typesetting Ltd., Hong Kong and was printed and bound in the United States of America.

Images of the metaphors are by Eric P. Stefik.

Library of Congress Cataloging-in-Publication Data

Internet dreams : archetypes, myths, and metaphors / Mark Stefik.
    p.   cm.
  Includes bibliographical references (p.   ) and index.
  ISBN 0-262-19373-6 (alk. paper)
  1. Information superhighway—United States. 2. Internet (Computer network)—United States. I. Stefik, Mark.
ZA3250.U6I58   1996
303.48′33—dc20   96-28249
                                                          CIP

Contents

Foreword

Metaphors ... schmetaphors? If you picked up this book, you probably already know and care about the Internet. Why then should you care about metaphors or archetypes or myths?

Why? Because the Internet can become anything we can imagine and program it to be. It is a most malleable and evolving infrastructure. Like the celebrated holodeck of the Star Trek Next Generation starships, it opens a truly endless frontier. At any given time, the net is limited by its computing power and communication capacity, but these are growing rapidly.

With such plasticity, it is how we think about the Internet that matters. The information infrastructure of the future (which is the real issue) is limited only by the vision of those who are making policy—economic, and technical decisions today. Limits to computing power and communication capacity may be the least of the problems we will face.

The Internet evolves in response to forces acting on it. Its heterogeneous structure exerts strong pressure to interlink applications, exchange digital contents, and integrate functions and services. The video function can be integrated with both e-mail and real-time meetings. The protocols that enable computers to talk to each other address critical issues of compatibility, security, and financial transactions, thus creating the open standards imperative without which little in the Internet would actually interwork.

So it works. But what is the net now and what should it be? As the Internet grows and becomes richer, both in content and in possibilities, more people care about what it becomes. Thinking about the Internet only in terms of protocols or video or meetings mixes levels and can be pretty limiting if not confusing.

So how should we think about the Internet? For a while, the "information superhighway" metaphor reigned in the press. But this metaphor has very little ability to explain either where the Internet arose or where it could go. In its place, Stefik teases out four other metaphors from current discourse about the net and puts them in perspective.

Stefik writes with a clarity of thought and with pithy, compelling examples that quickly draw readers in and encourage them to think beyond the surface meaning of the Internet. The potential social effects of immersion in Internet and Web culture are widespread, complex, and only dimly understood. Exploring this (cyber)space with Stefik is not only exhilarating, it is a growth experience for readers who are relatively new to the network. Even those of us (dinosaurs) who have been around since the Eocene of networking find it eye-opening to consider new metaphors to inform our thinking and to make facts become clearer in the telling.

Vinton G. Cerf
April 1996
Camelot

Acknowledgments

To all the people at Xerox and on the network who responded to my call for "examples of the use of the superhighway metaphor" I extend my special thanks. Warm appreciation is also due to the following friends and colleagues who participated in brainstorming sessions, read early drafts of the book, and offered their insights, suggestions, and URL's: Eric Bier, Dan Bobrow, Stu Card, Vint Cerf, Jim Davis, Marti Hearst, Giuliana Lavendel, Mark S. Miller, Matt Miller, Geoff Nunberg, Peter Pirolli, Bob Prior, Ramana Rao, George Robertson, Dan Russell, Jonathan Sheer, Stephen Smoliar, Bettie Steiger, Barbara Viglizzo, John Vittal, and Colin Williams.

Introduction

One helpful way is to think of the National Information Infrastructure as a network of highways—much like the Interstates begun in the fifties.
Vice President Albert Gore, National Press Club, December 21, 1993.

The essence of metaphor is understanding and experiencing one kind of thing in terms of another.
George Lakoff and Mark Johnson, *Metaphors We Live By*

We participate in the creation of our story. We can enact the personal myths of warrior, goddess, eternal adolescent, great mother, king or queen, master, slave, or servant of the divine.... In all these stories we choose and are chosen.... Yet we must ask: Is this who we are?
Jack Kornfield, *A Path with Heart*

We are told that the National Information Infrastructure (NII)—or, from a more global perspective, the Global Information Structure (GII)—will profoundly alter how we live, work, and play. Yet nobody knows what that infrastructure is, because it is still being invented. What it becomes depends in large part on how we think about it.

Some people see today's computer networks as the prototype of the NII. Others say it will be like cable television or the telephone system. In these views, the NII will be either more and better computers or more and better television channels or telephones. On the other hand, maybe the NII will be something altogether different and profoundly uplifting, something that taps into our collective dreams.

It's not that nobody is thinking about what the NII should be, could be, and will be. In fact, it sometimes seems that it is a matter of interest and speculation to everyone. It is the subject of Sunday newspaper columns, books, bills before Congress, hearings by various branches of government, and discussions in corporate planning sessions. Yet no article, piece of legislation, or small group in a closed room can define what the information infrastructure will be. What it eventually becomes is now emerging from *all* our collective imaginations and conversations.

When people talk about the information infrastructure, then, what do they say? One popular vision of the NII was stated in the technology position paper of the 1992 Clinton presidential campaign: "We must ... build Information Superhighways: to develop an advanced communications network, which will help companies collaborate on research and design for advanced manufacturing, allow doctors across the country to communicate, put immense resources at the fingertips of American teachers and students and much more." This quotation presents the NII in terms of what has become its most celebrated metaphor: the *Information superhighway* or the *I-way*. Although of course, it will not be a highway in the literal sense, the metaphor suggests that it will be *like* a highway. But in what sense?

The metaphors we use constantly in our everyday language profoundly influence what we do, because they shape our understanding. George Lakoff and Mark Johnson say that metaphors are pervasive because they reflect how we think, perhaps embodying deeply unconscious archetypes of personality and vision. When we change the metaphors, therefore, we change how we think about things. Because metaphors can guide our imagination about a new invention, they influence what it *can be* even before it exists. The metaphors we use suggest ideas and we absorb them so quickly that we seldom even notice the metaphor, making much of our understanding completely unconscious.

Giant Brains

In the 1950s, the main metaphor for describing computers was *giant brains*. The word *giant* was in one sense an apt description: computers were then very large. Throughout the 1960s and 1970s, most people thought of a computer as a big machine with flashing lights and spinning tapes that filled a secure, air-conditioned room and was attended by experts.

The giant brain metaphor was, however, wrong, and it was misleading. It did not tap into what we wanted to do with computers or what we could do. It failed to predict the actual future of computers or to guide their further development. It did not, for example, contribute to the vision of the personal computer, word processing, or spreadsheets, all of which came later. Computers were big, and bigness conveys the sense of power, awe, and fright we often associate with things much larger than ourselves. The metaphor would seem to predict that with progress, computers would get even bigger and more powerful. Instead, over the last twenty years they have become a lot smaller. Furthermore, their diminishing size did not correspond to any diminution in power; today's laptop computers are much more powerful than the giants of the 1960s.

The *brain* part of the metaphor was even less relevant. Brains think, but very little of what computers do corresponds to what we normally call thought. Furthermore, the term brain triggered fear. If computers are brains, what are they thinking about? Are they smarter than we are? Can they be trusted? Ultimately, the associations triggered by the metaphor of the giant brain were disempowering, for they undermined our sense of ourselves and led common wisdom astray.

The Information Superhighway Metaphor

The *information superhighway* metaphor goes back at least to 1988, when Robert Kahn proposed building a high-speed national computer network he often likened to the interstate highway system. Kahn is president and founder of the Corporation for National Research Initiatives, a not-for-profit organization created to provide leadership and funding for research and development of the NII. He is well known in the computer science community as the driving force behind the Internet and its predecessor the Advanced Research Projects Agency Network (ARPANET).

More recently Vice President Al Gore popularized the term information superhighway in his speeches. He claims he invented the term in 1979, which makes sense. The Vice President is the son of Albert Gore, Snr., who served as senator from Tennesee from 1959 through 1971 and was a force behind the Federal Aid to Highways Acts. These acts substantially increased federal funding for the national system of interstate and defense highways. Creating highways is in the Gore family tradition.

Frequently, the information superhighway is portrayed as an intricate tangle of communication lines connecting computer sites on a map of the United States. For an American, the graphic can be stirring, combining the image of the United States with a superimposed computer network that links everything together. The accompanying text describes vast quantities of data going places—life-saving medical data, pictures, and information from digital libraries. The image suggests that, like high-the network will connect us, bind us together. Why build hig' move goods around. Why build information highways?

mation. Nobody says it, but we can almost feel a subliminal message telling us: "It's the infrastructure, stupid!" Concrete highways were good things in the past. But why move only cars and trucks? Like the advertisement "It's not your father's Oldsmobile," the map speaks of a new age, the Information Age. Information highways are for the future.

The information superhighway metaphor shows up in virtually all speech and writing about the NII.

One helpful way is to think of the National Information Infrastructure is as a network of highways—much like the Interstates begun in the fifties.

Interpretation: Information networks should connect the country together and will bring economic prosperity.

On-ramps to the superhighway

Interpretation: Access to the I-way for doing business.

"... Traffic jams and gridlock"

Interpretation: Network congestion. When there is too much information travelling on the I-way, delivery is delayed.

Do you want to be in the fast lane or the slow lane?

Interpretation: Moving ahead quickly or being slowed down in traffic.

Highway robbery on the Internet

Interpretation: Unauthorized copying of digital works.

Detour the poor on the information superhighway.

Interpretation: People without money are disenfranchised because they cannot access the network.

Back roads of the information highway

Interpretation: Equivalent to slow country roads where not much business takes place.

National borders are just speed bumps on the information superhighway.

Interpretation: Information on a network can easily cross national borders without slowing down or going through customs.

Companies that hesitate risk becoming road kill on the information superhighway.

Interpretation: Businesses on the I-way will evolve quickly, and companies that do not invest quickly will be overtaken by those who act quickly.

Each example uses the highway metaphor to predict the future shape of the national information infrastructure in an attempt to influence people. Because, for example, the interstate highway system is widely credited with creating American prosperity, using the highway metaphor tacitly promises that large-scale investments in the Internet will similarly benefit the common good. The highway metaphor example also draws on the American driving experience, referring to traffic jams, gridlock, eight-lane turnpikes, toll roads, back roads, feeder roads, one-way roads, speed bumps, speed limits, and so on. A related metaphor equates a computer's user interface to the NII with an automobile's dashboard. The words *information superhighway* conjure up many other associated images.

The metaphor has become so popular that it offers serious challenges to people talking about computer networks, because it carries with it misleading meanings associated with roads. Mathew Miller, a Connecticut technology consultant, has a list of the ways regular highways differ from information highways. Highways, for example, are planned and designed, whereas information highways are self-organizing and have no central planner. Highways are constructed with taxpayer dollars; information highways will ultimately be financed mainly by private investment. Highways have fixed configurations and connect fixed physical locations; information highways have ever-changing configurations and link changing information sources. Miller uses these contrasts to help his clients avoid carrying over assumptions about highways to their thinking about information highways. He regards assumptions about the government's role in centralized planning and organization as particularly inappropriate to information highways.

The highway metaphor is, however, apt when it pictures information as traffic. Talking about one-way, two-way, and toll roads is descriptive of how bits and bytes travel on wires and gives us a mental image of information flowing around the country. Highway metaphors are thus useful for thinking about connectivity, speed, communications charges, and infrastructure. On the other hand, what is the purpose of all those bits and bytes? What do they have to do with everyday life? How adequate is the highway metaphor really?

Couldn't we, by analogy, describe the telephone system as the *voice superhighway*? Such a telephone metaphor would describe how voices travel around on wires. But when we think about the role of telephones in our lives, we're more likely to think about ringing telephones, cellular phones, answering machines, long distance rates, or how telephones let us save time, do business, and call relatives on holidays. The voice super-highway metaphor doesn't help us understand how telephones fit into our lives. In the same way, the information superhighway metaphor doesn't shed enough light on how the NII will affect our lives.

If, as we participate in the invention of the NII, we do not recognize that we are helping create it, our contribution will be unconscious. On the other hand, if we recognize that the NII is being collectively invented and reinvented, we can be aware of the possibilities and can voice our choices.

Multiple Metaphors, Richer Thinking

This book, then, is about more powerful and appropriate metaphors for thinking about the emerging information infrastructure and increasing our consciousness of invention by looking at the possibilities through different metaphors. Our focus is not current politics, nor is it a pre-scription of what the information infrastructure *should* be. In a period when new generations of digital electronics appear every year or two and when news about what's hot changes almost daily, some of the meta-phors we consider are ancient. They have appeared in various cultural forms for thousands of years and have influenced thinking about com-puters for at least fifty years. We refer to them as *metaphors for the I-way*. Here are the ones we explore in depth in the four parts of this volume.

• *The Digital Library*. The I-way as publishing and community mem-ory. This metaphor shows up in digital libraries, databases, and other archival information services. It emphasizes the publishing and storage of collected knowledge for preservation and access by a society.

• *Electronic Mail*. The I-way as a communications medium. This met-aphor shows up in the image of electronic mail used to send personal messages to each other and public messages to groups and communities.

• *Electronic Marketplace*. The I-way as a place for selling goods and services. This metaphor is used for thinking about issues of digital com-merce, digital money, and digital property.

• *Digital Worlds.* I-way as a gateway to experience. This metaphor shows up in descriptions of social settings on the network, group-ware, virtual reality, augmented reality, telepresence, and ubiquitous computing.

The goal of the work is not to create the one right metaphor for the I-way, for relying on a single metaphorical analogy would deprive us of a richer range of meanings and possibilities.

Archetypes and Myths

Metaphors connect with our consciousness in different ways and awaken our hearts in different ways. These awakenings correspond to the arche-types studied in Jungian psychology and mythology—inward elements of the psyche that reflect outward from our cultural experiences. The word *archetype* means an original model after which other, similar things are patterned. Among the numerous archetypes Jung identified are those of the hero, the child, the trickster, God, the demon, the wise old man, and the earth mother, as well as various natural processes, animals, and objects. Archetypes are not fixed; they appear in different forms, depend-ing on culture and context. Because they influence us without our being aware of them, archetypes are said to be part of the collective uncon-scious and are embedded in myths. The origins of most myths are lost in obscurity; in Greek, the word *myth* means "what they say."

In his writings about the role of myths, Mircea Eliade emphasizes their temporal qualities. Myths and fairy tales start out with "once upon a time" or "it could have happened this way." Such language seeks to create ambiguity about time, a sense of a mythical time that is qualita-tively different from ordinary, existential time. This ambiguity suggests that myths may be about the past but that they may also be about the present. Myths do not lose their relevance by virtue of being ancient because they are about how we view the world and, as such, may be outside of ordinary time.

The myths we remember and tell our children describe the kind of people we aspire to be. Many myths have central figures, and the stories of what these central figures do and what happens to them often says something important about how a community views the world. In psy-chological terms, the central figure of a myth corresponds to an archetype.

Archetypes for Internet Dreams

The four metaphors explored in this book correspond to four archetypes that have long guided our technological visions and currently figure in our thinking about the future shape of the Internet. By guiding our social invention, too, these archetypes create visions of what we want to be—as individuals and societies.

In Part 1 we consider the Digital Library Metaphor, which awakens the archetypal *keeper of knowledge* or conservator within us and reminds us to gather and preserve knowledge for future generations. Because we are a communicating species, we use information and ideas that other people, including our collective ancestors, have learned. As a species this gives us an enormous evolutionary advantage. Growing up and learning from others we come to understand and honor this archetype deeply. Variations on it include the keeper of ancient wisdom, the wise old one, the teller of stories in oral traditions, the curator of a museum, the scholar, and the librarian.

The Electronic Mail Metaphor explored in Part 2 appeals to the *communicator* within us and brings to mind our need to exchange thoughts with friends and community. There are many variations on this archetype: a person who draws extensively on interpersonal connections is called a *networker*; a *matchmaker* is someone who brings other people together; the *whistle blower* is someone who speaks out, calling public attention to a wrong. As communicators we try to keep in touch with our friends, especially on holidays, and to know what is happening in their lives. If we are politically active, we speak out on issues affecting the community. In the Internet community, the term *netizen* refers to just such a network citizen. These are all variations of the communicator archetype.

The Electronic Marketplace Metaphor in Part 3 refers to the *trader* within us, the archetype that prepares us for action and commerce. Because of its general role in getting things done, this archetype is also related to the older and more traditional archetypes of people who go out into the world to make a living, including the warrior, farmer, hunter, and gatherer archetypes. The merchant, the sea trader, the importer, the sales person, the business executive, and the bargain hunter are some of the other variations of this archetype.

In Part 4 we look at the Digital Worlds Metaphor, which awakens our inner *adventurer*, reminding us to explore new experiences and seek out the spice of life that fires the imagination. Variations on the adventurer archetype are the explorer, the ranger, the pathfinder, the mountain man, and the undersea treasure hunter. At all stages of life, people feel the need to seek out new experiences, but young people are especially eager to see the world before settling down. The person changing careers in mid-life and the older person who steps out of his or her accustomed role to give something to the community are also variations on the adventurer archetype.

The keeper of knowledge, the communicator, the trader, or the adventurer may be either male or female, as fits the occasion. To invent something as important as the information infrastructure we need to draw on all our best and fullest selves. These archetypes, with their deep and ancient roots in many cultures, represent what we see in others, but they are also parts of ourselves. This shared experience of cultural archetypes is part of what makes us what we are. Our goal in bringing them to mind is to enliven our imagination, so that when we make choices about the information infrastructure we draw on all the richness of the people we are.

Building the Highway

If, as we are told, the information infrastructure will have profound effects on how we live, work, and play, then what is at stake is not just ways of describing a technology but, more crucially, ways of describing ourselves as we wish to be. More potent than our view of technology is our view of ourselves. The I-way metaphors always refer back to ourselves—as the users of the computer networks or the participants in on-line communities. What do we see ourselves doing with the I-way? How do we see ourselves collectively as members of various on-line groups? Our search for understanding of the I-way is, ultimately, a search for ourselves and the future we choose to inhabit.

Highways connect civilization together. They are so important for moving people, goods, and services that they are usually fur???
of the infrastructure that serves a broad social good. In the

Robert Louis Stevenson persuaded the tribal chiefs of Samoa to cut a road through the wilderness. When it was opened, Stevenson said, "Our road is not built to last a thousand years, yet in a sense it is. When a road is once built, it is a strange thing how it collects traffic, how every year as it goes on, more and more people are found to walk thereon, and others are raised up to repair and perpetuate it" (*Vailima Letters*).

Some of the most important roads being built today are the information highways. These highways are entering our lives; they connect us to each other and reduce the distances between us. We can use them to create electronic communities and to discover our place in communities larger than our physical neighborhoods. They can help us to "think globally and act locally." In shaping what the information infrastructure will become, we are also choosing what we want to be.

Part 1

The Digital Library Metaphor: The I-Way as Publishing and Community Memory

We are in a transition between the print revolution, which is not yet over, and the electronic revolution, which is not quite underway; librarians are caught in the middle.

—Giuliana A. Lavendel, speaking on virtual libraries

The Goal of Project Gutenberg is to Give Away One Trillion Etext Files by December 31, 2001. [10,000 × 100,000,000 = Trillion] This is ten thousand titles each to one hundred million readers.

—From on-line information about Project Gutenberg

I will give the aphorisms as I go along, crediting them to a fictitious sage, "Kahuna Nui," and if they contain the words of great teachers of various ages, do not be surprised, for each one of those was indeed a "Keeper of the Secret."

—Max Freedom Long, *Growing into Light*

I have come to value the teachings, stories, and daily examples of living which they have shared with me.... I wish more people would share the ways of their grandmothers. I think it would help the present world situation if we all learned to value and respect the ways of the grandmothers—our own as well as everyone else's.

—Beverly Hungry Wolf, *The Ways of My Grandmothers*

We are born into a world rich in art, invention, and knowledge. Where does it all come from? According to many ancient myths, fire—the most common symbol of knowledge—came from the gods and was brought to mankind by a fire bringer. In western mythology, this fire bringer is usually Prometheus, a titan who stole fire from the gods on Mt. Olympus. In the Greek myth, he hid a spark in a stalk of fennel and carried it to his human friends. This legend is still celebrated on Easter Sunday in Greece, where people carry fennel stalks containing the Easter flame from their churches to their homes. In the Prometheus story, fire brought humanity power it would wield forever, and the gods were not pleased. Zeus punished Prometheus by chaining him to a rock for all eternity and sending an eagle to pluck out his liver, which grew back, every day.

In his *Universal Myths*, Alexander Eliot identifies several other legends about the fire bringer. In Peru, Australia, and Mexico, the fire bringer appears as a hummingbird. In the Peruvian myth of the Jivaro Indians a man named Takkea, invents fire but keeps it secret. One day his wife happens upon Himbui, the hummingbird, as he flutters helplessly on a path. She brings him into the house to warm him by the secret fire, but when she turns her eyes away for a moment, Himbui dips his tail in the fire and flies out of the house to share the flame with others. The fire bringer myth of the Djuan of northern Australia is similar and explains the origin of the hummingbird's two long flashing tail feathers. Although the fire bringer is not punished in these versions, the myths clearly identify fire as an important secret. Among the tribes of the American Northwest, the fire bringer is a raven; in the Plains tribes he is coyote; and on the Andaman Islands in the Bay of Bengal he is a kingfisher.

Other myths tell of the origin of metalworking, healing powers, weaving, agriculture, and fishing. In all these stories, knowledge is at first secret and is either discovered by a human being or stolen from the gods. As knowledge had to be kept safe for the people, early societies preserved it in their rituals and oral traditions, memorizing the myths and stories and passing them along from generation to generation.

Myths and Archetypes for Awakening the Keeper of Knowledge

The honor accorded this collective knowledge is reflected in attitudes toward the keeper of knowledge, who may be the teller of old tales, the wise elder, the singer of songs, or the priest. Modern stories sometimes see libraries as holy places and praise scholars who spend years in them doing research. At the Xerox corporation, where I work, stories about Chester Carlson, inventor of the xerographic process, tell how he spent years in the New York Public Library researching his invention. Today, we view often assign libraries the almost sacred trust of preserving and disseminating all knowledge.

Libraries collect information from the past and preserve it for the future. If libraries were only warm, comfortable places to read, they would be no different from the combination coffeeshops and bookstores that dot upscale neighborhoods across the country. But libraries have other properties that make them special. They let us pick up books, take them home, read them, and return them when we are finished; we never have to buy them. Libraries have catalogs that make it possible to find a book by topic, title, or author. Bookstores approximate this by arranging books by subject, but most do not use standard cataloging systems and simply order books within sections alphabetically by the author's last name. Libraries also offer a degree of comprehensiveness no bookstore can match. They contain many books and other materials that are too old or obscure to be commercially profitable. Finally, some libraries have inner sanctums where they keep rare books and unpublished historical archives. Thus, libraries, unlike commercial bookstores, play an important role in the preservation of our cultural and community memories.

As digital networks proliferate, the idea of a the digital library based on this keeper of knowledge archetype can also guide our intuitions about the new information infrastructure.

The Digital Library Initiative

In September 1993, the three largest federal sponsors of scientific research in the United States—the National Science Foundation (NSF), the Advanced Research Projects Agency (ARPA), and the National Space Agency (NASA)—announced a joint initiative to fund research on digital libraries. The term *digital library* goes back at least to 1988, when Robert Kahn and Vinton Cerf of the Corporation for National Research Initiatives published their "Open Architecture for a Digital Library System."

But what is a digital library? For people familiar with public libraries in big cities, a library is a massive stone building with steps leading up to the front door. There are rows of card catalogs and long shelves of books inside. The term *library* connotes an institution for collecting knowledge and keeping it in the public trust. Today, however, in computer-aware cities like Palo Alto, California, many library buildings are single story, and the card catalog is a row of computer stations. Nonetheless, the basic functions of all libraries are the same; they exist to collect worthwhile knowledge and information, organize and preserve it, and make it available to the community.

The digital library initiative reflects the elements of the library metaphor, updated for digital access. It begins by sketching an inventory of information sources already accessible on the Internet.

Today, the network connects some information sources that are a mixture of publicly available (with or without charge) information and private information shared by collaborators. They include reference volumes, books, journals, newspapers, national phone directories, sound and voice recordings, images, video clips, scientific data (raw data streams from instruments and processed information), and private information services such as stock market reports and private newsletters. These information sources, when connected electronically through a network, represent important components of an emerging, universally accessible, digital library.

The initiative statement also points to a key problem for research to address. It is not how to connect everybody to a network—analogous to "building more branches of the information highway"—but how to digitize even more information and organize it so that people can find it easily. The initiative is funding research in capturing and organizing the information—including text, images, sound, and speech—and in developing new ways to search for information and organize, index, describe, abstract, retrieve, and visualize it.

The creation of a major funded research program on digital libraries shows that the digital library metaphor is now being actively used to guide invention of the National Information Infrastructure (NII). The metaphor carries many of the older values and traditional assumptions about libraries over to the design of the new infrastructure.

The Deep Structure of the Library Metaphor

Because we are so familiar with book libraries, we look at them without seeing them deeply. The deep structure of the digital library metaphor lies in our assumptions about libraries and how they work in our lives.

We begin our discussion, therefore, by considering the books in a traditional library, looking first at the creation of those books. It is obvious (but not always taken into account) that the context of traditional libraries includes writers and editors. Writers write and editors determine which books are worth publishing. They control access to the printing presses and the distribution channels of publishers. Publishers publish the books, have them printed, and ship copies to wholesalers, libraries, and bookstores. Without writers and publishers, there would be no libraries. At the library itself, professionals select and purchase books for their patrons and catalog them.

When patrons come to a library, they search for books. Sometimes they use catalogs; sometimes they browse; sometimes they consult a reference librarian; and sometimes they look for a book that someone has recommended to them. The classification system used in many school and local libraries is the Dewey Decimal system; the Library of Congress (LC) system is used in most university and technical libraries. A book-classification system provides a number for each of a vast set of topics. Although no classification system is perfect, most users find that they work very well. If you don't know what book you want, you first you look up a topic and get the number for a particular book. Then you go to the bookshelf corresponding to that number. Even if the book you looked up is checked out, the chances are good that the neighboring books on the shelf will interest you; they might even be better than the book you were looking for. In this process, even if you start not knowing exactly what you want, you often end up with the information you need. Virtually all libraries also have sophisticated catalogs to their collections created by trained librarians. Traditionally, these catalogs are organized on cards in drawers and contain spelling variants and cross-references. When, for example, a name like Peter Ilich Tchaikovsky appears, there will also be cross-references to variants like Pjotr Iljics Csajkovszkij or Petr Il'ich Chaikovskii. If you look up a word like *bog* in the card catalog, you may find an entry saying "See also: Peatlands; Fens; Swamps, Northern; Muskeg; Forests, Semi-Open Lowland Needleleaf; Carbon Sinks; Carnivorous Plants; Sphagnum Moss; Vertical File: Bogs." In an April 1994 article in *The New Yorker*, Nicholson Baker and Michael Gorman characterize card catalogs as distinctive and important works of scholarship, developed over decades or even centuries. They are a real intellectual achievement by generations of librarians.

Without literacy, books would be unimportant. So digital literacy, whatever that turns out to mean, is an underlying assumption about digital libraries. Literacy is so ubiquitous in the modern world that we look at it without noticing it. Literate people often assume that almost everyone in the world is literate; when they learn otherwise, they do not understand why people lack literacy. Yet the widespread distribution of reading and writing skills literate societies require can only be achieved and maintained by a highly developed educational system. In the United States widespread—but far from perfect—literacy is largely a consequence of the nineteenth-century creation of public schools. Schools not only teach reading and writing but also how to look up information.

Printed books themselves have many deep connotations that can easily go unnoticed. In the printed book, there is an asymmetry of power between authors and readers. Once a book has surmounted the hurdles and quality checks leading to publication and distribution, it acquires a sense of permanence as "the printed word." It is often said that authors "write for posterity." Even if a book is vocally criticized when the shouting is over, the inked words on paper remain, and last longer than the spoken attack. The terms "author" and "authority" have the same linguistic roots. Over time the durability and immutability of print gives rise to a social attribution of authority to the author.

Modern print in most literate societies is also based on a notion of ownership of *intellectual property*. Intellectual property is governed by laws about copyright, patent, and trade secrets; of these, copyright is the most relevant to printed works. Because they require considerable effort and investment to develop, copyright law inhibits a second publisher from copying works and underselling the original book. This has not always been so, and copyright law has developed through a path of experience in trying other approaches to achieving the social good of making high-quality works available to the public.

The traditional library as we have described it is, therefore, far more than a place for storing collected knowledge; it is part of a social system involving social roles, literacy, and intellectual-property law—all of which are implied and assumed in the digital library metaphor.

Challenging Assumptions About Libraries

The digital library metaphor can mislead us, however, if we overlook what is different about the digital realm. To invent the NII, we cannot simply take the unexamined image of a traditional library, "digitize it," and assume that the resulting image reflects what the NII should be. To use the digital library metaphor to describe and understand the emerging national information infrastructure, we need to distinguish between what is fundamental about libraries and what is changing.

We can begin with the social roles surrounding the writing of digital works. In the traditional library context, writers write books. In a digital library, many different kinds of "writers" can record digital works. Thus, "writings" can include not only text and illustrations, but also music, animations, digital movies, video games, and computer software. These works are "all bits and bytes" in the digital realm, and multimedia forms intermingle the bits. This diversity fundamentally affects issues of literacy. The literacy required to watch a movie, listen to music, or use a computer program is different from the literacy required to read a book.

Because libraries have an enduring role in education and literacy, we usually assume that people have learned to read before they use a library. For a digital library, we would probably assume that people have to be trained in digital literacy before they can use a digital library. In practice, this has *not* been true, and the relative unavailability of such training has contributed to the mystique and frustration associated with first-time use of computer networks; the practical and technical hurdles inhibit many people from even trying. We underestimate the education needed to take advantage of digital libraries. Whereas many schools provide some training in the use of print libraries, there are far fewer corresponding classes for digital libraries. On the other hand, new ways to use digital libraries that require less literacy are being created; for example, software that reads text out loud could make computer-accessible libraries available to people with visual handicaps or a limited command of written language.

The changes that are creating the information networks may themselves fundamentally alter the publishing business. In paper-and-print publishing, publishers control access to expensive presses and choose which books to publish. In the desktop publishing world, and even more so in the digital and electronic world, access to production and distribution channels need not be so highly capitalized. Three of the fundamental economic factors affecting present-day publishing industry are printing costs, inventory costs, and transportation costs. Because digital works can be copied at nominal costs, stored in almost no space, and transported instantly anywhere in the world, writers can be their own publishers.

For digital library users, however, eliminating editors and publishers—who in the present system stand with the author to warrant the quality of a work—means facing a vast array of digital works of indeterminate quality and value. In addition, whereas traditional librarians are experts in selecting books that are both suitable and of high enough quality for their communities, a digital library that is part of a system that lacks not only editors and publishers but also human librarians, provides no evaluations of the works it supplies. Without publishers and librarians, the perceived value of the collection in a digital library can be very low.

Like traditional libraries, digital libraries need catalogs. Indeed, many libraries now use computers-created on-line catalogs, thanks largely to the Ohio College Libraries Center (OCLC), which shares its database of twenty-six million entries with libraries nationwide. Not all digital catalogs are as richly detailed as our examples of Tchaikovsky spelling variants or cross-references to bog suggest. There are, however, two important advantages of computer-based approaches. One advantage is that catalogs created by librarians can be augmented by automatic word analysis of texts. For example, when I searched under the term *bog* in a CD-ROM version of *Grolier's Multimedia Encyclopedia,* I found thirty-three articles including "swamp, marsh, and bog; bayou; heath; drainage systems; L'Anse aux Meadows; marsh; and peat moss." This analysis may not yet be as complete as human cross-referencing, but it is automatic and can be a useful supplement to other catalogs. A second advantage of computer catalogs is the ability to spread the cost of creating richly detailed catalogs through database sharing, as in OCLC, or through competition among commercial services that may in the future provide indexing services. *Encyclopedia Britannica,* which has an on-line information service with the slogan "your gateway to a world of information," sees the digital encyclopedia as only the starting point. They envision using the encyclopedia to let readers connect with other on-line information services, such as the wire services or on-line news magazines. The browsing and indexing services of the encyclopedia could then organize access to this larger world of information. It might, for example, include a synonym search in all queries; if I ask for articles about "public riots," it could automatically look for articles about "public disturbances," "civil disobedience," "campus unrest," and so on. If I ask for articles on Somalia, it could index historical summaries of the protectorates, articles about indigenous culture from archeological and religious sources, and news articles about current events. Although such knowledge-based search services are not yet generally available, they are well within the state of the art.

Libraries serve communities by making information available to the public and by preserving and archiving selected information. The Internet includes collections of material designated as digital libraries, but it also includes much transient information. Anyone with the right computer accounts can post information on the net, as either mail or web pages. But because only a small minority of people putting information on the network have the sensibilities of librarians, little of the information that appears there endures. Although the net offers the possibility of vast bodies of interlinked knowledge, a user following a link frequently learns from a network server that the information has disappeared. In this way, much of the network is more like a digital bulletin board than a digital library.

In all forms of paper publishing, the economics of mass production preclude publishing some works that appeal only to specialists. Electronic publishing need not work that way. Consider the electronic journal. A journal without printing costs could reasonably publish a twenty-thousand-word article about an obscure topic of interest to only a few specialists. With interactive user interfaces for reading, the average reader need not be burdened by the additional flood of information. The more obscure or specialized information would appear in interactive sidebars so that a reader would click for more information according to the degree of interest.

Books are intended to be easily accessible to everyone; to get a book at a library we need only a library card. We can read it in any reasonably comfortable and well-lit place, whereas reading a digital book requires a device such as a computer. A major advantage of a networked library is that it could be available twenty-four hours a day, a real treat where cutbacks in community services have reduced the operating hours of local libraries. However, there is a potential that many people would not have access to digital works. As long as expensive devices like computers are needed to read them, an economic barrier would prevent all but the privileged from gaining access to collections.

At present, the wholesale copying of books is inhibited both by copyright law and the bother of photocopying and binding books. On current general-purpose computers, however, it is very easy to copy digital works. With a single command, one can copy words, paragraphs, and even entire encyclopedias. In principle, of course, such copying is out-lawed by copyright law; yet, as publishers of computer software and video tapes understand, it is almost impossible to protect copyrights when the means of copying are readily available to millions. In 1996, it is still much more convenient and cost-effective for people to make copies dishonestly than it is to find the owners and pay the fees. Changes in technology that can completely change this situation may soon be available. We discuss these technologies in Part 3 in "Letting Loose the Light" (p. 219). These techniques, which allow for the "loan" of digital works, could provide new sources of revenue for libraries.

Beyond the Digital Library Metaphor

We began our discussion of the implications of the digital library meta-phor for the information infrastructure with an observation about literacy and preliterate societies. In literate societies literacy, which lets a person in one place convey information (via writing) to someone at a distant place and time, is often a matter of some considerable pride. People in literate societies tend to view preliterate societies as backward. It may surprise them to learn that preliterate societies often regard literacy as a step backwards. Egyptian mythology tells of the god Thoth, who had the head of an ibis. When he taught humans how to write, the sun god, Ra, asked him why he had done that, saying with a laugh that people would simply write things down and then forget them!

A wonderful account of a nonwriting society and its relationship to writing is in Malidoma Somés's *Of Water and the Spirit*. Nonwriting societies rely on oral traditions, in which learning is experiential and stories full of meaning are told by skilled keepers of tales. Such societies distrust readers and see writing as an inadequate method of conveying knowledge. For them, text is but a poor substitute for experience, as the frozen word of an invisible author is a poor substitute for a traditional story adapted by a trusted teller.

In an oral tradition, wisdom and knowledge are in the storyteller and are conveyed by stories. If a library is intended to contain knowledge and wisdom, could not a digital library also contain the storyteller? For example, the same networks that transport words can also transport audio recordings and movies and allow us to watch a recorded performance of a storyteller. Many community libraries, in fact, already lend out video tapes. In a culture of oral tradition, however, a storyteller is not a recording, and two tellings of a tale are never identical. Each one is modified in some way to fit the situation and the listeners. Obviously, a static recording lacks this variation and vitality. To regain the aliveness of the oral tradition, we need to reach back through the book to the author, or back through the tale to the storyteller. This process of reaching back through our metaphors of the information network would bring us closer to the fourth, the digital-world metaphor, which we explore in Part 4. In a digital world, we could interact with the storyteller and hear a story that is meant for us at the moment we hear it.

In modern society, libraries are not the only institutions that preserve knowledge for the future. A related institution is the museum; in fact, the very word *museum* harks back to western myths of fire bringers and purveyors of other knowledge. In the mythology of ancient Greece, the arts and sciences were presided over by the nine muses, whence *museum*, a place where fine art—and artifacts—are displayed. Thus, there are natural-history museums, art museums, technology museums, film museums, historical museums, and so on. On the network, museum collections of Civil War photographs are available through the U.S. Library of Congress; and Bill Gates, the founder of Microsoft, has bought the rights to distribute digital images of certain famous works of art. In India, a virtual museum to give digital access to art works from many periods and cultures is being planned. In 1990, Ranjit Makkuni of Xerox created a multimedia exhibit of Thangka paintings at the M. H. de Young Memorial Museum in San Francisco (described in an excerpt from Makkuni's article in this part). The exhibit, an experiment in the digital preservation of a disappearing cultural form, is a prime example of the keeper of knowledge archetype.

In the traditional library, books are passive and separate objects. Suppose that a library has books containing knowledge about X (hunting) and Y (the design of guided projectiles). Suppose that a reader wants to understand how to build a better bow and arrow for hunting (Z). In effect, the knowledge he wants is $Z = X + Y$. In the traditional library, this "knowledge additivity" takes place entirely in the mind of the reader.

Among artificial-intelligence (AI) researchers, there is a good deal of interest in finding ways to build knowledge servers that can work together as the human mind does in this example. Marvin Minsky, one of the founders of the field of artificial intelligence, imagined a few years ago a conversation between an old-timer and some children: "Do you remember when the books in the library did not even talk to each other?"

As yet, the prospects for such knowledge additivity are remote, although a few AI researchers have made some contributions in this area. What is most interesting, however, is that people are now asking this kind of question. If digital libraries can include storytellers, then they may also be able to contain experts. We can imagine bringing these experts together for discussion of a question; the session would probably begin by establishing a common terminology. Each person would bring different strengths, metaphors, and methods to the understanding of any given problem. On such an occasion, the digital library metaphor would overlap with the metaphors of communication in Part 2 and digital worlds in Part 4 of this book.

The examples above suggest how the digital library metaphor can spur the imagination of those—perhaps all of us—who will shape the National Information Infrastructure. The core values and archetypes of the digital library metaphor are about cultural preservation. The articles from which we have excerpted in this part carry forward these themes. Some of them were written before the term *digital library* was coined. Yet each one offers its own vision of what digital libraries could be.

Excerpt from "As We May Think"

Vannevar Bush

Connections

In myths of the origin of knowledge like the story of Prometheus, knowledge is a valuable, and rare thing. When we think about libraries, we do not usually think of them as overflowing with knowledge; somehow there is always enough shelf space. This is not the way Vannevar Bush saw the library in 1945 when he wrote the article this piece is taken from. For Bush, human knowledge is growing at a prodigious rate and greatly exceeds society's ability to make use of it. The value of knowledge is not in its rarity but in our ability to find the golden needle in the information haystack, and to make sense of the haystack as a whole. To address these problems, Bush argues that we need to reinvent the library.

His article reflects a visionary image of a digital library from a period long before computers were widely used in the public sector. His view also reaches back well beyond the traditional library to a library that merges personal and public records. The hypertext and personal computers that would make it possible to realize his ideas did not exist for another thirty years. Nonetheless, Bush's vision of how to handle information has inspired many people working in computer and information science. His ideas, though early, were not impractical; systems similar in their essential from to those he envisioned appeared in hypertext systems in the mid-1970s and on the Internet in about 1992.

Of what lasting benefit has been man's use of science and of the new instruments which his research brought into existence? First, they have increased his control of his material environment. They have improved his food, his clothing, his shelter; they have increased his security and released him partly from the bondage of bare existence. They have given him increased knowledge of his own biological processes so that he has had a progressive freedom from disease and an increased span of life. They are illuminating the interactions of his physiological and psychological functions, giving the promise of an improved mental health.

Science has provided the swiftest communication between individuals; it has provided a record of ideas and has enabled man to manipulate and to make extracts from that record so that knowledge evolves and endures throughout the life of a race rather than that of an individual.

There is a growing mountain of research. But there is increased evidence that we are being bogged down today as specialization extends. The investigator is staggered by the findings and conclusions of thousands of other workers—conclusions which he cannot find time to grasp, much less to remember, as they appear. Yet specialization becomes increasingly necessary for progress, and the effort to bridge between disciplines is correspondingly superficial.

Professionally, our methods of transmitting and reviewing the results of research are generations old and by now are totally inadequate for their purpose,

• • •

Our ineptitude in getting at the record is largely caused by the artificiality of systems of indexing. When data of any sort are placed in storage, they are filed alphabetically or numerically, and information is found (when it is) by tracing it down from subclass to subclass. It can be in only one place, unless duplicates are used; one has to have rules as to which path will locate it, and the rules are cumbersome. Having found one item, moreover, one has to emerge from the system and re-enter on a new path.

The human mind does not work that way. It operates by association. With one item in its grasp, it snaps instantly to the next that is suggested by the association of thoughts, in accordance with some intricate web of trails carried by the cells of the brain. It has other characteristics, of course; trails that are not frequently followed are prone to fade, items are not fully permanent, memory is transitory. Yet the speed of action, the intricacy of trails, the detail of mental pictures, is awe-inspiring beyond all else in nature.

Man cannot hope fully to duplicate this mental process artificially, but he certainly ought to be able to learn from it. In minor ways he may even improve, for his records have relative permanency. The first idea, however, to be drawn from the analogy concerns selection. Selection by association, rather than by indexing, may yet be mechanized. One cannot hope thus to equal the speed and flexibility with which the mind follows an associative trail, but it should be possible to beat the mind decisively in regard to the permanence and clarity of the items resurrected from storage.

Consider a future device for individual use, which is a sort of mechanized private file and library. It needs a name, and, to coin one at random, "memex" will do. A memex is a device in which an individual stores his books, records, and communications, and which is mechanized so that it may be consulted with exceeding speed and flexibility. It is an enlarged intimate supplement to his memory.

It consists of a desk, and while it can presumably be operated from a distance, it is primarily the piece of furniture at which he works. On the top are slanting translucent screens, on which material can be projected for convenient reading. There is a keyboard, and sets of buttons and levers. Otherwise it looks like an ordinary desk.

In one end is the stored material. The matter of bulk is well taken care of by improved microfilm. Only a small part of the interior of the memex is devoted to storage, the rest to mechanism. Yet if the user inserted five thousand pages of material a day it would take him hundreds of years to fill the repository, so he can be profligate and enter material freely.

Most of the memex contents are purchased on microfilm ready for insertion. Books of all sorts, pictures, current periodicals, newspapers, are thus obtained and dropped into place. Business correspondence takes the same path. And there is provision for direct entry. On the top of the memex is a transparent platen. On this are placed longhand notes, photographs, memoranda, all sorts of things. When one is in place, the depression of a lever causes it to be photographed onto the next blank space in a section of the memex film, dry photography being employed.

There is, of course, provision for consultation of the record by the usual scheme of indexing. If the user wishes to consult a certain book, he taps its code on the keyboard, and the title page of the book promptly appears before him, projected onto one of his viewing positions. Frequently used codes are mnemonics so that he seldom consults his code book; but when he does, a single tap of a key projects it for his use. Moreover, he has supplemental levers. On deflecting one of these levers to the right he runs through the book before him, each paper in turn being projected at a speed which just allows a recognizing glance at each. If he deflects it further to the right, he steps through the book ten pages at a time; still further at one hundred pages at a time. Deflection to the left gives him the same control backwards.

A special button transfers him immediately to the first page of the index. Any given book of his library can thus be called up and consulted with far greater facility than if it were taken from a shelf. As he has several projection positions, he can leave one item in position while he calls up another. He can add marginal notes and comments. taking advantage of one possible type of dry photography, and it could even be arranged so that he can do this by a stylus scheme, such as is now employed in the telautograph seen in railroad waiting rooms, just as though he had the physical page before him.

All this is conventional, except for the projection forward of present-day mechanisms and gadgetry. It affords an immediate step, however, to associative indexing, the basic idea of which is a provision whereby any item may be caused at will to select immediately and automatically another. This is the essential feature of the memex. The process of tying two items together is the important thing.

When the user is building a trail, he names it, inserts the name in his code book, and taps it out on his keyboard. Before him are the two items to be joined, projected onto adjacent viewing positions. At the bottom of each there are a number of blank code spaces, and a pointer is set to indicate one of these on each item. The user taps a single key, and the items are permanently joined. In each code space appears the code word. Out of view, but also in the code space, is inserted a set of dots for photocell viewing; and on each item these dots by their positions designate the index number of the other item.

Thereafter, at any time, when one of these items is in view, the other can be instantly recalled merely by tapping a button below the corresponding code space. Moreover, when numerous items have been thus joined together to form a trail, they can be reviewed in turn, rapidly or slowly, by deflecting a lever like that used for turning the pages of a book. It is exactly as though the physical items had been gathered together from widely separated sources and bound together to form a new book. It is more than this, for any item can be joined into numerous trails.

The owner of the memex, let us say, is interested in the origin and properties of the bow and arrow. Specifically he is studying why the short Turkish bow was apparently superior to the English long bow in the skirmishes of the Crusades. He has dozens of possibly pertinent books and articles in his memex. First he runs through an encyclopedia, finds an interesting but sketchy article, leaves it projected. Next, in a history, he finds another pertinent item, and ties the two together. Thus he goes, building a trail of many items. Occasionally he inserts a comment of his own, either linking it into the main trail or joining it by a side trail to a particular item. When it becomes evident that the elastic properties of available materials had a great deal to do with the bow, he branches on a side trail which takes him through textbooks on elasticity and tables of physical constants. He inserts a page of longhand analysis of his own. Thus he builds a trail of his interest through the maze of materials available to him.

And his trails do not fade. Several years later, his talk with a friend turns to the queer ways in which a people resist innovations, even of vital interest. He has an example, in the fact that the outranged Europeans still failed to adopt the Turkish bow. In fact, he has a trail on it. A touch brings up the code book. Tapping a few keys projects the head of the trail. A lever runs through it at will, stopping at intersecting items, going off on side excursions. It is an interesting trail, pertinent to the discussion. So he sets a reproducer in action, photographs the whole trail out, and passes it to his friend for insertion in his own memex, there to be linked into the more general trail.

Wholly new forms of encyclopedias will appear, ready-made with a mesh of associative trails running through them, ready to be dropped into the memex and there amplified. The lawyer has at his touch the associated opinions and decisions of his whole experience and of the experience of friends and authorities. The patent attorney has on call the millions of issued patents, with familiar trails to every point of his client's interest. The physician, puzzled by a patient's reactions, strikes the trail established in studying an earlier similar case, and runs rapidly through analogous case histories, with side references to the classics for the pertinent anatomy and histology. The chemist, struggling with the synthesis of an organic compound, has all the chemical literature before him in his laboratory, with trails following the analogies of compounds, the side trails to their physical and chemical behavior.

The historian, with a vast chronological account of a people, parallels it with a skip trail which stops only on the salient items, and can follow at any time contemporary trails which lead him all over civilization at a particular epoch. There is a new profession of trail blazers, those who find delight in the task of establishing useful trails through the enormous mass of the common record. The inheritance from the master becomes not only his additions to the world's record, but for his disciples the entire scaffolding by which they were erected.

Reflections

Although Bush's vision is expressed in the context of scientific literature, it also more generally relevant to the preservation of human knowledge, a key role of traditional libraries. But Bush's concept of the memex also extends the spirit of the library. As he says, "Science has ... provided a record of ideas and has enabled man to manipulate and to make extracts from that record so that knowledge evolves and endures throughout the life of a race rather than that of an individual." Bush foresaw the possibility of merging personal and public records through annotations and the value of recording not only the information but also trails through it created by users. His view of the memex as a desk-sized piece of furniture is not as crucial as the ability it provides to annotate documents and connect one idea to another across documents. In Bush's library you can write in the books, leave a trail of interesting places in the books without defacing them, and share annotated documents among colleagues—

perhaps creating new forms of encyclopedias. It is, in effect, a library of hypertext. Historically, Bush's idea draws on the practices of medieval scholars whose exegesis of texts, especially scriptural texts, consisted of marginal annotations and footnotes with embedded layers of commentary and explanation.

Bush's imagined trails can now be realized by using the ordinary links of hypertext. In a hypertext document, there are hotspots *that refer to related citations or forward references; these hotspots may appear as highlighted or colored text or icons. When you touch one of them, the system moves to the place in the document referenced by it. Hypertext is now used by many computer users as web browsers; and digital, multimedia encyclopedias with hypertext links on* CD-ROMs *and are now available to many schools and in homes. In this way, a computer network of hypertext documents can become an interlinked web of ideas.*

In Bush's memex, a researcher's trails are intended as guides, as pathways to learning for others. In the mid-1990s, however, only an educated few actively construct trails; many consumers use hypertext, but few create it.

Today's technology has advanced well beyond Bush's imagined microfilm-based memex. We can now build automated presentations that serve as multimedia guides to other works. The presentation concept goes well beyond hotspots and hopping along a trail; the juxtaposition of annotation and content that lets readers can see both at once is a crucial element. In simpler versions of trail hopping, touching a hotspot causes the commentary to disappear and replaces it with the referenced text, preventing the user from simultaneously viewing the trail and the document.

All sorts of special effects could be added for an effective teaching presentation. Consider the vocabulary of special effects used in the movies or the evening television news such as the establishing shot, zoom, freeze frame, time dilation, *and so on. In the animated environment of a graphics processor, a teacher could use such filmcraft effects to create an active teaching document that effectively utilizes many works in a library. The commentary text would appear in its own window, perhaps accompanied by audio, or even video, of the teacher. The cited document would fly in from the side, open to the appropriate spot, and the view would zoom in, highlighting the pertinent information. A comparable section from another document could then appear, and differences between the two documents might be summarized. The article by Ranjit Makkuni later in this section describes several examples of such interfaces.*

Appropriately enough, at the time of this writing, the full text of Bush's article is available on the Internet. Web mavens can find it at:

http://www.isg.sfu.ca/~duchier/misc/vbush/

Excerpt from *Libraries of the Future*

J. C. R. Licklider

Connections

In 1961 the Ford Foundation–funded Council on Library Resources selected Licklider to head a research team to investigate the characteristics of the library of the future. The study was intended to delineate the problems of libraries, especially those related to the increasing volume of scientific publication, and to consider how technology could be used to address these problems.

This study, conducted almost twenty years after "As We May Think," cited Bush's article as the main external influence on its work, revealing the power of Bush's dreams for technologists. In the foreword to Libraries for the Future, Licklider credits Bush for defining the "information problem" that is the focus of his study and quotes Bush's definition of it:

The difficulty seems to be, not so much that we publish unduly in view of the extent and variety of present-day interests, but rather that publication has been extended far beyond our present ability to make use of the record. The summation of human experience is being expanded at a prodigious rate, and the means we use for threading through the consequent maze to the momentarily important item is the same as was used in the days of square-rigged ships.

Although in the meantime, computers had become an important part of American business, in 1963—when the report was released—they were still primitive by today's standards. The primary means of input was punched cards. The report contains such occasionally quaint terminology as references to oscilloscopes, *which were added to research computers as display output devices, and* lightpens, *which made it pos-*

sible to draw on the oscilloscope screen. Even the most advanced computers then available for research were much less powerful than today's personal computers.

The future envisioned was the library of the year 2000, making the present time a particularly interesting one for reconsidering the assumptions and conclusions of the study. The study team agreed with Vannevar Bush that knowledge was increasing at a rate beyond society's ability to make use of it. Moreover, although team members saw the library as the most relevant institution for dealing with this growth, their interest went beyond the published information normally found in libraries. They asked broad questions about society's use of knowledge. Beginning with the most basic issues of technology for organizing and retrieving information, they went on to consider what computer aids could be devised for understanding it.

To do so, Licklider and his study team anticipated the future, projecting trends in technology and analyzing the limitations of books and paper as media for information. Their position was thoroughly grounded in the widespread technological optimism of the 1960s that expected engineering and science to lead the way to utopia. In the past thirty years, experience with the dark side of technology and automation has driven some of this enthusiasm underground. Nonetheless, it is still with us in our engineering schools and in the internal metaphors of those who work in science and technology. This is not a bad thing, for such faith inspires invention and motivates engineers and scientists to endure the many failures of research and design that precede finding approaches that really work. In that light, the article is refreshing in its boldness. It shows how some of the most influential technologists of the 1960s invented the digital libraries of the present and future by projecting forward from the technological innovations that were then emerging.

Technology is now sufficiently advanced to implement many of their suggestions, so that we now have very concrete actualizations of their vision in the forms of personal computers, the Internet, and so on. Reading these ideas about "future libraries" gives us a chance to see one version of the library dream in a purer form unconstrained by the particular directions technology has taken since 1961.

As a medium for the display of information, the printed page is superb. It affords enough resolution to meet the eye's demand. It presents enough information to occupy the reader for a convenient quantum of time. It offers great flexibility of font and format. It lets the reader control the mode and rate of inspection. It is small, light, movable, cuttable, clippable, pastable, replicable, disposable, and inexpensive. These positive attributes all relate to the display function. The tallies that could be made for the storage, organization, and retrieval functions are less favorable.

When printed pages are bound together to make books or journals, many of the display features of the individual pages are diminished or destroyed. Books are bulky and heavy. They contain much more information than the reader can apprehend at any given moment, and the excess often hides the part he wants to see. Books are too expensive for universal private ownership, and they circulate too slowly to permit the development of an efficient public utility. Thus, except for use in consecutive reading—which is not the modal application in the domain of our study—books are not very good display devices. In fulfilling the storage function, they are only fair. With respect to retrievability they are poor. And when it comes to indexing and abstracting it, books by themselves make no active contribution at all.

If books are intrinsically less than satisfactory for the storage, organization, retrieval, and display of information, then libraries of books are bound to be less than satisfactory also. We may seek out inefficiencies in the organization of libraries. but the fundamental problem is not to be solved solely by improving library organization at the system level. Indeed, if human interaction with the body of knowledge is conceived of as a dynamic process involving repeated examinations and intercomparisons of very many small and scattered parts, then any concept of a library that begins with books on shelves is sure to encounter trouble. Surveying a million books on ten thousand shelves, one might suppose that the difficulty is basically logistic, that it derives from the gross physical arrangement. In part, of course, that is true, but in much greater part the trouble comes from what we may call the "passiveness" of the printed page. When information is stored in books, there is no practical way to transfer the information from the store to the user without physically moving the book or the reader or both. Moreover, there is no way to determine prescribed functions of descriptively specified informational arguments within the books without asking the reader to carry out all the necessary operations himself.

We are so inured to the passiveness of pages and books that we tend to shrug and ask, "Do you suggest that the document read its own print?" Surely, however, the difficulty of separating the information in books from the pages, and the absence, in books, of active processors are the roots of the most serious shortcomings of our present system for interacting with the body of recorded knowledge. We need to substitute for the book a device that will make it easy to transmit information without transporting material, and that will not only present information to people but also process it for them, following procedures that specify, apply, monitor, and if necessary, revise and reapply. To provide those services, a meld of library and computer is evidently required.

• • •

The Size of the Body of Recorded Information

As a basis for thinking about precognitive systems, one needs an estimate of how much information there is to cope with.

• • •

During the first few months, a very rough estimate was made, based mainly on the work of Bourne (*The World's Technical Journal Literature: An Estimate of Volume, Origin, Language, Field, Indexing, and Abstracting*, Stanford Research Institute, 1961) and the size of the Library of Congress, together with some miscellaneous impressions.

• • •

If we accept 10^{15} as the present total, then we may take about 10^{14} as the number of bits required to hold all of science and technology, and 10^{13} for solid science and technology. Then, if we divide science and technology into one hundred "fields" and one thousand "subfields," we come out with 10^{11} bits or a billion characters for a subfield.

To relate the foregoing estimates to common experience, we may start with a printed page. If we assume pages with one hundred characters per line and fifty lines, we have five thousand characters per page. Thus the "solid" literature of a subfield is the equivalent of a thousand books, and the total literature of a subfield is the equivalent of ten thousand books. If one thinks of information theory or psychophysics as a subfield, the figures seem not to violate intuition.

• • •

Criteria for Procognitive Systems

Economic criteria tend to be dominant in our society. The economic value of information and knowledge is increasing. By the year 2000, information and knowledge may be as important as mobility. We are assuming that the average man of that year may make a capital investment in an "intermedium" or "console"—his intellectual Ford or Cadillac—comparable to the investment he makes now in an automobile, or that he will rent one from a public utility that handles information processing as Consolidated Edison handles electric power. In business, government, and education, the concept of "desk" may have changed from passive to active: a desk may be primarily a display-and-control station in a telecommunication-telecomputation system—and its most vital part may be the cable ("umbilical cord") that connects it, via a wall socket, into the procognitive utility net. Thus our economic assumption is that interaction with information and knowledge will constitute 10 or 20 percent of the total effort of the society, and the rational economic (or socioeconomic) criterion is that the society be more productive with procognitive systems than without.

Note that the allocation of resources to information systems in this projection covers interaction with bodies of information other than the body of knowledge now associated with libraries. The parts of the allocation that pay for user stations, for telecommunication, and for telecomputation can be charged in large part to the handling of everyday business, industrial, government, and professional information, and perhaps also to news, entertainment, and education. These more mundane activities will require extensive facilities, and parts of the neo-library procognitive system may ride on their coattails.

• • •

The criteria that are clearly within our scope are those that pertain to the needs and desires of users. The main criteria in that group appear that the procognitive system:

1. Be available when and where needed.

2. Handle both documents and facts.

3. Permit several different categories of input, ranging from authority-approved formal contributions (e.g., papers accepted by recognized journals) to informal notes and comments.

4. Make available a body of knowledge that is organized both broadly and deeply—and foster the improvement of such organization through use.

5. Facilitate its own further development by providing tool-building languages and techniques to users and preserving the tools they devise and by recording measures of its own performance and adapting in such a way as to maximize the measures.

6. Provide access to the body of knowledge through convenient procedure-oriented and field-oriented languages.

7. Converse or negotiate with the user while he formulates requests and while responding to them.

8. Adjust itself to the level of sophistication of the individual user, providing terse, streamlined modes for experienced users working in their fields of expertness, and functioning as a teaching machine to guide and improve the efforts of neophytes.

9. Permit users to deal either with meta-information (through which they can work "at arms length" with substantive information), or with substantive information (directly), or with both at once.

10. Provide the flexibility, legibility, and convenience of the printed page at input and output and, at the same time, the dynamic quality and immediate responsiveness of the oscilloscope screen and light pen.

11. Facilitate joint contribution to and use of knowledge by several or many co-workers.

12. Present flexible, wide-band interfaces to other systems, such as research systems in laboratories, information-acquisition systems in government, and application systems in business and industry.

13. Reduce markedly the difficulties now caused by the diversity of publication languages, terminologies, and "symbologies."

14. Essentially eliminate publication lag.

15. Tend toward consolidation and purification of knowledge, instead of, or as well as, toward progressive growth and unresolved equivocation.

16. Evidence neither the ponderousness now associated with overcentralization nor the confusing diversity and provinciality now associated

with highly distributed systems. (The user is presumably indifferent to the design decisions through which this is accomplished.)

17. Display desired degree of initiative, together with good selectivity, in dissemination of recently acquired and "newly needed" knowledge.

To the foregoing criteria, it may be fair to add criteria that are now appreciated more directly by librarians than by the users of libraries. Some of the following criteria are, as they should be, largely implicit in the foregoing list, but it will do no harm to make them explicit.

18. Systematize and expedite the cataloguing and indexing of new acquisitions, forcing conformity to the system's cataloguing standards at the time of "publication" and distributing throughout the system the fruits of all labor devoted to indexing and other aspects of organiation.

19. Solve the problem of (mainly by eliminating) recovery of documents.

20. Keep track of user's interests and needs and implement acquisition and retention policy (policy governing what to hold in local memories) for each local subsystem.

21. Record all chargeable uses, and handle bookkeeping and billing. Also record all charges that the system itself incurs, and handle their bookkeeping and payment.

22. Provide special facilities (languages, processors, displays) for use by system specialists and by teams made up of system and substantive specialists in their continual efforts to improve the organization of the fund of knowledge (This professional, system oriented work on organization is supplemented by the contributions toward organization made by ordinary users in the course of their substantive interaction with the body of knowledge.)

23. Provide special administrative and judicial facilities (again languages, processors, displays) for use in arriving at and implementing decisions that affect overall system policies and rules.

The list of criteria ends with two considerations that we think many users will deem extremely important in a decade or two, but few would mention now:

24. Handle formal procedures (computer programs, subroutines, and so forth, written formal, machine-independent languages) as well as the conventional documents and factions mentioned in criterion 2.

25. Handle heuristics (guidelines, strategies, tactics, and rules of thumb intended to expedite solution of problems) coded in such a way as to facilitate their association with situations to which they are germane.

Reflections

One of the most striking predictions in this article is that the average
person will have a personal information console,

his intellectual Ford or Cadillac—comparable to the investment he makes now in
an automobile, or that he will rent one from a public utility that handles information processing as Consolidated Edison handles electric power. In business,
government, and educations the concept of "desk" may have changed from passive to active: a desk may be primarily a display-and-control station in a telecommunication-telecomputation system—and its most vital part may be the
cable ("umbilical cord") that connects it, via a wall socket, into the procognitive
utility net.

The "console" predicted in 1963 corresponds to today's personal computer; the information system is either the Internet or one of the information utilities that connects to it. Thus, the technology appears to have
followed a path remarkably close to that expected by the study team.
However, the digital library it envisioned, containing the great works and
the expanding body of scientific literature, has not yet emerged. For the
most part, the greatest obstacles are not technological.

    To account for this, it is worth reviewing some of the report's criteria.
The library of the future stressed having information available to anyone,
any time, any where. Yet access to today's computer networks is by no
means universal. Nor does the network provide comprehensive access
to the expanding body of scientific works. Both issues are grounded in
economics—the cost of computer technology and the cost and value of
information. The study group did not consider the issue of intellectual-
property management. For them the requirement was mostly technological: "We need to substitute for the book a device that will make it
easy to transmit information without transporting material." Thus, the
study anticipates the technological requirements for passing information
around, but not the economic considerations related to creating knowledge in the first place. (One approach to address issues of usage rights
and fees for information are discussed in "Letting Loose the Light"
(p. 219) and in other articles in Part 3 on the electronic marketplace
metaphor.)

    Licklider's study also touches on a number of other questions and
recommendations that are examined more closely in the present work.

His suggestion, for example, that the library should contain a mixture of published and informal documents raises several issues, even in the context of scientific documents where publication is an integral and important part of the scientific process and of academic life. For a discussion of this question, see Joshua Lederberg's Communication as the Root of Scientific Progress *later in this part. Licklider also suggests that the digital library should facilitate collaboration by coworkers, which introduces another perspective on the production and use of knowledge as a social, rather than a solitary activity. We explore this theme in parts 2 and 4 of this book. On a technical level, Licklider's recommendation that future libraries should display initiative in disseminating recently acquired or newly needed knowledge coincides precisely with the function proposed by Robert Kahn and Vinton Cerf for "knowbots" in the next article, "The Digital Library Project."*

Finally, Licklider views the library not as a collection of passive documents, but as a potent and proactive information source. In a traditional library, it is sometimes possible to telephone a reference librarian to ask, for example, "How many computer workstations were sold last year?" A research librarian undertaking to answer the question would not simply list all the possibly relevant sources but would search the literature, synthesize facts from different sources, and give various qualified estimates as answers. Licklider's study team pondered the extent to which a computer system could perform this series of tasks and recognized that the ability to do so involves not only text processing, but also a complex synthesis of information.

They also realized that knowledge itself is not so well integrated. In the parts of the article not excerpted here, they survey the 1961 state of the art of natural language processing and artificial intelligence (AI). They point to promising directions but conclude that the underlying problems are deep. The thorniest issue, they found, was not the state of AI but the fundamental state of humanity's knowledge: "The most promising approach, it seems to us, is to accept the notion that, for many years at least, we shall not achieve a complete integration of knowledge, that we shall have to content ourselves with diverse partial models of the universe. It may not be elegant to base some of the models in geometry, some in logic, and others in natural language, but that may be the most practicable solution" (p. 78).

Licklider himself was a proponent of man-machine symbiosis, that is, systems for solving problems in which both people and machines take part. With more than thirty years of hindsight, this still seems like a sensible idea. Nonetheless, research on such matters has progressed slowly, and the issue is not presently widely recognized as central to the digital library project. By creating an on-line corpus of data on the question, digital libraries can present opportunities for research in these areas.

Excerpt from *The Digital Library Project,* volume 1: *The World of Knowbots*

Robert E. Kahn and Vinton G. Cerf

Connections

This article was written more than forty years after Vannevar Bush en-visaged the memex and more than twenty years after the Licklider study. By 1988 digital computers had come into their own and offered a tech-nology for realizing the interactive digital library far better than the microfilm technology Bush imagined. Progress in computer technology had also progressed beyond the feeble first prototypes available when Licklider's committee made its study. In addition, computer networks that can interlink libraries had developed, largely through the leadership of co-authors Kahn and Cerf. Their article describes the digital library as seen by two of its most visionary technical leaders.

Like Bush's, Kahn and Cerf's digital library works by interlinking personal libraries with public ones. The full text of the report is a high-level technical specification of how a network of separate but interlinked libraries may be made to work cooperatively as a large library. Because the network would combine public and private library sites, not all ser-vices would necessarily be free.

Kahn and Cerf focus on two key features of the digital library: its dynamic nature and its very large size. For the library user, it would be like having an ongoing working relationship with a team of very diligent and fast librarians.

Consider, for example, a scenario in which a user requests articles on a particular topic. Using an on-line information retrieval system, he or she might type in several key words that describe the content and context of the requested articles. The network then searches the catalogs of all the libraries and, after a short delay, reports back with a list of articles or books on the subject. A user whose interest is ongoing could post a permanent request in the network; whenever new articles on the subject appeared anywhere in the network, the digital library would gather them up and report them.

In Kahn and Cerf's digital library, such a search would be carried out by electronic agents they call knowbots, *knowledge robots that can find their way through the great size, heterogeneity, and complexity of a networked digital library. The following excerpt focuses on these knowbots.*

The term "library" conjures a variety of different images. For some, a library is a dim and dusty place filled with out-of-date texts of limited historical interest. For others, it is a rich collection of archival quality information which may include video and audio tapes, disks, printed books, magazines, periodicals, reports and newspapers. As used in this report, a library is intended to be an extension of this latter concept to include material of current and possibly only transient interest. Seen from this new perspective, the digital library is a seamless blend of the conventional archive of current or historically important information and knowledge, along with ephemeral material such as drafts, notes, memoranda and files of ongoing activity.

• • •

In its broadest sense, a DLS [digital library system] is made up of many Digital Libraries sharing common standards and methodologies. It involves many geographically distributed users and organizations, each of which has a digital library which contains information of both local and/or widespread interest.

Each user in the DLS manages his information with a Personal Library System (PLS) uniquely tailored to his needs. A PLS has the ability to act as a stand-alone system for its user, but under normal conditions it will be connected into a rich network of public, personal, commercial, organizational, specialized and national digital libraries.

The DLS provides each user with the capability to use other cooperating digital libraries and provides the necessary search, retrieval and accounting capabilities to support ready access to local and network-based information. The various digital libraries and the associated access to network based capabilities are integral parts of the Digital Library System. Convenient access to local and remote information, without regard for its location, is an essential goal of the system design.

The initial application of the DLS will be retrieval of specific documents for which a user may be able to supply only an imprecise description. For this purpose, we assume each retrieval request has a known target document which the user cannot describe or locate with precision, but can recognize when retrieved.

A Guide to the System

[The components of the Digital Library System] are Personal Library Systems for the users, Organizational Library Systems for serving groups of individuals or activities, new as well as existing Databases stored locally and across the country, Database Servers to handle remote requests, and a variety of system functions to coordinate and manage the entry and retrieval of data. The system components are assumed to be linked by means of one or more interconnected computer networks.

Local requests for information, if not satisfiable by the local Personal Library, are dispatched to other, larger or possibly more specialized sources of information available through the network. A single inquiry may spawn tens to thousands of exchanges among various parts of the full Digital Library System. This could easily happen if the system must first query several databases before responding to a particular inquiry.

These exchanges are, for the most part, mediated by *Knowbots*, which are active intelligent programs capable of exchanging messages with each other and moving from one system to another in carrying out the wishes of the user. They may carry intermediate results, search plans and criteria, output format and organization requirements and other information relevant to the satisfaction of a user's query.

A Knowbot is typically constructed on behalf of a user at his Personal Library System and dispatched to a Database Server which interfaces the network to a particular database or set of databases. To accommodate existing database systems which are not capable of direct interaction with Knowbots, these servers can assist Knowbots in translating their information requests into terms which are compatible with the existing database's access methods. In the future, we expect to witness the development of databases systems with built-in mechanisms for housing and catering to resident or transient Knowbots. It is possible, and even likely, that more than one Knowbot may be dispatched either directly from a Personal Library System or indirectly as a result of actions taken at a particular Database Server. These various Knowbots may rendezvous at a common server or all return to the originating workstation for assembly of the results.

Other Applications of the Digital Library System

Four possible applications of the DLS are described below. These are referred to as the Filter-Presenter, the Design Database Manager, the Researcher-Analyst and the Diagnostic Imager. Each of these uses would be implemented as an agent in the system.

The Filter-Presenter aids a user who is normally burdened by too much arriving information in the ordinary mailstream (e.g., magazines, newspapers, journals and electronic mail). If the material can be scanned electronically by the Knowbots, the user can be presented with only those aspects of the documentation he wishes to see. Of course, the user must first supply the Agent with sufficient guidance to carry out its task (including how he wants to see the results presented). Many research questions abound.

The filter may be too strong and therefore important items may be missed. Conversely, it may be too weak and the user will still be overloaded with irrelevant information. Irrelevant information may also be produced by a strong filter and relevant information missed by a weak filter, but both cases are much less likely.

The Design Database Manager couples a design program to an underlying database of relevant support information. It can also augment multiple design programs working collaboratively on a common design. In the case of VLSI design, for example, the elements in the database might be chip designs that could be used as subelements in a larger design. This could represent work underway by a team of designers. Or it could include standard designs such as simple microprocessors which may have limited use otherwise and could be used as pieces in a larger state-of-the-art chip. The advantage of this approach is that a new microprocessor design is not needed and users can be expected to be experienced in the use of existing designs for which software is already available. Alternately, the database manager could know about blueprints and how to use them and assist a user in retrieving and interpreting them.

The Researcher-Analyst assists a person who would normally search through large collections of documentation seeking specific types of information about a particular topic. It might identify hundreds of possibly relevant items that the user would have no time to explore. This agent could search all of them and develop information for the user depending on the nature of his research. For example, if the researcher was concerned about the history of infrastructure, he might ask the system to locate as many documented examples of early uses of electricity as possible. This task might normally take weeks or months to accomplish manually but the agent using the library might accomplish it in minutes or less.

Reflections

Science writer Bennett Davis summarized the idea of knowbots: "Imagine ... a willing corps of knowledge slaves at your bidding. You sit down with your morning coffee at your desktop computer. A knowbot brings you the morning news on the screen—your own personal edition, a composite of bulletins, patent developments, new journal articles, and stray tidbits all related to your field of work ... and edited to your own specifications" (Discover, April 1991, p. 21).

The term knowbot *has captured the popular imagination, perhaps because it rhymes with* robot *and appeals to the love of power. These agents augment the power of anyone using them, providing computational servants to find information and do other useful things. In mythological terms, the knowbots are like magical genies or, even, demons. If we use the right incantation, they will rise to do our bidding.*

The particular technical proposals in the article for realizing library services on computer networks are not necessarily the way things will work out. Sometimes simpler approaches are developed. For example, indexing services on the Internet can do some of the services Kahn and Cerf propose in the full technical report without all of the machinery. So-called webcrawlers *poll the network periodically, retrieving documents and noticing what words are used in them. Unlike knowbots, they stay at home and send out requests, creating profiles of the documents they receive and saving them in a master index. (While this book was being written such master indices increased their summaries of documents from about two million to thirty-four million.) Later, when a user asks a webcrawler to find all documents containing certain words, the system need only consult the master index and return a list of the relevant documents.*

Several aspects of Kahn and Cerf's vision of the digital library, especially the idea of building up a large library from a set of cooperating smaller ones, have been very influential. Although the database services presently operating on the network fall short of the capabilities Kahn and Cerf imagined, they do indeed achieve their strength through cooperation. Finally, perhaps the most potent aspect of knowbots right now is their ability to spark our imagination. Sophisticated operations such as those sketched by Bennett Davis may soon be implemented with knowbots. The very idea of knowbots has helped free people to think more deeply about what they want from digital libraries.

Excerpt from "Communication as the Root of Scientific Progress"

Joshua Lederberg

Connections

Scientists are among the greatest consumers of writings and libraries today. This article, the first of two in this book by biomedical researcher Joshua Lederberg, discusses roles for new information technology in the conduct of science. As a working scientist, Lederberg is engaged in finding and understanding scientific information pertinent to his own corner of the scientific universe.

In the myth of Prometheus and other stories about bringers of knowledge, knowledge of great value comes out of the ancient past to be treasured by humankind in the present. These myths, which emphasize the preservation of knowledge, may be misleading metaphors for the ways we create knowledge and use libraries today. Lederberg's description of his work introduces two themes about knowledge that are missing in the ancient legends. One is that knowledge is not created all at once, it is being constantly created, piecewise, by communities of scientists who propose, criticize, and build on each other's contributions to knowledge through systematic publication and review. A second theme is that specific information, even when filed away systematically in journals and libraries, is difficult to find or even to notice when so much is being created and stored. In the context of computer networks, people sometimes speak of a "firehose" of information to suggest the rapid rate at which information is created and flows down an "information pipeline."

In this article Lederberg characterizes himself as the principal reader for his laboratory group, the one who must keep on top of relevant scientific events. He goes on to describe how he does this, what tools he uses, and what frustrations he encounters—such as keeping track of ten thousand or so publications from the last decade that are not available on-line.

Compared with most people, Lederberg's vocation and informational needs are extreme, and they may seem irrelevant to many of us. Nonetheless they deserve the attention of anyone interested in or working on digital libraries. Society depends on having people who master information with Lederberg's dedication and intensity. Both the continuing growth in production of information and the increasing specialization of scientific fields suggest that the problems he and others like him face today will be confronted by more people in the future. A clear picture of the challenges we meet in searching, selecting, and making sense of information can help guide our idea of what a digital library should be. If a digital library with the capabilities Lederberg envisions could help him in his work, it could help the rest of us too.

He presented the following paper at the Sixth International Conference of the International Federation of Science Editors at Woods Hole, Massachusetts, on October 16, 1991.

I am very interested in scientific information. I don't do very much editorial work these days; I'm back working in the laboratory after a lapse of twelve years and that has kept me very busy trying to reacquaint myself with the literature of my own field. So I will offer you the perspective of a scientific reader. Now some people tell me that's a vanishing species! For anyone to say that, even with some sense of irony, is an atrocity.

One of my main functions with my own laboratory group is that I try to be its principal reader. If something goes on in the world outside and none of us has heard about it for two or three weeks, I'm the one who feels responsible. I want to be alert to events that might have a very important bearing on the way we think about our own research, our planning, of the data coming in, of the sources of error.

The Literature as Public Archive and Open Forum

Let me begin with a few truisms, just to be sure that we are operating on a common ground of reverence for the publication process. Publication is, to start with, just that! *Public*-ation. It converts private to public knowledge, in the service of registering a private claim of original authorship—in science, of discovery. Above all, the act of publication is an inscription under oath, a testimony. It is accepted as valid until firm evidence to the contrary; and there is an extremely high standard of accountability for what is published under a given person's name. Just look at the daily headlines. It is the essential ingredient to make scientific work responsible in the sense that one cannot readily retreat from assertions that have been signed, delivered to the printer and made available to thousands.

These publicly asserted claims also play an extremely important role in the allocation of resources, the ability of different scientists to survive in the competition with other legitimate claims for expenditures, for support of laboratories, for positions at the institutions, for space in the journals, for the attraction of students and collaborators. All these rest on those claims, the evidence for which in the end is in the public record. Both author and audience benefit from the successful assertion of those claims: especially credibility, that one doesn't have to spend an inordinate amount of time reexamining every detail of an individual's output if that person has established credibility through prior publication and exposure. Publication also results in a repository, constructing the tradition of science. Up to this point it can hardly be anonymous in order to perform the functions that I have just indicated. But as time goes by, we have the reassimilation of the content of scientific work and as it settles in and survives the criticism that it should have had at its early stages of the process, it becomes the common tradition, the unquestioned shared wisdom—often becoming anonymous by obliteration.

The literature is also a forum. It's a gladiatorial arena for competing claims, resolving discrepancies in data or interpretation. There used to be oral duels, and we revel in stories like Pasteur's confrontation with Pouchet that finally put spontaneous generation to rest in 1864. Today, our battles are more often fought out in print, which is indeed appropriate because the testimony then becomes available to the universe, not simply to the immediate onlookers. Despite the opportunity for very broad dissemination, there is the paradox, nevertheless, that broadcast restricts individuals' access to feedback. The publication system, at least in principle, should allow a dialectic to appear in more symmetrical terms where anyone with something purposeful to say has a way to get into the system. If the literature is a forum, it is also a rumen, a place for the digestion and assimilation of the variety of inputs where scientific claims go through a period of seasoning, modification, modulation. Even the truths look different five or ten years later regardless of explicit criticisms. We can expect a process of reinterpretation, a posthistorical reexamination of the meaning of their terms.

And now I only need to remind you of the term "imprimatur" (a wonderful metaphor): the imprinted witness that, an article having appeared in a refereed journal, it had survived a critical process, a conspiracy if you like, of the editors and the publishers and the referees— that something has appeared which is worthy of the shared interest and precious attention of the community.

Keeping Up with the Literature

May I tell you what I do as a reading scientist today? Reading the scientific literature has been my primary vocation for fifty years.

Books play a diminishing role. Today they are mostly for targeted reference. In the scientific domain, we rarely have the leisure today to read a book from cover to cover. A few biographies command attention. I just finished a proof copy of Carl Djerassi's life story: *The Pill, Pygmy Chimps and Degas' Horse*; another of that genre was François Jacob's revelation of the development of his scientific work: *The Statue Within*. These are obviously not very contributory to the details on how to do my next experiment, but they tell me a lot about the scientific personality, providing object lessons and models for emulation.

Rarely, I do see a work that compels total ingestion—for example *Physiology of the Bacterial Cell* by Neidhardt, Ingraham and Schaechter. This is such a magnificent synthesis at a fairly elementary level of exposition that I really marveled at the deliberation and distillation that went into the telling. Wonderful books like that are rare. In printed form they surely will be the survivors of any electronic revolution.

At an intermediary level of indispensibility as books in print format are the *Annual Reviews*. They are reference works for whatever you have to look up; but they also give a chance to browse through an enormous literature with some coherence.

Compare an *Annual Reviews of Genetics* with current issues of the journal *Genetics*. Even if I had the time to read every article, I wouldn't have the background to be able to place each one of them in the appropriate context of what comes through. And I regard this as my home discipline! People will spend varying amounts of their time and energy as well in trying to understand what is going on in science beyond the window of their own specific work in their research and teaching.

There are about a dozen journals that I subscribe to and maybe seven or eight of them that I do scan from cover to cover: *Nature, Science, Proceedings of the National Academy*—those are the very general ones. The *Journal of Bacteriology, Microbiological Reviews, Genetics, Biochemistry*. I pick up a hot paper now and then from *The Scientist*, and look at *The Sciences, New Scientist, American Scientist, and Scientific American* for general scientific culture. That is a textual sampling, not immersion. You couldn't read every article in a critical and detailed fashion in just the journals I have listed within the number of hours that there are in the week. What you can do within a couple of hours a day is to scan that range of material and try to pick out those things that might be of interest. To follow the structure of argument just in one's own specialty, you must go to the detail of trying to check the numbers on the graphs and see if they match the authors assertions—an arduous task.

We are well served by those kinds of journals in terms of maintaining a general currency about what is going on in the field. And they match very well the energy and interest and intellectual acuity that our scientific readers are able to put into the process. I see no occasion for those to be altered. Most scientists are very grateful for them: what thousands of scientists will share as common currency, to carry in their briefcase and read on the airplanes and the commuter rides, with all the convenience of the present print format.

Selective Retrieval and Managing a Personal Library

My main problem is how do you reacquire, retrace that intellectual traffic. What do you do with all of your marginal notes and, how do you synthesize a coherent system of what you've read? Well to try to deal with this on a current basis, I have Gene Garfield's wonderful products. I get the weekly *Current Contents on Diskette* with all of its embellishments. I eagerly await the five or six diskettes that have to be loaded, every week, and sometimes am impatient about how long it takes to load them and get going with that week's literature. My stored profiles work out reasonably well, but have to be embellished from time to time. You discover new keys, other notations that authors insist on in changing fads and idiosyncrasies of language. I can warrant that my profiles recover on a current basis about 96 percent of what I have read or would want to read. God help me if I lose my notes on the rest!

Then, how keep up with what's closest to my immediate specialty? Acquiring a couple or three papers a day is not hard. And even with a fairly detailed critical examination down to checking the points on the graphs and so on, reading them as they come in is entirely doable. My problem is the arithmetic of accumulation. After a decade, I've got about ten thousand papers that I have got to keep track of: the texts and my marginal notes and so on. And here my system is absolutely broken down! A technological fix is on the way: document scanners that can store page images and digitize scripts on searchable media. One or a few CD-ROM's will take care of the storage. But what a lot of bother for information, yes full text, that I should be able to acquire electronically in the first place. The more so for specialty journals and references to be searched on demand.

Within a given specialty there are usually one or two journals that specialists must see. There may be only a couple of hundred people who have such a level of interest that they will look at every article. There are the journals of broad appeal, and then a very flat distribution of the other sources. For my part, an additional thirty articles a month—perhaps half of them come from about fifteen journals; you can probably extrapolate with Bradford's Law to the rest. Ninety percent will come from about thirty-five, and then there is a gradual asymptote out to the vanishing returns from the total coverage that the system is going to offer.

Every now and then an article does pop up from an obscure place whence you had no systematic way to recover it; but in retrospect it was really quite important.

So each of us faces the task of selective retrieval from a cosmic domain of stuff that every other eager beaver in the world has been busily putting into the repository. Our present technology enables an approximation with reasonable confidence. Keeping track of what you have accumulated on pieces of paper is the frustration. That's not your bedside reading, well served by the print on paper version. The next step, to integrate that into your own private library of useful knowledge, is simply not achievable with last year's technology.

General Information Flood vs. Specific Information Drought

The fact is that scientific literature inherently has grown beyond the scope of any hundred people to have understood it and gone into it in some depth. It is built in to the growth of knowledge that past improvements in communication and storage aren't going to alter. What are the consequences? For one thing, the problematics of assessing the literature reinforces all the other drives to specialization. The ambitions of scientists have changed, to focus on ever narrower targets. It's just too much hard work to master an interdisciplinary area on top of all the other institutional obstacles. Never mind the intellectual conceptual problems. Never mind the problem of getting funding or moral and fiscal support, just to get hold of the necessary expertise and information! But that impediment is in principle remediable.

At the same time, are we drowning in information, inundated by the numbers of journals? You know, when you come to any specific issue, when there is some important special fact that you would like to know all about, the shoe is very often on the other foot. My usual experience in asking a new question: the odds are that the exquisite detail needed to take the next step has just never been done. So here, far from being drowned, I have a great deficit of specific and detailed knowledge of exactly what happens in such and such a system with such and such reagents, and so forth.

Our systems for acquisition of that kind of material is not perfect. But it is getting a lot better. And with devices like key word searching, articles related by bibliographic coupling, full abstract searching, which is just about what the technology does offer today, I can feel reasonably confident that explicit matters of factual detail, whether somebody has done that particular experiment can be retrieved, but often only with a lot of effort. Much more difficult, has anybody else had a good idea that would be pertinent to my search? Those keys are so much more difficult to catalogue. Often it takes great creative act to recognize that a concept developed in one context really is pertinent to another. So there will never be a guarantee that those can all be acquired. But there is at least the hope of finding it in that literature, and it is very important hope to try to preserve.

• • •

Editorial Review: The Essential Value-Added of Print and Electronic Journals

One direction things could take if we don't reform the system is that invisible colleges will take over as the principal but unreliable routes of communication. Archival copies of material will eventually be sent in to the repository. But there will be a limbo of material that doesn't know if it is going to go to hell or heaven for four or five years, while it is still cooking and unaccountably available, on a basis far from equitable. So, in due course there has to be a wholehearted exploitation of the new technologies and I don't have to plead for it. It's happening because electronic networks are becoming more and more available de facto to people working in a variety of fields. A couple of dozen of them now operate with a routine exchange of preprints (sic). The central problem facing the journal has been a radical change in the economics and technology of printing, without an adequate recognition of the essential value-added in the journal process.

• • •

The important value-added is the editorial process, including issues of selection, then of editorial work and improvement. And that very precious imprimatur. When something comes out in a journal of high repute (to make a circular argument), that's a journal worth my time and worth my attention. If it is just thrown up in the air without having undergone that kind of editorial review, it will not have been refined in terms of both the presentation, and perhaps even substance of the argument, and it won't have the imprimatur of other people, whose judgment I trust, that it's worth reading and can be relied upon for accountability.

Whether the article then gets into print is almost an irrelevancy at this point. Any of a variety of media of communication could follow on that editorial process. What we need to see more than has happened so far is the marriage—of that editorial role on the one hand, with a production role that uses the electronic technologies rather than the print, on the other. And that's where the spontaneous bulletin boards don't quite make it. They quickly get filled up with obscenities, literal and otherwise, for lack of that sort of control. I don't mind the obscenities as long as I don't have to plow through them. But I'd like a truth-in-advertising framework that tells me, as I say, what's worth reading. I'd like to know that *x*, *y* or *z* editorial committee had been established as a guide for what is worth capturing the priority of my attention.

A For-Profit and Non-Profit Alliance for Electronic Publishing

. . .

One feature of that kind of a system to which we have only a crude approximation today, is feedback, dialectic. It shouldn't take a federal case for reactions to a paper to be elicited from the scientific community—not just on the rumor network, but some place where everybody else can see it. This is the bulletin board system of commentary and would complement what the fixed board of editors would have to say.

If there is a good dialectical system and the critical community has an opportunity to express its views, even ex-post facto, that's how the scientific process works at its best. Here the economics and the technology for dialectic give a great edge on the electronic systems over the printed ones, if for no other reason than how to get propinquity? I mean, if an article has been printed and then a little later on, I write a critical reaction to it (even in the rare case that the journal accepts that sort of commentary and further dialogue), they do not adjoin one another on the shelves. It's a nuisance trying to find them. Let's say I write something six months ago; Gene Garfield wrote a blistering critique sometime after that. How are the two of them going to be brought together? That kind of reshuffling of the units is very hard with printed paper. It's trivial, of course, to do it with electronic media via the networks of linkage of material and commentary. That potential for reaggregation stands just after mechanized search and tempo of availability as the greatest advantage that these new kinds of media can offer.

Reflections

Readers have limited budgets of time for reading and searching for information. In his article, Lederberg gives an account of what he reads and how he spends his time deciding what to read. Peter Pirolli has coined the phrase information foraging *to suggest that the behavior of a person seeking information resembles that of an animal seeking food. Lederberg, as an information forager, tells us how he employs a mixture of specialized journals, general journals, and review journals for his information diet and uses citation and indexing services for long-range scanning.*

Where current technology cannot do what he would like, he struggles. Where does the system break down? Lederberg points to the ten thousand or so articles he collected over a decade; they are printed on paper, and covered with his notations. Even if he scanned them into a computer, he wouldn't have access to the notes. Why does he write notes in the margins of a paper in the first place? So that they are juxtaposed with the material they comment on, where the context is evident. But there is a price for this convenience! The notes are not part of an electronic publication. Lederberg wants a convenient means to write these notes, keep them attached to the pertinent content, and arrange them so that they become part of a digital record he can search and collect like any other documentation. Once again, we see Vannevar Bush's idea of trails and annotations, the merging of private notes and public records. Bush thought such a trail could connect ideas from distant fields to one another. Echoing this idea, Lederberg notes that it takes a creative act to recognize that a concept developed in one context is applicable to another.

One problem about writing in margins is that margins are small. In the 1980s the Annoland system for supporting the writing and revision work of a group of coauthors was developed at Xerox PARC. It supplied dig-

ital margins where coauthors could leave notes and facilities for keeping track of multiple proposed changes to a document. Because Annoland's margins were digital, they could be expanded to hold as much commentary as needed. Indeed, a fundamental design issue for annotated documents, whether new digital documents or ancient historical and religious texts, is the relative prominence in the display of source material and annotations. With digital annotations, a user can dynamically control the amount of space and detail.

The proliferation of hypertext on the World Wide Web has led to increased interest in issues of managing documents and providing for marginalia. For example, Roscheisen, Mogensen, and Winograd of Stanford University have proposed a system called ComMentor to enable people to share structured in-place annotations for arbitrary on-line documents. Their approach dynamically synthesizes documents from distributed sources, depending on the user context and the meta-information attached to them. They suggest that such facilities could, like Annoland, support structured conversation about paper drafts as well as collaborative filtering, seals of approval, tours of documents, usage indicators, and other things. Expanding such uses could easily produce an amount of commentary on a document greater than the document itself. In such cases, we could provide for the role of an editor. In hyperspace, even the choice of what things to link to can be an editorial judgment.

Lederberg's interest ranges from the creation of documents for scientific discourse to their publication and subsequent commentary. He observes that, given the long lead time in publication, much scientific communication takes place in invisible colleges, informal connections between working scientists in the same field who get to know each other over the years. They exchange ideas and scientific information informally, often long before the information appears in print. Much scientific discourse is also transacted through seminars, conference papers, exchanges of photocopies, and hallway conversations among colleagues. Among cliques of researchers, the latest papers circulate in a way that speeds communication but does not distribute information evenly in the community at large. Electronic journals, Lederberg observes, have the potential to help here, although various social issues need to be addressed first. One of the characteristics of a referred journal is that the editorial review board warrants each article that appears, thus assuring the reader of a level of quality control. Some electronic journals also follow this practice.

Moreover, Lederberg points out, an electronic journal can open the review process to the wider scientific community, so that articles, reviews, and commentary could be consolidated by automatic indexing. Appropriate user interfaces for browsing could arrange the display of articles and commentary both topically and historically, so that readers could find relevant citations and follow a trail of discussion and commentary. Again, this is reminiscent of Bush's trails, with the trails constructed by many colleagues visiting the same place. Both uses of trails—for showing connections among disparate works and for tracing commentary of work in progress—expand the content of the library from the public to the personal and from the formal to the informal. Both kinds of trails would make it easier to make sense of the knowledge accumulated in a collection of works.

A scientific community distinguishes among trial balloons, early drafts, nearly finished works, and archival versions. But if misunderstandings about the tentative status of an early draft risk damaging one's scientific reputation, what incentives are there to share early drafts? Of course, there will always be private, unpublished communications for exchanging preliminary comment and criticism within a circumscribed community. Such communication is inherently inequitable, however, and has a different standing and value—it is neither public nor scientifically "accredited."

Today, much science discourse takes place electronically. The 1994 edition of the Directory of Electronic Journals, Newsletters, and Academic Discussion Lists *published by the Association of Research Libraries, lists 440 electronic journals, including the widely read* Physical Review Letters. *The Association for Computing Machinery (ACM) is considering a radical change in the way it handles its publications to reflect the evolving needs of the computer science profession and the possibilities created by electronic distribution. They propose to create a digital library of ACM's entire literature, starting in the spring of 1995.*

One of the primary benefits of being an ACM member will be access to this database through ACM-supplied tools. Web mavens can find details of the proposal on the Internet at:

http://info.acm.org/pubs/epub_plan.txt

The journal Behavior and Brain Sciences *has always been based on a dialog format. When an article is selected, commentary articles from the community are also solicited, edited, and published. During 1995, the journal moved progressively toward electronic publication. Electronic preprints of articles can be obtained on the Internet from several addresses, including*

http://cogsci.ecs.soton.ac.uk/~harnad/ and
http://www.princeton.edu/~harnad/

There is active scholarly interest in on-line publishing and on-line commentary in the humanities and the arts, as well as in science. For example, the Society for Music Theory maintains an on-line journal and provides for short on-line commentary about articles that have appeared. A good starting point for exploring this material on the Web is

http://boethius.music.ucsb.edu/smthome.html

Finally, the University of Michigan Press has started an on-line archive for the Journal of Electronic Publishing, *which can be found at*

http://www.press.umich.edu/jep

Electronic journals are still in the experimental stage. At the time of writing, the experiment was beginning to take into account social issues related to academic publishing. So far, however, electronic publishing has been based on the economics of free distribution rather than on the stronger commercial possibilities of usage rights and usage fees (discussed in Part 3 of this book). Journal publishers were generally not aware of such possibilities when these electronic journals were started; they may not, in fact, have much merit for the average journal article, which is read by fewer than half a dozen readers. One journal editor remarked that the average article is read by 0.85 readers, including the reviewer! A familiar joke in the computer science community is that some of the more arcane journals are "write only"—meaning that nobody reads them at all.

In the world of academic publication, the economics of production and distribution are closely tied into the politics of science and promotion. Will publication in an electronic journal count as much in a close tenure case as publication in a traditional, paper-based journal? Part of the authority of paper-based journals derives from their ubiquity. Whenever you visit a worthwhile academic library, the relevant journals are on the display, conveying the impression that these journals are important. In scientific journals that publish articles from scientists in several fields, a particular reader may not be interested in articles outside his specialty, but when he sees the names of people in his field next to names of prominent scientists in other fields, he gets a sense of their relative importance. How can these subtle social effects work for journals that are seen only on the glowing displays of computers? How can a university department or a library tell if an electronic journal is important? How can it even tell if anyone reads it? Can it be sure that the papers it includes are adequately reviewed if a traditional publisher is not involved?

Scientific journals are almost unique in the publishing world because authors are willing to pay to have their work disseminated. Such costs are seen as a legitimate part of the cost of socially financed research, for disseminating the results is part of doing research. As journal prices rise, some people argue that journal publishers are misappropriating intellectual property for which taxpayers have already borne the brunt of the expense. Indeed, the rise of free electronic journals can be seen, in part, as a revolt against such publishers.

One important function of scientific journals has been to make public particular, unalterable statements signed by their authors. In this way, the date of publication becomes an undisputed point in claims of precedence of discovery or invention. With the advent of electronic documents, however, journal publication becomes only one way to certify such dates.

It is now possible to digitally notarize that a particular version of a document was written at a specified time. After creating a document (perhaps outlining an unpublished scientific discovery), an author can run a hash program that summarizes the document with a coded string called a digital signature. *Any change to the document would cause the hash program to produce a different string. Hash functions can thus be used to certify that published digital documents have not been tampered with.*

Hash functions can be used for the same purpose on unpublished digital documents, although the practice leads to some interesting twists on issues of publication and credit. Hash strings, because they are unintelligible, can be published without revealing the actual contents of the document; they can also be placed in a special electronic repository and dated to use in supporting claims of precedence for discoveries and inventions without public disclosure. Such methods seem to run counter to the free exchange of ideas for the public good that is generally espoused in science but could be very attractive to business. Any scientist could publish a large number of draft documents, each one containing a variation on a hypothesis. Later, after the dust has settled, an individual or corporation could claim great prescience by pointing only to those documents that have been vindicated. The hashing technology could exacerbate the situation by keeping the contents of this cloud of documents secret until the author chooses to release them.

Elsewhere, Lederberg has argued that if works are presented seriously enough that their authors expect to reap credit for them, the works must be irrevocable, subject only to whatever emendations authors or others choose apply to them. We might expect, further, that those whose work is kept secret would receive diminished credit for it. Scientific practice already gives more credit to those who prove ideas by experiment rather than speculation.

These examples suggest that several challenges are ahead for the digital library, which has to respect the functions of regular communication channels but not necessarily copy their forms. There is plenty of room for experimentation on the best ways to exploit the power and the new economics of digital media. The digital library, as well as the digital journal and the digital review process, may be transformed. As always, the challenge is not just in inventing the technology, but in deciding what shape we want it to have. The changes in scientific publication Lederberg foresees could fundamentally alter our processes of creating new knowledge, checking it, refining it, and making it accessible for others to build on.

Excerpt from "What Is the Role of Libraries in the Information Economy?"

John Browning

Connections

The books in conventional libraries are tangible objects. They carry the stamp of the library and can be checked out. When one patron has a book, another cannot read it. For John Browning, digital works are entirely different. They are, he argues, massless, and they can be copied and transported instantly. This point reflects both the common wisdom about digitization and many people's experiences with widespread unauthorized copying of digital works when the article was written. In 1993, approaches for controlling the copying and use of digital work (as described in Stefik's Letting Loose the Light, *Part 3), were not widely known or used in the library community. We don't yet know how much such approaches will affect libraries and the distribution of digital works.*

Browning wrote his article after the beginning of the Digital Library Project and, perhaps more importantly, after Gopher, Mosaic, and Netscape became available on the Internet. Users' experience with these programs has greatly enlarged public consciousness of the possibilities for digital distribution. The network, by creating a means for all sorts of people to file, publish, and browse digital documents on the network, is challenging traditional roles and, to some extent, putting them up for grabs.

Browning looks at how the digital transition is causing libraries, publishers, and book stores to reexamine these roles. Some libraries that have vast collections of works out of copyright are looking at digital distribution. Institutions such as the Library of Congress have made parts of their digital collections available on the network. What happens,

Browning asks, when libraries step into the business of publishing and selling works?

The world's great libraries share a great vision: Books once hoarded in subterranean stacks will be scanned into computers and made available to anyone, anywhere, almost instantly, over high-speed networks. A researcher in San Francisco might, without leaving the desk, reach into the database of the British Library to grab a copy of the Lindisfarne Gospels, while another researcher in London rummages through the collections of the Library of Congress trying to find various Federalist Papers. Instead of fortresses of knowledge, there will be an ocean of information.

Realizing this vision will transform libraries from guardians of tradition to catalysts of a vast change. By breaking down the walls that separate libraries from each other and from their users, librarians dissolve the barriers that separate libraries from publishers. This will change the economics of publishing, and with that, the way in which ideas are disseminated and culture is made.

The key step in this process is how the digitized images of books and journals are distributed from the libraries themselves. In the logic of technology, this is a trivial and obvious thing to do. Today, librarians spend increasing amounts of time and money copying text from paper— either to send it to some remote researcher, or to save the text from the decay of the paper on which it was printed. Many of those texts were created in electronic form. Why not, the logic goes, cut out unnecessary page-turning and work directly with the electronic version of the document?

Some libraries already are. Perhaps the most ambitious plans are being laid at the Bibliothèque de France, the French national library. Budget permitting, it hopes to make electronic copies of one hundred thousand of the "canonical works of the twentieth century" available electronically throughout France and, perhaps, throughout the world. But the Bibliothèque de France is not alone. At Boston Spa in Yorkshire, the British Library runs a service which finds hard-to-locate journal articles and other documents. Last year, it sent out more than three million bits of text worldwide, mostly photocopies, but also an increasing number of faxes. To cut down the sheer grunt work of copying text, the British Library is experimenting with new forms of service. Instead of receiving a printed journal from publishers, for example, it now receives a CD-ROM containing digitized images of the articles from which it prints out a new hard copy each time one is requested.

Such initiatives raise big questions. If someday in the future anybody can get an electronic copy of any book from a library free of charge, why should anyone ever set foot in a bookstore again? But if the books on a library's electronic shelves are not free, what is left of the distinction between library, printer and bookstore—and what is left of the library's traditional raison d'être: namely, making information available to those who cannot afford to buy it?

• • •

Books by the Numbers

From your local neighborhood Internet network terminal, you can now search the catalogs of thousands of libraries across the world. The Library of Congress catalog is there: containing more than twenty million entries. John Mahoney, head of computing at the British Library, says that twelve to fifteen million items in the British Library's electronic catalog will become available over the British research network, JANET, by this summer. By far the greatest contributions to online access to information, however, come from Ohio, of all places.

In 1967, academic librarian Frederick Kilgour had two insights: first, that all libraries soon would put their card catalogs on computer, and second, that it was senseless for them all to duplicate the work of typing text from cards into the machines. So he put together a consortium of academic libraries from Ohio, got a bit of seed money from the state legislature and began creating a cooperative card catalog based on a shared database.

Today the OCLC, descendant of Kilgour's Ohio College Libraries Center, enables more than fourteen thousand libraries, spread over forty-six countries, to share a database of about twenty-six million entries. Some five thousand of these libraries are general members that agree to share all of their catalog entries with other OCLC members—so that once one member has made a catalog entry for a new work, others can simply copy that entry rather than duplicate the same effort. Not surprisingly, OCLC also runs an inter-library loan service to help librarians get their hands on books that appear in the shared database, but not on their own shelves.

Automated catalogs are a boon to researcher and librarian alike. The OCLC has built a new service called EPIC that searches its online catalog and enables a researcher to track down information by any, some, or all sorts of indices—including author, title, publisher and subject.

But the sheer ease with which researchers can now find their way through vast collections often merely adds to their frustration. Though it takes only a few seconds to locate a book or article in an automated catalog, it then requires hours to bring it up from the stacks—or weeks to get it on inter-library loan. Nor is the impatience of researchers the only factor pressuring libraries to extend the scope of automation from the card catalog to the body of texts themselves.

On the contrary, more powerful forces are at work. One is the rapid decay of most paper made since the mid-nineteenth century, a time when papermakers switched to acidic wood pulp as their raw material. Joseph Price, head of technology at the Library of Congress, estimates that each year eighty thousand of the items on its shelves become so brittle that their pages can no longer be turned. The only way to save the text is to copy it onto another media. Today, the medium is typically microfiche, but Price reckons it will soon be some form of optical disk.

But paper decay is only one force pushing libraries to move text onto other media Another is the rising cost of paper publications and the difficulty in sharing them. Although many libraries can all plug into an electronic database, far fewer can have a given book or magazine on their shelves at any given time. Problem is, libraries can no longer afford to have all the books and journals they feel they should have on their shelves. Over the past few decades, the number and cost of academic journals has skyrocketed.

If publishers and researchers are not to be caught in a vicious spiral, whereby rising prices cause declining circulations and declining circulations push prices further up, the pressure grows on libraries and publishers alike to find new ways that enable researchers to get and to pay for only those journal articles that are needed. Here's where new technology can help.

Enter the Electric Book

Pushed from many directions, all of the world's libraries are moving towards electronic distribution of text. But each is moving into the electronic world in its own way. To see the differences, compare three of the world's great libraries: the Library of Congress, the Bibliothèque de France and the British Library.

The French, inevitably, approach automation with the most panache. They are engineering a whole new national library, called the Très Grande Bibliothèque, which will start from a grand new building and build a grand new foundation for France's libraries. According to Helene Waysbord, one of the creators of this new vision, the library hopes to strike a balance between conservation and diffusion—between protecting heritage and communicating it. To that end, the project has several strands. One is a new national library building: a monument to the book now being constructed on the left bank of the Seine. Its four towers stand at the corners of a sunken garden—at which researchers can gaze through two-story windows while they work.

But in addition to building new walls, the French are also trying to create a library without walls. Under the auspices of the Très Grande Bibliothèque (after the French high-speed trains, the Très Grande Vitesse), the automation of card catalogs has been accelerated. To go with automated catalogs, the Bibliothèque de France will install two hundred research workstations in the library's public areas when it opens in 1995.

The workstations will provide a network link to the card catalogs, notetaking and bibliography software, and, most ambitious, a sort of electronic notebook customized for work in electronic libraries. The workstations are still in the early prototype stage, but the plan is to allow a researcher to scan pages of text directly into a personal database instead of photocopying them for hard files. Scanned text can then be annotated, indexed, and searched by a variety of means.

Last and most ambitious of all, the Bibliothèque de France also has begun creating a new sort of electronic library based not on paper, but on the digitized images of books. It is busily scanning the pages of one hundred thousand great works of the twentieth century as chosen by a committee of notable French citizens. Through designated computer networks, these books will be made available far beyond the walls of the library—although the sheer amount of memory required to store the image and contents of a book means that, for now, the ability to read these electronic books will be limited to only those possessing both extremely high-powered computers and extremely high-powered network connections.

The task of digitization is one in which France's *dirigiste*, centralized bureaucracy can make rapid progress. First, as Waysbord points out, France worries little about political correctness. French academics use the phrase "cultural patrimony" without ducking or sneering, and all schools still teach the same lessons on the same day. Nobody is going to complain too loudly that the Bibliothèque's list of great books overrepresents dead white males.

Equally important, there is a French tradition to push ahead with a big idea and then sort out the commercial problems later. The bureaucracy can brush aside publishers' concerns over the implications of electronic distribution of texts with a speed and power that their English-speaking counterparts could never match. For better or worse, that is how the country got the Concorde. the Airbus. its nuclear power program. Minitel—and now the electronic book.

The Woe of Walls

By contrast, British and American librarians want to sort out the economics of the electronic library from the very beginning.

The commercial consequences of electronic libraries could be huge—and publishers' trade associations are already closely watching libraries with a suspicious eye. More simply, the libraries do not want to be stuck with loss-making electronic services that taxpayers are reluctant to support.

The British Library reached the end of its taxpayers' patience with the growth of overseas demand for faxes and photocopies of journal articles from the library's Document Supply Centre at Boston Spa in Yorkshire. So it evolved a three-tier pricing system.

Basic library services are free—including access to reading rooms, card catalogs, and most book, sound, map and picture collections. Charges for supplying documents from Boston Spa are limited to the costs of photocopying and transport when the service is provided to those within the United Kingdom. But providing documents to foreigners is run at a profit. Indeed, Boston Spa and a handful of other for-profit services now bring in about $50 million of the British Library's $150 million-a-year budget.

In theory, the experience with Boston Spa should put the British Library in an excellent position to blossom in the electronic world. Experiments with distribution of electronic documents from CD-ROM have been promising. So too has a link with the Colorado Association of Research Libraries, which faxes to American libraries copies of the actual journal articles whose citations have been found by searching online catalogs.

Although Mahoney and his colleagues at the library are eager to push ahead into the electronic world, a number of problems arise. One of the more vexing questions concerns copyright. Copyright payments for photocopied works in Britain are handled through a deal with the Copyright Licensing Agency (CLA), which, like its American counterpart, the Copyright Clearance Center, negotiates on behalf of publishers to set and collect copyright charges from high-volume photocopiers like libraries, universities and corporations. But publishers have not given the CLA authority to negotiate deals for electronic publication, not even for facsimile transmission.

The very idea of site licenses for photocopying is still a new one and faces much resistance among would-be licensees. Although the CLA is ready and willing to try to extend licensing to the electronic world, publishers want to move slowly—in part because they want to consolidate copyright deals with photocopiers, and in part because they have [not] arrived at a consensus among themselves over just how to face the electronic future. Until the publishers decide how they want to face the future, the future remains on hold.

• • •

Mega-markets, Meta-markets

On the other side of the Atlantic, the Library of Congress is just beginning its own budgetary debate. It is now forbidden by law for the Library of Congress to charge more than the cost of reproducing documents, plus 10 percent. As an add-on to experiments designed to test the longevity of optical discs as an archival medium, Price put photographs, sound and text onto an optical disc. The result made him enthusiastic about the prospects for electronic publications combining several media—marrying, say, Civil War photographs with letters and other documents from the Library of Congress's vast collections. But building such publications requires heavy research, the costs of which the Library alone cannot recover. So the Library has asked for legislation overturning the 10-percent restriction, but the proposal has run into controversy.

The Information Industries Association, representing publishers, fears that the legislation will unfairly set up government-subsidized competition. The American Library Association, meanwhile, fears that the legislation will set libraries on a slippery slope that will lead to the elimination of free services. The Library of Congress is talking compromise on both fronts. It says it will offer publishers a right of first refusal on all of its electronic projects—though it is not clear how this would work. Similarly it promises to give librarians a guarantee that certain basic services will remain forever free.

Libraries will be a powerful force in the emerging world of electronic information, so the debate merits time and attention. How, for example, might the cost and convenience of combining electronic clippings from libraries compare with customized electronic journals from publishers? What happens to the publishing industry when publishers can reduce their risks by not printing any copies of all but the most popular journals on paper—but instead can wait for interested readers to print their own copies of the articles they want from (taxpayer subsidized) library databases?

• • •

The logic of technology makes librarians and editors increasingly interchangeable. By lowering the costs of reproduction, and thus increasing the amount of information published, new technology increases the value of the judgments made by librarians and online searchers as they pick and choose what their customers might want to read. Eventually, publication may come to mean no more than somebody grabbing a document from the author's networked computer. Even before that, the editorial judgment of the librarian attains value and importance equal to that of the editor—and a paradox arises.

If libraries do not charge for electronic books, not only can they not reap rewards commensurate with their own increasing importance, but libraries can also put publishers out of business with free competition. If libraries do charge, that will disenfranchise people from information—a horrible thing. There is no obvious compromise. It is not really satisfactory either to cripple the technology so that libraries' digitized texts can be read on screen, say, but not stored; or to divvy information into two categories: the free (paid for by the taxpayer) and the commercial (paid for by the consumer). But compromise is badly needed—the technology is on the verge of transforming the great libraries' vision of paradise into a global reality.

Reflections

Browning's article closes with an apparent dilemma. Should libraries charge for electronic books? As he puts it, "If libraries do not charge for electronic books, not only can they not reap rewards commensurate with their own increasing importance, but libraries can also put publishers out of business with free competition. If libraries do charge, that will disenfranchise people from information—a horrible thing."

In effect, he is asking, should libraries go beyond their traditional roles? Does digital technology enable them to do it? Should fees be charged for digital works? In some ways the issues seem inherently mixed. Libraries have an understanding or modus vivendi with commercial players in publishing, but when they move into distribution they compete with bookstores, and when they put copy into readable form they compete with publishers. Should libraries compete with those they depend on?

In Browning's example of the Civil War materials, the Library of Congress became involved in creating and selling a new work by com-

bining and republishing old materials.* In doing so, the crossed the line between being a library and playing the roles of editor, publisher, and distributor. They also crossed the boundary between business and not-for-profit publicly subsidized institutions. The cry of "foul" arises from these crossovers. Charging fees is likely to make the cry louder, if—and when—the practice increases competition with conventional publishers.

Whether libraries should be allowed to charge fees to recover costs is an important one. Over the past few decades, American libraries have struggled to survive. A tug of war between civic pride, enlightened community interest, private donations, and concern about taxes currently govern the level of support for public libraries. The possibility of libraries digitally publishing and distributing works does not affect the issue of whether public libraries should charge for services. It does, however, affect the economics of the situation, as well as fundamental assumptions about how libraries work.

We cannot predict how it will all sort out in the end, especially since the effects depend on technologies that are only now appearing. In Part 3 of this book we show how the making of digital copies could be controlled by using technologies applicable to libraries as well as bookstores. They would enable libraries to reliably and securely loan copies of digital works while protecting them from unauthorized copying. These technologies could unravel at least part of the tangle in Browning's question: If unauthorized copying can be prevented, then some of publishers' fears about digital distribution can be allayed, libraries can distribute works digitally, and the public's free but limited access to information can be preserved.

---

* The Library of Congress distributes these materials as part of its American Memory collection, which contains archives related to American culture and history. At the time of this writing, Web mavens could find the home page for the American Memory project at

http://rs6.10c.gov/amhome.html

The electronic address of the Library of Congress is

http://lcweb.loc.gov/homepage/lchp.html

The plan to make available this (mostly) copyright-free property of old works and, ultimately, to include newer works came to a crashing halt wherever materials had unexpired copyrights.

Here are some of our own observations and predictions. The history of the Ohio College Libraries Center (OCLC) in automating catalogs and faciliting interlibrary loans suggests that the costs of digitizing works will not be borne by individual libraries. We predict that they will either be amortized among members of consortia or be paid by publishers.

Our second prediction is that patrons will pay some of the costs of electronic distribution. Those who access the library from the network will bear all the costs of their own workstations and, probably, most of the communications costs. Providing digital access within the library will require in-library workstations. It is curious that current plans for the Bibliothèque de France confine access to digital works to workstations in the library itself.

The capabilities possible with a usage-rights approach may also lead to new categories of library service and allow libraries to introduce new charges while maintaining some free access. Suppose, for example, that a library has the budget to buy ten copies of a digital book. The repository system described in Part 3 could allow these copies to be digitally checked out by patrons and returned automatically at the end of their loan periods. Suppose, further that an additional five copies of the work would satisfy a higher demand. In principle, the library could purchase the additional copies and loan them out for a fee, thus recovering their cost and perhaps a bit more. Patrons could decide whether to wait their turn for access to the free copies or pay for quicker access to the for-fee copies.

Part of the rationale for mixing for-free and for-fee services in a library is that the for-fee services could generate revenues to support the free public use of the library. This sort of two-level approach could also be used for paper books. What's different for digital works is that the practical matters of inventory and variable demand for copies could be handled automatically by computer systems while generating only nominal costs for long-term inventory. Five digital copies take no more space than one. By special arrangement with publishers, libraries could even make the digital copies they need on demand and pay the publisher for the actual usage of the book, which may rise and fall over time. This practice would serve the public interest by providing more people with access to books when they need them.

Even with these changed assumptions, however, important questions and ambiguities about the potential roles of libraries, as compared to bookstores and publishers, would remain. Bookstores too might provide digital works to their customers on a fee-for-copy or on a pay-for-play basis. Pay-for-play is a kind of metered use, in which the customer pays for the time to read the book, or perhaps pays to have it available for a given length of time. Such arrangements would be essentially the same as paying to borrow a digital book from a library; this suggests that the prospects of digital distribution will ultimately blur the differences between bookstores and libraries. Even if libraries do not "loan" digital books for a fee, bookstores will do so with metered-playing arrangements.

There are strong economic pressures to collapse the supply chain for publications. Academic journals are a case in point (as discussed in the Lederberg article). The high prices of journals are mostly a result of printing costs and the fact that their articles typically appeal to very small audiences. Prices would drop if the general overheads of printing, filing, and distributing paper were eliminated in favor of a system of printing articles on demand. The technology to use such a system is in reach, and some academic publishers are already distributing publications digitally by CDROM or network. Instead of photocopying them for interlibrary loan, the periodicals office at Boston Spa simply prints off a fresh new copy of the article in demand. Because the rising costs of journals are forcing libraries to cut back on subscriptions, the economic future of journals in their present form is now seriously in doubt. Publishers, however, continue to drag their feet for fear that collapse of the supply chain will lead irrevocably to self-publication.

Browning's essay demonstrates that traditional assumptions about the library cannot be simply transplanted to a digital context. Many underlying questions about the separation of roles among publishers, editors, printers, bookstores and libraries—as well as issues related to compensation for intellectual property—remain to be resolved. The traditional library functions of preserving intellectual property, cataloging it, and making it available to the public have an important place on the NII. The challenge lies in inventing appropriate new ways to carry them out.

Technological Revolutions and the Gutenberg Myth

Scott D. N. Cook

Connections

The information superhighway has often been described as the road to the information Promised Land. The idea is that as soon as it is developed, the general public will swiftly attain widespread access to all sorts of information. Similar predictions were made about the personal computer and, before that, about television. In these examples of the popular idea of a technological revolution a single new technology is introduced and rapid, far-reaching social changes quickly follow.

The most frequently cited technological revolution of this sort is the invention of the movable-type printing press by Gutenberg around 1450. According to the usual account, the revolution in printing led to widespread literacy and played an important role in triggering the transformation of western civilization.

As a philosopher interested in technological change, Cook takes a special interest in the printing revolution. The popular account of the effect of the printing press has become the exemplar of technological revolutions in general. It is also wrong. Cook calls the popular account the Gutenberg myth and examines in some detail the actual unfolding of events that led to general literacy in the western world.

As Cook describes it, the printing press was itself several inventions, including new techniques of casting pieces of type and development of an ink that would adhere to metal type. Yet, even counting all of this as a single invention, other critical breakthroughs were required to complete it. When did they occur? How long did it take for the general public to become literate? What factors governed the pace of social change that gave the "common man" a use for and an interest in books? The examination of the Gutenberg myth is, we suggest, especially timely for understanding our present expectations about digital libraries and our goals in establishing the information infrastructure.

The dream of a digital network linking people and information around the globe is commonly considered *the* technological revolution of the 1990s, with the shape of the twenty-first century issuing from it. The Internet, the World Wide Web, and their next-generation cousins have captured the imagination of the public and of specialists in numerous fields. What is imagined is nothing short of revolutionary changes in our lives, our society and our world. Ultimately, we are told, the scale of these changes will be even greater than those of the Gutenberg revolution—the changes commonly associated with invention of movable type printing in fifteenth-century Europe.

The new technologies of our time are indeed exciting and powerful. Much good (or much evil) could be done with them. But the claim that we are seeing a new Gutenberg revolution is a dangerous one. It is dangerous because the picture of the Gutenberg revolution found in histories, encyclopedias, and the popular media is historically inaccurate and conceptually misleading. It would have us believe that rapid and far-reaching changes in literacy, learning and social institutions were caused by a single new technology. This is what I call the Gutenberg Myth; it is not accurate history (as we will see below). Yet, the Gutenberg Myth has become the most commonly used model for making predictions about the directions new technologies will take and for identifying what we need to do to avoid being left behind.

As a model for understanding other revolutions the Gutenberg Myth can be dangerously misleading. Using a faulty sense of printing as a way of understanding other powerful innovations guarantees neither their wise development nor responsible use of them. A better model for technological revolutions, especially the digital revolutions going on around us, is suggested by a broader, more realistic understanding of the Gutenberg revolution itself.

The Gutenberg Myth

The appearance of printing has been celebrated as a major step in the advance of technology and the development of western civilization. Charles Babbage. the nineteenth-century inventor of calculating machines, remarked that "the modern world commences with the printing press." Today, it is commonly held that the invention of movable type made possible the mass distribution of the printed word, brought about a string of broad and rapid social advances through an explosion in literacy and learning, and ultimately "democratized knowledge" (Burke 1978). *The McGraw-Hill Encyclopedia of Science and Technology* states that the invention of movable type printing "... was one of the most important inventions in human history. It was significant, even revolutionary, in two respects." The first was the principle of movable type itself. "A second and more important aspect [was that it] ... made it possible to put more information into the hands of more people in less time and at lower cost, and thereby to spread literacy and learning more widely and rapidly than ever before" (Bruno 1987). As historian of science Derek de Solla Price put it, "By 1500 ... the printed book had become a quite new force. The momentous effect, of course, was that the world of learning, hitherto the domain of a tiny privileged elite, was suddenly made much more accessible to the common man" (de Solla Price 1975, p. 99).

This is the traditional view of the Gutenberg revolution. It is the image that comes to mind when printing is suggested as a model for other technological revolutions. It does not, however, reflect the realities of European history. The process by which the world of learning became "accessible to the common man" entailed several factors in addition to movable type. I will focus on two of them that are particularly central. The first was paper: bringing the printed word to the masses required a medium to print on which was available in quantities and at a cost amenable to "mass distribution." The second factor was literacy: the "common man" needed to be able to read. Neither of these requirements obtained in 1500. These discrepancies point to the need for a richer, more accurate account of the story of movable type and its relationship to the spread of literacy and learning to a broad population in western civilization. It is, after all, the achievement of broad literacy and learning that makes the story of printing revolutionary. This story can begin with the Gutenberg Bible itself.

Gutenberg Revisited

The invention of movable type printing is usually credited to Johann Gutenberg of Mainz, Germany, who used it to produce one of the most famous masterpieces of the fifteenth century: the book now called the Gutenberg Bible. As with many important inventions, when, where and by whom the invention actually came about has been the subject of considerable debate. One theory, for example, holds that the first person in Europe to develop movable type was not Gutenberg, but Laurens Janszoon Coster, a contemporary of Gutenberg's living in the Netherlands. (This theory has a good measure of historical merit; as well as a great deal of popularity among the Dutch.) In fact, Gutenberg was not the only person in Europe working on the idea of mechanical printing. It is also quite likely that Gutenberg drew on the work of others in such allied crafts such as metal alloying and casting. Further, it is possible that the work of Gutenberg, Coster, and others in Europe owes a significant debt to the development of print blocks in Asia, which by the fifteenth century had been in common use in China, Japan, and Korea for generations (including their use in the printing of books). With these qualifications in mind, we can take the advent of movable type printing in mid–fifteenth century Europe as a starting point of the 'print revolution'' associated, symbolically at least, with the printing of the Gutenberg Bible.

The principle of movable type used in printing the Gutenberg Bible is elegantly simple. Gutenberg took as his basic unit the single letter, making type blocks that carried one letter each. The blocks were of standard size in all their dimensions so they could be set one-by-one, in any combination, into consistently straight lines on a flat printing bed in an arrangement of text making up an entire page, which in turn offered a consistently level printing surface. After being used to print any number of copies of that page, the arrangement could be broken down and the type blocks reused. Gutenberg's chief technological accomplishments included developing techniques of metal casting and alloying that made this process economically and technically practical.

In keeping with the principle of movable type, each letter of the Gutenberg Bible was set by hand. The pages, over one thousand of them. were printed one at a time onto hide parchment or rag-fiber paper. Next, in the spirit of the manuscripts of the day, hand illuminations and lettering, details were added to each of the printed pages. Letters at the beginning of chapters, for example, were written in by hand and elaborately illumined and every capital letter in the entire text had a red highlight scribed through it. Finally, the leaves were bound, again by the hand of the craftsman, into large, elegant volumes. The whole project, from casting the first type to binding the final volume, took several years.

Looking at the Gutenberg Bible and at Gutenberg's practice as a craftsman, one does not sense the invention and exploitation of a revolutionary technology but rather the conservative use of an innovative technique for the mechanical production of manuscripts. In fact, the very aim of movable type printing and the technical innovations Gutenberg brought to it were directed at producing volumes that looked as much as possible like manuscripts. Within the printing craft in general, moreover, the same standards of craftsmanship and aesthetics associated with manuscripts were applied to printed books for at least two generations beyond the Gutenberg Bible. Had the new technology not met these old standards, it might well have been dismissed as a failed experiment. Indeed, a judgment like this seems to have been made in China. Type blocks containing a single character were developed, but the Chinese abandoned them in favor of plate blocks containing entire texts; they felt that the type blocks were not sufficiently consistent in shape to produce a printed page that met the high aesthetic standards of their calligraphy. This suggests that the initiation of a technological revolution may often depend on *new* technologies being functionally compatible with *old* craft practices and *traditional* values of the surrounding culture.

Since printing the Gutenberg Bible on fine parchment entailed the use of hundreds of pieces of hide, raw materials alone could be a costly factor. A single copy required the skins of fifty to seventy-five sheep. Likewise, the paper Gutenberg used (most copies were on paper), though less costly than parchment, was nonetheless a valuable commodity. It was produced a single sheet at a time by skilled craftsmen dependent on often scarce supplies of waste rag or scrap from garment manufacture.

Gutenberg's finished product, then, was a marvelously fine piece of craftsmanship, a beautiful and valuable example of the printer's art. And it remains so to the present day. But it was also an artifact for elites, chiefly the aristocracy and the Church. The Word as printed by Gutenberg was not distributed to the masses. In fact, only about two hundred copies of the Gutenberg Bible were ever produced. Meanwhile, printed books in general remained far too costly for de Solla Price's "common man" well beyond 1500.

Not only were most people in the fifteenth century unable to buy a Gutenberg Bible, they were also unable to read it. This is an essential element in assessing the course of the printing revolution; any potential mass social change associated with printing must be weighed against the extent of mass illiteracy.

Although difficult to define and measure, even a cautious estimate places illiteracy in fifteenth-century Europe at well over 90 percent of the general population. Further, since those who could read were concentrated among clergy, scholars, and aristocrats—and there almost entirely among men—illiteracy in most other segments of society was close to universal. Even among those who could read, not all were schooled in Latin, which was, of course, the language of the Christian Bible.

In the light of such factors. Gutenberg's efforts appear far from revolutionary—indeed, they are quite in keeping with the social, religious, political, and economic institutions of his day.

Printing and Mass Illiteracy

Even so, printing was much faster and less expensive than the copying of manuscripts. This fact, along with the aesthetic quality of printed texts, came to present a significant challenge to traditional manuscript production. Indeed, the displacement of calligraphy by movable type as the preferred means of creating documents resulted in a dramatic spread of printing technology. By the middle of the sixteenth century, presses were operating in most major centers of Europe and had begun to appear in the Middle East and Asia. In the New World, the first press was established at Mexico City in 1539; the second, a century later in 1638, at Cambridge, Massachusetts.

Within literate communities, the press helped bring about a greater availability of texts and a vastly expanded number of individual titles. It is estimated that some thirty thousand editions were printed in the first fifty years following the advent of the press, equaling the number produced in the previous one thousand years. Moreover, in scholastic communities, the press became a key element in a remarkably rapid growth in the translation and publication of classical texts—a phenomenon that was to fan the glowing coals of the Enlightenment.

By 1650, movable type technology was a fact of life in hundreds of communities throughout Europe. But the spread of the technology did not carry with it a broad social revolution in literacy and learning. Although levels of literacy rose in some sectors of the population (in connection with the Reformation, for example), illiteracy in Europe in general stood at about 80 percent in 1650, and the ability to read and write remained significantly associated with class and gender. At this point, two hundred years after Gutenberg, access to the world of learning was *not* a fact of life for the masses.

In the eighteenth century, illiteracy began to decline at a greater rate. By 1700 it had fallen to between 65 and 70 percent. As the nineteenth century approached, the figure neared 50 percent. Among the factors associated with this improvement was the growing role of reading and writing in work, especially in the trades. In fact, one of the earliest exceptions to the exclusion of literacy to all but social elites was its appearance among the trades. Reading and writing became a growing part of work as the increasing organization of society expanded the need to keep records. Treatises on craft skills, meanwhile, became one of the largest categories of printed books (third after religion and law).

Significantly, the spread of literacy to more people and more classes of people during this period (approximately 1650 to 1800) occurred alongside some rather remarkable changes in both the idea and reality of social equality. The notion that individuals are equal within a human community found strong expression in the political, literary, and philosophical writings of the time. Philosophical propositions like Hobbes's argument that all people are equal in "a state of nature" and Locke's contention that all people are by nature equally free found broader expression in Jefferson's declaration that "all men are created equal" and Rousseau's insistence that social inequalities are unnatural creations of our institutions. Claims of a political right to specific forms of social equality became banners of the American and French Revolutions. Kant gave these themes a stronger moral sense with his argument that all people are (or ought to be) moral equals as legislators within a "kingdom of ends." Similarly, various notions of equality were explored in the art, architecture and music of the period.

Ultimately, this sweeping reevaluation of the idea of equality entailed nothing less than a recasting of what was to be understood as the entitlements of membership in society and the beginnings of a parallel redesign of the social institutions associated with providing and guaranteeing those rights. All this made the spread of literacy, as a prerequisite of citizenship rather than of privilege, more "thinkable," and thus more feasible. The decline in illiteracy during this period, therefore, must be understood as much more the product of changing social, political, and moral values than as a consequence of the continued presence of the centuries-old technology of printing. That is, this aspect of the printing revolution was due more to social than technological factors.

The Paper It's Printed On

From the time of Gutenberg until the early nineteenth century, paper was the product of costly materials and highly skilled craftsmanship. No major advance had been made in the painstaking, sheet-by-sheet hand work of the ancient craft since it entered Europe from the Islamic world in the twelfth century.

Correspondingly, the value placed on paper is reflected in numerous laws and customs from the time of Gutenberg to the nineteenth century. A 1666 English law, for example, decreed that only wool, being unsuitable for papermaking, could be used in burying the dead. An early New England periodical, in encouraging readers to save rags for papermakers, suggested that each housewife make a rag bag and keep it next to the family Bible—a wonderfully symbolic connection emphasizing the value placed on paper. The *Boston News Letter* printed an announcement in 1769 that "... the bell cart will go through Boston about the end of each month ... " for the purpose of collecting rags. Readers were further encouraged to fulfill their civic duty with the following poem.

Rags are beauties which concealed lie,
But when in paper, how charms the eye!
Pray save your rags, new beauties to discover,
For of paper, truly, everyone's a lover;
By the pen and press such knowledge is displayed
As wouldn't exist if paper was not made.
Wisdom of things, mysterious, divine,
Illustriously doth on paper shine.

In 1776 the Massachusetts General Court required that in each community a person be appointed to collect rags. To conserve paper, it remained until 1818 a punishable offense in England to print newssheets or broadsides larger than 22 by 32 inches (roughly the current size of the *New York Times*).

The search for a reliable, less expensive alternative to rag scrap as the raw material for paper had been unsuccessful—though not for want of effort. Several materials were tried experimentally, including hemp, pine cones, used shingles, potatoes, and asbestos. A particularly imaginative source for rag, itself, was found in the mid-nineteenth century in Egyptian mummies. Shiploads of mummies were sent from Egypt to paper companies in the United States, where their linen wrappings were taken off and recycled, so to speak, into paper. This practice continued for some time, apparently without the intervention of concerned health officials, outraged clergy, or jealous archaeologists. The only competition the papermakers had for the mummies was from the new Egyptian railroad, which, reportedly, used them as fuel.

That mummies could be shipped all the way from Egypt to the United States solely for the use of their wrappings is a gauge of the value and cost of paper at the time (as well as a measure of deficit in respect for the dead). The availability of rag and the cost of paper were clearly serious obstacles to printing on a mass scale well into the nineteenth century.

Mass Printing and Mass Society

Through the course of the nineteenth century, several technological and social innovations combined to produce dramatic changes in printing and literacy. By the turn of the century, wood pulp had been identified as a reliable and plentiful fiber source for papermaking. The first experimental techniques for producing pulp-fiber paper by machine were operational by the 1810s. In the 1840s, a machine designed specifically for the mass production of paper-quality pulp was introduced. By the 1860s, wood pulp paper was being made commercially in mills that could turn out paper at dazzling speed in continuous rolls of indefinite length. The development of machine-made pulp and paper made possible a rapid drop in the cost of paper. The price of newsprint, for example, fell by a factor of ten between the 1860s and 1890s.

Printing itself developed remarkably through the nineteenth century. Steam power was introduced to press operation in 1810. In the middle of the century, the flat reciprocating printing bed was displaced by the development of the stereotype cylinder, the molded and curved printing surfaces now associated with the "rolling press." A major step in the printing craft was made in 1884 with the invention of the linotype. With this machine, the highly time-consuming hand work of setting type one letter at a time could be replaced by a mechanized operation that cast type by the line. This principle dramatically increased the speed and reduced the cost of typesetting. In doing so, the linotype became an important factor in making possible the mass production of the printed word. With respect to printing technology, meanwhile, the linotype represents a significant step away from the principle of movable type, since it treats the line rather than the single letter as its basic unit.

Resting on expanding notions of social equality a fundamentally important social innovation of the nineteenth century was the introduction of public education. From the middle of the century onward, state-supported elementary education became a reality in country after country. By the end of the century, it was accepted, at least in principle, throughout Western Europe. The parallel decline in illiteracy was dramatic. In 1800, half of the general population was illiterate. By the century's end, the figure was under 10 percent.

With the advent of mass literacy and the development of technologies for the rapid and relatively inexpensive mass production of paper and printed materials, the mass distribution of the printed word became a meaningful and practical possibility. It was not until the latter decades of the nineteenth century, therefore, that the social and technological elements for making "the world of learning ... accessible to the common" person through printing were fully in place—four hundred years after the appearance of the movable type press.

All of these factors combine to help us sketch out a fuller, more accurate understanding of the printing revolution; they also point to the need for a broader, multi-dimensional model of the structure of technological revolutions to replace the Gutenberg Myth. At the very least, this account of the printing revolution suggests that the traditional, one-dimensional model of new technologies (or a single new material gadget) causing broad social change must be regarded with deep suspicion.

A healthy skepticism about the Gutenberg Myth is also called for in our efforts to understand the social changes associated with new technologies in our own time. Clearly, we need a new model of the structure of technological revolutions in order to assess the role of technological change in our lives and cultures in a way that avoids the political and moral myopia of the Gutenberg Myth. It is to the exploration of some examples of these pitfalls that I now turn.

Illiteracy in the Shadow of Technology

The story of the spread of literacy and learning in western civilization is an important one, as is the role of the printing press within it. At the same time, the call for making "learning ... accessible to the common" person is still heard today in the broader context of making literacy and learning accessible to the peoples of the world.

Approximately 90 percent of the illiterate people alive today live in the developing world, where the average level of adult illiteracy is around 40 percent. Many of these countries have literacy programs, and there are internationally sponsored literacy initiatives through the United Nations and private organizations. Progress is being made, but neither the "problem" nor the "solution" is simple. Nor is it simply a matter of technological need. The level of illiteracy in these countries fell by almost 10 percent between 1970 and 1980, yet (because of population trends) the absolute number of illiterate people increased during that period by nearly seventy-million.

Just as the Gutenberg Myth fails to capture the realities of western history, so too it fails as a model for assessing the current realities of the developing world: The image of literacy and learning emerging on a mass scale from the introduction of printing technology would, indeed, be a very misleading model for these nations. The situation in the developing world is neither well understood nor effectively addressed by assuming that mass literacy can emerge from the introduction of a single technology. Today, print and other technologies such as computers are readily available, but this has not made it possible to "put more information into the hands of more people ... and thereby to spread literacy and learning" throughout the developing world (as the McGraw-Hill encyclopedia's formulation of the Gutenberg Myth might suggest).

Exciting New Technologies, Same Old Myth

The printing revolution is often evoked as a model for understanding the social importance of new technologies. The structure of technological revolutions implicit in such analogies is typically the Gutenberg Myth: a single technology being the sole cause of rapid and far-reaching social change. Throughout the 1980s, for example, the personal computer was depicted in the popular and scholarly press as single-handedly revolutionizing the whole of society. By the early 1990s the same was being said about the "data superhighway." Not surprisingly such discussions of exciting new technologies reflect the same sorts of historical and conceptual distortions found in nearly all references to the printing revolution.

Conclusion: Revolutions Recaptured

This brief look at the printing revolution suggests that the structure of technological revolutions is neither simple, technologically determined, nor everywhere the same, either historically or culturally. It is clear that

the model of sweeping social change being caused by a single technological innovation is historically and conceptually faulty and misleading.
Such changes are not *caused* by the appearance of a single gadget; they
are *constituted* in multiple, mutually influencing technological and social
innovations. A new model of the structure of technological revolutions
must reflect these facts. Moreover, it must be able to embrace the deeply
held values that inform our cultures and underlie the choices we make
about the direction our technologies ought to take—even when those
choices are made by default rather than by design. The technological
determinism inherent in the Gutenberg Myth forecloses discussion of just
these social, political, and moral values—which are ultimately the only
means by which we can distinguish between an appropriate and inappropriate role for any of the exciting new technologies of our day.

Reflections

*Cook's retelling of the Gutenberg story shows us that the role of tech-
nology in social transformation is not a simple process of introducing
new technology, then watching things happen. For Cook, exposing the
Gutenberg Myth means debunking technological determinism. Rather
than seeing changes as caused by the appearance of a new technology, he
sees them as constituted through multiple, mutually influencing technological and social innovations. What lessons should we take from the
account?*

*One possible lesson is that social transformation often takes longer
than the spread of a given technology. In Cook's revised account, several
centuries went by before widespread literacy prevailed and before the
price of paper became low enough to make books and other printed
materials broadly affordable. The time required for a technology to come
into wide use need not, however, always be measured in multiple centuries. The present century has seen many technologies—including automobiles, radio, television, microwave ovens, compact discs, video games,
and personal computers—move from their first demonstrations to worldwide used by millions of people. Social change is cumulative. The development of commercial radio required broadcasting stations, dealerships
to sell the radio sets, advertisements to pay for the programs, and the*

willingness of people to set aside time to listen to it. Given this context, commercial television did not have to start from scratch, for the social innovations brought about by radio prepared the way for television. Every change, technological or social, builds on and modifies previous ones.

Cook's account focuses principally on two factors, the development of paper and the spread of literacy, which we can examine for analogies to the case of computers and network. In the case of printing, paper was the medium whose price and availability affected the production of printed works; as Cook noted, the price of paper was high when the printing press was invented and it stayed high for centuries. In contrast, the price of computers has declined rapidly since the 1950s. According to many analysts, the price of key computing elements like memory and processors drops by half every eighteen to twenty-four months. Between 1992 and 1994 the number of personal computers in use in the United States grew from about eight million to about forty million. Although not yet available to everyone, it is clear that they are rising in popularity much more quickly than books did in the thirty years after Gutenberg's invention.

Cook's account of how other inventions combined with the printing press to produce the print revolution is a variant on the theme "everything is connected." Inventions, of course, do not come from nowhere; they are constructed out of things that already exist. But the larger part of the story is that no invention stands alone. An invention also needs to arise in a context that can create all the other inventions necessary for its use. For example, the widespread use of the automobile required numerous other inventions, such as reliable tires and automatic starters, as well as service stations to make fuel available for long trips and good roads to travel on.

To understand the development of roads, though, requires us to look beyond technological developments to what might be called social inventions. Initially, good roads had to be built to accommodate the greater speeds of cars over horses. In the 1950s, however, an important shift in value occurred that came in part from post–World War II concerns about national security. Combined with the interests of the oil companies, this shift brought about the interstate highway system. As social invention and the infrastructure for automobiles continued to evolve, gas stations installed self-service pumps and they now take credit cards.

Displacing an invention with an entrenched infrastructure can be more costly than building infrastructure in the first place. New inventions compete with old ones embedded in their existing infrastructure. Today, one of the obstacles to cars using alternative fuels is the lack of a distribution system for these fuels. It is not that we have forgotten gasoline service stations weren't here when the first settlers arrived but that people who buy cars now expect an infrastructure to be in place before they buy them.

In the story of printing, the social invention that led to widespread literacy was a shift in social values regarding equality that arose from the French and American revolutions and fostered state-supported elementary education. The literacy analogy for computers is computer literacy, although it is not clear what computer literacy *means. If we examine what was entailed in* radio literacy *and* television literacy, *we find that they built on all sorts of cultural innovations already in place. This is also true for computer literacy, which builds on not only literacy in written language but also on people's experiences with radio, television, and video games.*

In fact, we do not know everything included in computer literacy, or even in television literacy, because they keep changing. Is television literacy simply the ability to channel surf? Is it the ability to recognize the difference between fact and fiction? In print literacy, there is generally a clear distinction between them; libraries even keep works of fiction and nonfiction in different sections. In radio and television, however, the immediacy of drama seems to stir different sensibilities, and sometimes to confuse them. Consider the often-discussed phenomenon of public panic that took place when some people mistook Orson Welles's radio broadcast of H. G. Wellis novel War of the Worlds *as a news broadcast of an actual invasion from Mars. With a book, it is usually a simple matter to look at the cover to determine whether it is presented as fiction; but on television reenactments of historical events and crime scenes (sometimes called "faction") arouse public debate because, some people complain, they dangerously blur the distinction between fact and fiction.*

A turning point in computer literacy occurred the 1990s with the popular introduction of reference material on CD-ROMs and on-line, allowing users to search for information rapidly and automatically. The ability to use a computer as an information retrieval tool, once the domain of specialist librarians, spread to other professionals, and even to schoolchildren. For many people accustomed to using computers mainly for word processing, this new use marked the first time they could expect to get more out of their computer than they had put into it. It marked a shift in our understanding of what it means to know how to use computers, to be computer literate.

Cook tells us that most people did not immediately see a use for reading after Gutenberg invented the printing press. In the twentieth century, it seems, the rapid spread of the computer reflects no such doubt about its value. Something seems to happening quickly. Part of our challenge is to understand what that is.

Excerpt from "Libraries Are More than Information: Situational Aspects of Electronic Libraries"

Vicky Reich and Mark Weiser

Connections

The stereotypical vision of a patron using a digital library is a person seated at a computer workstation consulting on-line catalogs and retrieving information. The following article blends the experience of a professional librarian with the vision of a world-class technologist to take a contrarian perspective on what digital libraries could be. Reich and Weiser begin by drawing attention to functions of libraries that provide no information but meet human needs—such as serving as centers of community culture. Their analysis demolishes the stereotypical vision by helping us see much more of what libraries do now and what they could do electronically.

A new national information infrastructure is inevitable. Many papers have been written on the technical and economic issues that are part of creating this infrastructure. The issues dealt with are usually those of gathering, storing, and retrieving the information; or distributing it; or charging for it; or preserving the intellectual properties rights of the creators, distributors, and users of the information. A national information infrastructure, though, is not just about information.

The United States has a national information infrastructure today. The wire services, the newspapers, the radio and television broadcast systems, and the national telephone system all provide a national grid of information. More importantly from the point of view of large, reliable, distributed information systems, our national information infrastructure today consists of tens of thousands of public and school libraries all across the country. These libraries are in nearly every elementary, junior high, and high school; and they are in nearly every community, even the very small. In the long run, it is these widely scattered and local community information sources that will be strongly affected by the NII. For instance, already many community pubic libraries are networked via the FreeNet system.

Community public libraries provide more than information. If one is considering replacing or augmenting them with electronic information systems, then it is important to consider the effect on the situational aspects of the present and future NII. We believe that these situational functions have come to exist because they fill a valuable role in the community. Their existence provides valuable lessons for the policies that should govern electronic information systems.

The most easily available source of networked library information today is the catalog; and yet 35 percent of library visitors have never used the catalog. Up to 12 percent of library visitors use no information in the library at all, but bring their own material. Clearly libraries now are doing much more than providing information, and as they become more networked they will need to continue to provide more. This paper is about some of that "more," and how to carry it forward to networked libraries.

• • •

Marshall McLuhan once described a thermonuclear explosion as information, but we think it is dangerously misleading to say that everything is information. There is an important difference between things considered as information, and things that are simply part of everyday activity without any imputed purpose of conveying knowledge. While a dictionary also has situational aspects, such as its distinctive smell and weight, its informational aspects dominate, and so dictionaries were computerized early. While a library reading room has informational aspects, such as a clock or posters on the wall, the situational aspects dominate; greater posters do not make up for uncomfortable chairs. This paper is about to what extent networked libraries can have comfortable chairs.[1]

Situational Functions of Libraries

Public libraries know they are not only about information. A widely used planning guide for public libraries lists eight public library roles: *community activities center, community information center, formal education support center, independent learning center, preschoolers' door to learning, popular materials library, reference library*, and *research center*. The first of these is completely non-informational, the next four have large non-informational components. Only the last three are predominantly informational and so are easily convertible to networked libraries. For instance, *preschoolers' door to learning* requires common comfortable space for parents and children to come together and to have fun; *community information center* requires arrangements for casual walk-by and for the display of physical objects; *formal education support center* and *independent learning center* require the ability to move objects (like car repair manuals) to their source of need (under the car). Below we discuss three ways that existing public libraries server non-informational functions: community identity, community culture, and minutiae of life.

Community Identity

We name by "community identity" the ways in which a library has impact merely by its existence in a common space, similar to how a park or mountain (or very ugly building) might function. ... A library is not just an information source, it is also a place to go after school, a place at which to "turn left" when giving directions, a part of the community skyline and streetscape, a place for interesting trees and gardens.

• • •

We believe that the networked library should strive to provide the following functions for community identity: distinctive "places"; geographically local networked meeting rooms, and a physical community presence.

Distinctive "places" If communities continue to enjoy local identity (we think this diversity is very valuable and will not vanish) then their networked versions ought also to be distinct. Thus one should have a different feel when connecting on-line into Harvard's Widener Library versus the Palo Alto Children's Library. For instance, Palo Alto might offer a cheery message, a bit of community news, and a weather report; while Harvard might present a dignified message of intersession operating hours and guest access rules. (We are not proposing incompatible interfaces, just interesting variety. The wide variety in library architecture doesn't prevent people from finding the front door or checking out books.)

Local meeting rooms   Many network services contain chat rooms and bulletin boards where people of similar interests can talk. Libraries should be the providers of network rooms for their community. Special rooms could be created for issues of temporary interest, like a one-time referendum. Some communities have experimented with these services already.[2]

Going one step further, there could be networked rooms for very local areas, such as people living on the same block or same street. This is similar to branch libraries (even tiny storefronts) that provide the primary function of bringing information to local areas, but also secondarily create social spaces for small local groups.

• • •

Browsers from other communities might be able to look at the topic headings and how much activity each has, without actually joining. This is not unlike the information a visitor gleans while driving through a town and noticing how "alive" it is. The Internet community could get the feel for a "place" that one can get visiting a vibrant town without really being a member of it. Scholars and expatriate community members might still be permitted access, providing a vital extended community of neighbors.

Physical Presence   The networked world has a physical presence through displays and keyboards. This need not, and should not, be its only physical presence. A community proud of its on-line library might make its downtown a showcase of free, ubiquitous information access. Anyone walking through the downtown could be constantly in touch with information about weather, national events, or local sales. This information could come either from small and large displays everywhere through the downtown, or from handheld information terminals that we may all carry on our person someday.

The community might also put up on street corners large electronic displays of the results of continually operated queries on national databases. Examples of such queries are those that mention the community in the national press, or a topic of the week chosen by the library staff. For instance, a large downtown display might be continually scrolling through articles that are relevant to some local community concern, such as clean water or health care. The choice of articles could be manual, or the librarians could choose the search query of the week, and have the full text of the query results show up on the community display screens, with new matches replacing old once each day.[3]

These physical presences would make the community unique, as does distinctive building architecture. They could become significant sources of community pride and competition much as the electrification of downtowns once drove the spread of electric networks early this century. They could serve the simple community function of places to meet, excuses for gardens and landscaping (such as pleasant seating near the large electronic displays), and references for directions (turn left at the kiosk).

• • •

Community Culture

When a group of people behave similarly and share the same institutions and ways of life, they can be said to possess the same culture.

Public libraries contribute to culture by nurturing the distinctive culture of their local place, by providing homes for minority community cultures, and by providing access to other cultures. Some of this nurturing is by access to information sources, such as books and newspapers, that are already the focus of the networked library. But situational aspects of libraries are also part of their cultural presence.

A community culture is formed in part by its common institutions and ways of life. Coffee houses in Berkeley and deli's in New York are situational cultural institutions that also enable certain ways of life. Libraries contribute to cultural ways of life in at least four ways:

- Providing bulletin board space
- Providing display space for local artists and community groups
- Providing selected and organized displays from the local collection
- Providing non-interactive parallel work space (e.g., carrels)

The first three items above are a regular part of library life. Ten percent of library users view the bulletin boards, 15 percent the displays. While not a large percentage, it is a large number of people nationwide. The first three items also do provide information via their posters, artworks, and organization of information. But the information is of a situational sort that is often overlooked in thinking about networked libraries: it is primarily of local interest, and its value is very transient. The items posted on bulletin boards ("guitar lessons for children, $20 per half hour") are of no interest nationwide. The interest of local artists is often that they are local (e.g., your neighbor), as is their subject matter. And the selections from the local collection assume their interest especially because they are from the local collection, selected by local librarians. Our fourth item, parallel work-spaces, is distinctively non-informational. We discuss each of these below.

Local library bulletin boards are special in part because of where they are   Any posting there was probably by someone in the community, certainly by someone who has visited a library. Already one knows a little about who it was, how easy they will be to contact, and so on. Networked library bulletin boards will want to preserve some of this implicit context to the postings.[4]

Local artists and community groups also help generate community interest   The subject matter of the art may be of local interest, as is simply knowing that the person lives in the neighborhood, and so cannot help but be working out of a context partially shared by the community. For instance, postcards and landscapes of a particular area sell more copies at the site.

A related local context is implied when a display from a local collection is organized by the local librarians   Not only is it these librarians, in this building, paid for by this town, for this community, using this collection who created it, but I know that my friends and neighbors who come to this library are all going to see this same display. This locality and commonalty of exposure are a crucial part of community culture.[5]

Networked systems already have bulletin boards, chat lines, ASCII art forums, and constructed displays of interesting information (digests). However, these are almost never community localized. The over twenty thousand FidoNet and K12Net nodes are all locally based (accessed by a local phone call), but our sampling of them leads us to think that their primary service is their interconnection with other nodes around the country. Most of their offered services do not mainly work to promote a local community culture for local residents.

Another situational activity enabled by libraries is non-interactive parallel work spaces   That is to say, a place to work alone, but in the presence of others. This kind of participation in shared work is common; providing for it is part of good architectural design. Coffee houses are a more public form of locations for non-interactive parallel work. It is interesting that, so far, computer systems have not very well provided such spaces, except in some multimedia experiments. We predict that going on-line to do one's own work, while being peripherally aware of others on-line with you, will be an important characteristic of future networked systems. (Perhaps already part of the attraction of CompuServe and America Online is in part being there with others, even if one is just checking the encyclopedia.)

• • •

Minutiae of People's Lives

Libraries provide services that enter intimately into people's lives. We bring books home to read in our bedrooms, and to share with our children. We care for our gardens, our homes, our pets, and our parents with advice from our libraries. We carry a little bit of library with us when we carry around a checked-out book. The physical resources of a community library therefore exist both in its buildings and their contents, and also in the homes of the community members. This spreading of library items throughout a community, in a sense the diffusion of the library into the community, we call its participation in minutiae.

The past few years have seen the beginning of work on a new kind of relationship between people and electronic information. Sometimes called "ubiquitous computing," this relationship is based upon the computer as invisible, as getting out of the way so that people can get on with their lives as effortlessly enhanced by the computer and its information. The most powerful information is that which we do not need to attend to in order for it to affect us. For instance, a very important part of a novel is the choice of the author's voice. Yet for most novels this choice of voice must recede into the background for the reader in order for the author to achieve her intended effect.

Ubiquitous computing predicts that there will be several hundred little information-providing devices around the home in twenty years. These are a medium by which the networked library could continue to participate in the minutiae of life. Here are some ways this might work:

• The library could loan physical devices to members of the community who wanted to follow some community activity, such as local soccer or city council. The devices would be programmed to follow that activity. The patron would not need to log on, know any commands, or do anything other than glance at this physical item in their home from time to time. The devices would be reusable with reprogramming that would require bringing them back to the library.

• The library could distribute and maintain networked posters of community activities. These posters would physically reside in the community, perhaps even in people's homes, but would be continually connected to a steady source of community information, perhaps via paging. Then, in one's home, to see what activities are happening in your community that day, just glance at this poster hanging in your kitchen. It always shows today.

• • •

Specific Recommendations for the NII

To summarize our remarks, we recommend that planners for the NII and networked libraries adopt the following recommendations:

• Encourage and fund the development of distinctive and diverse community information nodes. The NII is not just the wires, but what is at the ends of them. Let each community be unique.

• Creatively use widespread community information displays. Think beyond the terminal to the community posterboard as an additional model of community network information access.

• Encourage community members to create, and post, distinctive community information. Let each community create its own network culture.

• Provide a way for network access to be controlled on the basis of physical proximity, so only those physically in a community could access some of the community information.

• Encourage, and fund, library loan programs for electronic access. Loan out pagers, as well as books.

Conclusion

Many may think it strange for us to be arguing for the preservation of local substance, and sense of place, when it is exactly to be free from the limitations of a particular place that causes people to be attracted to the Internet. But like anything else, absence of place can come in excess. The creation of various kinds of "placeless" communities like the National Academy of Sciences in our society have not obviated either people still needing homes and communities, or these "placeless" communities themselves needing distinctive places (such as the NAS retreat in Woods Hole). As network resources replace placeful resources, we will reach the point that we need more electronic "places." This paper tries to head off going too far with placelessness, to add constraints to internet architecture today so it can be placeful tomorrow, and to temper naive enthusiasm for a completely placeless existence.

• • •

Reflections

The preceding articles have asked whether the role of the library should be stretched from lending books to potentially publishing them and selling them. Reich and Weiser's focus, however, is not on books. Forget the patron of a digital library browsing on-line catalogs and retrieving information. If Reich and Weiser are correct, the main visible presence of a community library will not be hidden away in workstations but will be visible at kiosks on the main street, on electronic bulletin boards in homes and schools, and in other places. This interconnection of libraries, newspapers, and schools is more than a town resource; it is an organizer of a networked community.

Consider, for example, the work of the career or college counsellor. How do you find jobs, be they new professional positions or summer jobs for high school students? Human networking is a key to this. In an electronically networked community, the bulletin board that at the local store or library can be transformed into digital kiosks or home computers.

Reich and Weiser found several roles for public libraries in a town-planning guide: community activities center, community information center, formal education support center, independent learning center, and preschoolers' door to learning. These roles go beyond what we might expect from just the keeper of wisdom archetype. If, for example, you use the library as a community information center, are you looking for information or are you trying to connect with community activities? Both answers may be correct, but the second one takes us into the realm of the communicator. The example suggests two things: that social institutions adapt to serve the needs of a community; and keeping in mind the metaphors we need to understand real libraries may help us design good digital libraries.

In the later parts of this book, we discuss digital libraries in the wider context of the different I-way metaphors. Digital libraries are related to on-line discussion groups in the electronic mail metaphor; to the economics of publishing and lending of works in electronic marketplaces; and to places for meeting and working with people in the digital worlds metaphor. For example, where is the librarian when the library is a kiosk? With digital networks, the librarian may be accessible in the same way that information is—via a display on the kiosk. At the same time, if librarians are very accessible, will there be enough of them to handle the potential demand? What kinds of service requests should have priority? Should there be a fee for library services?

The technological portion of this vision of libraries draw on work with "ubiquitous computing" that Weiser has led at Xerox PARC. Ubiquitous computing is the idea that we may one day have hundreds of information-providing devices in our environment—in homes, cars, workplaces, and public spaces. In terms of our metaphors for thinking about the NII, this idea pervades all the metaphors—from the metaphor of the digital library to the metaphor of digital worlds.

Notes

1. Some early reviewers of our paper took us to be arguing for the preservation of physical libraries. While we do believe that physical libraries should be preserved, not least for their situational features, our arguments may not be taken at full force if they are only applied to physical preservation. This paper argues for something different: that we early make room for the new forms of comfortable chairs that will be needed by online information.

2. It is important for the library and the librarians to play a leading role in providing this service. Librarians are familiar with handling information. They understand confidentiality and free speech, and although many libraries are government-funded, librarians strongly value being independent of political special interests.

3. These kinds of facilities would enable the library to present to the community such information as weather or local-access TV programming. These are not services the library currently provides; whether libraries will or should take a more proactive role in providing "real time" information to the community, as opposed to "information suited for repositories," is open.

4. Of course, there is a context to many networked bulletin boards now: that the poster is likely male, computer-oriented, and a college student. Encouragement by both social and technical means to achieve truly wide use will eliminate this particular context while adding a variety of others.

5. Researchers working on [ideas about] newspapers of the future have remarked on a similar significance of shared context. The fantasy of a custom newspaper is just a fantasy because it deprives the reader of reading what everyone else has read.

Excerpt from "The Electronic Capture and Dissemination of the Cultural Practice of Tibetan Thangka Painting"

Ranjit Makkuni

Connections

Not all of the collective experience of a nation is manifest in writing. Museums recognize this with special and historical exhibits of paintings, sculpture, inventions, historical settings, and—more recently—films, records, and other media. In this way museums reflect a variation of the archetype keeper of knowledge in which "knowledge" takes a broad set of forms. As noted in the introduction, the word museum *has mythological roots; in the mythology of ancient Greece, the arts were presided over by the muses.*

Just displaying an artifact in a museum, however, does not convey much about its significance, or even its identity or use. Artifacts need to be interpreted and put into a context.

Imagine, therefore, a museum that wants to explain a dance that has a deep cultural significance expressed in a group of rituals and stories. If the museum showed only the dancer's shoes, or even the dancer's costume, we would understand none of this broad significance. If it exhibited the costume on a manikin in a pose next to a musical instrument used to accompany the dance, we still could not imagine the dance. If it showed a movie of the dance with the music playing, we would begin to get more, but we still would not understand how the dancer's movements tell the story. All this is a preview of what Makkuni thinks a museum should and *could do by using interactive multimedia technology that could also carry the exhibit to patrons over the network. Makkuni's goals for exhibits derive from his understanding of how stories and rituals are usually passed down in living cultures, rather than on what is usually done either in museums or on computers. In this way, he stretches past conventional limitations and, in the process, shows us what can be done when we have a vision and when we connect it with long-held cultural practices and dreams. In this excerpt from a longer paper, Makkuni explores the potential for preserving tradition with technology.*

Its subject is a multimedia exhibit celebrating the creation and meaning of Tibetan Thangka paintings. When China annexed Tibet in 1959, the exodus of Tibetans from their homeland uprooted many ancient traditions. One threatened tradition is the method of making scrolled paintings that had been handed down from master to pupil for over two thousand years.

The article was written near the beginning of the project, which later received international acclaim.

To glance for the first time at a Thangka painting of Sakyamuni Buddha (Figure 1) is to be transported to an evocative world charged with fantasy and symbolism. The image depicted is not a portrait, but a symbol of Sakyamuni, Buddha, or the Enlightened One. The painting is called Thangka. Typically, images on Thangka paintings, like those expressed in stone and metal, represent the various deities that populate the Tibetan artistic pantheon. Blazing with symbolism, their purpose is to transport the viewer into the supernatural and paradisiacal world of the deity, a world conceptualized by theologians and visualized by artists for countless generations conveying the Tibetan Buddhist ideal of self-realization and harmony with the cosmos. The paintings are invested with special powers, and are dedicated in an attempt to secure both material benefits and spiritual well being for the donor, the donor's family, and the greater community.

Visually expressive and stimulating as these images are, the depiction of the various deities on Thangkas is regulated by very precise rules of composition. Some of these rules of composition were represented in canonical treatises describing verbally the basic iconography of the various deities. Other rules were expressed visually through proportioning diagrams and example sketches of deities. The sketches demonstrate, for example, various compositional schemes of Thangkas, the postures of deities, the gestures that deities make with their hands, the symbolic

Figure 1
Thangka painting of Sakyamuni Buddha, sixth century BC founder of Buddhist teachings. Painted by Jampa, Dharamsala, 1979. Dorje Chang Institute, Auckland, © 1979. Courtesy of Wisdom Publications, London.

objects that their hands clasp, the rendering of the deities' garments and accessories, and landscape elements that echo the deities' spiritual qualities. These rules of composition are timeless as they were passed down from master to pupil through successive generations, the medium of transmission consisting of proportioning diagrams, example sketches, and verse in Tibetan canonical treatises.

A variety of forces threaten the practice of Thangka painting, moving the craft toward irrevocable simplification. The Electronic Sketch Book of Tibetan Thangka Painting project is conceived as a way of using interactive computing and video technologies to preserve in electronic form Thangka expertise and the cultural context in which Thangkas are created, and use the records in educating people about the world of Thangka painting. The project is a creative collaborative effort between groups: systems designers of Xerox PARC, art historians and Tibetologists of the Asian Art Museum of San Francisco, a renowned Tibetan monk, and a master Thangka painter.

The electronic sketch book is seen as having two roles: a preservation role, and a dissemination role. In the preservation role, the sketch book takes form as a chronicle, an audio-visual diary of Thangka imagery and expertise similar to traditional manuscript illuminations and narrative paintings. In the dissemination role, the sketch book serves as a medium of transmission, one that can connect Thangka masters with beginning students, and, in museum settings, serve as an interpretive guide to both the cultural context and process of Thangka paintings. On a philosophical note, the sketch book relates the sense of "contemporary time" with the "traditional time" of Tibet.

The introduction of a new communication and representation medium is bound to affect the practice of Thangka painting. We present our motivations for the use of electronic technologies for preserving and disseminating Thangka painting. We examine the relationship of the art to the rich cultural practice, illustrating the relationship between media, ritual and the designed artifact, and point out the limitations and benefits of electronic technologies in the capture and transmission of Thangka painting. Focussing on process as well as product, our research illustrates themes of characterizing the design expertise behind the artifact, and the electronic transmission of cultural presence. Specific to how people interact with electronic media, we address expressive means to interact with computers, and the re-creation of the cultural experience using electronic media.

• • •

Keeping in mind the broader vision for the use of electronic technologies in the world of Thangka painting, we describe a particular implementation of the sketch book for a western museum educational setting—the galleries of the Asian Art Museum of San Francisco. For the museum setting, the focus of the sketch book is on the preservation of the cultural practice of Thangka painting, and public dissemination aimed at the general museum-goers who have no prior experience with Tibetan art, and who have little or cursory knowledge of computers.

The sketch book takes form as a museum installation by which general museum-goers can gain a glimpse of the world of Thangka painting—its sounds, sights, processes, and cultural context. Associated with the general museum audience we faced particular challenges which shaped the form and content of the sketch book: for the general museum audience, the sketch book must be easy to use; its user interface model must be simple to understand; it must allow museum-goers open-ended explorations. With respect to the sketch book's construction, the presentation materials had to be authored by museum curators who had little exposure to computers.

The sketch book contains a video database of sounds and images of the process of Thangka composition including: images from the museum's rare painting collection, images of rules of composition, techniques, and Tibetan cultural life, live recordings of a master Thangka painter's composition process, curatorial analyses of paintings, and a monk's discussion of theology. Mediated by a computer system, this database is used in two modes: authoring and presentation. In the authoring mode, museum curators collect video source material of Thangka imagery, edit and condense the source material into video records, create a computational model of the video records in the database, organize the records, and create presentations of Thangka related topics for the public. In the presentation mode, an interactive graphic interface allows museum-goers to explore the curator's presentations.

The museum setting of the sketch book consists of a wall containing three video monitors and a computer screen. By pointing at and touching elements of a Thangka painting on the computer screen to play back video records, the museum-goer gains access to the different elements of the video database—paintings, live sketches, discussions, curatorial analyses.

Motivations

The word *Thangka* literally means "something that is rolled up," hence, a rolled-up image or a painting scroll. The Tibetan words for *to paint* literally translate as "to write Gods." A cross between symbol, ornament, and design, the Thangka is a way of "seeing" the world from both aesthetic and spiritual points of view.

The center stage of a Thangka painting is usually occupied by a deity. In the painting, the Buddha, dressed in a monk's robes, is shown meditating in still repose, and turning away from all attachments to seek a cure for the world's sorrow. A lotus supports his body for, indeed, his feet cannot rest on the physical earth. His right hand extends over the length of his body and touches the cushion upon which he meditates, calling the earth to witness the occasion of his enlightenment. This expression is called the gesture of "earth witnessing" or "earth pressing." Similarly, his left hand, expressing the gesture of "meditative equipoise," accepts in its palms a begging bowl. Positioned around the perimeter of the throne, although greatly reduced in scale, are acolytes and attendants, goddesses and demons, leaves and flowers, dragons and deer, whose purpose is to emphasize the majesty of the central personage. Various offerings—the symbolic wheel, conch shell, bowls, jewels, auspicious birds—are laid before the Buddha. Motifs of landscape, evoking mystery—steep mountains and canyons, turbulent lakes with dancing waves, and whirling clouds—form the background of the painting. These symbols of expressive gestures, auspicious offerings, and mysterious landscapes form a rich visual language, which is the medium of communication between the painter and the viewer.

Despite the bewildering complexity of the painting, the technical basis for Thangka paintings is a series of rectilinear diagrams. The depiction of the various deities on Thangkas is ordered by very precise rules of composition, among them the theories of the bodily proportions of the various deities that make up the Tibetan artistic pantheon. These theories of proportion, handed down, generation through generation, from master to pupil, have been the means of transmitting the craft for the last two thousand five hundred years. These theories are not the work of one artist or generation, but the work of generations of craftsmen, the fruit of communal thought. According to art historian Coomaraswamy:

This communal thought is not only the popular thought, but that of the greatest and wisest minds seeking to impress their vision on successive generations. However there is a fatal weakness of communal art: it has no power to resist the corruption from without. It is beautiful by habit, rather than by intention, so a single generation under changed conditions is sufficient to destroy it. (*The Crafts of India and Ceylon*, 1964)

The annexation of Tibet in 1959 by China led to the exodus of Tibetans from their homeland, among them their spiritual and temporal leader, the Dalai Lama. Tibetan monasteries, once the rich repositories of Thangka paintings and other cultural artifacts, were impoverished and many of their paintings destroyed. Many of the painters and other craftsmen were scattered in various refugee settlements all over the world. In a battle to preserve and reconstruct the cultural continuity, the Dalai Lama has asked painters and craftsmen to disseminate the traditions in the West. Thus the painters have become wanderers, traveling the world as a living archive. It is in these painters, more than in collections of Thangka paintings in museums, that we find the knowledge of the "ways of painting."

The Electronic Sketch Book project suggests the potential of electronic technologies—computers and video—to preserve and disseminate long standing craft-traditions, such as Thangka painting, endangered by external forces. Museum exhibitions preserve the artifact of craft. Scholarly work in academic institutions illustrates skills and techniques and shows relationships between culture and craft. While there has been a considerable and exemplary effort in preserving artifact and illustrating techniques, our work offers some support for the community that practices the craft, assisting the human carriers of the ways of creating artifact. While craft has been disseminated by academic (literary) means, we

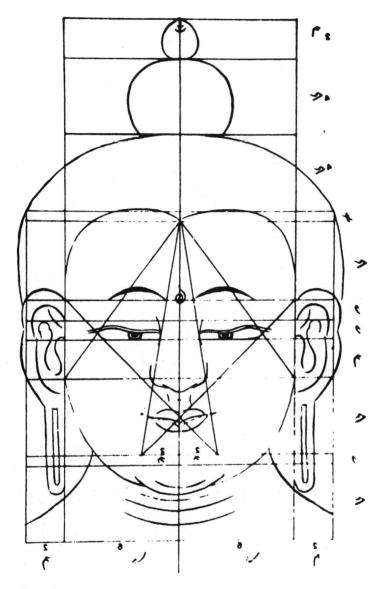

Figure 2
Proportioning diagram of Buddha's face. Drawn by Wangdrak.

recognize the need to incorporated—rather than exclude—the genius of the community of craftsmen in building tools for preserving and disseminating their craft. The best designers and judges of any tools that preserve and disseminate craft are the members of the community that actually practices the craft.

• • •

Based on these explorations and studies, we believe that representations of process, when repeated and re-enacted across situations, connect members in a design group across time, communicate experience between members and across projects, and provide a basis for formalized design craft. In addition, the representations of design experience are valuable in educating people about the craft. They can provide beginning designers with a rich library of previously preserved scenes, which, in turn, may be assimilated into future design practice. When viewed over long periods of time, design craft can be viewed in a state of flux: some in the process of formation, experimentation, simplification, or, as in the case of Thangka painting, in the process of deterioration.

Our support of Thangka painters in preserving and disseminating their craft is an extension of work in representing process. While traditionally Thangka painting has been transmitted by structured rules of composition, these rules are highly evolved and stable, they do not exclude artistic exploration.

The images of deities commonly depicted on Thangkas, along with their counterparts expressed in a variety of media—such as stone, metal, or wood sculptures, ink manuscript illustrations painted on paper and cloth, acrylic and watercolor painting on cotton and silk banners, and mural paintings and inscriptions on the walls of monasteries—certainly illustrate the technical prowess of the artists in adhering to the rules of composition, but at the same time, also illustrate the artists' imaginative power of visualization. Though all artists obey the rules of composition, no two paintings or sculptures are alike. The many different executions of the same deity illustrate the delicate relationship between, first, the artists' technical virtuosity in the medium to express the theologians' visions, and second, the imaginative power of the artists in rendering these visions to reflect the artists' love, devotion and admiration of the deity being depicted. This relationship, between the remarkable conformity to basic iconography and the ethnic stylization of the deities, is also felt in the various countries where Buddhism flourished. The artist reproduces a design handed down unchanged over centuries in a practice of aesthetic fidelity to angelic prototypes. But, within the language of the craft, there is incredible freedom to improvise. These images, regardless of medium, time, and place, illustrate the artists' faithfulness to the well-established rules of composition, and ability to accommodate artistic exploration within those rules. This, notwithstanding the preservation and dissemination of the craft as it has been practiced in traditional media, makes even the expression of Thangkas by applying structured computing and video machinery a domain worthy of examination.

Admittedly, it would be a scholarly conceit, blinded by optimism, to believe that, in bringing electronic technologies to the craft of Thangka painting, change is escapable. Electronic technologies herald change with the potential of both improvement and degradation of the process of craft. Amidst this dilemma of change, we cannot remain satisfied by avoiding the use of electronic technologies to preserve and disseminate the craft of Thangka painting. In any event, our use or avoidance is measured against the forces endangering the craft: rapid collecting of Thangkas, commercializing Thangkas, simplifying the process of creating Thangkas to meet the tourists' demand for mementoes, and painters abandoning their craft in search of economic opportunity. These forces are already moving the practice of Thangka painting toward irrevocable simplification, transformation, or degradation. Timeliness is important; delay might leave only an extinct craft. Hence, we propose to bring electronic technologies to Thangka painting now, and to do so with great reverence for the craft, as did countless generations of painters who produced these ageless, admirable paintings.

• • •

Electronic Capture and Dissemination of Thangka Painting

The purpose of the electronic sketch book is to aid in the capture and dissemination of the cultural processes of Thangkas. The craft environment will still include actual paintings, but the purpose here is not to study or display the finished paintings, for museums and books do that well enough. Rather, the purpose is to introduce into the craft environment a medium that is fundamentally about process, and hence about the sense of time. A craftsman takes actions toward a Thangka, such as generating an element, identifying with the theme to be depicted, or composing a whole painting. Unlike the scholar or museum curator who examines and collects these finished paintings, we are concerned with representing and collecting the scenes of actions in which the craftsmen create the Thangkas, and tying those to scenes in the communal use of the Thangkas.

Through these scenes, each action, however large or small, whether it is the shading of a deity's eyes, the invocation of a deity, or examining the different compositional schemes for a whole painting, will be capable of re-enactment. By re-enacting process, aspiring painters or spectators can retrace and re-experience the actions of the Thangka master, and learn the craft through action. By replaying scenes showing communal use and discussions with Thangka practitioners and craft-persons, beginning students and museum-goers can gain an understanding of Thangkas in their cultural context, and learn how to interpret the Thangkas. The research challenge is to examine the nature of a craft process that is being renewed—and altered—using the electronic sketch book.

• • •

Reflections

The Electronic Sketch Book of Tibetan Thangka Painting *was the stepping-stone to an even more ambitious project for Makkuni. His next project, the* Gita Govinda *project, reexamines the approaches and technologies that can play a part in the digital library metaphor.*

The Gita Govinda *is an ancient love poem depicted in painting, music, and dance. These different forms—what Makkuni calls "traditional multimedia" have coevolved and influenced each other over the centuries. Perhaps echoing the tradition of apprenticeship in India, Makkuni recognizes the role of the Master or teacher in cultural preservation. For Makkuni, a digital medium must be able to capture the spirit of the teacher in guiding the student's learning. What does a teacher do? The teacher presents and explains. The teacher directs the student's attention.*

The teacher puts up presentations and compares things—how a theme is depicted in painting, how it is shown in dance and music.

Makkuni's exhibit of the Gita Govinda embraces music, dance, and literature. To get a sense of how he uses computer technology in the exhibit helpful to bring to mind filmcraft, special effects in the movies, the zooming in on pictures and instant replays of televised sports. Zoom into the dancer appearing in a window; freeze frame and slow down. The teacher may highlight the dancer's gesture with overdrawn animations, little colored arrows showing exactly how the hands are moved or how the dancer bows. Instant replay and slow motion make it easier to see slowly what the dancer did quickly. On one part of the exhibit screen the teacher explains something; on another part he or she highlights the dance with animations, or illuminates the musical notation as the music plays. Maybe the teacher amplifies certain instrumental parts separately to show their particular contributions. Gestures can be coordinated with other elements so that we see exactly how the music corresponds to the dance, or how the dance corresponds to part of a written story.

A presentation this rich has important implications for other uses in digital libraries. The purpose of Vannevar Bush's memex was to help master information that had become overwhelming and to enable one information forager or "sensemaker" to make trails for the next. The user could follow the shared trails in the memex to engage in collaboration and make sense of collected information. Makkuni's example transforms the trailmaker into a teacher or master. Here, too, each trailmaker teaches the next. What does the trailmaker leave for his successors? For Bush, it was just a trail. For Makkuni, it is the full range of communication between teacher and student. The teacher gestures, and moves, and presents material. Makkuni's focus on culture and dreams lifts him beyond the confines of conventional hypertext. He shows us that the tools for teaching in the digital media are more powerful when they move beyond text. In effect, he is creating multimedia teachers. Instead of just putting class notes on the network, Makkuni puts the teacher—or at least the teacher's vibrant performance—on the network.

This innovation comes at a time when most of the information on the Internet is based on text. In the user interfaces provided by today's HTML-based browsers, when you follow a link you loose the annotations; that is, the teacher is not there. You cannot even see the class notes and the subject matter at the same time; the teachings utterly disappear when you click on a link! In the Gita-Govinda project, and in other imaginative multimedia presentations, the teacher remains to help control the display and to provide emphasis and gestures. Through explanation and demonstration, the teacher brings the artifacts and practices to life.

Why is this important? One assumes that better presentations mean more effective learning. Digital works that are easier to access and understand, encourage people to explore. Moreover, not all readers have the same skills. Might a network of such teachers enable curious non-readers to expand their horizons? Makkuni's teacher embodies perfectly the keeper of knowledge archetype and expands our imagination about what kind of information infrastructure we can create.

Part 2

The Electronic Mail Metaphor: The I-Way As a Communications Medium

Stories are medicine. I have been taken with stories since I heard my first. They have such power; they do not require that we do, he, act anything—we need only listen.

Clarissa Pinkola Estés, *Women Who Run With the Wolves*

Communication ends separation.

A Course in Miracles

In a few years, men will be able to communicate more effectively through a machine than face to face to face.

J. C. R. Licklider and Robert Taylor, "The Computer as a Communication Device"

You cannot do anything in the Internet by yourself. This derives from the basic observation that all the interesting communication connections in the world have at least two ends.

from a flurry of e-mail messages on an Internet mailing list

As a messenger, the Trickster is likewise a sponsor of computer networks, cellular phones, and satellite television, linking the diverse people of the world.

Allan B. Chinen, *Beyond the Hero*

In his *Just So Stories* for children, Rudyard Kipling wrote a story called "How the First Letter was Written." In this story, a hunter goes down to the river with his precocious daughter to spear catfish. He accidentally breaks his spear and sits down to repair it. The daughter becomes bored and, unknown to her father, encounters a friendly stranger from a neighboring tribe that speaks a different language. On a piece of birch bark she draws a series of pictures intending to show her father fishing, his broken spear, where they are, and so on. Somehow she convinces the stranger to run to her house to give the "letter" to her mother, so that someone will bring her father another spear. The wife, never having seen a letter before, puzzles over the meanings of the childish drawings and symbols. Thinking the writing means that her husband is under attack, she dispatches warriors to save him. This is just the first in a sequence of confusions in a story that is all about misunderstanding writing.

For us, understanding writing is not generally as hopeless as it is in Kipling's story. Language and the conventions of writing are created and used by communities—and that connection is no coincidence. Indeed, the words *communicate* and *community* have the same roots. If everyone lived as a completely isolated and independent individual, we would have no use for communication or, perhaps, even language.

The language used in messages ranges from the mundane to the profound. Spoken messages, unless they are recorded, last for a shorter time than written ones. What is spoken fades from our ears quickly, whereas what is written can be read again and again. Writing is useful for preserving communications for later reading or even future generations, as reflected in the digital library metaphor and the keeper of knowledge archetype. It is also useful for communicating at a distance, as in the Kipling story, and for everyday messages and small talk. Messages knit us together in communicating communities.

Myths and Archetypes for Awakening the Communicator

In terms of archetypes, the need to communicate—to hear and be heard—is reflected in the communicator archetype. The best-known communicator archetype is the messenger. There are many tales of messengers. For example, in the fifth century B.C., when the ancient Greeks defeated a much larger army, they sent news of the victory across the plain of Marathon by runner. After delivering his message the messenger collapsed and died. The length of a marathon race today, twenty-six miles, is the length of the plain of Marathon. In colloquial speech, the phrase "don't kill the messenger" refers to not taking out anger on someone who brings bad news. In Elbert Hubbard's "A Message to Garcia," a brave messenger-soldier faces the nearly impossible task of carrying a note to a general through dangerous jungles and enemy territory. The story, written in 1899, sold over 50 million copies.

In western culture, the most famous messenger archetype is Greek mythology's Hermes, the son of Zeus and Maia. He was Zeus's messenger and a bringer of good luck. Known for his speed, eloquence, cleverness, and protectiveness, Hermes was aided by wings he wore on his sandals and cap. Hermes is also the patron of orators, writers, athletes, merchants, and thieves. Advertisers use his image as a symbol of speed. His Roman mythological counterpart is Mercury, the son of Jupiter; in the Celtic pantheon, the god Lug plays a similar role as the swift communicator. In his discussion of African spiritual systems in *The*

Drummer's Path, Sule Greg Wilson suggests that there are correspondences among Hermes, Mercury, Elegba, Tehuti, Exu, and Ifa.

Hermes is often associated with e-mail and communication. One of the first e-mail systems on the ARPANET was named HERMES and was developed at Bolt Beranek and Newman (BBN) between 1975 and 1977. It was used as part of DARPA's Military Message Experiment and introduced the idea of arbitrary message headers and mail filters, among other things. Interestingly, a competing message system called HG was created at BBN around 1976. According to Austin Henderson, one of the designers of HERMES, HG is a lovely reference to a reference: *Hg*, the chemical notation for the element mercury, alludes to Hermes's Roman name. The image of Hermes is also used as an icon by a British telecommunication company.

Another important story about communication and communities is the biblical account of the Tower of Babel, which was built by the descendants of Noah to reach up to heaven itself and make them like God. To prevent them from completing the tower, God caused them to speak many languages so that they could no longer understand one another. Then he scattered them over the earth. The story of the Pentecost in the New Testament is an opposite kind of story. The word *Pentecost* is Greek for *Shavuot*, the spring harvest festival of the Israelites. When the disciples were together in Jerusalem after Jesus's resurrection, there appeared to them tongues of fire, and they were filled with the Holy Ghost and began to speak other languages. Because of the harvest festival, Jerusalem was filled with crowds of foreign visitors speaking many languages. When the disciples moved among the visitors, they spoke to them in their own languages and many were converted to Christianity. Both stories illustrate the theme of the separation of human communities, divided by distance and language.

The communicator archetype can take many forms, reflecting different relationships between the communicator and the community: the orator is the citizen speaking out; the pen pal is the friend known intimately only through writing; the matchmaker is a networker who brings people together as couples. Some communicators carry negative connotations in a community because they tell secrets; these include the tattletale, the informant, the traitor, and the spy. Ultimately, of course, we are all communicators—whether as teachers, as prolific writers of office memos, or as faithful correspondents with our friends.

The communicator is also one of the archetypes that can guide how we think about information infrastructure. In our time, it is embodied in the electronic mail metaphor. Electronic mail (e-mail) is the most popular function on the Internet. For most computer users, it is either free or much cheaper than using a telephone. Some e-mail users call the regular postal service the "snail mail," referring to the fact that when everything is working, e-mail is delivered in minutes instead of the days required by regular mail. You can read e-mail whenever and from wherever you want, and you don't need a stamp. Since the 1970s e-mail has been a widely used feature of the Internet.

In spite of its relatively long history, new users of e-mail are often surprised—by things people say in e-mail they would never say in person and by the amount of junk mail they receive. Different media have different properties that affect how we use them; because e-mail is different from postal mail, we end up using it differently. The electronic mail metaphor can help us understand why this is so and why e-mail seems to break down our assumptions about regular mail.

The Deep Structure of the Electronic Mail Metaphor

Because people are already familiar with mail, the electronic mail metaphor brings with it a lot of prior meaning. The deep structure of the electronic mail metaphor, therefore, lies in our assumptions about regular mail and how it works.

We begin by looking at the process of sending a letter. First, someone writes the letter, perhaps even rewriting it several times; then, when satisfied with it, he or she folds it and puts it in an envelope. Of course, people write letters for various reasons. A letter to a pen pal or a distant friend is for many a time of reflection and intimacy. A writer may relax, perhaps listen to music while composing it; or go to a serene setting to write it. Some people write to their friends mainly when they are traveling, to describe what they are seeing and doing. In these examples, people write to particular individuals to say personal things; the letters are private. Social custom treats the sealing of an envelope as a guarantee of privacy.

The mechanics of sending a letter take advantage of the knowledge and resourcefulness of the post office. The sender writes the recipient's address on the envelope; the post office will usually deliver the letter correctly, even if the address is not complete or exactly correct. Letters are sent by taking them to a mailbox and usually reach their destinations in a few days. On the receiving end, letters arrive at a mailbox in a fixed physical location. If we move, we get a new address and a new mailbox. Even though mail can be forwarded, it is best to let correspondents know our changes of address.

Many people receive a substantial amount of junk mail, which is generally sent by organizations, not individuals. Junk mail is easy to recognize: it may say "bulk mail" on the stamp or "crd sort" or "pre-sorted" on the envelope. Some people use these cues to discard junk mail without even opening it.

Individuals do not usually send large mailings because of the costs of postage, materials, and handling. Saying the same thing to several people requires one to make multiple copies of the letter and put each one in an addressed envelope.

The mail metaphor, like the digital library metaphor, carries with it certain assumptions about protocol and literacy; and different kinds of letters have different forms and protocols. For example, if your are writing to someone you don't know, you begin by explaining who you are and why you are writing. Such letters tend to be very polite. In contrast, letters to the editor of a newspaper need not be especially polite and must be very short and to the point. For most kinds of written letters, a writer will be careful about titles, referring to the recipient as *Dr.* or *Professor* or *Ms.*, as appropriate. When my grandmother wrote to me as a child, she used the title *Master.* We also assume that when we write letters to people, we will get a response.

Challenging Assumptions about Mail

The electronic mail metaphor can mislead us if we overlook what is changing or different about the digital realm. We begin by writing a letter in a different way. Electronic mail is composed on a word processor, making it routine to cut and paste words and use spelling checks. Of course, these tools can lend themselves to large-scale mistakes when authors paste together sentences hastily from other letters. One widely observed consequence of e-mail is that writings often contain errors of grammar and content caused by the accidental deletion or inclusion of information. Because word processing invites us to casually reuse blocks of text, we may run the risk of accidentally including in a personal e-mail letter inappropriate material originally intended for someone else.

With regular mail, if we get a personal letter it comes from an individuals, whereas a form letter is probably from an organization trying to sell us something. In e-mail, however, some people are experimenting with using personal form letters. In their *Understanding Computers and Cognition*, Winograd and Flores suggest that a conversation for action can often be understood in terms of a series of stages. An initial request may be followed by promises, counter proposals, acceptance of offers, and so on. At each point in the conversation there is a small set of possible actions, and these are linguistic. This idea was taken to the next logical step in an experimental e-mail system called the Information Lens, which was devised by Tom Malone and colleagues the Massachusetts Institute of Technology. The Information Lens contains forms for many different kinds of letters. For example, general categories of forms include action requests, commitments, and notices. An example of a notice might be a meeting announcement or a publication announcement. The lens was partly intended to automate the writing of electronic mail and to facilitate its automatic processing by a computer. For example, a computer could update a personal calendar when a particular seminar is either announced or canceled.

With regular mail, you are reminded of cost whenever you write a letter because you have to find and attach postage stamps. Long-distance mailings cost more, and big heavy letters and packages cost still more. By contrast, sending an e-mail seems free, and its cost does not depend on its length or on how far it must travel. Because we do not need to find stamps, we do not think about costs.

Another difference relates to unclear addresses. Knowing roughly where somebody works or lives usually doesn't help a lot in determining that person's e-mail address. E-mail addresses are full of strange symbols; sometimes they contain last names, sometimes first names, sometimes initials, and sometimes nonsense strings assigned at the convenience of the e-mail provider. The Internet links many different e-mail systems that use a variety of naming schemes in different institutions and mail systems. If the e-mail address is not exactly right, the message will not reach its intended recipient.

With regular mail, sending the same letter to several people costs more and requires substantially more handling. With many e-mail systems, sending a letter to a list of people is as easy as sending it to one person and costs the same. We say that e-mail has easy *fan-out*: you do not need to make multiple copies of a letter; you just include all the addresses. E-mail can be a powerful tool for getting the word out to lists of people and to on-line discussion groups.

The ease of sending e-mail to a group means that people do it more often. Nearly every user of e-mail has at one time or another sent out a message to people not intended to get it. E-mail users also tend to use available lists for making announcements without making sure that the message is appropriate to everyone on the list. This means that most people receive several messages a day that they consider to be junk mail.

On e-mail, a letter from a private individual need not be private at all, a possibility that has led to the development of on-line discussion groups, in which all members get all group e-mail that is sent. These special-interest groups organize themselves around all sorts of topics, ranging from music reviews, to movies, to gardening, or to any other definable topic.

Interest groups are *virtual communities* in which e-mail diminishes the usual effects of distance. It is not unusual for members of interest groups to communicate with each other on a daily basis; sometimes they have more conversations with people across the country or halfway around the world than they do with people in the next office. In these virtual communities, the sense of community and communication is real enough. What is virtual is that the people do not necessarily live or work near each other in space. Rather, they are neighbors in cyberspace. We touch on this theme further in Part 4 on the digital worlds metaphor.

Many messages to a discussion group are responses to a message sent by someone else. Most of the people reading the message exchange, however, are simply readers who do not actively participate in discussion. In contrast with regular mail, reading a discussion group's mail is considered a legitimate part of the public process, rather than a violation of privacy. It is analogous to reading the letters to the editor in a newspaper.

With ordinary mail, privacy is signaled and usually ensured by the use of a paper envelope. With e-mail, privacy has recently become a contentious issue. Some organizations have taken the position that, as computers are company equipment, e-mail is about company business. Some executives have used various computer programs to read e-mail between employees; in some cases where an employee was in conflict with management, this practice has led to disputes about privacy. For individuals who desire privacy in situations like this, some e-mail systems provide "privacy-enhanced e-mail"—systems that use encryption techniques that make it very difficult to read other people's mail. Privacy-enhanced e-mail is said to be sent in "digital envelopes" that are analogous to the envelopes used in ordinary mail. E-mail in these systems is encrypted in a coding key that can be unlocked and read only by a recipient who has the decoding key. Such keys can also be used to establish the identity of the sender.

The most-experienced users of e-mail may use programs that display the name of the sender as well as the topic. This is often enough to discard e-mail, especially if the topic is stale or the message was sent to a wide-distribution mailing list. Some sophisticated e-mail systems include facilities for automatically filtering and sorting mail. Thus, users can write filters that discard mail from certain sources or on certain topics and can prioritize mail, marking messages as needing prompt action or as requiring no immediate attention.

With regular mail, you may carry a letter around with you until you find a mailbox. In fact, some people use this extra time to decide whether to send a letter, perhaps one written in haste. With e-mail, though, there is no walking around and waiting. You simply click a button and the e-mail is sent; once you send it, it is out of your control. A few e-mail systems make it possible to recall a letter, but this ability is not generally available on the Internet. When everything is working well, e-mail reaches its destination in a few minutes. Receiving regular mail, like sending it, takes time. You have to go to a physical mailbox to pick it up, whereas e-mail is massless. You can log into the e-mail system from any telephone or network connection, read your mail, and send replies.

Although e-mail has expectations and protocols, they are not the same as for regular mail, and they leave more room for confusion between senders and receivers. For example, because e-mail is delivered immediately, some people expect an immediate response. One of the advantages of e-mail, however, is that you can read it at your convenience. Still, it is generally considered impolite not to respond to e-mail for days at a time. One colleague of mine had a series of personal and family emergencies that put him out of e-mail contact for about three months. When he returned and found that thousands of messages had accumulated, he decided to discard them, on the grounds that anything important would be sent again. When he failed to respond to my request for a favor, however, I misunderstood his silence as an unexplained "no" until I talked to a mutual friend and heard about his problems. Some people set up programs that automatically respond to mail with a brief explanatory note while they are away on vacation, a practice similar to changing the message on an answering machine or voicemail system during extended absences.

In general, e-mail is less formal and more anonymous than regular mail. People say things in e-mail they would not say in ordinary mail, perhaps because it is so easy to send mail to large numbers of people. They seem to press the send button without thinking about it and without the cooling-off period that would follow if they carried a letter around with them until they reached a mailbox. The term *flame* refers to e-mail that rants on about some subject; in the following articles, we include some examples of flames and a form letter for responding to them.

Finally, it is possible to write e-mail in when you're not at your desk. I occasionally see people at coffeehouses in the Bay Area writing on a laptop computer; it seems to me that doing that is much less relaxing than writing a short note on paper in the same setting. It's easy to write a postcard or note on a wedge of space on the table or on a book balanced on one's knee. Using a laptop, by contrast, means placing it in the middle of the table, right where you would otherwise put a slice of pie and a cup of coffee. Instead of writing with an elegant pen, and focusing on the content of your note, you have to use a four-to-six pound computer and keep an eye on the battery-charge indicator—unless you've found a table near a power outlet. Furthermore, you might not want to leave a portable device worth as much as a used car unattended while you go to refill your coffee cup. At least today, the devices for writing e-mail in public places fall short in several ways.

E-mail Today

The electronic mail metaphor is the second of four metaphors we present for thinking about the national information infrastructure. Unlike digital libraries, e-mail is already used by millions of people for hundreds of hours each. Indeed, some observers of computer networks and other new technologies say that the term *information age* is a misnomer; rather, we should call this the *communication age.* The electronic mail metaphor is not so much a guide to what the communication infrastructure could be like as an example of what computer networks are already like. The articles in this section discuss how e-mail is used today and how these uses affect people and their organizations.

At present, e-mail augments but does not replace other forms of communication. Sometimes in their enthusiasm for new technology, people use e-mail when they could as easily or better use more established means of communication. I recently saw a letter to the editor in which someone complained that e-mail users "sit alone in a room in front of a computer screen typing like hell to people far away whom they never need meet in person and acting like together they are solving the problems of the world. This while the garbage needs to be taken out and the dog has his legs crossed because he needs a walk."

So, does it make sense to use e-mail to talk to someone in the next office? This question made me think of my own recent behavior. The other day I sent a request for technical information about software to a mailing list of about fifty people. As it turned out, a colleague two offices away had the answer. When his e-mail response came back, I walked over to ask him for some further details in person; but he was not in his office, or even in the building. He had responded to my message while working at home. So I walked back to my office, and sent him another e-mail asking for more information. A few minutes later, I received another answer from a different person. My colleague had not had the answer to my question at hand but had forwarded my query to someone who did. In cases like this, e-mail is not a refuge from life or an illusion about solving world problems when the dog needs a walk. It has its own unique advantages of fan-out, electronic distribution, and asynchronous communication. Fan-out enabled me to poll a large number of people quickly; electronic distribution got my message to my colleague, even though he was working at home; and asynchronous communication meant that each of us could read and respond to the e-mail when we wanted to, instead of playing "phone tag."

The use of e-mail to find information makes it potentially an alternative to a library. Simply put, we can either look something up in a library or book we can ask someone by, often, sending our question to a mailing list. This is similar to what happens on radio talk shows when a caller or the host asks the millions of listeners a question and someone who can answer it calls in. Like radio, e-mail has a natural fan-out, albeit typically with smaller numbers. For example, when I started writing this book I sent out a message to all the approximately two hundred people on the "ComputerResearch" list at the Xerox Palo Alto Research Center, where I work. I asked then to send me examples of the use of the information superhighway metaphor like "information speedbumps" or "taking the on-ramp." I sent the e-mail on a Friday night at about 5:30 P.M. Before 7:00 P.M. that night I had six responses; replies then crescendoed for a couple of days and tapered off after two weeks. Altogether I received about twenty-five replies.

Another use of e-mail that relates to digital libraries and publishing is the exchange of drafts in the informal and early stages of writing. (In Part 1, Lederberg explores this theme in his article "Communication as the Root of Scientific Progress"; he continues the discussion in "Digital Communications and the Conduct of Science" later in this part.) E-mail and other computer facilities make it convenient to distribute drafts of papers to colleagues and solicit peer reviews, as well as to collaborate with colleagues. There is something about e-mail that facilitates informal collaborative exchanges. Unlike formal publishing and review, e-mail supports a real-time dialog in which colleagues can take the time to ask questions, negotiate the meanings of terms, and work through misunderstandings. Because it can be personal, e-mail is not subject to review by an editor or to examination by colleagues.

E-mail is used heavily in many corporations. Several of the articles in this section examine the effects on organizations when e-mail becomes one of the principal communication channels. Several observers have noted that e-mail opens up lateral communications in organizations, which allow for better coordination than when communications must follow strict management hierarchies.

This connectivity also gives people the opportunity to use the network to respond to global events. In the 1980s, during the political uprisings in the former Soviet Union and in China eastern computer organizations exchanged news with westerners through e-mail and fax machines, which replaced ham radio as a means of keeping in contact during an emergency. Hermes had found a new technological embodiment.

Finally, the boundaries of e-mail use inevitably overlap with our other metaphors for thinking about the information infrastructure. Consider again the Information Lens experiment in which some e-mail gets processed automatically. Using form letters makes automatic processing practical and ensures that messages will include certain kinds of data and will convey standardized information on their location. Indeed, automatic processing of such messages is routinely used on the Internet for subscribing and unsubscribing to mailing lists. What this means is that the medium of e-mail is now being shared, not only by people but also by *computational agents*. Imagine, for example, a situation in which 90 percent of the messages received by my computer concern me but are not actually intended to be read by me. Instead, they would be read by my computational agents, which are busily arranging various things for me—managing some parts of my calendar, collecting information from earlier bibliographic search requests, or saving and grouping interesting news items. The possible functions of these agents point to different metaphors and provide different perspectives for understanding emerging network technologies. The digital library perspective shows the agents as knowbots that provide knowledge services; the e-mail perspective shows them functioning in the mail medium and processing routine messages; in the digital worlds perspective, such agents would participate in creating the experience of an information space portrayed as a digital reality.

Some Consequences of Electronic Groups

Lee Sproull and Samer Faraj

Connections

Lee Sproull, along with Sara Keisler, is well known for her work on what happens when organizations introduce new technologies. When e-mail took root in organizations in the late 1970s and early 1980s two things occurred regularly and predictably. One was that e-mail users spontaneously organized their own discussion groups on topics of interest; the second was a kind of organizational flattening as people developed e-mail cross-links that did not necessarily follow hierarchical lines of management.

The trend in e-mail has always been toward greater connectivity, and it has now gone well beyond company boundaries. Few e-mail systems operate within a single company. In the past few years, dial-up e-mail providers have realized the advantages of interconnection for reasons that are not hard to understand. Nobody would tolerate a telephone system that would only let them call people who use the same company. Similarly, information providers found that their customers were often lured away because they wanted to exchange e-mail mainly with people using a different provider.

In the following article, Sproull and Faraj consider the social phenomena associated with e-mail in the wide-open territory of interconnected networks. In this context, the organizational rationale for e-mail has largely disappeared. People use e-mail for their own purposes, and those purposes are largely social. In the earlier organizational setting, the introduction of e-mail was rationalized in terms of its functionality. Company executives and corporate information managers argued for e-mail the same way that they argued for new computing tools, databanks, or libraries. Sproull and Faraj call this attitude the techno-logical view. *Applying a technological view to computer network leads to thinking in terms of metaphors like information highway and the digital library, which emphasize the speed of information or facilities for storing and retrieving it. In the technological view, people cruise or browse the network independently to seek information.*

However, the use of e-mail for social purposes suggests that a techno-logical point of view sheds much less light on the use of networks than a social view. *In the* social view, *people search for affiliation, support, affirmation, and community. They gather together, chat, and confide. They look for others with common interests and form groups. Sproull and Faraj focus on these electronic discussion groups, which are one of the major ways people use e-mail on the computer networks. The most popular discussion groups on the Internet are part of a system of elec-tronic bulletin boards known as Usenet. Every day more than twenty thousand messages are posted to Usenet newsgroups on an ever-widen-ing tree of topics.*

On-line discussion groups exploit properties of e-mail that are unmatched by any other medium. A message posted to a discussion group may reach hundreds or even thousands of readers. Not only does the sender not know these people personally; he or she may not even be aware of how many people there are on a mailing list. On any given morning, thousands of people send messages to mailing lists. You can visualize this phenomenon as raindrops falling on a map, each drop spreading out and carrying the message to people in cities all over the country or, even, the globe. The map becomes covered by these trails, as copies of the messages stream out to subscribers to their particular topic.

Even a person reading a message a minute every minute of an eight-hour working day could read only 480 messages in a day. Clearly, nobody can read them all. What makes this flood of information useful is that the messages are directed to people interested in a particular topic—maybe old cars, human rights, science fiction movies, or jobs in engineering. The produces a cooperative, efficient system of distributing information from a large number of senders to a large number of inter-ested receivers. If discussion in a newsgroup is inhibited by too many subscribers, the group may be split into subgroups that limit their attention to messages with a narrower focus.

This combination of features—personal transmission, easy fan-out, and filtering by topic—is achieved by no other medium. Media like radio and television have fan-out but not transmission by citizens of average means. Telephones have personal transmission but no fan-out or filtering. The post office has personal transmission and fan-out for a price, but no automatic filtering by topic. The result of all this activity is a more richly connected society. Just as people in a company exchanged e-mail with those in other branches of the organization, people on computer networks now exchange e-mail with people in different parts of the country or the world, people they would never talk to otherwise. This article gives a quick tour of what some of these people are doing.

In the real world, groups benefit their members (and vice versa) by providing physical, economic, cognitive, and emotional resources. Electronic groups do not provide direct physical or economic resources but they frequently offer information that may lead to them, such as leads or advice about jobs or items for sale. Most electronic groups offer information or cognitive resources for their members. For example, on "comp.databases," one can ask questions such as:

I am looking at products for pulling data from an Ingres database running on a VAX (VMS). We currently use PCLIN1C to get data to PC's but want to access this data through Ethernet instead of asynch ports. Does anyone have any advice on products from companies like IQ Software or Gupta?? What Ingres products on the PC do I need (Tools for DOS, ...)? Any help would be appreciated.

The "comp." groups frequently offer technical advice. On "comp.databases" members exchange opinions about the technical merits of new database packages. On "comp.object," people struggling with trying to write programs using object-oriented methods appeal to the wisdom of more experienced members. On "comp.c^{++}," members discuss the intricacies of the c^{++} programming language. They post portions of code, saying they "think it should work but it does not." These messages challenge other members to identify the problems and post a corrected version. In the technical groups some people expend significant effort to collect and provide technical information. Some people maintain and circulate bibliographies. Members who receive many answers to interesting questions often publish a summary of them.

The social and political groups also offer information. "Soc.feminism" for example provides impromptu reviews of new feminist books and movie reviews. These reviews are the catalyst for lively discussions regarding current cultural issues. On "soc.culture.lebanon" hard-to-find information is frequently posted: the text of U.S. travel advisories to Lebanon, the daily exchange rate of the Lebanese pound, news stories about Lebanon from the UPI and AP news feeds. People exchange advice about how best to prepare Lebanese dishes and suggestions for good bicultural baby names. Jokes, many in poor taste, are frequently posted and either enjoyed or disparaged by readers.

Many electronic groups offer entertainment, which can be an emotional resource. Three of the largest Usenet newsgroups, each with more than one hundred thousand readers, have entertainment as their primary purpose: "alt.sex," "alt.sex.stories," and "rec.humor." The technology policy community sometimes seems mildly embarrassed by such groups. They do not match lofty views of the net as a resource to elevate intellectual discourse; moreover, many people find the contents offensive. Nevertheless, they are extremely popular.

Electronic groups also offer affiliation. Despite the fact that participants in electronic groups may be surrounded by people at work or school, at least some of them feel alone in facing a problem or a situation. If their situation is problematic, it is easy to believe it must be their own fault since no one else around them has the same problem or a similar perspective. Even though electronic groups are usually composed of strangers, because they share a common interest, they are also likely to share common experiences. A result of finding others in the same situation or with the same problem can be the realization that, "I am not alone!" Thus, electronic groups can provide emotional support to their members. Here are three examples.

In 1990, a postdoctoral physicist began a public electronic mailing list, the Young Scientists' Network, for scientists like himself, who faced the prospect of being unable to find permanent jobs in physics. The Young Scientists' Network includes weekly messages from the founder on such topics as job tips, funding possibilities, and relevant news stories [J.

Morell, *Science*, May 1, 1992, p. 606]. Subscribers send in their own tips and scoops. Although it was created to provide information to unemployed or underemployed scientists, it rapidly became an informal support group. One physicist said, "The main value was in confirming the trouble I was having finding a job." Another offered, "It helps save your sanity, it helps to know that it's not because of a personal failing that you can't find research work." The Young Scientists' Network, which had about 170 members a year ago, has grown to 3,000 members today.

In 1987, a computer scientist began a private mailing list, Systers, to share information with her colleagues about events and topics in the world of operating systems. Systers expanded to become a "forum for discussion of both the problems and joys of women in [computer science more generally] and to provide a medium for networking and mentoring" [Borg, cited in K. Frenkel, *Communications of the ACM*, November 1990, p. 36]. There are messages about job openings, book reviews, conferences, and general conversations. One of its members says, "There's a feeling of closeness, so it's easy to talk" (field notes, 1/9/92). She believes that the closeness was established early because the group was private and people were careful to show positive regard for others in their messages. She says that even today, when the interaction starts getting contentious, "somebody always sends mail that's soothing." Systers currently has over fifteen hundred members in one hundred fifty companies, two hundred universities, and eighteen countries around the world.

"Misc.kids" is a Usenet group for discussing the joys and sorrows of kids and parenting. It's a mix of information, jokes, discussion, and debate, with topics ranging from diaper rash to corporal punishment. One reader describes misc.kids as "a support organization, a debate-team, an encyclopedia of information, and a social group all rolled into one. Even the people I never agree with, I care about" (field notes, 5/92). Another confided, "When I had problems in pregnancy (the baby had a chromosome abnormality), I posted about it and received support from all over the world—an amazing experience" (field notes, 5/92). Misc.kids sees about sixty messages a day and has about forty-eight thousand subscribers world-wide.

These electronic groups do much more than provide information. They offer the opportunity to make connections with other people. They provide support and a sense of community. To be sure, they also provide information. But, as one group member said, it is "information with an attitude."

In the real world, mutual benefit is the social glue that sustains face-to-face groups over time; members who benefit from others reciprocate. Direct reciprocity is difficult if not impossible in the electronic context, but more generalized altruism is relatively easy to sustain. When one person asks for help, it is very likely that one or more group members will provide a helpful or supportive response. (A much larger proportion might be able to help but might be too busy, too diffident, or too selfish to respond.) With membership of thousands, the proportion responding can be extremely small and still yield one or more beneficial responses. Furthermore, responses can be seen by all group members, thereby helping others who had the same question or problem but did not post a message about it.

Moreover, even people who receive no direct benefit from any particular helpful message see the process of helping behavior modelled in the group. And finally, with large groups, no one person need spend much time being helpful: a small number of small acts can sustain a large community because each act is seen by the entire group.

The benefits provided by electronic groups often extend beyond the direct participants when members act as conduits of information to people outside the group. Requests for information are frequently posted to a group "for a friend who doesn't have net access." Group members sometimes forward pertinent posts to friends or colleagues. In the case of technical groups at least, we hypothesize that employers benefit from their employees' group membership when information gleaned from the group is applied or passed on in the workplace.

. . .

Of course, the consequences of electronic group membership are not all positive, just as the consequences of affiliations in the real world are not all positive. Erroneous or poor information can be promulgated as easily as high-quality information. People can spend a lot of time reading group messages. Lively discussion can degenerate into frustrating conflict and rancor. But, for several million members, the benefits apparently outweigh the costs.

. . .

Reflections

I once got a fortune cookie that said "A wise man knows everything; a shrewd man everybody." This distinction between knowing facts and knowing people blurs with e-mail and on-line discussion groups. When you browse through a set of messages from a discussion group, is this more like communicating with people or more like searching through a digital library? Are we entering the information age or the communication age? Both answers are approximations. From the perspective of the fortune cookie, the answer depends on whether you are trying to make contacts or get information.

Peter Pirolli and others have suggested modeling people using computer technology as information foragers, a concept that supports both the technological and social views characterized by Sproull and Faraj. Foraging behavior is a general term describing the ways how hunters and grazers go after their food. Different animals in different settings use different foraging strategies; spiders sit and wait for game to come to them, and wolves chase their game. Different strategies work best in deciding long to stay in a given region before moving on and how much to cooperate. In a desert setting, there may be enough food and water to survive, but supplies are uncertain. Human populations in such a setting increase their chances of survival by sharing essentials. Thus finding food and finding other people turn out to be tightly coupled behaviors. In more plentiful environments, hunters tend to be more territorial. In other settings, when the game moves, hunters follow. Thus, foraging strategies can produce either solitary and territorial behavior or social and cooperative behavior, depending on circumstances.

On the network, people use different foraging behaviors in different situations. When a topic is hot and new, information is scarce. The behavior of information foragers in this setting is like the behavior of foragers in the desert, where it makes sense to share things. The best way to connect with scarce information is to connect with the small group that is creating it. Over time, as a topic becomes more crowded, things change. People, seeing less value in getting every bit of news on a topic, create smaller subgroups and become more specialized and territorial.

Different kinds of electronic tools foster different kinds of foraging behaviors. Joining newsgroups and waiting for useful information is akin to spider behavior. A newsgroup spider waits for useful information to arrive in the newsgroup e-mail. Switching from spiders to humans, we could say that joining a newsgroup is like fishing. Selecting what newsgroups to join is analogous to deciding where to put fishing nets. On the other hand, a person following links and references in a digital library in pursuit of interesting information may be better described as a lion or a hunter. The hunter archetype generally characterizes people who go out and do things in the world. (In Part 3 we explore the hunter-trickster as one of the archetypes for doing things related to the electronic marketplace metaphor.)

When large groups of new users join the Internet, veterans of on-line discussion groups complain. Here is an example excerpted from a newsgroup discussion during a period of initial confusion caused by finding an arithmetic bug in the Pentium chip in late 1994:

Years ago, Alex Chorin, a math professor at Berkeley, began a book review with one of my all-time favorite quotes, "This book detracts from the sum total of human knowledge."

I am afraid we may have now reached that point with the activity in comp.sys.intel. I will be looking to comp.soft-sys.matlab and sci.math.num-analysis for future discussion of the aspects of this problem that I am interested in.

From the perspective of veterans, hordes of new users have invaded their discussions over the past few years, using bad etiquette and asking dumb questions. The social problem is analogous to the problem of assimilation when natural disasters or wars lead to mass movement of people to new lands. When the rate of immigration exceeds a certain amount, the resulting chaos and need for adjustment in the host country can evoke resentment and backlash from the resident population. This suggests that one problem has to do with rates of assimilation.

Other issues have to do with size, not just rates of growth. Suppose, for example, that the number of people likely to send bizarre e-mail messages on a given day is one in a thousand. When the population doubles, the number of bizarre messages also doubles. This characteristic can lead some networkers to push for greater exclusivity of membership. From an information-foraging perspective, the value of hanging out in a particular newsgroup goes down when too much of the message *traffic is concerned with off-the-wall comments, simple questions, or old information.*

A new activity that may threaten the viability of on-line discussion groups is called spamming. To spam a discussion group is to flood it with junk mail about something, especially things that have nothing at all to do with the group's discussion topic. Junk mail can be advertisements to sell a product or just outlandish messages that impede normal discussion. To get at the relevant news, a newsgroup reader must find a way to step through the messages, avoiding the junk mail. When the time needed to find useful messages gets high, the perceived value of the newsgroup goes down. In the lingo of net users, many newsgroups that used to be interesting have now been spammed and are no longer worth subscribing to. Various fixes are possible. A human editor can filter out the advertisements but might also filter and delay the discussions. Various automatic procedures could also be invoked to delete messages by known spammers. Although no preferred solution to the spamming problem had emerged at the time of this writing, netizens' resiliency and desire to communicate will, I believe, lead to one or more solutions.

The lifetimes of a newsgroup depends on its topic. Activity in groups focused on a particular current event usually drops as the event fades from public view. Newsgroups on new technology specialize into subgroups as the technology matures, while newsgroups on enduring topics probably achieve steady states as different people move through them.

Sproull and Faraj note that some newsgroups form around adult and sexual themes, which inevitably raises issues of community standards and freedom of speech. Some people argue that the relevant community for establishing standards is not the community of one person who happens to read a group's e-mail, but rather the network community—a changing collection of group members from all over the world. The thrust of this argument is that if you don't like the topic, or the content of the discussion, you shouldn't join it. Others have raised concerns about children gaining access to pornographic materials and even making unsupervised contact with adults on sexual topics. In response to such concerns, some network service providers have begun to regulate discussion groups by limiting access to some groups, banning certain topics, and expelling offending members of groups.

Exclusive discussion groups are not like public forums but like private clubs that offer membership by invitation only or by a fee. In exclusive clubs, people may be willing to say things in private that they would not be willing to say in public. Private mailing lists are common among professional working groups. For example, at work I am on several mailing lists of people interested in computer science research, working in a particular laboratory, and belonging to a particular working group. Membership on such lists is controlled.

To take the private-club idea another step forward, consider the possibility of private clubs with exclusive memberships, rules about confidentiality with real bite, and limits on the ability of the excluded public to post to the newsgroup. There might be private newsgroups for people who are generally inaccessible—for example, major financiers, philanthropists, leaders of powerful companies, or even scientists. Suppose it was known that these members read the messages on their exclusive newsgroup every day and that a nonmember could send a message to the group, only through a broker. What would someone be willing to pay to ensure that members of such an exclusive club read a message? This sort of newsgroup might function somewhat like a newspaper of limited distribution, with the broker as editor or, perhaps, advertising manager. (The value of network advertising is explored in articles on the electronic marketplace metaphor in Part 3.)

We have seen that e-mail is a very flexible medium. It can be adapted for personal conversations, public newsletters, and private discussion groups. As the network continues to grow, other possibilities will be discovered and explored. When e-mail is used for group conversations, the network takes on the characteristics of place—like the office coffee pot or the local watering hole. In this way, the electronic mail metaphor overlaps with the digital-worlds metaphor we discuss in Part 4.

Netiquette 101

Jay Machado

Connections

The dark side of the rapid delivery and fan-out properties of e-mail is the opportunity for widespread distribution of angry and foolish messages. Sometimes users react so vehemently to something on the network that they are tempted to release their emotional energy in an e-mail message and, to get the maximum punch, blast it far and wide. This phenomenon is widely enough recognized to have a special name: it is called flaming. *According to Guy Steele's* Hacker's Dictionary, *to flame is "to speak incessantly and/or rabidly on some relatively uninteresting subject or with a patently ridiculous attitude."*

Healthy communities often cope with such extreme expressions with humor. Humor on the network tends to be dry. The following article includes two examples that deal humorously with flaming and other kinds of e-mail misuse. The first example, Chip Rowe's tongue-in-cheek guideline to flaming, provides tips about how to be most annoying. It originally appeared in Spy Magazine. *The second example is an antidote to use when you yourself are flamed on the network. Jay Machado found this form letter to send back to flamers on various network humor lists. Like much of the humorous folklore on the network, the letter is anonymous. The term* thread *in the letter refers to a thread of discourse and to the common practice in network discussion groups to use the same subject line for a series of responses to a topic by different people. A sequence of such messages is called* a thread.

How to Be Annoying On-line (Chip Rowe)

Make up fake acronyms. On-line veterans like to use abbreviations like IMHO (in my humble opinion) and RTFM (read the freaking manual) to show they're "hep" to the lingo. Make up your own that don't stand for anything (SETO, BARL, CP30), use them liberally, and then refuse to explain what they stand for ("You don't know? RTFM").

WRITE YOUR MESSAGES IN ALL CAPS AND DON'T USE PERIODS OR RETURNS SO THAT EVERYONE HAS TO SCROLL ACROSS THEIR SCREENS TO READ EVERY LINE ALSO USE A LOT OF !!!!!!!! AND DDOOUUBBLLEESS TO SHOW THAT YOU'RE EXCITED ABOUT BEING HERE!!!!!!!!

cc: all your email to Al Gore (vice-president@whitehouse.gov) so that he can keep track of what's happening on the Information.Superhighway.Internet.

Join a discussion group, and tie whatever's being discussed back to an unrelated central theme of your own. For instance, if you're in a discussion of gun control, respond to every message with the observation that those genetically superior tomatoes seem to have played an important role. Within days, all discussion of gun control will have ceased as people write you threatening messages and instruct all other members to ignore you.

The Flame Form Letter

[The following has been making the rounds on the net, and is presented here for informational purposes only.]
Dear

[ ] sir [ ] clueless one [ ] twit [ ] great man on campus
[ ] madam [ ] dweeb [ ] twerp [ ] comrade
[ ] Elvis [ ] moon beam [ ] boor [ ] Obergruppenfuehrer
[ ] citoyen [ ] Geek [ ] grad student [ ] cur

You are being gently flamed because.

[ ] you continued a boring useless stupid thread
[ ] you repeatedly posted to the same thread that you just posted to
[ ] you repeatedly initiated incoherent, flaky, and mindless threads
[ ] you posted a piece riddled with profanities
[ ] you advocated Net censorship
[ ] you SCREAMED! (used all caps)
[ ] you posted some sort of crap that doesn't belong in this group
[ ] you posted the inanely stupid "Make Money Fast" article
[ ] you threatened others with physical harm
[ ] you made a bigoted statement(s)
[ ] you repeatedly assumed unwarranted moral or intellectual superiority
[ ] you are under the misapprehension that this group is your preserve
[ ] you have repeatedly shown lack of humor
[ ] you are apparently under compulsion to post to every thread
[ ] you are posting an anonymous attack

⟩Thank you for the time you have taken to read this. Live n' Learn.⟨

Reflections

Perhaps using a flame form letter to squelch a flamer is using fire to fight fire. While I was writing this material I received a flame letter. The following excerpts from it omit names at the request of its sender, who told me the network has a short memory and he doesn't want to be memorialized in hard copy for this particular episode. I selected this flame because it is relevant the to topics of e-mail and marketplaces on the Internet—and because of the way the message spread. For brevity, I have eliminated most of the seventeen hundred words of the original message.

A few words of explanation may aid those not yet familiar with the network. HotWired is an electronic magazine on the network, and Mosaic and Netscape are names of network browsers.

```
From: ⟨name deleted⟩
Date: Thu, 3 Nov 1994 09:49:03 -0800
Mime-Version: 1.0
To: ⟨stefik@parc.xerox.com⟩
```

Subject: CONSPIRACY: Is HotWired ashamed of its advertising?

FORWARD AND REPOST THIS MESSAGE AS FAR AND WIDE AS YOU CAN.
It took me about five minutes of using HotWired to figure out a number of interrelated mysteries:

1) Why Mosaic Communications got such a big plug in WiReD 2.10;
2) Why HotWired won't admit MacWeb users;
3) Why Netscape (by Mosaic Communications) doesn't let you selectively load inline images....

1) I recognize the vital economic function of advertising. I enjoy not having to pay $7.50 for today's Mercury News. I appreciate the risk an advertiser takes in spending advertising dollars on a medium that may or may not reach the advertiser's target audience (I seldom buy a newspaper, so money spent to advertise in the Merc is wasted on me).
2) I recognize the need to commercialize the Internet; it has already been "free" (see below) to too many people for so long that the Great Unwashed are starting to demand that you and I pay for terminals for the homeless in the public library....

 What I object to is SNEAKINESS and HYPOCRISY....
 If my suspicions are correct, ... I submit that choosing the same economic model as television will inevitably lead to the same crap-dominated content as television....
 ... what really makes the Net great is that it's the first medium in the history of communications that is *any-to-many*....

I hope to hell I'm wrong, ...

Please reply to me personally; I may not subscribe to mailing lists where this ends up.

Why I left out most of the letter will become clear in the following messages I received. There are several things instructive about this flame. First of all, the writer experienced something on the network—"it took me about five minutes"—and became indignant. What he saw pushed him over the edge, releasing feelings and perceptions that may have built up over a considerable period of time. He suspected a devious conspiracy and felt it was time to be heard. People who received of the letter were supposed to spread the message, which was complex, far and wide. It was all about how advertisements and graphics are handled by network browsers, but its implications spread out to touch on issues of freedom, network economics, what makes the network great, and what's wrong with television. It accused the conspirators of being sneaky and hypocritical and used a vocabulary of high-handed oratory handed down from a superior moral position: "I submit that ... I recognize...." Four hours after I received it, I got a second message from the same sender.

From ⟨⟨name deleted⟩⟩
Date: Thu, 3 Nov 1994 13:27:42 -0800
Mime-Version: 1.0
To: ⟨stefik@parc.xerox.com⟩
Subject: CORVVS CORDON BLEU: Netscape found to be not exceptional

I forgot a maxim that I've repeated often enough to plenty of people: "Never attribute to conspiracy what can be equally well ascribed to stupidity."

It only took about twenty-five minutes for me to get the answers to the questions I wanted: ...

One correspondent who informed me of this ...

So I retract any imputation of connivance on the part of HotWired and Mosaic Communications....

Please resend this message anywhere you saw my earlier message.

... I will admit to having been *uninformed*, and an ass, and I wish all my correspondents well.

I was disappointed by the number of people who replied with "Attaboy; you tell 'em; those damn advertisers should get lost," ...

Having blasted off his flame in all directions, the flamer attracted some attention and got back a number of responses. If you send a message to several tens of thousands of people and even one person in a hundred answers, you still get lots of replies, often within a few minutes. This particular flamer was polite about retracting his original flame, although people who received and simply discarded it got hit again. The second message, however, was not the end of it. Half an hour later, a third message arrived from the same person.

From: ⟨⟨name deleted⟩⟩
Date: Thu, 3 Nov 1994 14:04:58 -0800
Mime-Version: 1.0
To: ⟨stefik@parc.xerox.com⟩
Subject: IT GETS WORSE ...

I'm going back to bed. Today has been a total loss.... ⟨⟨name deleted⟩⟩ wrote:

⟩ An interesting and unexpected fact arose along the way: if you ⟩ access HotWired via lynx, you can't see the advertising even if you want to. This doesn't seem fair to the advertisers.

Turns out this isn't the case either. Shows what I get for believing indignant people just because they're indignant. Good night ...

So it was not only the original message that contained errors; the replies did too. We can imagine that the energy released by the original flame triggered responding flames, perhaps thousands of them from all over the world. Perhaps fighting fire with fire can have a quenching effect, even for network flames. The original sender retired from the debate after the third message, and the flame apparently died out.

Reflecting on the incident in terms of the e-mail metaphor and arche-types, it became clear to me that no other medium—telephone, postal mail, or radio—provides comparable power or a corresponding respon-sibility for using it wisely. The original sender's experiences on the net-work had obviously aroused feelings of indignation, and he had not thought about his message very long. The e-mail system provided him with an irresistible temptation to broadcast his message to thousands of people—but also, ultimately, to learn from his mistake.

Net mavens interested in seeing what others have written about neti-quette may want to check out Arlene Rinaldi's Netiquette home page:

http://rs6000.adm.fau.edu/faahr/netiquette.html.

Or Chuq Von Rospach's primer on how to work with the Usenet community:

http://www.eff.org:80/ftp/Net_info/Introductory/netiquette.faq

For a satirical piece by Brad Templeton called the "Dear Emily Post-news," see

http://www.eff.org:80/ftp/Net_info/Introductory/netiquette.faq

Jay Machado's Bits and Bytes *is a newsletter delivered by e-mail. Net mavens interested in more samples of it can subscribe to* B&B *by sending e-mail to*

(text: SUBSCRIBE bits-n-bytes) listserv@acad1.dana.edu

To unsubscribe send a message to

(text: UNSUBSCRIBE bits-n-bytes) listserv@acad1.dana.edu

Excerpt from "The MPC Adventures: Experiences with the Generation of VLSI Design and Implementation Methodologies"

Lynn Conway

Connections

Flaming, as we noted above, is the dark side of e-mail fan-out. But fan-out can also be a very powerful positive force. The following article illustrates how the properties of e-mail can be used in socially constructive ways. E-mail is not simply a communication tool for individuals; communication happens only in communities. E-mail can foster the formation, organization, and coordination of communities.

As a young girl, Lynn Conway was fascinated with telescopes. The essence of a telescope is that it enables us to see things at a distance, just as e-mail enables us to say things at a distance. When she looked at the ARPANET in the late 1970s, Conway saw not only individual stars but also constellations. She saw not just individuals, but groups of people who organize themselves to do things together. E-mail, she realized, could trigger and amplify activity. In her article, she explains how she used e-mail to create and organize a community of electrical engineers and to change the way computers are designed.

Prior to 1980, electrical engineering students interested in designing chips might take a course and carefully design a single transistor, focusing on its detailed layout rather than larger system-design issues. Conway and colleague Carver Mead believed that the traditional teaching of system design made the design process too slow and tedious. They proposed a radically different approach in which the rules for laying out individual circuit elements were greatly simplified. Their goal was to make it possible for students to design entire computers consisting of thousands of transistors.

The acronym VLSI stands for Very Large Scale Integration, the art of making computer chips by laying complex patterns of materials on silicon. VLSI makes it possible to put an entire computer processor on a single chip. Essentially all modern computers now use VLSI technology.

To change design practice, Mead and Conway needed to radically simplify the rules and to find ways to compose elements at all levels. They wanted design methods that could be easily learned by digital system designers, and that would allow the full architectural potential of silicon to be realized. Naturally there was a great deal of skepticism and resistance to the idea. To succeed, Mead and Conway needed not only to develop and present new design methods, but also to test them on a large scale and to find a way to motivate participants to engage in the adventure.

E-mail played a crucial role in realizing the potential of their idea. Conway recognized that e-mail has easy fan-out, what she calls high branching ratios. *By using e-mail she could maintain contact with hundreds of participants without the time-overhead of telephoning them individually or the delays of writing and mailing separate letters. When activity in one place triggers more activity in another place there can be a chain reaction as a critical mass of a community organizes itself around related goals. In the hands of someone who understands communities in action, e-mail can guide and accelerate community activities. Lynn Conway is a keen observer of communities at work, and her understanding of how they work makes her an effective leader.*

The MPC adventures (multiproject chip network) had many far-ranging social effects. One was that the project stirred a great deal of innovation and economic growth; several of the design projects mentioned in the article ultimately were used to found important high-technology companies. For example, chip designs from the various MPC adventures became the intellectual capital that initiated Sun Microsystems and Silicon Graphics, among others. The Advanced Projects Research Agency ultimately followed Conway's lead and established its own implementation services on the ARPANET. Another product of the social experiment was the textbook Introduction to VLSI Systems, *published in 1980 by Lynn Conway and Carver Mead. The book and the design methods it advocates were developed and tested in communities of designers before being published. The textbook soon came to dominate courses in system design electrical engineering departments around the country.*

When new design methods are introduced in any technology, especially in a new technology, a large-scale exploratory application of the methods by many designers is necessary in order to test and validate the methods. A lot of effort must be expended by a lot of people, to debug the primitives and composition rules and their interaction with the underlying technology. A similar effort must also be expended to generate enough design examples. That is the first point: *A lot of exploratory usage is necessary to debug and evaluate new design methods.* The more explorers that are involved in this process, and the better they are able to communicate, the faster the process runs to any given degree of completion.

Suppose some new design methods have been used and fairly well debugged by a community of exploratory designers, and have proven very useful. Now consider the following question: How can you take methods that are new, methods that are not in common use and therefore perhaps considered *unsound methods*, and turn them into *sound methods*? In other words, how can you cause *the cultural integration* of the new methods, so that the average designer feels comfortable using the methods, considers such usage to be part of their normal duties, and works hard to correctly use the methods? Such cultural integration requires a major shift in technical viewpoints by many, many individual designers. Changes in design practices usually require changes in the social organization in which the designer functions. These are difficult obstacles to overcome. We see that numbers are important again, leading us to the second point: *A lot of usage is necessary to enable sufficient individual viewpoint shifts and social organization shifts to occur to effect the cultural integration of the methods.* The more designers involved in using the new methods, and the better they are able to communicate with each other, the faster the process of cultural integration runs.

When methods are new and are still considered unsound, it is usually impossible in traditional environments to recruit and organize the large numbers of participants required for rapid, thorough exploration and for cultural integration. Therefore, new design methods normally evolve via rather ad hoc, undirected processes of cultural diffusion through dispersed, loosely connected groups of practitioners, over relatively long periods of time. (Think, for example of the effect of the vacuum-tube-to-transistor technology transition on the design practices of the electronic design community, or of the effect of the discrete transistor-to-TTL technology transition). When the underlying technology changes in some important way, new design methods exploiting the change compete for market share of designer mind-time, in an ad hoc process of diffusion. Bits and pieces of design lore, design examples, design artifacts, and news of successful market applications, move through the interactions of individual designers, and through the trade and professional journals, conferences, and mass media. When a new design methodology has become widely integrated into practice in industry, we finally see textbooks published and university courses introduced on the subject.

I believe we can discover powerful alternatives to that long, ad hoc, undirected process. Much of this talk concerns the application of methods of experimental computer science to the particular case of the rapid directed creation, validation, and cultural integration of the new VLSI design and VLSI implementation methods within a large computer-communication network community.

First I will sketch the evolution of the new VLSI design methods. The new VLSI design courses. and the role that implementation played in validating the concepts as they evolved. Next I'll bring you up to date on the present status of the methods, the courses, and the implementation systems. Finally, I'll sketch the methods that were used to direct this evolutionary process. We'll reflect a bit on those methods, and look ahead to other areas where such methods might be applied.

Evolution of the VLSI Design Courses: Role of the MPC Adventures

In the early 1970's, Carver Mead began offering a pioneering series of courses in integrated circuit design here at Caltech. The students in these courses in MOS circuit design were presented the basics of industrial design practice at the time. Some of these students went on to do actual design projects, and Carver found that even those without backgrounds in device physics were able to complete rather ambitious projects after learning these basics. These experiences suggested that it might be feasible to create new and even simpler methods of integrated system design.

In the mid 1970's, a collaboration was formed between my group at Xerox PARC and a group led by Carver here at Caltech, to search for improved methods for VLSI design. We undertook an effort to create, document, and debug a simple, complete, consistent method for digital system design in nMOS. We hoped to develop and document a method that could be quickly learned and applied by digital system designers, folks skilled in the problem domain (digital system architecture and design) but having limited backgrounds in the solution domain (circuit design and device physics). We hoped to generate a method that would enable the system designer to really exploit the architectural possibilities of planar silicon technology without giving up the order of magnitude or more in area-time-energy performance sacrificed when using the intermediate representation of logic gates as in, for example, traditional polycell or gate-array techniques.

Our collaborative research on design methodology yielded important basic results during '76 and '77. We formulated some very simple rules for composing FET switches to do logic and make registers, so that system designers could easily visualize the mapping of synchronous digital systems into nMOS. We formulated a simple set of concepts for estimating system performance. We created a number of design examples that applied and illustrated the methods.

The Mead-Conway Test

Now, what would we do with this knowledge? Write papers? Just design chips? I was very aware of the difficulty of bringing forth a new *system of knowledge* by just publishing bits and pieces of it in among traditional work.

I suggested the idea of writing a book, actually of *evolving a book*, in order to generate and integrate the methods, and in August 1977 Carver and I began work on the Mead-Conway text. We hoped to document a complete, but simple, system of design knowledge in the text, along with detailed design examples. We quickly wrote a preliminary draft of the first three chapters of this text, making use of the Alto personal computers, the network, and the electronic printing systems at PARC. In parallel with this, Carver stimulated work on an important design example here at Caltech, the work on the "OM2." Dave Johannsen carefully applied the new design methods as they were being documented, refined and simplified, to the creation of this major design example.

We then decided to experimentally debug the first three chapters of material by interjecting them into some university MOS design courses. An initial draft of the first three chapters was used by Carlo Sequin at U.C. Berkeley, and by Carver Mead at Caltech in the fall of '77. During the fall and winter of '77–'78, Dave Johannsen finished and documented the new OM2 design. The OM2 provided very detailed design examples that were incorporated into a draft of the first five chapters of the text. We distributed that draft in February '78 into spring semester courses by Bob Sproull at CMU, and by Fred Rosenberger at Washington University, St. Louis.

We were able to debug and improve the material in these early drafts by getting immediate feedback from the '77–'78 courses. We depended heavily on use of the ARPAnet for electronic message communications. Our work rapidly gained momentum. A number of people joined to collaborate with us during the spring of '78: Bob Sproull at CMU and Dick Lyon at PARC created the CIF 2.0 specification; Chuck Seitz prepared the draft of Chapter 7 on self-timed systems; H. T. Kung and several others contributed important material for Chapter 8 on Concurrent Processing. By the summer of '78 we completed a draft of the manuscript of the entire textbook.

The MIT'78 VLSI Design Course

During the summer of 1978, I prepared to visit MIT to introduce the first VLSI system design course there. This was to be a major test of the full set of new methods and of a new intensive, project-oriented form of course. I also hoped to thoroughly debug the text prior to publication. I wondered: How could I really test the methods and test the course contents? The answer was to spend only half of the course on lectures on design methods; then in the second half, have the students do design projects. I'd then try to rapidly implement the projects and see if any of them worked (and if not, find out what the bugs were). That way I could discover bugs, or missing knowledge, or missing constraints in the design methods or in the course contents.

I prepared a detailed outline for such a course. and printed up a bunch of the drafts of the text. Bob Hon and Carlo Sequin organized the preparation of a "Guide to LSI Implementation" that contained lots of practical information related to doing projects. including a simple library of cells for I/O pads, PLA's, etc. I then travelled to MIT and began the course. It was a very exciting experience, and went very well. We spent seven weeks on design lectures, and then an intensive seven weeks on the projects. Shortly into the project phase it became clear that things were working out very well, and that some amazing projects would result from the course.

While the students were finishing their design projects, I cast about for a way to get them implemented. I wanted to actually get chips made so we could see if the projects worked as intended. But more than that, I wanted to see if the whole course and the whole method worked, and if so, to have demonstrable evidence that it had. So I wanted to take the completed layout descriptions and very quickly turn them into chips, i.e. implement the designs (We use the term "VLSI implementation" for the overall process of merging the designs into a starting frame, converting the data into patterning format, making masks, processing wafers, dicing the wafers into chips, and mounting and wire-bonding the chips into packages).

We were fortunate to be able to make arrangements for fast implementation of those student projects following the MIT course. I transmitted the design files over the ARPAnet from MIT on the east coast to some folks in my group at PARC on the west coast. The layouts of all the student projects were merged together into one giant multiproject chip layout, a trick developed here at Caltech, so as to share the overhead of maskmaking and wafer fab over all of the designs. The project set was then hustled rapidly through the prearranged mask and fab services. Maskmaking was done by Micro-Mask, Inc., using their new electron-beam maskmaking system, and wafer fabrication was done by Pat Castro's Integrated Circuit Processing Lab (ICPL) at HP Research, in Palo Alto. We were able to get the chips back to the students about six weeks after the end of the course. A number of the MIT '78 projects worked, and we were able to uncover what had gone wrong in the design of several of those that didn't.

The MIT course led to a very exciting group of projects, some of which have been described in later publications. The project by Jim Cherry, a transformational memory system for mirroring and rotating bit map image data, is particularly interesting, and was one of those that worked completely correctly. Jim's project is described in detail in the second edition of the Hon and Sequin Guidebook. Another interesting project is the prototype LISP microprocessor designed by Guy Steele, that was later described in an MIT AI Lab report.

As a result of this course and the project experiences, we uncovered a few more bugs in the design methods, found constraints that were not specified, topics that were not mentioned in the text, that sort of thing. You can see that the project implementation did far more than test student projects. It also tested the design methods, the text, and the course.

The MPC Adventures: MPC79 and MPC580

I'll now describe the events surrounding the multiproject chip network adventures of the fall of 1979 and spring of 1980. I remember thinking: "Well, ok, we've developed a text, and also a course curriculum that seems transportable. The question now is, can the course be transported to many new environments? Can it be transported without one of the principals running the course?" In reflecting on the early work on the text by communicating with our collaborators via the ARPAnet, and by thinking about which schools might be interested in offering courses, I got an idea: If we could find ways of starting project-oriented courses at several additional schools, and if we could also provide VLSI implementation for all the resulting student projects, we could conduct a really large test of our methods. The course might be successful in some schools, and not in others, and we could certainly learn a lot from those experiences. I began to ponder the many ways we could use the network to conduct such an adventure.

We began to train instructors from a number of universities in the methods of teaching VLSI design....

We coordinated the MPC79 events by broadcasting a series of detailed "informational messages" out over the network to the project lab coordinators at each school.

Just twenty-nine days after the design deadline time at the end of the courses, packaged custom wire-bonded chips were shipped back to all the MPC79 designers. Many of these worked as planned, and the overall activity was a great success. I'll now project photos of several interesting MPC79 projects. First is one of the multiproject chips produced by students and faculty researchers at Stanford University. Among these is the first prototype of the "Geometry Engine," a high-performance computer graphics image-generation system, designed by Jim Clark. That project has since evolved into a very interesting architectural exploration and development project.

• • •

As I think back over the origins of the VLSI implementation system, it's clear that we didn't initially set out to create such a system. It was really a serendipitous result. We were extremely motivated and driven to provide VLSI implementation to a large university community. I thought that it just might be possible to do that. I realized that pulling off VLSI implementation on such a vast scale would generate and propagate a lot of artifacts, and thus announce the presence of the new design culture, and help to culturally integrate our methods. So, we began working very hard at PARC to create ideas to bring down the cost per project and the overall turnaround time, and to scale up capabilities for handling as many designers as possible.

Somewhere along the line I began to use the metaphor that "we're creating something for mask and fab that was like the time-shared operating system was for computing systems." Our idea was to create a system that provided remote-entry, time and cost-sharing access to expensive capital equipment, and that also managed the logistics of providing such access to a large user community.

• • •

Sketch of and Reflections on the Research Methods Used

How was all of this done? Let's reflect on these events, focussing on the research methods used to direct and help all of these different things jointly evolve. You'll notice a common idea running through all of these events: Fast-turnaround implementation provides a means for testing concepts and systems at many levels. It isn't just used for testing the project chips. It also tests the design environments, the courses and instructional methods, the text materials, and the design methods.

I'll now describe a basic method of experimental computer science, and sketch how this method was applied to the generation of the VLSI design and implementation methodologies. Later I'll describe the resources required in order to direct this sort of large scale, experimental evolution of engineering knowledge and design practices.

Experimental Method

There is a basic experimental method that is used in experimental computer science when we are exploring the space of what it is possible to create. The method is especially applicable when creating computer languages, operating systems, and various kinds of computing environments, i.e., applications where we provide primitives that many other people will use to generate larger constructs. Suppose that you've conceived of a new system concept, and want to try it out experimentally. The method is simple: You build a prototype of a system embodying that concept, run the system, and observe it in operation. You might immediately decide, "Hey, this is just not feasible," and scrap the idea right there; or you may think, "Well, maybe we can improve things," or, "Let's try something slightly different," make some revisions, and run the system again. This simple, iterative procedure is sketched in Figure 1. After the experimentation has generated sufficient knowledge (for example, has demonstrated the feasibility of the concept), you may make a transition into some later phase in the evolution of the concept.

What might such later phases be? Suppose you've successfully taken a new concept through a feasibility test, perhaps experimenting with a quick implementation that you ran yourself. You may think, "Well, let's build an improved prototype, and have some other user run it. I'll watch the user use it, and see what happens." After going around that loop a few times. and making further refinements, you may make the transition to building a prototype to be placed into extensive field trials by many users. Thinking back, you can see how the design course was taken through a succession of such phases, from feasibility to transfer to a few other "users" and on to full scale "field trials." By obtaining feedback

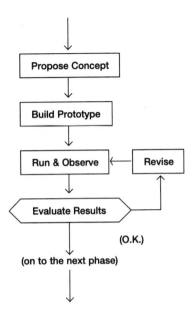

Figure 1
An experimental method.

from users and observating results at each step, you move on to the next phase (see Figure 2) of refinement and integration of that particular system.

If we study the development of the VLSI design methodology, its validation, and its social propagation, you'll notice that the following has happened: The methodology involved a multilevel cluster of systems that were being jointly evolved. Each system in the cluster runs through the experimental loops, and passes through the various phases of its own evolution. Entries at the higher levels, for example the methodology, or the text, or the documents to support a course, might be more solid and in later phases of their evolution at any given time than, for example, a course in a particular school, or the design environment for that course.

The Network Community
Some key resources are required in order to organize such an enterprise. Perhaps the most important capital resource that we drew upon was the computer-communications network, including the communications

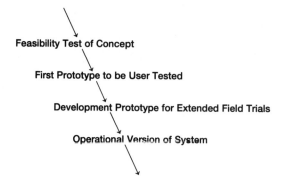

Feasibility Test of Concept

First Prototype to be User Tested

Development Prototype for Extended Field Trials

Operational Version of System

Figure 2
Some phases in the evolution of a system.

facilities made available by the ARPAnet, and the computing facilities connected to the ARPAnet at PARC and at various universities. Such a computer-communication network is a really key resource for conducting rapid, large scale, interactive experimental studies.

The networks enable rapid diffusion of knowledge through a large community because of their high branching ratios, short time-constants, and flexibility of social structuring; any participant can broadcast a message to a large number of other people very quickly. It isn't like the phone, where the more people you try to contact, the more time-overhead is added so that you start spending all of your time trying to get your messages around instead of going on and doing something new.

The high social branching ratios and short communications time constants of the networks also make possible the interactive modifications of the systems, all of these systems, while they are running under test. If someone running a course, or doing a design, or creating a design environment has a problem, if they find a bug in the text or the design method, they can broadcast a message to the folks who are leading that particular aspect of the adventure and say, "Hey! I've found a problem." The leaders can then go off and think, "Well, my God! How are we going to handle this?" When they've come up with some solution, they can broadcast it through the network to the relevant people. Thus they can modify the operation of a large, experimental, multi-person, social-technical system while it is under test. They don't have to run everything through to completion, and then start all over again, in order to handle contingencies. This is a subtle but tremendously important function performed by the network, and is similar to having an interactive run-time environment when creating and debugging complex software systems.

There is another thing that happens in the network: it's relatively easy to get people to agree to standards of various kinds, if the standards enable access to interesting servers and services. For example, CIF became a *de facto* standard for design layout interchange because we at PARC said "if you send a CIF file to us we will implement your project." Everybody put their designs in CIF!

We answered our own questions: "Is CIF documented well enough to be propagated around? Does it really work anyway? Does it have the machine independence we've tried for?" That way we debugged CIF and culturally integrated CIF.

Such networks enable large, geographically dispersed groups of people to function as a tightly-knit research and development community. New forms of competitive-collaborative practices are enabled by the networks. The network provides the opportunity for rapid accumulation of sharable knowledge. Much of what goes on is captured electronically—designs, library cells, records of what has happened in the message traffic, design-aid software and knowledge—all can be captured in machine representable form, and can be easily propagated and shared.

One reason for the rapid design-environment development during '79—'80 was a high degree of collaboration among the schools. Often, as useful new design aids were created, they were quickly shared. Many of the schools had similar computing environments, and the useful new knowledge diffused rapidly via the ARPAnet.

Another reason for rapid progress was keen competition among the schools and among individual participants. The schools shared a common VLSI design culture: during '79–'80 all used the same implementation system, and batches of projects from the schools were often implemented simultaneously. Therefore, project creation, innovations in system architecture, and innovations in design aids at each of the schools were quite visible to the others. Students and researchers at MIT, Stanford, Caltech, CMU, U.C. Berkeley, etc., could visualize the state of the art of each other's stuff. These factors stimulated competition, which led to many ambitious. innovative projects.

Successful completion of designs, and thus participation in such competition, depended strongly on the quality of the design environment in each school. Therefore, there was strong pressure in each school to have the latest, most complete set of design aids. This pressure tended to counter any "not invented here" opposition to importing new ideas or standards. The forces for collaboration and for competition were thus coupled in a positive way, and there was "gain in the system."

Now, think back to the question, "How do *unsound methods* become *sound methods?*" Remember, you need large scale use of methods to validate them, and to produce the paradigm shifts so that the methods will be culturally integrated. In industry, it's very difficult to take some new proposed technique for doing things and put it in use in a large scale in any one place; a manager trying such things would be accused of using unsound methods. However, in the universities, especially in graduate courses in the major research universities, you have a chance to experiment in a way you might not in industry, a way to get a lot of folks to try out your new methods.

A final note about our methods: The major human resources applied in all of these adventures were faculty members, researchers, and students in the universities. The research of the VLSI System Design Area has often involved the experimental introduction and debugging of new technical and procedural techniques by using the networks to interact with these folks in the universities. These resources and methods were applied on a very large scale in the MPC adventures. There are risks associated with presenting undebugged technology and methods to a large group of students. However, we have found the universities eager to run these risks with us. It is exciting, and I believe that it is appropriate for university students to be at the forefronts sharing in the adventure of creating and applying new knowledge. The student designers in the MPC adventures not only had their projects implemented, but also had the satisfaction of being part of a larger experimental effort that would impact industry-wide procedures.

Reflections

A *few years after the Mead-Conway textbook was published, I happened to talk with Conway's editor. The book had done quite well, and he was reflective about the events surrounding its publication. He turned to me and said, "Lynn was not just writing a textbook. She was running a revolution." He described a map of the United States Conway worked with. It had pins marking all the places her book was being used. She kept in touch with course instructors and made sure that seminars for them were offered periodically. She introduced new instructors to each other so they could share materials and conduct design competitions between their classes. Early in the semester she sent them examples of chips and wafers they could show off as design artifacts and as warrants of their own credibility. In effect, Conway managed the growth and development of a community of designers and helped many new professors gain stature in their departments.*

Lynn Conway was more, however, than an accomplished communicator. John Heider's book, The Tao of Leadership, *talks philosophically about Tao. Tao means how: how things happen, how things work. Conway did not strive to be a leader; she simply led. She saw how things worked and acted with them. As Heider observes, good leadership consists of motivating people to their highest levels by offering them opportunities, not obligations.*

Heider's identifies two archetypes of leadership: warrior and healer. As a warrior, the leader acts with power and decision. That is the Yang, *or masculine, aspect of leadership. Most of the time, however, the leader must act as a healer and be an open, receptive, and nourishing figure. This is the feminine, or Yin, aspect of leadership.*

In the Part 3 of this book we look at myths and archetypes for going out into the world and doing things. The healer archetype, a feminine archetype, is often part of the hunter-trickster-shaman complex archetype associated with hunter-gatherer societies. The warrior archetype is typically associated with patrilinear, hierarchical societies. In the current context, we can see how the archetypes of leadership blend with the communicator archetype when someone like Conway uses e-mail creatively to get things done.

She did this by welding a set of geographically separated people into a community with a mission. Professors and students both competed and collaborated. They exchanged examples and analyses of each other's designs and traded computer software. Conway and Mead broadcast informational messages to the participating schools, which resulted in a pacing and coordination of the larger enterprise and a method of conveying administrative details as well as information about bugs and newly discovered methods. E-mail knitted the community of designers into an organic whole in which the processes of knowledge creation, propagation, and testing ran much faster than they usually do.

Part of the attraction of developing design methods in this way was the opportunity to be part of an important movement. Lynn made sure that participants' contributions became known to their colleagues, again, through e-mail. Messages about the project often contained news about, and by, people who were designing chips or finding bugs in design methods. As participants got to know each other, they became a community.

Ultimately, this article isn't so much about VLSI design as it is about the social construction and use of knowledge. Its value lies in seeing how Conway accelerated and amplified the social processes of constructing and using knowledge by exploiting the properties of e-mail. E-mail helped the VLSI design community become conscious of its role in creating knowledge by letting them see new designs and learn new ways of designing things in silicon. They saw both designs that worked and ones that didn't work and experienced the subsequent extension, debugging, and revision of design knowledge. Lynn Conway saw that people with a mission could coordinate their work and collaborate in creating wider knowledge. The processes of knowledge creation and testing have time constraints that depend on various parameters. Some of the parameters are related to communication—especially time needed for fan-out and synchronization. Conway shows us that using e-mail and communications networks can change these time constraints and make the social processes of community formation and knowledge generation run faster.

The stories of the Tower of Babel and the Pentecost are also relevant to her achievement. When Mead and Conway began their project, the designers were not yet a community. For one thing, they used many different kinds of computers at many different sites. Left to evolve on their own, they probably would have produced a collection of different and incompatible chip design languages. A crucial part of the enterprise, therefore, was to devise a single language that would work on all computers: a language that would describe circuits for all interactive design programs, work for testing design rules, and be used by the implementation server to fabricate chips. A common language ensured that ideas and tools developed at one site would work for designs developed at another. The MPC project created the "Caltech Interchange Format" (CIF) for circuit descriptions. CIF, the methods of the draft textbook, became the languages that defined and knitted together a new community.

Excerpt from "Digital Communications and the Conduct of Science: The New Literacy"

Joshua Lederberg

Connections

Historians say that the most interesting time to study cultures is when they are undergoing profound changes. As an inventor, I have found that the most interesting time to study inventions are when they are new and just being introduced. At those moments, people are most open to the possibilities. Often they see things that are forgotten later in the press of immediate practical realities and do not reappear for some time.

Lederberg wrote this article in 1978, shortly after the ARPANET became operational and long before it evolved into the Internet. As a geneticist and computer scientist, Lederberg is deeply concerned with long-term issues and is necessarily a futurist. In the article he reflects on the future possibilities of e-mail and the national computer networks that were then emerging. Since then, many of the things he foresaw have become realities. Perhaps even more interestingly, some of them were premature and are yet to be realized. Nonetheless, they are still part of a wide open future that many of us have forgotten.

In 1978 university computers were large, extremely expensive mechanisms that could only be purchased when groups at a campus pooled their resources and used them on a time-shared basis. Often the groups had little more in common than their desire to use a computer. The ARPANET changed community practice around computers in two important ways. First, it let people distant from a computer use it almost as if it were located nearby. This change enabled those with common interests who were spatially separated to share a computer. Second, it allowed

them to communicate through e-mail with people who used any com-
puter on the network, however distant. Together, these changes in con-
nectivity radically altered the culture and experience of researchers; it
put them in daily electronic contact with a much larger group of people
interested in the same kinds of questions. In this way, it increased the
"critical mass" of researchers engaged in similar research.

The SUMEX-AIM computer facility was the first national shared-
computing resource for medical research. It was established in January
1974 to serve a community of specialists doing research on the applica-
tions of artificial intelligence to medical research. As leader of the facility
and a working scientist, Lederberg was interested in the effects of the
ARPANET and the implications for scientists of widely available com-
puter networks. Here he presents his thoughts on the introduction of
networks and predicts how they would be used in the following twenty-
five years.

• • •

This essay is written from the perspective of an enthusiastic *user* of
packet switched communications. The system itself is here regarded as a
black box that accomplishes efficient transfer of digitally encoded information in near-real time among terminals that interface both to human
users and to computer-manageable files. The economical integration of
user, file, processor, and distance-indifferent communication link is the
novel capability of what I shall call a EUGRAM system. EUGRAPHY
thus embraces not only electronic despatch of mail but also a panoply of
computer-augmented text handling tools and protocols. This account is
informed by my experience over the last five years in the development of
the SUMEX-AIM community for research in artificial intelligence related
to biomedical science. However, it will be primarily concerned with the
expected impact of, and needs for, the elaboration of EUGRAPHY in the
conduct of scientific research generally over the next twenty-five years.

Conduct of Science: Computers and Communications

• • •

The past twenty years have witnessed a growing self-consciousness
about the structure of scientific activity, impelled in part by Malthusian

concerns over the long term implications of a geometric increase in publications—a ten-fold expansion over the 40-year typical career of the scientist. Much more has been written than implemented about so means of helping scientists keep up with the "information-explosion." One must acknowledge the utility of recent introductions of literature-searching and alerting services, many of which crucially depend on computer support and EUGRAM-like communications.

• • •

In practice, frequent personal encounters facilitated by grant funding, jet aircraft and invisible colleges seem to play an increasingly important role in the exchange of information within scientific specialities, but without any systematic inquiry as to the costs, efficiency, and equitability of these modes.... The long-distance telephone surely has its role also, but more for operational detail than serious intellectual discourse; and the use of the mails is as idiosyncratic as is the performance of the US Postal System, with the notable exception of the exchange of xerocopied preprints of forthcoming publications.

In the face of this inertia, one should be skeptical about the marketability of new systems like EUGRAPHY, regardless of their technical virtues. Indeed, scientists may be the last to adopt them on a comprehensive scale, except for demonstrations that may arise from a) computer science, b) research management, c) military requirements, d) the ever graver collapse of conventional mails, and e) business applications like EFTS. With respect to c), we of course owe a great deal to the ARPANET as showing the way, and with the potential for a spillover into civil technology perhaps comparable only to [the] jet engine. The sheer economy of EUGRAPHY, and the diffusion of microprocessors and displays into the laboratory and into everyday life, are bound to force an encounter with the challenges of new systems despite the traditional conservatism of the scientific establishment (with respect to its own way of doing business, and its attention to change outside the academic discipline). Nevertheless, the history of the medical and engineering sciences both show many instances where a reluctant marriage of theoria and praxis has engendered major enrichments of the basic sciences.

All the above notwithstanding, our own experience with EUGRAPHY at SUMEX-AIM has been extraordinarily good. Individual users of course rely upon it routinely for access to computer processing. More surprising was the utility of EUGRAPHY for research management, involving the exchange of texts even over relatively short distances — offices down the corridor or in nearby buildings. This phenomenon has provoked introspections about EUGRAPHY as a qualitatively different method of interpersonal communication from conversation, the telephone, the handwritten memo, the dictated letter or the published report, and some speculations about the further evolution of EUGRAMs as part of scientific communication.

Comparing the EUGRAM with the Telephone

When telephone usage is limited to a few calls per day, and the connecting parties are reliably locatable, the telephone may indeed fulfill its image of instant, spontaneous communication. In current practice, beleaguered by time zone shifts, lunch hours, conferences, and competing calls, the reality of phone usage is exemplified by the employment of secretaries to make and receive the calls. The very instantaneity of the phone connection generates a queuing problem that defeats the basic motive. In due course, the two way conversation may disappear, to be replaced by messages stored on tape recorders. The information density of speech may be viewed as very low, or very high, depending on how much of the burden is carried by the text, how much by inflection, phrasing, and other personal qualities. It may be only with respect to communications that have high affective content that audio can compete with digital channels, and to do this well may require better than the average channel quality than is now readily available between metropolitan centers. Even here, the enhancement of literary competence might go a long way to permit the EUGRAM to compete with the song.

The EUGRAM, furthermore, has all the advantages of digital storage and accessibility to archiving, sorting and searching mechanisms that are far easier to implement, and require far less bandwidth than do voice messages. The EUGRAM itself can be composed quickly with a text-editor on the user display, where it is readily rehearsed, corrected and re-edited before being transmitted. The same EUGRAM can be fanned out simultaneously to a large number of recipients, or it can be revised and perfected through several versions with similar broadcast, or with selective distribution.

From the receiver's perspective, he has the advantage of a literate spatially oriented medium. In contrast to the time-fluent telephone, radio or TV, he has the option of perusing his mail at his own pace, of interruption, backtracing and cross-checking the text, even of marking it for reexamination and further rumination. He retains mastery of the use of his own time, and can coordinate attention to a coherently chosen set of tasks. He is liberated from the tyranny of synchronizing his own mental processes to those of the external actor. This freedom of course reduces the impact of that actor, just in proportion to the responsible autonomy it returns to the reader.

In framing responses, entire messages or selected extracts together with added comments can be forwarded to others, or returned to the sender—lending focus to a "discussion" and providing unambiguous texts for the development of a consensus. EUGRAMs can be filed and retrieved efficiently, or transcribed into hard copy as required. Text editors may be embellished with elaborate formatting aids, spelling correctors, even an online thesaurus to aid in composition. When quantitative calculations are in question, numbers can be mechanically copied directly from program outputs, avoiding pestiferous typographical errors. The same computer is likely to be the user's research tool and give access to shared data-bases: the EUGRAMs can then refer to common files by names that are themselves machinable. The user will also have access to other conveniences, such as desk-calculator-like programs for the checking of figures. He can even track the growing size of a EUGRAM-script (like this one) to be sure it fits into the assigned space. These word-processing capabilities can of course be consummated with hard copy sent through the mails, but with some additional effort, and the degradation of the machinability of the product at the other end.

The paradoxes of instant telephony are most manifest when several parties are involved. In our experience, several weeks prior notice (or other rigid prearrangement) has been needed to schedule teleconferences if four or more people were required simultaneously. EUGRAMs to groups are sent in real time supported by conveniences like group labels. Stored in the receiver's file areas, EUGRAMs are exchanged among an active community like SUMEX-AIM within a few hours, often within minutes. Users also remain in ready communication with each other, via their respective EUGRAM files, even when either or both have travelled away from their customary homes. Lightweight, portable terminals give any user full access to the system from any point which connects to the global telephone and other communications networks. Some facilities offer a fair amount of directory assistance, in locating and identifying the EUGRAM addresses of users; files may also be used to contain blocks of addresses that can be addressed by group names. At SUMEX-AIM, publicly accessible bulletin boards are also available for broadcasting information or posting queries, without obtrusion, to a large audience. No doubt, "junk mail" will become a problem in this medium, as it may in any other. However, the recipient has as powerful a technology for filtering unwanted messages as the broadcaster has for disseminating them. The struggle is more evenly matched, and there is then less economic incentive for abuses than applies, for example, to the distraction of one's attention by automated telephone sales technology.

• • •

EUGRAMs and Complex Communications

• • •

In many instances, it might still be possible to read a journal article over the telephone and garner some degree of comprehension of the argument even without visible records: but consider how often we have to ask simple names to be spelled out and numbers repeated in phone discourse. Imagine then communicating a computer program of more than ten instructions over the telephone! Indeed, it is precisely for the sharing of such program source texts that EUGRAMs have been most manifestly indispensable for groups like the ARPANET and SUMEX-AIM communities.

These program texts, which may reach hundreds of thousands of instructions are among the most complex records of human logical effort—and more than any other production, the information is manifestly all in the text. However, they also typify the information content of other scientific efforts like mathematical proofs, structural analysis in chemistry, and other arguments. Some of these also resemble program sources in becoming almost impossible to criticize as written records alone, viz., without exercising them on the computer or in the laboratory. The recent demonstration of the four-color-map theorem comes to mind.

One of the facilities offered under SUMEX-AIM is the CONGEN system. This is an aid to the organic chemist. offering him the computer generation of a hypothesis-tree of structures under given constraints. It can also be used as a verifier of claims of new structures, as a proof-checker. As an exercise in advanced organic chemistry, graduate students were assigned the verification of a set of structures recorded in the recent literature. Many of the proofs were found to be incomplete, usually for lack of tacit stipulations that were still plausible in the immediate context. We have no firm statistics, but perhaps one "proof" in ten contained a substantive fallacy, unnoticed by the author and reviewers, that invited a critical reexamination of the conclusion. This suggests that organic chemical analysis has already become too complex for the existing media, that a significant part of the literature is shaky, and that computer-augmented proof-checking of complex structures should be part of the process of editorial review. The prevalence of statistical fallacies in the biomedical literature, often deeply rooted in careless experimental designs, has provoked much critical comment. Certainly, it is responsible for a redoubled waste of resources, in the primary efforts, in faulty policy and practice, and in the further work needed for criticism and rectification.

Probably it is wrong to say that chemistry is so complex; to the contrary this finding is more likely a result of the simplicity and transparency of the logical argument in its proofs, which makes them more amenable to computer emulation. Outside of mathematics, very little scientific reasoning has been subjected to formal analysis and representation. EUGRAM publication now affords the opportunities and incentives to undertake more rigorous formulations both by providing more convenient media for depositing illegible proofs and offering access to symbol-manipulating machines to digest them. Increasingly, hardware engineers will find themselves companions to linguists and philosophers of science; they have long since shared profitable joint ventures with formal logicians.

Emergence of the New Literacy

. . .

Most of these remarks have concerned EUGRAMs between identified persons. The use of EUGRAMs for communication with archives opens up additional opportunities and foreseeable problems. In our experience at SUMEX-AIM, EUGRAPHY has been indispensable for the division of labor in drafting and criticizing complicated research proposals: twenty people may be closely involved in a product of 250 print pages.

. . .

This discussion has intentionally focussed on the difficulties and side effects that may attend the introduction of challenging new technologies of communication. Surely others will emerge as difficult to foresee as the impact of the internal combustion engine on the structure of cities. The problems should not obscure the constructive implications of steps toward the realization of an effective "world brain," which had already obsessed Leibniz, and which may be the defining attribute of technological culture: the efficient refinement and sharing of human knowledge. We do well to question our moral capability of enjoying the fruits of such cooperation; but this is not to damn ourselves in advance, especially if we acknowledge that anticipating the human problems is a task of equal priority to engineering the hardware.

Reflections

It can be fun to keep score when reading older articles predicting the future of technology and its uses. In this regard, Lederberg's 1978 predictions hold up well. Among other things, he foresaw the appearance of telephone answering machines as well as the risk of junk e-mail and the technical defense of automatic mail filters.

His most interesting observations, however, are timeless. Lederberg is interested in the process of science and in scientific discourse at all levels. For him, the processes of collaboration, peer review, and exchange of draft documents are as important as published works. His term EUGRAM encompasses many of the tools for producing intermediate-level works—not only e-mail but also hypertext bulletin boards and, more generally, the means (including computer programs) for creating and exchanging digital works of all kinds.

The article also provides a counterpoint to Lederberg's article in Part 1 on the digital library metaphor. The first article concerns writing for posterity and the problem of keeping up with the increasing number of articles available to a researcher, in an era of scientific specialization and rising journal costs. In this article his attention shifts from communications in the broad scientific community to communications within a working group. The shift in timespan and community size is also a shift in the voice of the archetype—from the keeper of knowledge to the communicator and contributor. Lederberg finds the state of the art of tools for the communicator much more satisfactory than those for the keeper of wisdom.

Perhaps the most extraordinary account in the article is the use one professor made of the CONGEN system as a proof-checker. This is an example of a technological idea that was tried in a specialized, but practical, setting but was, apparently, far ahead of its time. Carl Djerassi enlisted his graduate students to use a computer program to check the published results in a chemistry journal for correctness and completeness. He himself reported on the event at greater length in his autobiography, The Pill, Pygmy Chimps, and Degas' Horse *(1992):*

The computer programs our AI group had developed were designed to accomplish a task for which the computer is best qualified, and that is, at the same time, most difficult to perform manually; the exhaustive generation of all possible structural candidates consistent with the isolated bits of information.... I asked each student to search the chemical literature for a publication in which the structure elucidation of some natural product was based on conclusions derived from a variety of physical methods.... After each student had selected such a paper, I asked that they subject the literature data to scrutiny by our computer program. Did the computer agree with the chemist's conclusion that no other structural alternative was consistent with the published data? Or was some straw man lurking in the background which had not yet been eliminated by the evidence at hand? Had a straw man possibly been overlooked by the chemist?...

The results of this pedagogic experiment were even more dramatic than I had anticipated. Without exception, each student discovered that the evidence cited in the published literature was consistent with at least one structural alternative that the authors had not considered. In one instance, the computer generated over two dozen structural straw men that had not been eliminated by the experimental evidence in the literature! I wrote to each author—in Japan, Italy, Spain, England, and North America—describing the student's (really the computer's) con-clusions and asking whether the author had any comments about the ambiguity of his or her published results.... I suggested, only partly tongue in cheek, to one of the journal editors that our computer program could become a completely auto-mated and totally unbiased journal referee for any manuscript dealing with struc-ture determination ... but to my knowledge no journal has so far had the courage to try such an experiment (pp. 141–42).

As yet, there are no practical applications of computer programs for checking the quality of published research data, and the very idea is astonishing. However, the design-rule checkers in electronic design men-tioned in Lynn Conway's article can also be used to check communica-tions and to verify the correctness of circuit designs communicated by e-mail. These uses suggest that computers could play a role in checking knowledge, either in the context of the keeper of knowledge—as in the CONGEN example—or in the context of advisers—as in the electronics design example. In terms of ancient archetypes, perhaps these ideas are modern-day variants of the ancients' oracles and seers reborn as knowl-edge-based systems. (The reader interested in learning more about such systems may consult my textbook, Introduction to Knowledge Systems.)

Finally, it is instructive to look at the mythological ideas Lederberg refers to obliquely at the end of his article—"the constructive implication of steps toward the realization of an effective 'world brain.'" He notes that the philosopher and mathematician, Leibniz, was obsessed with the idea of the world brain. In the late 1970s, Lederberg gave a talk about the MOLGEN research project at Stanford University—a knowledge-based system for reasoning about plans for experiments in molecular genetics. At the time, he was intrigued with Leibniz and the possibility of creating both a knowledge base and calculus of scientific reasoning; he was inspired, in part, by the MOLGEN project. For him, the term world brain seems to refer to the efficient refinement and sharing of human knowledge, a suitable obsession for scientists, who see their role as extending human knowledge. If computers and knowledge-based rea-soning systems are nodes in a world brain, then the computer network must surely be the nervous system.

In recent years, environmentalists, science-fiction enthusiasts, and others have discussed the "Gaia hypothesis," the idea that the earth as a whole is a coherent living system and seeks to correct imbalances in *its ecosystems. The name* Gaea *is a variant of* Gaea *of Greek mythology, the goddess of the earth who bore and married Uranus and became the mother of the Titans and the Cyclops. Gaea, therefore, was older than the other gods of the Greek pantheon. One interpretation of the hypothesis that combines mysticism and technology sees mankind and technology coevolving toward a point where the human race will be ready to take mature responsibility for caring for the earth. Lederberg's slant on this issue, however, focuses on a scientific perspective; that is, it is shaped by the keeper of wisdom archetypes of the digital library metaphor more than by a view of humanity as the explicit conservator of the earth.*

The adjustment of the scientific community to the computational infrastructure is still ongoing. Certainly the potential and practice for long-distance scientific collaboration have both expanded since the article was written. Some of the articles in Part 4, on the digital world metaphor, illustrate the potential an increasingly digital and interconnected world presents for communication and joint efforts in a "national collaboratory."

Part 3

The Electronic Marketplace Metaphor:
Selling Goods and Services on the I-Way

We are committed in that transition to protecting the availability, affordability, and diversity of information and information technology as market forces replace regulations and judicial models that are no longer appropriate.
Vice President Albert Gore, December 21, 1993

When in the market place you toilers of the sea and fields and vineyards meet the weavers and the potters and the gatherers of spices, —
Invoke then the master spirit of the earth, to come into your midst and sanctify the scales and the reckoning that weighs value against value.
Kahlil Gibran, *The Prophet*

Business makes the world go round. This sentiment may not be good physics, but it honors people who get things done. We have all heard someone described as a "man of action" and know the proverb "action speaks louder than words." In the physical world action sustains life.

Doing things in the world is crucial for the survival of any culture, and every culture has stories that teach how to do it. The stories change over time as the conditions of life change. For men, the teaching focus of the stories have shifted from the ideals of the hunter to the ideals of the farmer to the ideals of the warrior, reflecting different cultures and different values for getting things done. As we will see, in the digital age the values appear to be shifting again. To understand the nature of the shifts and how the archetypes arose, we look to the record in archaeology and mythology.

Myths and Archetypes for Awakening the Trader

Hunter-gatherer cultures represent the original form of human society; these societies are also called nomadic cultures, or simply hunting cultures. Such cultures dominated in Paleolithic times and persist in some parts of the world. A much-studied example is Mesopotamia, "the land between the rivers." Mesopotamia is the Greek name for the triangular area between the Tigris and Euphrates rivers, which stretches from a little above Baghdad to the mountains of Armenia. Nomadic hunting cultures thrived there until about 8000 B.C., when the agricultural revolution brought about the domestication of plants and animals as well as fundamental changes in the social roles of men and women.

In nomadic hunting cultures the dominant archetype in stories about action in the world is the shaman-hunter-trickster. Evidence for this archetype comes from both the archaeological record and observation of such contemporary peoples as the Kung of Africa, the Inuit of North America, and Australian aborigines. Tricksters are hunters, and hunters are usually men. Women are typically the gatherers of fruits, roots, vegetables, and nuts. Men and women in these cultures work together to create a subsistence livelihood. Hunters depend on wile and cooperation; for example, Australian aborigines masquerade as emus to hunt those birds, just as the Bushmen of Africa use feather disguises when hunting ostriches. Thus, hunters resort to trickery out of necessity; and to survive—because hunting is uncertain and dangerous—they often use magical preparations for the hunt. Before hunters leave on an expedition, a shaman may draw a picture of the quarry with an arrow flying into its heart. Inuit shamans appeal to the spirit guardians of animals; Bushmen use ecstatic dances, entering trances in which they turn into great animals in a spirit realm. When a society stops hunting, the hunting archetypes decline and are replaced by new archetypes.

The discovery of agriculture produced a cultural revolution. Grain and bread became staples. Hunting became less important as domesticated pigs, cows, and other animals provided meat. Masculine hunter traits of spontaneity and risk-taking became less valued, because agriculture demanded different values, like a steady work ethic. Whereas for hunters, extra, unskilled children were an impediment to the hunt, for farmers many children mean more helping hands. Many societies become matrifocal when they became agricultural. When the Navajo migrated from Alaska and Canada to the American southwest, for example, they lost their traditional hunting grounds and learned agriculture from the nearby Pueblo Indians. They also shifted to the matrilineal society that is typical of early farming cultures.

Starting in about 4000 B.C., patriarchal cultures in Mesopotamia began to displace matrifocal farming cultures. As documented in Gerda Lerner's *The Creation of Patriarchy*, the population rose steadily, and farmers accumulated property. In Mesopotamia, people began to move from the mountains to the grassy uplands. By 6000 B.C., the area between Assyria to the Euphrates was dotted with villages. At the same time, a climate change toward colder weather in many parts of the world increased the competition for fertile land, making rich settlements tempting targets for invasion. Warfare, the deliberately planned use of violence to capture resources, was invented. In the archaeological record, the first images of battle scenes appear at the end of the Paleolithic period. Warriors then became necessary for the survival of a culture, and this fundamentally changed manhood ideals. Boys were taught to deny fear and pain, and ordeals were invented to toughen warriors. New rituals were invented to remind warriors returning from a battle to be gentle and loving at home.

The invention of warfare and increases in population led to the creation of larger, more-organized societies. In Mesopotamia, political organizations and centers of trade and government were established. Trade between groups to supply stone, wood, metals, and other materials increased. By 3100 B.C., there were cities, and by 2000 B.C. the civilizations of Mesopotamia had devised systems of flood control and irrigation. Over time, the country was overrun by more warlike neighbors, and ancient names for the area changed from Mesopotamia, to Sumeria, to Babylon. By 745 B.C. much of the region was part of the Assyrian empire.

The pattern of development from hunting and gathering to agriculture to organized society in Mesopotamia was similar in other parts of the world. Everywhere it occurred, this sequence, replaced the ideals of the hunter-gatherer with the ideals of the warrior-hero.

From Tricksters to Heroes: The Evolution of Myths and Archetypes

In his *Beyond the Hero*, Allan Chinen traces how the shaman-hunter-trickster archetype arose in the Paleolithic era, was buried under the goddess traditions of agricultural societies, and was buried still deeper under the hero-warrior-king archetype of patriarchial society.

The trickster is known in the myths of many cultures; he is Hermes of Greek myth, Legba of Africa, Coyote of North America, and Maui of Polynesia. His image is connected with hunting, healing, and shamanism. Many Paleolithic images portray dancers that are half men and half animals. This symbolism is consistent with the shaman's role in hunting cultures, in which he talks to prey animals and calls on their powers to achieve success in the hunt. Paleolithic art shows tricksters dancing and wielding magic; it also focuses on wounded men. In shamanic traditions, being wounded is part of becoming a shaman. The image may also refer to the danger that hunters of large animals confront. The wounding theme might also reflect the trickster's ability to survive, despite physical blows or symbolic blows to pride.

Coyote of Native American tradition is one of the most famous tricksters. He is a mischievous, cunning, and sometimes destructive force. The Maidu and other southwestern tribes expect to suffer from his endless trickery, especially his powers to control the hunt and to change his shape at will. Mythological tricksters can be recognized by the way they live by their wits. Like hunters, they are wild but not brutal; they are fierce, but they avoid violence.

Old archetypes never disappear completely, although their relevance waxes or wanes with social conditions. The shaman-trickster is embodied in three Greek gods: Hermes, Hephaestus, and Dionysus. Hermes, who is well known for his cleverness, is still linked to hunting; the moment he was born, he hungered for meat. Hephaestus brought to humanity such crucial inventions as fire and metalworking. His traits are similar to those of the Raven of North America, Maui of Polynesia, and Legba of Africa. Hephaestus's image also reflects the wounded tradition of the shaman-trickster. Although Dionysus is not usually considered a trickster—but the god of wine and revelry—like the other more typical tricksters, he is associated with uninhibited impulses. Like Coyote, or the Celtic Cerunnos, he comes back to life alter being killed.

As patriarchal culture replaced farming and hunting cultures, three new archetypes appeared in various combinations involving a hero, a warrior, and a king. The various characteristics and variations are discussed in Joseph Campbell's *The Hero with a Thousand Faces*. In a patriarchal society, some changes and conflicts, such as the changing and ultimately competitive relationship between a father and a son, are inherent. In various myths, the young man succeeds the older patriarch either by peaceful means or by violent overthrow. In these myths, the hero is often the patriarch-to-be and the patriarch is a former hero. The patriarchal form frequently mirrors the strict hierarchies of military organizations. In many myths, aging patriarchs become tyrants.

Getting Things Done in the Electronic Marketplace

Which of these archetypes are relevant to teaching us how to get things done in modern society? Specifically, which archetypes are relevant to the electronic marketplace?

Hierarchical business organizations tend to resemble patriarchal organizations and their warrior ideal. On the other hand, small organizations and so-called virtual corporations often require leaders to coordinate, complex activities, take the initiative, and work in collaboration with others. These qualities are closer to those of the trickster archetype.

In the second article in this section, Malone and his colleagues argue that electronic communication is changing the costs of doing business in ways that favor marketplace organizations over hierarchical organizations. As this shift takes place, we may expect to see a change in the ideals that are valued, a downplaying of the warrior archetype and a reemphasis on trickster characteristics of communication and coordination. Such a shift in ideals may also play an interesting role in making corporations more responsive to social and ecological issues. Allan Chinen suggests that the world is threatened by ecological collapse, sectarian strife, and a growing gap between rich and poor. Many people have pointed out that these problems arise from the spirit and archetype of the warrior, who fights enemies and seeks to conquer nature.

Because electronic commerce is new to the Internet, much of what is being tried now is experimentation. In the original research-oriented ARPANET, commerce was heavily discouraged. Using e-mail to advertise was considered a misuse of the facilities. There were no ready means to send or spend money on the network. In the 1990s commerce on the network has moved from being forbidden, to being tolerated, to being encouraged and promoted. Many different approaches for using credit cards or digital cash on the network have been proposed; the question is not whether money will be spent on the network so much as which of the competing approaches for doing so will prove most workable. In 1993 the CommerceNet consortium was organized in northern California to conduct market trials of technologies and business processes to support electronic commerce on the Internet. Its charter is to facilitate interactions among customers, suppliers, and development partners to create an open electronic marketplace. Its very purpose reflects a vision of the national information infrastructure as an electronic marketplace.

The Deep Structure of the Electronic Marketplace Metaphor

The electronic marketplace metaphor carries over from earlier conceptions a good many assumptions about how a market works. In traditional towns, producers bring things to a central place on market day. Most town markets focus on agricultural goods and other locally produced goods, although some traders sell things from around the world. The economic benefit of markets is that people with different skills from different regions can produce different kinds of goods. When people specialize, goods are cheaper, and the standard of living rises.

Another element of the marketplace metaphor is money. Long ago, trade and barter may have been the norm, but currencies make trade easier. In some markets, goods can be purchased by delayed payment or credit schemes. Goods also have prices. Over time, prices adjust according to supply and demand. On any given market day in a particular market, prices may be flexible—subject to negotiation or to formal bidding processes such as those used at auctions and in the stock market.

When markets grow more complex, some people begin to specialize in trade rather than in producing goods, making a profit on the difference between a purchase price and a sales price. When distributors combine things from different suppliers and add perceived value to a product, they support their work by adding additional fees. As the number of things for sale in a market increases, competition for consumers' dollars rise. Because consumers spend only a limited amount of time in the market, competitors vie for their attention by way of hawking and advertising.

Challenging Assumptions about Marketplaces

Like the digital library and electronic mail metaphors, the electronic marketplace metaphor can mislead us if we overlook the differences between the traditional market and the digital realm. The same technologies and historical trends that are leading to the National Information Infrastructure (NII) are changing other parts of our lives at the same time. We cannot invent the NII by simply taking the idea of a traditional market, digitizing it, and using it as model of what the NII should be and do.

The differences begin with the concept of a market as a place to go on market day to sell or buy goods. It is immediately obvious that an electronic marketplace has a very different sense of place that relates to the fact that it is easier and cheaper to move bits than to move people. We do not travel to a market in a physical sense; the electronic market comes to us. In fact, the electronic market's sense of place is an illusion created for our benefit.

Time and the scale of regions can also be quite different. In traditional farmer's markets, people from a small community agree to meet at a particular place and time to set up the market. Shoppers make short local trips to get there. With electronic markets, communication costs are so low that they may attract people from distant areas, even different time zones. Electronic markets may also be staffed by computational agents rather than people. These changes mean that in many cases electronic markets can serve very large regions and be open all the time.

Money on the network may also come in forms different from the familiar cash, check, or credit card. Although new varieties of these forms of payment are being tried on the network, some people are interested in other possibilities that provide increased privacy and security—for example, a system that lets a customers write personal electronic checks without divulging their identity to the receiver. The value and market for such instruments has yet to be determined.

In traditional markets, manufacturing and transportation costs are paramount constraints. In electronic markets that sell physical goods, these constraints still operate. Although electronic markets can also be used to sell digital goods, the original creation costs may still be high. A sobering lesson from corporate investment in office automation is that the savings and productivity gains from computer technology can be elusive. In some product areas, however—for example, digital publishing—the replication of digital works can be cheap, since the goods are made out of patterns of bits. Thus, in contrast with traditional book publishing, the unit cost of a copy of a digital work is low and does not decrease with the number of copies made. This fact will decrease price differences between works of broad and narrow appeal. Finally, transportation costs are low for digital goods, which diminishes the advantages of local producers and opens the way for distribution over very large, possibly global areas.

Creating the Electronic Marketplace

To illuminate some of the choices ahead in creating electronic marketplaces, we consider three issues: the price of advertising, brand loyalty for information goods, and the shopping experience. These topics are interesting in part because they provide bridges between our experiences in physical and electronic markets.

In print advertising, the price of an advertisement varies tremendously. For example, advertisements sent directly to particular professional audiences may cost as much as $110 per thousand. These are among the most expensive print advertisements; because they are focused they are thought to be the most effective. Advertisements in an upscale trade magazine cost around $40 per thousand people; these are still focused, but not as sharply. In consumer-oriented magazines, the price drops to about $30 per thousand, and in daily newspapers it is under $20 per thousand. Conventional wisdom says that getting the price under $10 per thousand requires a shift from paper-based distribution to broadcast distribution, such as radio and television. What is the value of advertising on a computer network? The price might be low, because it is transmitted rather than printed; the value might be high if the audience is highly focused. As electronic marketplaces are created, the answers to such questions will be sorted out by experience. At the time of this writing, there is much speculation about the value of advertising on digital media.

In physical goods, manufacturers and retailers work hard to establish brand loyalty. Brand loyalty and name recognition are significant factors in goods and services ranging from fast-food restaurants to automobiles to music to brands of travel guides. Will there be brand loyalty in an electronic market? Magazine and newspaper publishers work hard to establish a certain look and coverage that appeals to a market, and radio and television producers work hard to produce a similarly recognizable quality in programming. Not surprisingly media developers also work to develop recognizable identity and brand loyalty in their on-line and interactive information services. One of the significant events of the 1990s is that the experience of usefully looking up information on the computer has moved from the sole province of the librarian to the wide province of schoolchildren and others who use CD-ROM reference works and the World Wide Web. What this means is that sellers have new opportunities to create brand loyalty to information sources. For example, the National Broadcasting Company recently discussed the possibility of producing interactive news for the Microsoft network. Using the war in Bosnia as an example, it cited the possibility of linking the daily news normally associated with newspapers and television news, the kind of monthly analyses that appear in news magazines, and archival information from encyclopedias and history books. All this information could be integrated in a network-based information service. If such a network attracts loyal customers of school age, it might establish a brand loyalty for information that continues into adulthood.

The experience of the shopper in the electronic marketplace is also being invented as I write. Consider some of the possibilities.

Shopping by the Yellow Pages.   Today, many people shop by telephone. They pick up a telephone book and a pad of paper and "let their fingers do the walking" by calling different vendors. A shopper reading the Yellow Pages is often on the verge of making a purchase decision, which makes an advertising there very effective from a marketing point of view. Such advertisements may cost as much as twenty thousand dollars. This is much higher than the price of an advertisement in a newspaper, which is ignored by the vast majority of readers not considering a relevant purchase on the day the paper comes out. Shopping on the information infrastructure could be very much like shopping in the Yellow Pages. You could use the network to check a directory of services carrying the goods you are looking for and to scan the advertisements that appear. The advertisements could be multimedia presentations describing and demonstrating the virtues of particular products and vendors. Click for more information. Click to order. Click to speak to a salesperson.

Shopping by Catalog. Another variation on the shopping experience is catalog shopping, which, unlike the Yellow Pages, focuses on the goods of a particular distributor. There are already several catalogs on the network for ordering books, musical instruments, and other sorts of things. They mimic paper-based catalogs and typically include pictures, descriptions of goods, and price and ordering information. With an on-line catalog, you do not need to fill out an order form; you just click to order. In a seamless network environment, you could click your way from the Yellow Pages to the catalog of a particular merchant.

Shopping by Broker. Another variation on the shopping experience is the practice of using a broker. People who already know exactly what kind of car they want to buy night call a broker, who would then contact various dealers and negotiate the best buy. The consumer could benefit when distributors are willing to bid against each other to compete for a lowest price. On the network, brokers could be a combination of real people and automatic agents. A shopper could select an item from a catalog or other source and ask a broker to obtain it at the best price. Brokers might also provide advice and information to guide the customer's choice. Imagine, for example, having *Consumer Reports* on-line organized to easily display comparative reviews of the product being considered. A broker could combine these reviews with prices from actual distributors to give the buyer information and flexibility.

Shopping at the Mall. In our era, perhaps the most common shopping experience people have is going to a shopping mall. A mall has many different stores, and there are people to talk to at the stores. Both customers and salespersons at, for example, a store selling recorded music have an interest in music. Thus mall shopping is very different from catalog or Yellow Page shopping, because it is a social experience. Imagine that shopping on the network included a video connection to a physical store, or made it possible to communicate with other shoppers. Interfaces that could allow real-time text-based or even video communication could let us talk to other shoppers and salespersons who are discussing the goods we are interested in. This vision of the marketplace touches on the digital world metaphor discussed in Part 4 and also refers back to the social aspects of traditional markets. In one variation on the digital mall shopping experience, we might take a friend shopping—perhaps one who is physically distant from us; the on-line digital world would keep us together as we explore the mall or catalogs and talk things over.

At the time of this writing, on-line marketplaces are still in their early stages. Catalogs for many kinds of goods—ranging from books to clothing to musical instruments—are available on-line. Such services as on-line information brokers are starting to appear. On-line delivery of content is still somewhat problematic, however, as there are few safeguards preventing the redistribution of proprietary information.

The articles in this part describe some of the first steps being taken to develop commerce on the network. The first article, an excerpt from the home page of CommerceNet, outlines its goals in the form of a scenario. The next article discusses changes in the structure of business organizations that occur as they decentralize and become internally market-oriented by using an information infrastructure. The third article chronicles the firsthand experiences of an on-line entrepreneur trying to sell books on the Internet. The last article describes an approach to protecting copyrighted digital property in a way that could remove some of the key barriers to on-line commerce.

Excerpt from "Electronic Commerce on the Internet"

From the CommerceNet Home Page

Connections

The CommerceNet is a consortium actively engaged in the introduction of commerce to the Internet. To this end, they are engaging in consulting and building network infrastructure and also in on-line teaching. The following excerpt from their home page is a visualization of how the network could support commerce, a scenario from the not-too-distant future....

Bill owns a small company that designs printed circuit boards. His four-engineer design group is located ten miles outside of Boulder Creek in the Santa Cruz, California, mountains. This morning, he checked his electronic mail box on the Internet and found a message from Irene, a design engineering manager at a large computer company in San Jose. She asked him to look at a sensitive request for quotation (RFQ) she had just posted. The RFQ was open only to three firms, and the message was encrypted in such a way that only those three firms could read it.

After analyzing the RFQ, Bill again used the Internet to check for current prices for the integrated circuits needed to build Irene's board. He accessed several online catalogs for IC manufacturers and made rough estimates of the cost of materials. There was one thing left to deal with: a sticky design issue he didn't quite understand. He queried several engineers he knew at Irene's company via the Internet as well as an engineer in Amsterdam he had met at COMDEX. The Amsterdam engineer referred him to an article in a back issue of an electronics association journal, which he promptly downloaded from the journal's Internet forum.

After lunch, Bill prepared a quotation and sent it, encrypted, to Irene. The bid not only was secret—it was also a legally binding offer. He mused about how his access to the Internet enabled his company to get jobs that used to go only to the "big boys" on the other side of the hill. His quotations were extremely accurate; he could always look up the most up-to-date prices and inventories via online catalogs. His designers were highly efficient; they accessed the latest applications and utilities from colleagues all over the world. And his cash flow was improved because he could send invoices and receive remittances via the Internet.

Irene, at the other end of the "electronics food chain," often remarked about how using the Internet had helped her company's profitability. The publications group cut printing costs by putting its data sheets, catalogs and data books online. Her engineering group could take advantage of independent board designers; the other two firms bidding on her boards were in Oregon and Taiwan.

The bottom line: for Bill and Irene, the Internet is easy to use and secure. It provides access to services and information sources around the globe. It is a commercial tool, as fundamental as a spreadsheet or telephone, that they both need to stay competitive.

Reflections

In Neal Stephenson's Snow Crash, *the Metaverse is an electronic place that mirrors the real world, including both its watering holes and its markets. You don goggles and technology whisks you there. Appearances in the Metaverse are programmed; virtual real estate is bought and sold. In the virtual-reality version of direct manipulation interfaces actions in the Metaverse can cause changes in the real world. If a virtual person hands you a card saying twenty-five million Hong Kong dollars, taking it into your virtual hand causes two computers somewhere on earth to swap bursts of electronic data to transfer the money.*

The marketplace envisioned in the CommerceNet scenario is not steeped in virtual reality, but it is steeped in the idea of the virtual corporation. In virtual corporations, projects and products are put together by groups of people who organize themselves to carry out specific proj-ects. A successful project uses the best people available, rather than limiting staff to those available in a particular corporation. A virtual corporation reaches out into the larger world through computer net-works, taking advantage of their inherent properties of fan-out and efficient communication. Relationships among working groups are nego-tiated, contracts are signed, and technical data are exchanged on the net-work. As groups finish their parts of the work, they leave the project and look for the next thing to do—possibly with different people.

The companies in this scenario can make use of several kinds of transactions on a network. So what are the transactions necessary to carry out electronic commerce? Dan Schutzer of Citibank distinguishes nine kinds of activities.

1. *Shopping and advertising*
2. *Negotiating*
3. *Ordering*
4. *Billing*
5. *Payment and settlement*
6. *Distribution and receipt*
7. *Accounting*
8. *Customer Service*
9. *Information and knowledge processing.*

Most of these activities involve communication and can be realized on the network, either asynchronously or in real time, and can employ voice, video, or graphics. In short, the network can marry the abilities of telephones, televisions, electronic wirelines, and regular mail to conquer time and distance. Although social and business practices need to evolve before networks can become significant elements in the world's com-merce, even now the inherent advantages of the digital and electronic medium are starting to pull it into competition with the established alternatives. Those advantages will bring electronic commerce into its own.

One common reaction to a proposal to carry out these business activ-ities on the network is simply "We don't do things this way." This reac-tion reminds me of a story a friend told me about cooking a ham with his girlfriend. They were preparing the ham in the kitchen when she asked him if he had a hacksaw. "What for?" he asked. "To saw off the knuckles," she replied. "Why do you do that?" he asked. She paused, and then said. "I don't know. My mother always did." A little later they called her mother. "Why do we saw off the knuckles of a ham with a hacksaw before cooking it?" they asked. "I don't know," the mother replied. "That's what my mother always did." A little later they called the grandmother. "Why do we saw off the pig's knuckles with a hacksaw before baking the ham?" they asked. "Oh that!," she said. "That's because otherwise my oven was too small to fit the ham in."

Some businesses today have similar reasons for the ways they manage the nine activities on Schutzer's list. The networks offer them new, and sometimes advantageous, ways to organize these functions, especially for projects undertaken by virtual corporations. The company gets a bigger oven, and some groups find improved methods of doing business.

With digital goods and services, the distinction between the electronic market and the physical world blurs. What form might digital services take? Perhaps they will become the digital answer man—a network of people and electronic databases that will bid to answer any question for a price that depends on how fast you want it. Perhaps they will deliver video or music entertainment any time anywhere, for a price. Today in rural Georgia, medical examinations of certain kinds are sometimes conducted in the privacy of a remote-television examination room with a doctor at one end and a patient at the other end hundreds of miles away. Although these examples involve goods and services that fit the electronic marketplace metaphor, of they also border on the metaphor of the digital worlds.

In one view of the future information infrastructure content is free and is distributed by information providers as advertisements for the services they charge for. In another version, content circulates in the marketplace as digital goods whose price, like that of physical goods, follows the laws of supply and demand. At the time of this writing, electronic marketplaces are still in the earliest stages of exploration and invention and have plenty of room for creative experimentation.

Net mavens interested in seeing more about CommerceNet may consult its home page:

http://www.commerce.net/information/about.html

Excerpt from "Electronic Markets and Electronic Hierarchies"

Thomas W. Malone, Joanne Yates, and Robert I. Benjamin

Connections

In the South Seas there is an indigenous culture that once used massive stones as a kind of currency; weighty gold reserves are still used by banks and governments to back up their currencies and as a hard form of wealth. Increasingly, however, financial transactions involve no movement of rare or expensive objects or even paper; they are conducted electronically.

The electronic transfer of funds was pioneered by Electronic Data Interchange (EDI), which focuses on high-volume transactions between businesses with long-term relationships. EDI supports prearranged, business-to-business transactions. It was developed initially for the financial industries, but has now spread to cover many repeatable and routine transactions between companies and suppliers.

In recent years, transactions systems have evolved from single-source channels to electronic marketplaces. For example, in 1976 United Airlines created a sales channel that allowed travel agents to book flights on United directly, which provided a competitive advantage until American Airlines upped the ante. American developed its own booking system, not only for its own flights but also for the flights of other airlines. To prevent agents from switching to American, United quickly followed suit. This evolution from single-source channels to electronic markets became a trend in a number of industries. At the time of this writing, the Internet is emerging as a broad electronic marketplace. More and more on-line services are connecting to it, and several novel ways to carry out financial transactions are coming on-line.

The idea of the electronic marketplace is transforming businesses inside and out. Since the 1980s, it has contributed to the trend toward downsizing, decentralization, and increased outsourcing. Several industry watchers have predicted that the future of the corporation lies in the virtual corporation. In a rapidly changing and increasingly global economy, inflexible and fixed entities are being superseded by dynamic groupings in which business teams respond to business opportunities by coming together to carry out specific projects. Why should this be? As Malone, Yates, and Benjamin see it, the replacement of hierarchies by marketplace forces for coordinating economic activity is not accidental. It is driven by the effects of the technology—the increased flexibility and reduced costs made possible by information technology.

Analytic Framework

Definitions of Markets and Hierarchies

Economies have two basic mechanisms for coordinating the flow of materials or services through adjacent steps in the value-added chain: markets and hierarchies. *Markets* coordinate the flow through supply and demand forces and external transactions between different individuals and firms. Market forces determine the design, price, quantity, and target delivery schedule for a given product that will serve as an input into another process: The buyer of the good or service compares its many possible sources and makes a choice based on the best combination of these attributes.

Hierarchies, on the other hand, coordinate the flow of materials through adjacent steps by controlling and directing it at a higher level in the managerial hierarchy. Managerial decisions, not the interaction of market forces, determine design, price (if relevant), quantity, and delivery schedules at which products from one step on the value-added chain are procured for the next step. Thus buyers do not select a supplier from a group of potential suppliers; they simply work with a single predetermined one. In many cases the hierarchy is simply a firm, while in others it may span two legally separate firms in a close, perhaps electronically mediated, sole supplier relationship.

Variants of the two pure relationships exist, but can usually be categorized as primarily one or the other. When a single supplier serves one or more buyers as a sole source of some good, the relationship between the supplier and each buyer is primarily hierarchical, since the buyers are each procuring their supplies from a single, predetermined supplier, rather than choosing from a number of suppliers. On the other hand, the relationship between a single buyer and multiple suppliers serving only that buyer is governed by market forces, since the buyer is choosing between a number of possible suppliers. As the number of suppliers is reduced toward one, relationships that have characteristics of both types may exist.

Factors Favoring Markets or Hierarchies

A number of theorists (e.g., O. E. Williamson's *Markets and Hierarchies*) have analyzed the relative advantages of hierarchical and market methods of organizing economic activity in terms of various kinds of coordination or transaction costs. These coordination costs take into account the costs of gathering information, negotiating contracts, and protecting against the risks of "opportunistic" bargaining. Building on this and other work, Malone and Smith have summarized several of the fundamental trade-offs between markets and hierarchies in terms of costs for activities such as production and coordination. Table 1 summarizes the part of their analysis that is most relevant to our argument here.

In the table the designations "Low" and "High" refer only to relative comparisons within columns, not to absolute values. Production costs include the physical or other primary processes necessary to create and distribute the goods or services being produced. Coordination costs include the transaction (or governance) costs of all the information processing necessary to coordinate the work of people and machines that perform the primary processes. For example, coordination costs include

Table 1
Relative costs for markets and hierarchies

Organizational form	Production costs	Coordination costs
Markets	Low	High
Hierarchies	High	Low

determining the design, price, quantity, delivery schedule, and other similar factors for products transferred between adjacent steps on a value-added chain. In markets, this involves selecting suppliers, negotiating contracts, paying bills, and so forth. In hierarchies, this involves managerial decision making, accounting, planning, and control processes. The classification of a specific task as a production or a coordination task can depend on the level and purpose of analysis, but at an intuitive level, the distinction is clear.

Table 1 is consistent with an analysis of both the simple costs involved in information search and load sharing and the costs resulting from "opportunistic" behavior by trading partners with "bounded rationality." As Williamson summarizes, "tradeoffs between production cost economies (in which the market may be presumed to enjoy certain advantages) and governance cost economies (in which the advantages may shift to internal organization) need to be recognized."

In a pure market, with many buyers and sellers, the buyer can compare different possible suppliers and select the one that provides the best combination of characteristics (such as design and price), thus presumably minimizing production costs for the desired product. One of the obvious benefits of this arrangement is that it allows for pooling the demands of numerous buyers to take advantage of economies of scale and load leveling. The market coordination costs associated with this wide latitude of choice, however, are relatively high, because the buyer must gather and analyze information from a variety of possible suppliers. In some cases, these costs must also include additional negotiating or risk-covering costs that arise from dealing with "opportunistic" trading partners.

Since hierarchies, on the other hand, restrict the procurer's choice of suppliers to one predetermined supplier, production costs are, in general, higher than in the market arrangement. The hierarchical arrangement, however, reduces coordination costs over those incurred in a market by eliminating the buyer's need to gather and analyze a great deal of information about different suppliers.

Various factors affect the relative importance of production and coordination costs, and thus the relative desirability of markets and hierarchies. We focus here, however, on those that are particularly susceptible to change by the new information technologies. Clearly, at a very general level, one of these factors is coordination cost. Since the essence of coordination involves communicating and processing information, the use of information technology seems likely to decrease these costs. Two other, more specific, factors that can be changed by information technology are also important in determining which coordination structures are desirable: *asset specificity* and *complexity of product description....*

Asset Specificity

An input used by a firm (or individual consumer) is highly asset specific if it cannot readily be used by other firms because of site specificity, physical asset specificity, or human asset specificity. A natural resource available at a certain location and movable only at great cost is site specific, for example. A specialized machine tool or complex computer system designed for a single purpose is physically specific. Highly specialized human skills—whether physical (e.g., a trade with very limited applicability) or mental (e.g., a consultant's knowledge of a company's processes)—that cannot readily be put to work for other purposes are humanly specific. We propose yet another type of asset specificity: time specificity. An asset is time specific if its value is highly dependent on its reaching the user within a specified, relatively limited period of time. For example, a perishable product that will spoil unless it arrives at its destination and is used (or sold) within a short time after its production is time specific. Similarly, any input to a manufacturing process that must arrive at a specific time in relation to the manufacturing process to avoid great costs or losses is also time specific.

There are several reasons why a highly specific asset is more likely to be acquired through hierarchical coordination than through market coordination. Transactions involving asset-specific products often involve a long process of development and adjustments for the supplier to meet the needs of the procurer, a process that favors the continuity of relationships found in a hierarchy. Moreover, since there are, by definition, few alternative procurers or suppliers of a product high in physical or human asset specificity, both parties in a given transaction are vulnerable. If either one goes out of business or changes its need for (or production of) the product, the other may suffer sizable losses. The greater control and closer coordination allowed by a hierarchical relationship are thus more desirable to both.

Complexity of Product Description

Complexity of product description refers to the amount of information needed to specify the attributes of a product in enough detail to allow potential buyers (whether producers acquiring production inputs or consumers acquiring goods) to make a selection. Stocks and commodities, for example, have simple, standardized descriptions, while those of business insurance policies or large and complicated computer systems are much more complex. This factor is frequently, but not always, related to asset specificity; that is, in many cases a highly specific asset, such as a specialized machine tool, will require a more complex product description than a less specific asset. The two factors are logically independent, however, despite this frequent correlation. Coal produced by a coal mine located adjacent to a manufacturing plant is highly site specific, though the product description is quite simple. Conversely, an automobile is low in asset specificity, since most cars can be used by many possible consumers, but the potential car buyer requires an extensive and complex description of the car's attributes in order to make a purchasing decision.

Other things being equal, products with complex descriptions are more likely to be obtained through hierarchical than through market coordination for reasons centering on the cost of communication about a product. We have already noted that coordination costs are higher for markets than for hierarchies, in part because market transactions require contacting more possible suppliers to gather information and negotiate contracts. Because highly complex product descriptions require more information exchange, they also increase the coordination cost advantage of hierarchies over markets. Thus buyers of products with complex descriptions are more likely to work with a single supplier in a close, hierarchical relationship (whether in-house or external), while buyers of simply described products (such as stocks or graded commodities) can more easily compare many alternative suppliers in a market.

Items that are both highly asset specific and highly complex in product description are more likely to be obtained through a hierarchical relationship, while items that are not very asset specific and have simple product descriptions are more often acquired through a market relationship. The organizational form likely for items in the other two cells of the table will depend on which factor dominates.

Historical Changes in Market Structures

To illustrate the application of our analytic framework, we briefly examine the historical evolution of market structures in America, paying particular attention to the effects of a key nineteenth century information technology, the telegraph.

Until the mid-nineteenth century, small-scale local and regional markets, not hierarchies, coordinated adjacent stages of American industrial activity. The three major functions of manufacturing—procurement, production, and distribution—were generally handled by different parties. By mid-century the dramatic improvements in communication and transportation provided by the telegraph and the railroads created a network for exchanging information and goods over great distances, thus effectively increasing the area over which markets or hierarchies might be established.

Our analytic framework helps explain how these developments encouraged larger and more efficient markets in some cases, and larger, multifunctional hierarchies in others. On the one hand, as Table 1 illustrates, markets are more communication intensive than hierarchies. Therefore, reducing the time and cost of communication favored—and thus encouraged—the growth of markets. On the other hand, the growth in market area increased the number of economic actors potentially involved in transactions as well as the total amount of communication necessary for efficient markets to operate, thus favoring hierarchies. The net effect of the telegraph in different industries depended largely on the other factors from our framework.

Just as our framework would lead us to expect, nationwide markets mediated by telegraph developed for products such as stocks and commodities futures. These products were nonspecific assets with many potential buyers. In addition, they were easily describable and consequently susceptible to standardized designations that reduced telegraph costs further. The commodities futures market, for example, only emerged on a national scale after a uniform grading scheme that simplified product description was adopted.

The detailed evolutionary path of large integrated hierarchies was more complex than that of national markets and involved several factors other than the telegraph. Nevertheless, our framework again proves useful in the explanation of which conditions led to which forms. The growth of market areas, encouraged manufacturers to increase their output, frequently by developing new techniques of mass production that offered economies of scale. Such firms, however, often found that existing procurement and distribution mechanisms did not support the high-volume throughput necessary to realize the economies, especially when specialized equipment or human expertise were required.

The first companies to vertically integrate procurement, production, and distribution within a hierarchy were those with asset-specific products, such as meat packers with perishable products requiring railroad refrigeration cars and rapid delivery, and manufacturers of complex machine tools with specialized sales and support needs. In the first case, high time specificity outweighed low complexity of product description. In the second case, the product description was complex, and the sales process was high in human specificity. For these firms, the telegraph provided a mechanism by which close hierarchical coordination could be wielded over great distances. Although the economies of scale were the major factor driving this integration, asset specificity and complexity of product description played a role in determining which firms were likely to integrate, using the telegraph as a mechanism of hierarchical coordination rather than of market communication.

Thus our analytic framework is useful in interpreting the impact of communication technology on past changes in organizational form, even when non-communication factors also played a large role. In the next section, we apply the framework to contemporary developments.

Contemporary Changes in Market Structures

We can now give a fuller explanation of the nature of electronic hierarchies and markets, the conditions under which each is likely to emerge, and the reasoning behind our thesis that the balance is shifting toward electronic markets.

Emergence of Electronic Interconnection

Let us begin by looking briefly at the technological developments that make electronic interconnection of either type possible and desirable. New information technologies have greatly reduced both the time and cost of communicating information, just as the telegraph did when it was introduced. In particular, the use of computer and telecommunications technology for transferring information gives rise to what we term the *electronic communication effect*. This means that information technology may (1) allow more information to be communicated in the same amount of time (or the same amount in less time), and (2) decrease the costs of this communication dramatically. These effects may benefit both markets and hierarchies.

In addition to these well-known general advantages of electronic communication, electronic coordination can be used to take advantage of two other effects: the electronic brokerage effect and the electronic integration effect. The *electronic brokerage effect* is of benefit primarily in the case of computer-based markets. A broker is an agent who is in contact with many potential buyers and suppliers and who, by filtering these possibilities, helps match one party to the other. A broker substantially reduces the need for buyers and suppliers to contact a large number of alternative partners individually. The electronic brokerage effect simply means that electronic markets, by electronically connecting many different buyers and suppliers through a central database, can fulfill this same function. The standards and protocols of the electronic market allow a buyer to screen out obviously inappropriate suppliers, and to compare the offerings of many different potential suppliers quickly, conveniently, and inexpensively. Thus the electronic brokerage effect can (1) increase the number of alternatives that can be considered, (2) increase the quality of the alternative eventually selected, and (3) decrease the cost of the entire product selection process.

When a supplier and a procurer use information technology to create joint, interpenetrating processes at the interface between value-added stages, they are taking advantage of the *electronic* integration *effect*. This effect occurs when information technology is used not just to speed communication, but to change—and lead to tighter coupling of—the processes that create and use the information. One simple benefit of this effect is the time saved and the errors avoided by the fact that data need only be entered once. Much more important benefits of close integration of processes are possible in specific situations. CAD/CAM technology, for example, often allows both design and manufacturing engineers to access and manipulate their respective data to test potential designs and to create a product more acceptable to both sides. As another example, systems linking the supplier's and procurer's inventory management processes so that the supplier can ship the products "just in time" for use in the procurer's manufacturing process, enable the latter to eliminate inventory holding costs, thus reducing total inventory costs for the linked companies. The benefits of the electronic integration effect are usually captured most easily in electronic hierarchies, but they are sometimes apparent in electronic markets as well.

Electronic interconnections provide substantial benefits. The recipients of these benefits—either buyers or suppliers (or both)—should be willing to pay, either directly or indirectly, for them. The providers of electronic markets and electronic hierarchies should, in many cases, be able to realize significant revenues from providing these services.

The Shift from Hierarchies toward Markets

Our prediction that information technology will be more widely used for coordinating economic activities is not a surprising one, even though our analysis of the three effects involved (electronic communication, brokerage, and integration effects) is new. In this section we move to a more surprising and significant prediction: that the overall effect of this technology will be to increase the proportion of economic activity coordinated by markets.

Although the effects of information technology discussed above clearly make both markets and hierarchies more efficient, we see two arguments supporting an overall shift toward market coordination: The first is a general argument based on the analysis summarized in Table 1; the second is a more specific argument based on shifts in asset specificity and complexity of product descriptions.

General argument favoring shift toward markets   Our initial argument for the overall shift from hierarchies to markets is a simple one, based primarily on two components. The first is the assumption that the widespread use of information technology is likely to decrease the "unit costs" of coordination. As noted above, "coordination" refers to the information processing involved in tasks such as selecting suppliers, establishing contracts, scheduling activities, budgeting resources, and tracking financial flows. Since, by definition, these coordination processes involve communicating and processing information, it seems quite plausible to assume that information technology, when used appropriately, can reduce these costs.

The second component of our argument is based on the trade-offs summarized in Table 1. As we noted above, markets have certain production cost advantages over hierarchies as a means of coordinating economic activity. The primary disadvantage of markets is the cost of conducting the market transactions themselves, which, for a number of reasons, are generally higher in markets than in hierarchies. An overall reduction in the "unit costs" of coordination would reduce the importance of the coordination cost dimension (on which markets are weak) and thus lead to markets becoming more desirable in some situations where hierarchies were previously favored. In other words, the result of reducing coordination costs without changing anything else should be an increase in the proportion of economic activity coordinated by markets. This simple argument does not depend on the specific values of any of the costs involved, on the current relative importance of production and coordination costs, or on the current proportion of hierarchical and market coordination.

We find the simplicity of this argument quite compelling, but its obviousness appears not to have been widely recognized. There is also another, less obvious, argument that leads to the same conclusion. This second argument is based on shifts in our key factors for determining coordination structures: asset specificity and complexity of product description.

Changes in factors favoring electronic markets versus electronic hierarchies   Some of the new, computer-based information technologies have affected both of our key dimensions so as to create an overall shift from hierarchies to markets. Databases and high-bandwidth electronic communication can handle and communicate complex, multidimensional product descriptions much more readily than can traditional modes of communication. Thus the horizontal line between high and low complexity has, in effect, shifted upward so that some product descriptions previously classified as highly complex, such as those of airline reservations, may now be considered low in complexity relative to the capabilities of the technology to communicate and manipulate them. The line should continue to shift upward for some time as the capabilities of information technology continue to evolve.

The dimension of asset specificity has undergone a similar change. Flexible manufacturing technology allows rapid changeover of production lines from one product to another. Thus some physically asset-specific components that are similar to other, nonspecific components may begin to be produced by more companies. Companies that in the past would not have tooled up for such a small market now may produce small numbers of these components without significant switch-over costs. The vertical line therefore moves slightly right because some asset-specific components have become, in essence, less specific.

Both these changes increase the region of the chart in which market modes of coordination are favored, lending more support to our argument that there will be an overall shift in this direction.

Examples of the shift toward electronic markets   A dramatic example of the shift toward electronic markets has already occurred in the airline industry. When airline reservations are made by a customer calling the airline directly (and the commission is received by the airline's own sales department), the selling process is coordinated by the hierarchical relationship between the sales department and the rest of the firm. When airline reservations are made through a travel agent, the sale is made (and the commission is received) by the travel agent acting as an external selling agent for the airline. In this case, the selling process is coordinated by the market relationship between the travel agent and the airline. Due, presumably in large part, to the greater range of choices conveniently available through the electronic market, the proportion of total bookings made by travel agents (rather than by customers dealing with airline sales departments) has doubled from 35 to 70 percent since the introduction of the American Airlines reservations system.

Similarly, there are many recent examples of companies such as IBM, Xerox, and General Electric substantially increasing the proportion of components from other vendors contained in their products. This kind of "vertical disintegration" of production activities into different firms has become more beneficial as computerized inventory control systems and other forms of electronic integration allow some of the advantages of the internal hierarchical relationship to be retained in market relationships with external suppliers.

• • •

Conclusions and Strategic Implications

A casual reading of the business press confirms that electronic connections within and between organizations are becoming increasingly important. The framework we have developed here helps illuminate many of these changes. We have shown how the increasing use of electronic interconnections can be seen as the result of three forces: the electronic communication effect, the electronic brokerage effect, and the electronic integration effect. We have analyzed how factors such as the ease of product description and the degree to which products are specific to particular customers affect whether these interconnections will take the form of electronic hierarchies or electronic markets.

Finally, and perhaps most importantly, we have argued that, by reducing the costs of coordination, information technology will lead to an overall shift toward proportionately more use of markets rather than hierarchies to coordinate economic activity. By applying this framework, it is possible to see how many of the changes occurring today fit into a larger picture and to predict some of the specific evolutionary changes that are likely to occur as information technology becomes more widely used.

Our analysis has several implications for corporate strategy:

1. All market participants should consider the potential advantages of providing an electronic market in their marketplace. For some participants, providing such a market may increase the sales of their current products or services. For all participants, it provides a potential source of new revenues from the market-making activity itself.

2. All organizations should consider whether it would be advantageous for them to coordinate some of their own internal operations more closely or to establish tighter connections with their customers or suppliers using electronic hierarchies.

3. Market forces make it likely that biased electronic sales channels (whether electronic hierarchies or biased electronic markets) for non-specific, easily described products will eventually be replaced by unbiased markets. Therefore, the early developers of biased electronic sales channels for these kinds of products should not expect that the competitive advantages these systems provide will continue indefinitely. They should instead be planning how to manage the transition to unbiased markets in such a way that they can continue to derive revenues from the market-making activity itself.

4. All firms should consider whether more of the activities they currently perform internally could be performed less expensively or more flexibly by outside suppliers whose selection and work could be coordinated by computer-based systems.

5. Information systems groups in most firms should begin to plan the network infrastructure that will be necessary to support the kinds of internal and external interconnections we have described.

6. Advanced developers of computer-based marketing technology should begin thinking about how to develop intelligent aids to help buyers select products from a large number of alternatives. Such intelligent aids may eventually be able to act, in part, as automated agents for the buyers. They may also, in some situations, be able to provide detailed information to suppliers about their customers' preferences.

In short, if our predictions are correct, we should not expect the electronically interconnected world of tomorrow to be simply a faster and more efficient version of the world we know today. Instead, we should expect fundamental changes in how firms and markets organize the flow of goods and services in our economy. Clearly more systematic empirical study and more detailed formal analyses are needed to confirm these predictions, and we hope the conceptual framework presented here will help guide this research.

Reflections

This article suggests that computer networks are leading to a shift in the way corporations are organized and business is completed. Malone,

Yates, and Benjamin consider two extremes in an organization: tradi-tional hierarchical corporations and marketplace structures for virtual and distributed corporations. In their analysis, each approach has ad-vantages. Hierarchical organizations have high production costs, because of inefficient in-house sources, but low coordination costs. Marketplace organizations have low production costs but high coordination costs. Electronic communications, however, can lower the costs of coordina-tion and thus favor the virtual corporation.

This shift in organization corresponds to a shift in relevant archetypes. Hierarchical organizations favor the patriarchal warrior archetype, whereas market organizations favor interchange and coordination, char-acteristics of the trickster archetype. Like a military organization, the warrior archetype favors domination and conquest to gain power and wealth. Such predatory characteristics do not always work well in busi-nesses that requires alliances, coordination, and repeat business. This is not to say that virtual corporations are less competitive; indeed, the marketplace is usually seen as the epitome of the competitive arena.

Old archetypes do not, however, disappear. Some manufacturing busi-nesses, for example, require a large, dedicated capital investment. The capital may be gathered from many sources, but the manufacturing plant is typically organized hierarchically and for the long term. Groups working in such a facility do not wander off at the conclusion of a project to work elsewhere on something else.

New combinations of personal traits appear as society determines the characteristics needed for success. If the warrior archetype is best suited for the hierarchical organization, the trickster archetype is better suited for the virtual corporation. The warrior takes orders and works on a single well-defined mission, but the trickster needs to be flexible and resourceful. Digital communications are shifting the balance away from the hierarchical organization and toward the market organization. Thus, the trickster may be reborn, making a comeback from the time when farming cultures diminished the importance of hunting and, again, when the need to defend farm land led to a hierarchical, patriarchal society.

The electronic marketplace requires mechanisms for facilitating com-merce. Malone, Yates, and Benjamin focus on electronic funds transfer, but in the Release 1.0 *newsletter of January 1995, Jerry Michalski divides electronic commerce into three tiers that need different mechanisms. The top tier includes very complex commercial transactions that need specific one-time services and customized contracts. He gives as examples acquisitions of companies, set designs for a Broadway musical, and buying custom components. These transactions are hard to represent in catalogs and standard order forms. As you might expect, this tier of commerce has resisted automation in electronic marketplaces.*

The vast majority of automated transactions occur in the middle tier. It includes many kinds of business-to-business processing and the emerging on-line shopping malls. This is the area EDI makes computer-to-computer links from one corporation's inventory system to another's order-entry system. This tier, which Malone, Yates, and Benjamin discuss in their article, is where some people expect the Internet to shine.

The bottom tier involves very simple transactions that are so low in value that it is uneconomical to record and bill them with traditional billing systems. Digital works could easily produce many transactions within this tier. Imagine paying, for example, a nickel to include a digital photograph in a school report, or a fraction of a cent per page to print a digital newspaper on a home printer. Or imagine on-line services offering microtransactions *that cost a few pennies per operation. If enough people take advantage of them, the total market could be very large.*

Changes in digital communication on all these levels are enabling electronic commerce to expand. On a very broad scale, society is figuring out how to do business and what new models and values will define the electronic market place.

Excerpt from "Slaves of a New Machine: Exploring the For-Free/For-Pay Conundrum"

Laura Fillmore

Connections

Sociologists say that the interesting time to study a social group is when it is experiencing major changes. For publishing, as it faces a possible digital transition, these are times of much confusion and experimentation. To be successful, digital publishing requires good cheap reading devices, a way of handling money, and a method to distribute digital property securely. None of these prerequisites existed when Laura Fillmore created the Online Bookstore. Even now, computers are still too expensive for most people to purchase casually. Desktop computers are about as portable as large television sets, and laptop computers have batteries that need recharging every few hours. No computer display is as easy to read as print on paper. Although digital payment on the network is getting started, there are as yet no widely accepted methods of protecting digital property.

Fillmore's speech is interesting not only for its account of the travails of starting a digital publishing business, but also for her wonderful inventiveness about possible new forms of network publication that would be very different from conventional book publishing.

• • •

I am *not* making money by publishing on the Internet. And I don't know anyone who is. Since 1992 our company, the Online BookStore, has been involved in Internet publishing, and we have found it an exercise riddled with paradox and the unexpected; frequent bouts of optimism and what-if idea sessions—a conundrum whose parameters keep shifting.

We have enjoyed commercial success from publishing *about*, talking and meeting and consulting *about* publishing on the Internet; but are we making money from the real live act of on-line publishing for a price? Not yet. As far as I can tell, publishing intelligently in the distributed Internet environment still *costs* money. I don't think I am alone in this realization. I am coming to suspect that there may be no such as thing as publishing on the Internet, or, rather, publishing according to the definition of publishing as we know it from our familiar paper reference points. This may not be the news you came to hear, but I am happy to share what insights I have with you.

The Online BookStore started out under the umbrella of Editorial Inc., a profitable publishing services business which I started in 1982, and which produced hundreds of books for publishers. In 1991, we had nineteen employees, three offices, three shifts around the clock, and used desktop computers to produce such titles as *The Sports Illustrated Almanac* for Time/Warner, Andy Warhol's biography for Bantam Books, and *Doing Business in Kuwait* for Ernst and Young. We were part of a services industry trafficking in paper. Using computers, we were able to integrate the various publishing disciplines under one roof, calling on hundreds of freelancers to supplement our in-house working staff and become a publisher's publisher of sorts, a virtual corporation.

We caught the desktop publishing wave when it was just a swell out at sea in the mid-eighties; and, in the resulting shift in the typesetting business from large centralized composition companies to distributed PC-based typesetting platforms, we rode the wave, and produced books using page composition systems such as PageMaker, Ventura Publisher, Scribe, TROFF, T_EX, and Polaris PrintMerge. Polaris PrintMerge was my favorite, not only because it was the first and crudest PC-based typesetting platform, but because it introduced me to the notion of electronic slavery, our topic of the day.

Turn the clock back ten years, when my company was five-people strong and I was salvaging a typesetting job someone had abandoned in frustration before the machine; it was a manual for hospital custodians, arranged in three columns, detailing how to keep a hospital clean and sanitary. The janitors, our future readers, were supposed to start on the upper left-hand column of each page with the instructions to don their uniforms, and then by the bottom right-hand entry, they had to "clock out wearing uniform." Every page had the same layout for a different duty—mopping the floors, emptying the trash—all items in all columns had to align three across. Before the days of WYSIWYG, assessing one's success as a typesetter meant printing out again and again, at about five minutes per page. The deadline loomed. I would type and wait, type and wait, a period here, a comma there, a drone before the keyboard, caught up in the electromechanical semi-idiot production cycle. When I finally clocked out, called the Fed Ex man for the finished package, I vowed never again to wear the uniform of typesetter. I would hire typesetters.

This was my first personal experience with electronic servitude in the publishing context, though I didn't realize it at the time: I saw it as a business opportunity instead; which, from a commercial standpoint, it certainly was. I learned that users of Polaris PrintMerge, no matter how smart, would become the victims of badly designed software, would turn into drones, because that was their inevitable function vis-à-vis their task and the tools afforded them for completing the task. The humans workers functioned as the erring component, the wetware, charged with coaxing a right-or-wrong result out of a desktop computer.

This was the much-touted cutting edge, offering profit without honor and the opportunity to hire others to work Polaris PrintMerge till a better program came along—which happened startlingly fast. I hired others to stay up all night staring into screens, printing out, cursing the widows and orphans, and printing out again. This first generation of servitude involved securing output from single, unconnected machines, getting desktop computers to emulate the work of the large dinosaur machines lumbering reluctantly off into typesetting antiquity. We were selling output from these PCs, trying to recreate type of such quality that it did not appear to be what it was—computer byproduct. So, busily formatting the output of computers gave us a way to use and begin to understand the machines; but of course, in hindsight, how could we have been anything else but servants to the machines? We did not apprehend the utility of our machines; using computers to wrestle with the static and formatted output of single machines was an error few perceived and many committed, are still committing. We do what we know, and, with the gift of hindsight, can see that this act of manufacturing type on paper, produced by distributed computers sited in decentralized locations, constituted an intermediate step from static to kinetic publishing.

As so often happens with computers, the cutting edge of Desktop publishing became a swamp and then a backwater.

• • •

I'm painting a grim picture, but the tide is about to turn. In the late eighties, we began to produce and typeset books about computer networking, books focusing on the structure and function of globally interlinked computers, which seemed to elicit life from people when used as a communications medium, rather than demeaning them when used as an output medium. One such title, probably the first book on computer networks worldwide, was John Quarterman's book *The Matrix*, published by Digital Press, which concerns computer networks and conferencing systems worldwide. In 1989, when we were working on the production of this book, the author introduced me to the then-alien concept of electronic mail.

• • •

Some of the messages he would send had nothing to do with the text of the book itself, however: messages posted to mailing lists from students in Tianaman Square during the uprising that spring; messages from Alaskans offering first-person accounts of what the oil company wasn't telling us about the Valdez disaster. Fresh and unmediated communication about things that mattered from far corners of the world—news just hours old, unsanitized by the media. Here was information, digitally recorded voices, coming out of the new machine, which itself is a vast collection of interconnected machines being used as conduits for human thought. Where the Haitain freelance typist was hidden and voiceless behind four middlemen and had no hope of a phone, let alone an Internet connection, the students in Beijing and citizens of Alaska could talk electronically; and there were millions around the world who could and did listen, immediately, electronically; and no one stopped them. The Internet is an open network, distributed, not contained, not owned by anyone.

I don't know if any Chinese students or Alaskan citizens profited in a commercial sense from their posting or "publishing" on the Internet— for, after all, what is publishing but writing for public consumption, regardless of the means of distribution or, in the case of Internet publishing, access. But they profited in other, perhaps more valuable ways by making their voices heard as witnesses to events of their time. Clearly, in this case, the new and networked machine did not function simply as an output facilitator, a means of replication for familiar words on a paper page. It functioned as a kind of worldwide broadcasting medium.

Call it an epiphany, thanks to insight from the above incident, or call it simply local economic necessity; our business shifted in the direction of electronic publishing, and away from paper-based publishing. Another shift in the tide. The first major step in the new direction, which involved creating work rather than producing it for publishers, was *The Internet Companion: A Beginner's Guide to Global Networking* by Tracy LaQuey, which was the first popular trade book about the Internet back in 1992. This book, produced with lightning rapidity and penned by a very gifted and knowledgeable author, seemed to grow beyond itself even before it was born and soon became a bestseller. At a time when there was precious little current copyright information on the Internet, and acceptable-use policies stood in the way of for-profit publishing on the Net, we couldn't just put a book up there with a price tag on it. It was a brave act for Tracy LaQuey to take the innovative leap, to take the words we both wanted people to pay for in the bookstores and give them away, in ASCII, on the Internet. That was the beginning of the Online BookStore (OBS) in 1992. Many thousands came and grabbed those files; many wrote in asking for more. None of the users paid a dime.

However, a conundrum is a paradox of sorts, and counterintuitive as it may seem, giving the ASCII files away by anonymous FTP spurred the print sales of the book. Who wants to read hundreds of pages in ASCII, anyway? Even our publisher was supportive of our effort and happy with the resulting sales figures. They are not alone. Prentice-Hall publishes Brendan Kehoe's *Zen and the Art of the Internet*, which is available for free on the Net. His book continues to sell very well. The same applies to the MIT Press's *Hacker's Dictionary*, which is available for free on the Net and sells briskly in paper as well. This leads to conundrum number one: that giving something valuable away for free can make money. It points to a richness not found in the tangible world quite so readily: the more I give you the more I have. Some call this a new kind of marketing, and this was a pleasing lesson to learn. But was this experience really on-line publishing, or was it the success of an early hybrid of on-line/paper publication?

The popularity of the on-line *Internet Companion* ASCII files drew my attention further away from paper, and I was seduced by the prospect of the then ten million people on the Internet—ten million literate people with disposable incomes—attached to the Net. Why not acquire lots of Internet rights to lots of books and put them on-line at the Online BookStore? Surely some percentage of those people would buy files of a popular author's books for a reasonable price. So, to test the concept that people would pay for books on-line, we approached one of the best-selling authors on the planet, Stephen King, and acquired first serial rights to a story from his new book, *Nightmares and Dreamscapes*. The numbers were enticing: if only 1 percent of the ten million people paid $5 for Stephen King's story, available only at the OBS and only on the Internet, then that's half a million dollars!

We tried to make it as widely appealing and usable as possible: we formatted it as a Voyager Expanded Book, in plain ASCII for those with only e-mail access, in Adobe Acrobat, in HTML format for Mosaic affi-cionados. We acquired the German rights, did a dual-language edition, and released it in time for the 1993 Frankfurt Book Fair, the largest book fair in the world. The result: they all came—the radio, the TV, the print media, creating lots of smoke and a nice firm footprint in the sand of Internet history. But sales? The half a million dollars in per-copy sales? The companies who participated in bringing this story into its Internet incarnation—the Internet Company, Texas Internet Consulting, Viking Penguin, Hodder Stoughton, EUnet Germany, Hoffman und Campe, Aldea Communications, Bunyip, and the Online BookStore—didn't pull in enough in per-copy sales to pay the phone bills for setting up the deal. A vast amount of smoke, a tremendous marketing boost for the printed book, again, lots of noise—and by extension, lots of profit for the pub-lisher and for the author—but handfulls of per-copy sales. The per-copy sales model for a contained publication, a publication which is complete in and of itself and is not linked to anything else of significance on the distributed network, does not seem to work. The OBS is not the only on-line publishing site which has shown these results.

However, where per-copy faltered, site licensing proved a far better option, which resulted in some commercial satisfaction on all sides. We have sold site licenses to networks and organizations with good results. Site licensing offers exclusivity to the organizations and networks which optioned the work, while offering the author the reassurance of having a defined set of users and a certain hedge of protection against rampant copying and posting for a profit of his work. One key element in site licensing seems to be timeliness; one publishes first on-line, before the information or ideas grow old and gather moss. Perhaps this site-license model proves more lucrative than the per-copy sales model because it enables the licensor to give the information away for free (after paying for it), while achieving a defined benefit, a market advantage over its competitors, by giving away scarce information on an exclusive or semi-exclusive basis.

This same combination of for-free/for pay can be seen in the sponsorship model, the third commercial model after the per-copy and the site license, where, in the same way that Mobil Oil brings you Masterpiece Theatre, a company might sponsor a particular publication distributed for free on the Net. The familiar economy of having the book buyer, the purchaser of information, pay for the information, is reversed in sponsored publishing. The sponsor wins by having his name, his product, associated with the freely distributed text. A discreet screen of product information, a company logo attached to a file is all it takes. The money then flows thus: the sponsor pays a certain amount, probably pennies, each time someone picks up a file by anonymous FTP. The taker pays nothing at all. What is being sold here is not the information, but the "attention" of the reader; the information or the ideas function as a conduit for ... marketing, again. Sponsorship is an easy and risk-free model, for the sponsor. What is at risk, of course, is the objective sponsorship of truth. Which company might have sponsored the students in Tianaman Square, for example?

We see this sponsorship model in frequent practice around the Net today, vast electronic for-free Internet sandboxes such as SUNsite, funded by Sun Microsystems and Cisco Systems and others. The sponsors gain by providing their equipment to people making creative use of it, so others will come and see what they are doing, and ... buy the sponsors equipment or products. So, as the freely available ASCII files for the *Internet Companion* fueled the sales of the printed book; so too the freely available playground sandbox at SUNsite spurs the sales of the sponsors' wares. It is kinetic advertising at its best, and it capitalizes on the fundamental shift in economics which fuels the new machine, the shift from the economy of scarcity, of buying and selling things, ideas incarnated as physical things, to the economics of abundance, where what is for sale isn't a thing at all, but the minds, the attention, of those paying attention to the ideas and information. Such an apparently "free" on-line environment makes for a welcome change, away from our common human penchant for owning and hoarding things with price tags on them. In the economy of abundance, the status of *having* shifts to the status of *having access*.

The notion of having access points to a fourth possible business model of publishing on the Net: subscription-based publishing. In the globally distributed multimedia hypertext environment—that's a mouthful, but how else do you say it?—an environment where the traffic increases in the hundreds of thousands of percent annually and nothing is but what it not, a subscription seems like another logical approach. Think of the digital stream analogy—does one want to buy a piece of the stream in a bottle, or does one want to subscribe to the stream and with that monthly subscription fee get all the fish, the pollywogs, the flowing water in which to bathe—as well as the flotsam and the jetsam from the guys upstream.

But even the subscription model comes up wanting in the Mosaic environment. Mosaic is, at this point, a free multimedia "browser" on the World Wide Web of interconnected computers. Widely hailed as the "killer app" for on-line publishing, Mosaic enables the users to navigate around the computers of the world, accessing, picking up, customizing anything that can be digitized—for free. But even were there tollgates firmly in place on every server in the world, still, I think the traditional subscription model would at least need adaptation from what we think of today when we think of a subscription to, say, cable TV or *The New Yorker*; because Mosaic epitomizes the three defining aspects of the on-line publishing environment which are not found together in other broadcast and print media: its distributed, interactive, and recorded nature.

A year ago, in the pre-Mosaic boom days, it seemed to the point to say that "Content is King," and to think that successful on-line publishing meant offering easy and commercially viable access to content. It only takes a short journey with Mosaic, which has a learning curve of under half an hour for the beginning user, to realize that content is everywhere, and more is available every day. Content alone fast becomes irrelevant in the absence of context. What good are a hundred novels on-line, if the Net, the means of access, is not exploited to create a context, a way of thinking about and reading these novels? Might we not learn from the above for-free experiences, and consider a publishing model where readers are allowed free access to those novels, in return for the readers allowing a publisher to record and study their thought paths, the links they make while reading, thinking, and studying on-line? One may not want to pay $5 for an on-line "contained" or finite, static, linear text of James Michener's *Chesapeake*, but one might pay considerably more if one could follow the electronically generated thought path resulting from a course taught by the author himself about factual fiction, a course where one could navigate the links students make in their critical thinking about the novel, navigate and link to related documents, graphics, videos, sounds, experiences, and the author himself—all in real time. How does one charge for such a contextual experience? What is in fact being published, and what is for sale? In the kinetic publishing environment, apparently, the static text, the words, become subsidiary to their context as determined by each individual user.

• • •

On-line publishing is commercially successful today in the marketing sense, successful for those of us who still try to own and hoard, owning things as a bastion against mortality perhaps—such marketeers are successfully protecting their back-end business by doling out carefully controlled portions in obvious marketing efforts: a chapter here, a blurb there—and then selling the printed book or the manufactured product. Publishing on the individual level, however, might be more spontaneous, more complete, a freer marketplace of ideas that will enable the testing of the concept that time and attention can indeed prove valuable currency—currency which may not be defined in dollars—on-line. Such an individual as a publisher might make a living on the Net, make his own home page, turn his "E" drive into a fast-food joint or a used-book shop along the Infobahn, into a public sandbox for people to link to and peruse, while maintaining a private segment to which real-time access is licensed or sold, like having "This Space For Rent" (point to head).

Charging for thought, kinetic, real-time thought, combined with recorded thought, what we used to call publications, might make money on the Internet. Again, as with the first *Internet Companion* example, this model is a hybrid, between what is living, real-time thought, and what is dead, that which is already recorded. We think by association, and associations are links. By thinking about something or someone we give it value. The World Wide Web of computers, where traffic in 1993 increased 341,000 percent, is a hypertext environment allowing for the globalization of associative thought, the accessing and weaving together of chunks of information into customized sets. Anything that can be digitized can be linked to: texts, graphics, videos, sounds, experiences such as on-line museum exhibits and libraries. And people as well can be linked to texts in real time via e-mail. What is for sale in this hyperlife environment is the naming and pointing to resources, either live or dead, kinetic or static. If I were a net architect tasked with building an Ethernet and my boss wanted it done by tomorrow morning, I would pay dearly for the name of and on-line access to Bud Spurgeon, an Ethernet expert here at United Technologies, and pointers to his on-line documents. I would pay most of all for access to him in real time to help me solve my problem. This problem might be worth a thousand dollars tonight, and nothing tomorrow if I lose my job because I couldn't get the network up and running. If the on-line publisher offered this access to Bud—access which travels right up the chain of the hierarchy of intimacy from email to phone and even face-to-face—that publisher would be capitalizing on the multimedia capabilities of the webbed environment.

We are talking about buying and selling people in real time. This gets me back to the topic at hand: slavery. But no longer are we simply talking about typesetting a janitor's manual in Haiti, of tying people to keyboards so they can make the machines spit out pages in a highly regulated format. We are talking about selling the digitized mind of a human being who chooses to sell access to his own real-time interactive original thought.

. . .

If we look around us now, we can see lots of other people making money from the Internet. People selling hardware, connectivity, and software; they are making money. They are the means-makers. But once acceptable means are in place for, say, W3, what then? Will we see trading in the form of link brokers and URL futures? Will humans be bought and sold for their minds rather than for their ability to wash dishes or pick cotton? The Internet today is a multimedia environment, and it might be useful to consider the record industry for a final thought about where all this is going, for the conundrum before us involves assigning value to both recorded and live information. Recorded thought, ideas, or music, is in a sense dead. It is live when it is reciprocal, as a concert is reciprocal, or as, in a way, karioke is reciprocal. As soon as the rock band The Doors recorded *Break on Through*, it became posterity, static, a commodity to be bought and sold, a commodity which increased in value after Jim Morrison himself was dead at a young age. In the New Machine, the recording of *Break on Through to the Other Side* might be available for free, while access to Morrison would cost dearly, and access to karioke interaction with the Doors would cost as well. These are the living, interactive links I am referring to, the links that bind us to our new on-line environment and enrich us, rather than the links that fetter us in servitude to the Great Records machine we are in the process of creating.

Reflections

Laura Fillmore's article is about a marketplace that does not work yet. Unlike Browning, she is not confused about whether there should be a charge for intellectual property on the network. Her problem is to find a way to make it profitable! In terms of the archetypes for action in the world, there is little question where Fillmore fits. She is a consummate hunter-trickster: resourceful, enterprising, and scrambling to make a living. Her suggestions in this article show the amazing depth of her search for viable ways to do business on the network.

Most fascinating, however, are her accounts of the value of the most transitory information on the network. In traditional publishing, there is a hierarchy of permanence for works published in a hierarchy of materials: hardbound books, paperback books, magazines, newspapers, and fliers. The more durable the package, presumably, the longer-lived the information. On the Net, however, when the value of information is very time-sensitive the risks to the digital publisher of having information pirated and resold are minimized. In the extreme case, the information might be a packaged, real-time experience, either in personal consulting or in social group participation.

One of Fillmore's compelling conjectures is that readers might not "pay $5 for an on-line "contained" or finite, static, linear text of James Michener's Chesapeake, *but might be willing to pay even more to "follow the electronically generated thought path resulting from a course taught by the author himself about factual fiction, a course where one could navigate the links students make in their critical thinking about the novel, navigate and link to related documents, graphics, videos, sounds, experiences, and the author himself—all in real time."*

The transition leaps across our classifying metaphors. What amounts to an on-line writer's workshop goes beyond the digital library metaphor, through the electronic marketplace and into the digital worlds metaphor we discuss in the last section of this book. The changes at hand challenge us to understand the possibilities. Fillmore, the hunter-trickster, hunts cleverly for business possibilities, using multiple metaphors to make sense of the search.

Given Fillmore's conundrums about fees, it is ironic that net mavens can find the full text of her speech on the Internet (for free) at

http://cism.bus.utexas.edu/ravi/laura_talk.ht

The Online BookStore can be found at

http://marketplace.com/obs/obshome.html

Letting Loose the Light: Igniting Commerce in Electronic Publication

Mark Stefik

Connections

In "The Digital Library Project: The World of Knowbots" in Part 1, Robert Kahn and Vinton Cerf ask, "If a thousand books are combined on a single CD-ROM and the acquirer of the CD-ROM only intends to read one of them, what sort of royalty arrangement is appropriate to compensate the copyright owners? How would compensation be extended for cases in which electronic copies are provided to users?" Their questions show how, in 1988, issues about copyright protection and payment for using information arose in the context of early CD-ROM distribution.

By 1994 copyright issues not only had not been settled, they were coming to a boil. Laura Fillmore's effort to build a successful publishing business on the Internet reveals the limitations of what was practical in May of 1994. Although digital works were being sold on the Internet, provisions for commerce were primitive. Furthermore, the ease of copying digital works had led many people to believe that digital information should be free. Fast access to the network had made trading programs or other data as easy as mixing songs on audio tape. In short, it had become much simpler for network users to infringe copyright than to uphold it.

This is the context for the oft-quoted statement by John Perry Barlow of the Electronic Freedom Foundation, "Copyright is dead." Advocates of free information argue that because you don't lose the original when you make a copy of a digital work, there should be no charge for copying information. The conventional wisdom among publishers in late-1994, when this article was written, was that digital containers for software were inherently leaky vessels and that no viable solution would ever be found. The article suggests, however, a way to sustain commerce for those who want to sell information on the network.

Throughout the time I've been groping around cyberspace, an immense, unsolved conundrum has remained at the root of nearly every legal, ethical, governmental, and social vexation to be found in the Virtual World. I refer to the problem of digitized property. The enigma is this: If our property can be infinitely reproduced and instantaneously distributed all over the planet without cost, without our knowledge, without its even leaving our possession, how can we protect it? How are we going to get paid for the work we do with our minds? And, if we can't get paid, what will assure the continued creation and distribution of such work?

John Perry Barlow, "The Economy of Ideas"

No problemo.

T-101 (Arnold Schwarzenegger) in *Terminator 2*

It all depends on whether you really understand the idea of trusted systems. If you don't understand them, then this whole approach to commerce and digital publishing is utterly unthinkable. If you do understand them, then it all follows easily.

Ralph Merkle

Across many cultures, knowledge and inner knowing are described as light. *Letting loose the light* refers to spreading knowledge in the world, typically in written form. Consistent with this metaphor, the period in the eighteenth century characterized by a burst of writings in philosophy and science is called the *Enlightenment*. In the present century the metaphor of knowledge as light is both poetic and physically realized. Books, pictures, movies, musical performances, and other works can be conveniently represented digitally. With fiber optics, digital works are actually transmitted by the shining and pulsing of light.

The digital representation of works and their nearly instantaneous transmission has profound consequences for commercial publishing. Three of the fundamental economic factors affecting the publishing industry—printing costs, inventory costs, and transportation costs—can be drastically reduced. Digital works can be copied at minuscule costs, stored in almost no space, and transported instantly anywhere in the world.

This portability opens up visions of a greater information age. For libraries, universal access to the world's written knowledge is a centuries-old vision. Today many libraries have electronic catalogs accessible to anyone with a computer. Articles can be delivered to anyone with a fax machine. In the technophile's idealized vision, books and magazines need never be printed on paper at all; any digital work could be made available to anyone, anytime, anywhere in the world.

However, the dream of universal digital access to high-quality works dangles just beyond reach. Such works are not usually available, because of publishers' concerns that uncompensated copying will infringe and erode their ability to make a living. History suggests that this problem will not go away. Publishing thrives only when it is profitable, and profitability depends on limiting uncompensated copying.

The conventional wisdom—based on the way computers are used for word processing, electronic mail, and computer networking—is that copying digital works is easy and, therefore, inevitable. There appears to be a clear, inherent conflict between representing works digitally and honoring the commercial and intellectual property interests of creators and publishers. Fortunately, computers need not be blind instruments of copyright infringement. Properly designed digital systems can be more powerful and flexible instruments of trade in publications than any other medium. The seeming conflict between digital publishing and commerce is merely a consequence of the way computer systems have been designed to date.

The technological means for commerce in digital works are now at hand. New and unconventional when compared with today's uses of computers, these means will enable us to buy, sell, and lend digital works much as we now buy, sell, and lend printed books and other publications. They will change the way digital works are purchased and delivered and will give consumers access to all sorts of works at any time of the day—though not necessarily for free. Consumers will be able to sample works, borrow them, rent them for nominal fees, and make copies for friends. Creative people will be able to circulate their works to networks of friends while earning a reliable living from people who make copies of them. This technological system will affect everything from digital books to digital television, from digital music to digital video games. It will radically change our concepts of digital libraries, digital bookstores, digital music stores, digital newspapers, and digital television stations. Moreover, any competent technological company will be able to implement the required systems.

Here is a road map to this new land. First, we discuss the history of copyright law and the reasons for the widespread, but incorrect, belief that works represented digitally will be copied without permission. We then describe the technological innovations that can enable and support commerce in digital publishing. Finally, we introduce the institutional and business challenges that lie ahead. What we require to overcome them is the wit, will, and means to create institutions that provide the necessary security, convenience, vision, and longevity.

The Origin and Rationale of Copyright

It is harder to be honest than to cheat when copying digital works on general-purpose computers. The license printed on the package of most purchased computer software authorizes a buyer to load the software into one computer and use it there. Getting another legal copy for a friend involves driving to the computer store and buying it. It is much easier, faster, and cheaper to simply load the same software into another computer. Such copying is so private and easy to do that most people do it without thinking, and without guilt.

Unauthorized copying on computers is not, of course, limited to purchased software. With a few keystrokes, it is often possible to copy a paragraph, an article, a book, or a life's work without compensating its creators or publishers. Nor are unauthorized copying and use new phenomena. Anyone who ignores the FBI warning message on video tapes to make copies for friends infringes a copyright, as do people who copy compact discs onto cassettes. As a practical matter, it has not been feasible to enforce the copyright law in these cases. There are simply too many people with recording devices to make rigorous enforcement practical or cost-effective.

It is widely believed that there is no viable technical solution to this problem for digital information. John Perry Barlow, a prominent spokesperson in the computer industry, says that the idea of patents and copyrights needs to be rethought in the digital age. Information, he argues, cannot be contained or owned. It wants to be free. Cyberspace is the new frontier, and its leaders and pioneers are today's radical thinkers about freedom of information. Barlow suggests, in fact, that we abandon all notions of intellectual property and market regulation. This solution was tried at least once, and it didn't work. Apparently, for high-quality works to spread in the world people need to be able to make a living from creating and distributing them.

Barlow's arguments are reminiscent of the intense debates about intellectual property that took place in France during the French Revolution. Like Barlow, revolutionaries argued that ideas cannot be owned and should not be regulated. During the revolution, many writers and underground publishers emerged as civic heroes of public enlightenment by arguing against tyranny and for freedom of the press. The revolution of the mind, they said, required the dismantling of the laws and institutions governing authorship, printing, publishing, and bookselling. Absolutely free communication was one of the most precious rights of man. All citizens should be able to speak, to write, and crucially, to print freely. According to this philosophical ideal, people had a will to know and should be allowed to read and learn from anything they liked. The wide availability of books and the right to publish were seen as keys to this spread of knowledge.

In 1789, the revolutionary government wholly deregulated the press, believing that the works of the great writers of the Enlightenment would thus be made universally and cheaply available. The writers and publishers certainly never expected what actually happened. Instead of works of enlightenment, the presses turned out mostly seditious pamphlets and pornography. Printers also competed with each other to bring out cheap editions of books others had spent money developing. So little money could be made producing the good books that quality declined; most editions were abridged and contained many errors. Publisher after publisher went into bankruptcy and then out of business. The disastrous nature of an unregulated press, largely unanticipated in the heat of the revolution, became blatantly obvious as the publishing industry fell into shambles. The same leaders who had clamored for the freeing of the presses came belatedly to understand the folly of their action. In the chaos of the unregulated press, some prominent and popular writers even stopped publishing; because they could not control the printing of their works, they could not make a living by writing.

In 1793 legislation to restore order to publishing was passed. It recognized the rights of authors and grounded the publishing industry in the principles of the marketplace, establishing the author as creator, the book as property, and the reader as an elective consumer. This law reflected a fundamental shift in the Enlightenment perspective, which now saw that the widespread creation and publication of creative works was better served when the authors could own the products of their minds. This history of the treatment of intellectual property in France is discussed by Carla Hesse in her book *Publishing and Cultural Politics in Revolutionary Paris, 1789–1810.*

Today, most people see the infringement of copyright on digital systems as unavoidable. In the remainder of this section, we describe the assumptions about computer design behind this belief and argue that we need to go beyond conventional ways of thinking to solve the problem.

Three main factors currently inhibit the development of digital publishing: (1) the absence of high-contrast, low-power, cheap flat-panel displays; (2) lack of an inexpensive and reliable way of handling money digitally; and (3) the need for a widely accepted means of accounting for the use and copying of digital works. Improvements in technology will almost certainly solve the display problem in the next five to ten years. Most people see such displays as crucial to making electronic books and newspapers portable. They matter less, however, in applications for which desktop displays are satisfactory or where displays are not necessary—such as in transmitting musical works. The second factor—methods of handling money digitally, in the form of checks, credit cards, or anonymous cash—has recently become the subject of much field experimentation. Our focus is on the third problem, techniques for commerce in what we call *digital property* rights or *usage rights*, a generalization of the idea of copyright that delineates several kinds of rights besides copying.

Some publishers see illicit copying as too big a business risk and do not publish in digital form at all. Digital newspapers often leave out important and high-value content such as the pictures or graphics, and consumers of these lower-quality papers are unwilling to pay much for them. The perception of low quality leads to a chicken-and-egg problem in which the publishers make little money and consumers have few choices. Ironically, publishers of works that need periodic upgrading, such as computer software, have found that some leakage increases their customer base, even though it is often reported that there are more unauthorized copies of a program in use than authorized ones. Software publishers have decided that the revenue losses of illegal copying are affordable, although they lead to unfair billing. Software publishers charge all users the same price, regardless of the use to which they put the program, arguably overbilling people who use the work infrequently.

As computers and computer networks have proliferated, the need for a better approach to protecting digital works has become more widely appreciated. Moreover, as new kinds of works—such as music, video, and multimedia works that mix these forms—are now available digitally, people from different industries are searching for solutions. Given this wide acknowledgment of the need, why have solutions seemed so elusive? Apparently, we are stuck in a rut, assuming that things must be done the way they have always been done with electronic mail, word processing, and other current applications.

Conventionally, we use general-purpose computers with general-purpose operating systems and general-purpose programs. The computer industry, grounded on the premise that computers can do anything that can be programmed in software, produces a wide range of programs—word processors, spreadsheets, databases, calendars, graphics programs, and computer games. Manufacturers accept no liability when someone uses a computer to copy a copyrighted file. After all, one company builds the computer, another writes the software that does the copying, and both hardware and software are intended for general purposes—that is, any purpose the user wants to put them to. The manufacturer wants no responsibility for someone who uses the computer in a way that just happens to infringe a copyright, nor does the software publisher. The perpetrator is the consumer, who finds it easier to make an unauthorized copy than to be strictly honest.

Stuck within this framework the community of computer users protests against any attempt to regulate the copying of digital property. If we continue to accept this framework, with all of its assumptions, no party will be motivated or empowered to break the cycle and no effective way to protect digital property will be developed. At present, without enforceable property rights, the writers of words, interactive games, and songs often are not compensated for their work. And without their works the world is a darker, poorer place. Honoring their creative work in the digital systems of tomorrow requires us to challenge the design assumptions of the systems we use today.

A New Design for Digital Publishing

The technical core of the approach we propose is based on two ideas: (1) that digital works can be bought and sold among trusted systems, and (2) that works have attached usage rights that specify what can be done with them and what it costs to exercise those rights.

Trusted Systems

The term *trusted system* refers to computers that can be relied on to do certain things. For example, suppose that a creator or publisher forbids all copying of a particular digital work. A trusted system in this context would reliably and infallibly carry out that stipulation; no amount of shouting or coaxing would coerce it to copy the work. The trusted system might be very polite, but ultimately it would always refuse to make an unauthorized copy. Similarly, suppose that a trusted system *could* copy a work but only if it reliably records a set fee to be paid when it has done so. A trusted system would always record the fee whenever the work was copied. If the copying process is interrupted part way through, the trusted system would follow a standard policy; for example, it might delete the partial copy, record no fee, and note that a copying attempt was begun but not completed. Again, no amount of coaxing would change its behavior. It could always be counted on to follow the rules of the trust.

A common but false analogy claiming to show why digital works cannot be protected in computers is that of genies and bottles. In this analogy, a valued digital work corresponds to a genie and the bottle is a place to store it When a digital work is sent to a computer, for example, it may be sent in coded form, so that even if the transmission is intercepted it is useless to a wiretapper. Once people have a legal copy of a digital work, however, they can make more copies of it. Since they have a key, they can just decode the work and make copies of it. Alternatively, they can copy the coded version and give away copies of the key. Once the content genie is out of the bottle, according to this scenario, you can't put it back in and unauthorized digital copies are sure to circulate. This is the problem trusted systems can fix.

Trusted systems speak a communications protocol with other trusted systems and will not transmit information to any system not recognized as another trusted system. This strategy ensures that copies of digital works are either inside trusted systems or they are encrypted. When they are inside trusted systems, usage is controlled. When they are outside trusted systems, usage is practically impossible without breaking the code. The important issue, however, is not just protection and containment. The greater good is not served by simply limiting the flow of information. It is served by supporting and encouraging a lively trade in information. *Rather than just confining genies to specific bottles, we want to encourage them to travel between bottles under rules of commerce.*

A very concrete question about such a system is "Why couldn't I just copy a file onto a diskette and give that away?" Unless there is permission to do so, a trusted system would never copy a work to a diskette or anywhere else. Even if permission to copy a work is given, a trusted system would not make a copy on a diskette, because a diskette is not a trusted system. Nor are magnetic tapes, compact discs, or, even, the disk drives of trusted systems. Trusted systems contain computers, have internal protected storage, and communicate by protocol. From a user's point of view, the trusted system is the storage device. Trusted systems only make copies of a digital work on themselves or on other trusted systems. Putting an unencrypted copy on a diskette is letting the genie out of the bottle onto an unprotected medium that can be accessed by a general-purpose computer that does not honor usage rights.

There is an important issue about the perception of trusted systems. One way of looking at them is to say that trusted systems presume that the consumer is dishonest. This perception is unfortunate, and perhaps incorrect, but nonetheless real. Unless trusted systems offer consumers real advantages they will probably view them as nuisances that complicate our lives. A more favorable way to look at trusted systems is to compare them to vending machines. They make it possible to order digital works any time of the day and get immediate delivery. Faster than a telephone-order pizza, a digital work can be delivered immediately over the same telephone line it was ordered over.

In summary, the first key to commerce in digital works is to use trusted systems. We have spoken of these systems as computers, but they are not limited to devices like personal computers and need not seem like computers at all. They could be personal entertainment devices for playing music, video game devices, laptop reading devices, personal computers, devices for playing digital movies at home, credit-card-sized devices that fit in your pocket, or whatever. In the following discussion we refer to these trusted systems as *repositories*, an architectural plan that can have different embodiments. Repositories communicate digitally with other repositories and not with anything else. In contrast to such current passive media as compact discs, repositories have no externally defined limits on storage capacity; so successive generations of repositories could increase in capacity while remaining completely compatible with earlier systems. Digital works would be communicated between repositories using secure coded protocols. Repositories would read the rules that apply to a given digital work and follow them. This brings us to the next issue: How do repositories know what the rules are?

Attached Usage Rights
We start with an analogy. When we go to a store to buy a shirt, there are various tags attached to it. One kind of tag is a price tag. If we want to buy the shirt, we must pay the amount on the tag. Another tag gives cleaning instructions: for example, wash by hand in cold water or dry clean only. Still another tag might say something about the style of the shirt or the history of the shirt company.

This is roughly the idea of *usage rights* on digital works. Digital works would come with tags on them. The tags—put there by the creators, publishers, and distributors—would describe the usage rights for the digital work: what can be done with it and what it costs.

There are some important differences from the shirt's tags. The first is that the tags are digital and intended to be read and used by the repository itself, although consumers can also read the tags through the repository's user interface. They are written in a machine-readable language and give the repository the rules for using the work; they are an electronic contract enforced by the repository. Another difference is that the tags are not removable. Finally, there can be tags attached to different parts of a work. For a shirt, it is as if there were tags on the pockets, tags on the buttons, tags on the collar, tags on the sleeves, and so on. Each tag would grant rights to that part, and different rights could pertain to different parts of a work. For example, a digital newspaper might have certain rights on local stories, others on photographs or wireline stories or advertisements, and so on.

Suppose that the digital work is a piece of music. A statement describing a right might say the following:

This digital work can be played on a player of type Musica-13B. This right is valid from February 14, 1995 to February 14, 1996. The repository must have a security level of three. No other authorizations are needed. The fee for exercising this right is one cent per minute with a minimum of five cents in the first hour. Usage fees are paid to account 1997-200-567131.

Of course, such an internal statement would not be in English, although it should be in a well-defined computer language. Here is an example of a machine-readable statement in a usage rights language:

Right Code: Play Player: Musica-13B

Copy Count: 1

Time-Spec: From 95/02/14 Until: 96/02/14

Access-Spec: Security-Level: 3

Fee-Spec: Fee: Metered $0.01 per 0:1:0
               Min: $0.05 per 0/1/0

Account: 1997-200-567131

Computer languages are more precise than natural languages and have formal grammars and semantics that define how to interpret each phrase in the language. Computer languages are not at all poetic, but they are much less ambiguous, if less expressive than natural languages. Because the sentences of a digital property language are parts of potential contracts between the creators of digital works and consumers, clarity and simplicity are exactly what we want. Interpreting a usage rights language is quite simple. In level of difficulty, it is more like reading bar codes from packages at the supermarket checkout than it is like reading and understanding an English sentence in a story.

A digital property language needs to define several different kinds of rights, mainly those concerned with how the work can be transported, how it can be rendered, and whether it can be used in derivative works. Other, special rights relate to making and restoring backup copies to protect against hardware failure. The easiest way to understand usage rights is to consider some examples.

Transferring Digital Works   When we copy files for friends on a general-purpose computer, we increase the number of copies of a digital work, fail to compensate the work's creator, and infringe the copyright. A repository, in contrast, never infringes copyright.

Our first scenario illustrates how copy and transfer rights would work in a repository system. Suppose that Morgan buys a copy of a digital book, perhaps at the book kiosk at the supermarket. To do so, he exercises a right to copy the book and pays a fee; copying the book records a transaction between the seller's repository and (say) a card-sized repository that Morgan carries with him. Alternatively, he could buy a copy of the digital book from home by telephone. In either case, the digital book is delivered electronically by a communications protocol between the vendor's repository and Morgan's repository. At the end of the transaction, Morgan has spent some money, has a copy of the digital book in his repository, and can now read it on a reader. The book arrives with all its usage rights intact.

Now suppose that, when Morgan finishes reading the book, his friend Andy asks to borrow it. They plug their repositories together, and Morgan exercises a *transfer right* to move the digital book to Andy's repository. With paper books, once we have bought a book we can give it away or dispose of it in any way we please, and the same right could apply to Morgan's digital book. At the end of the transfer transaction, the digital book resides on Andys repository and not on Morgan's, and no money has been exchanged. Andy can now read the book, but Morgan cannot. The crucial point is that the transfer transaction preserves the number of copies of the digital book.

We now consider a scenario involving a loan right. Again Morgan has a digital book that his friend Ryan wants to borrow for a week. They plug their repositories together and Morgan exercises a *loan right*. Again, while the digital book is loaned out, Morgan cannot use it. Suppose, however, that Ryan goes off on vacation and, while he is playing volleyball on a beach thousands of miles away, the week's loan period runs out. He has completely forgotten the book. Because both repositories have clocks in them, Ryan's repository deactivates its copy when the week is up. Meanwhile, Morgan's repository also notices that the loan time is up and marks its temporarily deactivated copy as usable again. Without any action by either person, or even any communication between their repositories, the digital book has been returned automatically. If Ryan still wants to access it later, he could pay a nominal fee to rent the work or to make his own copy. The point of both scenarios is that the repositories follow rules, which in this case mimic and improve on the rules of loaning for paper books. The ability to return loaned materials automatically would probably be widely used in digital libraries.

Rendering Digital Works   To read a digital book you have to be able to see it; to listen to digital music you have to be able to hear it; to enjoy a digital video game, you have to be able to see and hear it. We use the term *render* to mean the processing of a digital work so that it can be experienced. Like copying, transferring. and loaning, rendering is controlled by usage rights.

We distinguish two forms of rendering: playing and printing. When we play a digital work we send it to another person through some kind of transducer so that he or she can experience it. The term play, usually employed in phrases like *playing music* or *playing a movie*, is also used to denote displaying part of a book, running a computer program, or running an interactive video game. The term *print* in the digital context means to make a copy of the work on media outside usage rights control, either on paper or by writing a file to an external storage device.

The concept of usage rights allows great flexibility in marketing digital works. Today, when you buy a compact disc at the music store, you pay for the copy and play it for free. The same is true for a book. You buy the book and read it as often as you want; generally, you aren't supposed to make copies of it, but you can give it away. By contrast, keeping digital works in repositories would provide more flexibility.

Suppose for example that Andrea's mother is at the music store but does not know exactly what music her teenage daughter wants to buy. She transfers a selection of music to her own repository, choosing collections by half a dozen bands that she knows Andrea likes. At this point she does not need to pay anything for the right to make the copies. When she gets home, she transfers the music to Andrea's repository for her to checks out at her leisure. Like all repositories, Andrea's home repository has a built-in credit server that transfers funds electronically. She can listen to short demonstration samples for free or listen to pieces she selects for twenty-five cents an hour; or she can pay for five years of unlimited playing for $10. Thus, Andrea exercises a pay-for-play right rather than a pay-for-copying right. If pay for play has an infinite term, there are no fees for playing the music as often as she likes. The terms and alternatives for usage rights and usage fees would be set by the music's creators and distributors. What Andrea gains by this arrangement is flexibility and the convenience of trying out different digital works. She might even be able to use technology similar to a cellular telephone to order music and download it from the music store to her car repository.

For books, however, the idea of pay for play may not seem very useful if the typical book we have in mind is the paperback novel. As it is already cheap, it does not seem worthwhile to charge for the time needed to read it. Besides, why should slow readers pay more than fast readers? On the other hand, consider large, expensive reference works like encyclopedias. People do not casually pay out hundreds of dollars for these works; nor do they usually read them from beginning to end. Paying a small fee for each hour of actual use may make it feasible to bring high quality digital encyclopedias into many households that could not otherwise afford them. As in the music example, purchasers could decide whether to pay by the hour or for large or infinite blocks of usage time.

As yet another example, consider the digital newspaper, which could, in principle, be delivered in several ways: bought at the corner newsstand, downloaded over the telephone, or broadcast by a digital radio station. It could be available though pay-for-play usage rights or by monthly subscription. Suppose, however, that a particular newspaper is reluctant to allow its customers to make paper copies of the newspaper, even for a fee, for fear that some enterprising person will print up enough copies for the entire neighborhood and cut into circulation. To prevent this occurrence, usage rights could be designated so that people trying to print the newspaper would discover they have no printing rights.

Suppose, again, that a month later customers find that they can print the newspaper's old news without hindrance but not its new stories. In that case, the usage right for printing would be dated to prohibit printing until a month had passed since publication, perhaps because the publisher figures that printouts of old news are more like advertisements for the newspaper than threats to circulation. Variations in what the publishers might allow or encourage are virtually endless. The rights granted on stories or photos or whatever could even become a basis for competition among digital newspaper publishers.

Making Derivative Works Distributors add value to products by advertising and selecting works and presenting them to consumers, making a living by performing these functions and requiring compensation for them. Today bookstores and music stores operate on a per-copy basis, charging for "hard copies" of books or compact discs. If pay for play became popular for digital works, how would distributors make money? What is needed, of course, is a mechanism for paying distributors when a consumer chooses to pay for play. This mechanism, called a *shell*, would enable distributors to modify rights and add new usage fees.

We can understand shells as analogous to gift boxes of different sizes. A common and amusing trick is to put a present in a small box, wrap it, and put that box in a bigger box, wrapping that box and putting it in a bigger box, and so on, perhaps attaching a gift card to each package. In digital work, the boxes would correspond to digital containers (shells) and the gift tags would correspond to attached usage rights. Putting a digital work into an empty shell, or into a shell containing another digital work, is called *embedding,* and it is controlled by an *embed usage right.*

Consider the following case. Nick has written a novel and offers it in digital form. He determines what he wants to charge per copy and attaches usage rights to it, specifying the fee to be paid into his account every time a copy is made. His publisher agrees to publish the book and puts another shell around it directing that when the work is copied, an additional fee is to be paid to the publisher. The publisher may help the author improve the book in various ways and spend money advertising it. Finally, a bookstore puts an additional shell around the publisher's shell, directing that when the kiosk makes a copy of the book, a fee should be paid to the bookstore. Thus when a customer buys a copy of the work, he or she pays, automatically, a fee to the bookstore, to the publisher, and to Nick. This works because the accounting system follows the instructions embedded in every shell of the copied work.

Or consider Paige, a college professor at a business school that bases courses on case studies collected into a reader. Paige chooses the cases of interest for her course as digital works with attached rights. If an interesting case has an extraction right, she can remove a copy of it from its digital source; if it has qualified editing rights, she can make certain kinds of changes to it; if it has embed rights, Paige can add it to her own collection. At each stage, the continuing rights to the work are controlled by its creator's specifications. Paige can put all the works she has collected into a shell and add her own usage right specifications to the shell. When a student buys a copy of her course reader, fees are paid to the creators of each case study and to Paige herself.

It is interesting to compare this process of controlled reuse to the existing practice in which one author requests reprint permission for an article by another author. The process of granting and obtaining permissions is tedious and time consuming and is often assigned to editorial assistants by publishers who do not expect to earn much from reprint requests. This approach assumes that they are willing to agree to the most usual rights, fees, and conditions for reprinting a work. By lowering the perceived hassle and cost of reuse, usage rights may trigger a substantial increase in the commercial reuse of works.

Consumer-based Distribution   One of the most radical possibilities for distributing digital works is *consumer-based distribution*, sometimes called super distribution. With ordinary media, consumer copying and sale of works is considered a problem, because creators and publishers receive no compensation for such copying. In contrast, consider what would happen in our earlier scenario if Morgan, instead of giving or lending his digital book, makes a copy of it for his friend Andy. The repositories would record the transaction and bill Morgan or Andy for the new copy. Depending on how the shells have been set up, fees would be collected for the store where Morgan originally bought the work, for the distributor, for the publisher, and for the creator, even though none of them are present at the transaction. Every consumer would become a potential salesperson, a word-of-mouth sales channel.

This possible future is in radical contrast to the problem foreseen by Barlow in the quotation at the beginning of this piece. Digital property can be anywhere on the planet without the knowledge of its creators and still make money for them whenever it is used or copied by a repository.

Licenses and Tickets   In a trusted system, licenses and tickets would be special kinds of digital works that play direct roles in commerce. *Licenses* would be digital certificates that enable someone to exercise certain usage rights. Think of them as similar to driver's licenses or identification cards that authorize someone to drive a car or enter a restricted area. A digital license would let someone exercise certain rights, such as copying or printing a particular work. When a consumer asks to use a licensed work, an authorization server or "digital authority"—a program on a repository—would check his or her digital license. *Digital tickets*, a kind of coupon offered by publishers for prepaid uses or discounts, would enable a possessor to exercise a right exactly once. Think of digital tickets as comparable to movie or train tickets; once you have entered the theater or boarded the train, the ticket is punched and cannot be used again. A digital ticket is punched by a digital ticket agent that is a program on a repository.

When an author creates a work and specifies its usage rights, he or she can require buyers to have particular licenses or tickets to exercise certain rights. These digital licenses and tickets would be essentially impossible to forge; would let consumers exercise usage rights in living rooms, school dormitories, or anywhere else; and would assure authors that fees will be collected and that the tickets and licenses specified will be required.

Different areas of publishing have different crucial problems for which digital licenses and digital tickets could offer solutions. In some industries, there is an advantage in ensuring that only authorized distributors can sell digital works. The author of a computer game, for example, may want his or her game sold only through distributors licensed to advertise, promote, and demonstrate it. If a dealer without that license tries to copy and sell the game, the repository would refuse the transaction. By determining who gets distributor's licenses and arranging that licenses cannot be transferred between repositories without authorization, the author could maintain control over distribution. Such digital licenses could also restrict distribution rights to a certain time period.

In the music and video industries, companies try to limit the playing of their recordings to home use. While current technology provides no effective way to enforce this provision, trusted entertainment systems using licenses could distinguish between equipment for home use and equipment for theater or broadcast use. Equipment for playing digital recordings would come with different licenses and fee schedules for home and public use. Alternatively, radio transmitters and receivers might all be linked to repositories; a station might broadcast a work but require each listener to pay a nominal fee for receiving it. Trusted systems could provide a basis for many different kinds of relationships between creators, broadcasters, and the public than are feasible today.

In the book publishing industry, it is common to offer big discounts on books that remain unsold after a certain period of time. Imagine a usage right that allows a copy of a digital book to be made for nothing in exchange for a certain ticket. Later, a book club might offer these tickets for sale and let a holder get any three digital books in exchange for three tickets. The price of a digital book could thus be determined later by the price of the ticket, which could vary according to demand.

In the computer software industry, it is common to release new versions of software to fix bugs in earlier versions and to offer the upgraded software for free or for low prices to purchasers of the original version. The problem lies in making sure that the upgraded versions are not given to people who did not purchase the original software. Digital tickets would offer a solution by allowing vendors to bundle upgrade tickets with the original works. Consumers could use any copy of the upgrade versions of the software to make their own new copy by simply using their tickets; this approach lets consumers upgrade their software without going back to the dealer. Because digital tickets get punched when they are used, the approach would allow exactly one upgrade per original version.

Because metered and per-copy fee arrangements can make usage budgets unpredictable for organizations, they may prefer *site licenses*. Such licenses would grant members of an organization the right to use a digital work subject to restrictions. For example, a site license would generally preclude making copies for use by people not in the organization; or it might distinguish between different kinds of uses in different departments. It might also limit the number of people who can use a work at the same time, perhaps leaving its administration to someone in the organization. The supplier of the digital work would specify in the usage rights that the organization's site license be recorded on a repository before the work could be used. If different departments require different regulated uses, then each department would have its own specialized license. To monitor such global constraints as the number of copies of a work simultaneously in use, a digital license could instruct the repository's authorization server to communicate periodically with a site authorization server that registers and counts users.

Licenses and tickets could be established for diverse categories and purposes, including social purposes. For example, a charity or governmental organization could issue certificates to low-income people or inner-city youth. Socially conscious publishers could then offer discounts or limited free use of certain digital works to people holding such certificates. From a profit perspective, they may assume that offering the certificates will increase the potential base of customers by contributing to public literacy and that, in any case, these consumers would not buy the work. The same digital-license mechanism could provide special rights to certified librarians, researchers, and teachers; and certificates could be dispensed at libraries to allow readers to browse works for limited periods.

One area that has been much discussed recently is control of access to works on computer networks. In the present free-wheeling environment of computer networks, interested people can set up discussion groups on explicit and adults-only topics. The same computer network that offers on-line museums and information sources for kids may also offer on-line pornography. Controlling access to such materials requires an approach that balances social interests in free speech and commerce with community interests and responsibilities regarding adult materials.

In public settings off the network, the issue of adult material usually arises in reference to magazines and videos. It is common practice for dealers to display adult magazines so that passersby need not see suggestive covers. Video distributors generally follow the movie rating system: G for general audience, PG for parental guidance advised, R for restricted, and X for adult movies. Both these approaches have analogs to digital licenses. Thus, works can come with ratings established by appropriate institutions or community organizations. For example, a G-rated movie would require no license, whereas viewing a digital movie rated PG-13 would need either an identity certificate specifying that the consumer is over 13 or a permission ticket issued by his or her parent.

The foregoing examples show how central digital tickets and licenses are to the usage rights approach and how one overall infrastructure could serve a wide range of social and commercial purposes.

Foundations of Trust in Repositories

Next we explore the question, what is it that we want to trust about repositories and what is the basis for such trust? In general, a trusted system is one that can be relied upon to take responsibility for a given operation or set of operations. In the case of digital works on repositories, the requirement for trust is that the repositories follow—at all times and in every instance—the rules about how digital works are used. They must be accountable for all uses of the works and for the fees charged for those uses. Responsibility is, fundamentally, an issue of *integrity*. For repositories that integrity has three parts: *physical integrity* refers to the soundness of the physical device itself; *communications integrity* means roughly that repositories cannot be easily fooled by telling them lies; and *behavioral integrity* means that repositories will exercise their functions exactly as they are supposed to, 100 percent of the time.

Physical integrity applies both to the repositories and to the digital works they protect. One threat to a repository is that someone will pry open the case and gain access to what is stored inside. In a trusted system different repositories could have different levels of security. A repository that can be compromised with a power drill and a screwdriver would have a low security level. A somewhat higher level of physical security would be a system with sensors that enable it to detect a threat and erase certain key data. A still higher level of security, suitable perhaps for a real life James Bond, might be a system that self-destructs when it detects that it is under threat, perhaps setting off alarms and telephoning for help.

Even at its lowest level, security for a repository would be much higher than the security for such passive media as videotapes, compact discs, or computer diskettes. These media record their information out in the open where it can be accessed by any general-purpose reading device; they cannot detect intrusion or take any kind of protective or evasive action. Repositories, on the other hand, would never present data to any device that fails to establish itself as a bona fide, qualified repository.

The second kind of system integrity, communications integrity, would ensure that repositories could not be easily fooled by being connected to illegitimate computer systems masquerading as legitimate repositories. When repositories connect with each other, they would go through a registration process identifying themselves to each other and establishing their bona fides. Imagine, for example, two secret agents unknown to each other who meet by arrangement. What's the secret word? How do I know you are who you say you are? Are we sure that nobody else is listening? These are the kinds of concerns two repositories would have when they are connected. They would put each other through a series of tests intended to weed out impostors and protect the works with which they are trusted. Only when registration succeeds would they establish a trusted session.

A few words about how this works are in order. At the heart of the registration process is a security concept called *public key encryption*, a well-known and much-studied system for secure and secret communication. In this approach, each repository is given a private key or code, which it keeps secret, and a public key. In a trusted system, these keys would be given to a repository when it is manufactured and would be certified by a master repository known to be highly secure. (One of the principal requirements for the system architecture—discussed in the last section of this paper—is an institution that can control and safeguard the master repositories.) Communications integrity is ensured because all communications among repositories are in codes that are extremely difficult to break. In addition, provisions to detect attempts to tamper with communication and to isolate repositories identified as compromised can be built into the protocols.

Finally, we come to behavioral integrity. Even if the repositories have not been physically compromised and can prove their identities to each other, how do we know they will work properly? In the secret agent analogy, how do we know that the other agent hasn't been compromised or turned? Because the behavior of computers is determined by their programming, the programs used in repositories must be thoroughly tested and certified, which is a lot of work. What makes the certification task easier for repositories than for computers in general is that repositories would have limited functions. They would need to carry out a limited number of very specific operations relating to usage rights, protocol handling, and accounting. Furthermore, there would be procedures that guarantee that all installed software is inviolable to tampering or modification. Finally, even if a repository were compromised, it would need to identify itself for any transaction with a certificate from a master repository; other repositories, given the identity of the compromised repository, would refuse to carry out further transactions.

In summary, the physical integrity, communications integrity, and behavioral integrity of a repository are the foundations of a trusted system. A repository is designed with the ability to detect tampering and communications errors and to ensure certified behavior. These characteristics could be achieved by computers. Until now, however, the value of these attributes has not been appreciated, so that elements of the technology are not widely available and computers are designed without these goals in mind.

The Accountant Inside When someone makes a copy of a digital book and the repositories record the charges, what's to say that the author or publisher will ever get paid? Suppose, for example, that the repository is a credit-card-sized device. Why not just throw it away when a large enough bill accumulates on it? Also, if repositories contain the equivalent of money, what will prevent theft of that money?

There are many ways to approach these questions. During 1994 several groups conducted field trials of the national computer networks that operate digital checking accounts, cash, and network credit cards. These trials provide a base of experience relevant to usage rights.

Repositories would have a substantial advantage over such systems because they would record a transaction without requiring an immediate telephone or computer-network connection to a financial clearinghouse. This is especially relevant for billing tiny amounts, microtransactions, for which the cost of a telephone call would dwarf the amount of the payment. Monthly connections to a clearinghouse would be more convenient. A repository could be connected to a clearinghouse in any of several ways: by plugging it into a bank teller machine or a special telephone or connecting it to a computer network through a personal computer. In such an operation, the repository would open a channel to a clearinghouse with a registration protocol similar to the ones used when two repositories connect to each other. During the monthly session, all transactions could be reported in a single communication and a fresh credit limit for the repository could be set.

Some security measures would be necessary. First, a personal identification code similar to those used at automatic tellers would be required before charges could be accrued. Second, all transactions would be reported by both parties; this would not prevent cheating but would require two people to collude in losing their repositories. Third, the repository itself, which is likely to be more expensive than a credit card, would require insurance to replace it. Finally, as happens with credit cards today, anyone who regularly reports the loss or theft of a repository would eventually have difficulty getting a replacement or would be forced to use a repository with more stringent security arrangements.

Implications and Institutional Challenges

Stakeholders in digital publication will ultimately come from many industries, walks of life, and parts of the world. For a variety of reasons, they are now accustomed to different versions of copyright law and have different conventions of what constitutes fair use of copyrighted material. As more and more kinds of publication go digital, people's different expectations are likely to create a tug of war. Digital property rights may provide a way to manage this evolving situation. Because copyrights traditionally last a long time, we need to create and shape institutions governing usage rights that will serve us well for a long time.

Usage Rights and Copyright Law

Copyright law is not static. Over time, there have been various changes. Notable copyright reforms were made as recently as 1976, and several more are currently under active discussion. Defining a few terms will bring us to the nub of many copyright issues and show how digital usage rights are relevant to them.

Copyright law has provisions for what is called *fair use*, the amount and kind of quotations from a copyrighted work that can be made without permission. In general, creators and publishers have an interest in limiting free use of their own materials under fair use so that they can require extra fees for particular uses. Consumers, librarians, and scholars, on the other hand, have an interest in ensuring that certain uses are unencumbered.

Here are some examples. A person who buys a copy of a work is permitted to use it in a variety of ways. Although making copies of the work to sell or give away is generally not legal, some copying is allowed—at least for certain kinds of works and in some contexts. For example, it is usually all right to make a copy for personal use and to quote passages from a book in a book review or scholarly work, as long as the original source is cited. As new media have become important, similar issues have arisen about fair use in quoting from recorded music and movies.

Sometimes more than one kind of use is distinguished for a work. An easily understood example is that of a play script. The usual copyright provisions govern the copying of a script. The right to create a stage production from the script and to perform it publicly for profit is not, however, covered by fair use. A public performance requires a different kind of right, a *performance right*. Similar issues arise for musical scores and recorded music. When we buy a compact disc or cassette tape of music, fair use includes playing it at home, whereas a radio transmission constitutes a public performance. Because performance rights are not included in the purchase, radio stations are supposed to pay for putting such works on the air. The small print on a compact disc generally includes the phrase "all rights reserved," the publisher's way of claiming all rights not explicitly granted.

The fair use doctrine arises when possessing a copy of a work gives a person the potential to use it in ways its creator thinks are unfair. In such cases, usage rights could provide for different kinds of uses and fees, distinguishing between copying rights, loan rights, transfer rights, play rights, broadcast rights, print rights, extract rights, embed rights, editing rights, and several others. On a trusted system, these specific rights could be granted by requiring particular digital licenses or tickets and different fees. Some kinds of digital players, for example, might have built-in licenses and codes that determine whether they can be connected to public broadcast systems or only to home systems.

In many fair use scenarios, the gap between what is fair use and what is infringement is exacerbated by the fact that there is nothing in between. Fair use costs nothing. Other uses cost fees; and even when the fees are small, the cost and bother of obtaining and accounting for them is high. The digital property rights approach, however, could permit transactions for even nominal amounts of money, changing the confrontational issue of fee versus free to a practical issue of "how much?"

Usage rights could also make it possible to grant rights to designated categories of users for social reasons. Digital certificates could be made available to librarians, library users, teachers, students, impoverished people, and so on. Some interest groups are already drafting position papers about fair use in the electronic age, spelling out certain rights that they believe should incur no fees, such as the right to print temporary paper copies for personal use. Curiously, the concept of usage rights reverses our conventional assumptions about making copies; printing a paper copy, we can now recognize, is moving digital content out of repository control. In a usage rights context, paper copies would have greater potential for unauthorized copying than digital copies would.

In summary, the usage-rights approach provides repository-mediated contracts to govern the various uses of digital works. It creates specific language for common kinds of uses and their fees. It is a tool never imagined by the creators of copyright law, or by those who believe laws governing intellectual property cannot be enforced. What copyright law protects is the expression of ideas. As John Perry Barlow put it, "The point at which this franchise was imposed was that moment when the 'word became flesh' by departing the mind of its originator and entering some physical object.... Protecting physical expression had the force of convenience on its side. Copyright worked well because, Gutenberg notwithstanding, it was hard to make a book.... Unlike unbounded words or images, books had material surfaces to which one could attach copyright notices, publishers marques, and price tags (*Wired*, March 1994).

The ability to attach appropriate tags proclaiming the rights and fees for different uses is exactly what repositories do for digital works. Such tags, permanently attached and honored by the trusted systems, would enable us to experience the works. With these tags, the basic concepts of copyright law seem to work just as they are. In this way, an unconventional redesign of computer operation can preserve and even improve the now conventional social contract between those who create and those who consume works of the mind.

What Repositories Can and Can't Do

Repositories cannot, of course, prevent all unauthorized copying of digital works. No technology can keep someone from reading a digital book, then laboriously typing the words verbatim at a keyboard. A plagiarizer could even use technological aids, for example, a television camera aimed at a display and feeding its output into a computer equipped with an optical text reader. Digitally published music could be played through a repository's speaker and recorded through a microphone. Recordings of interactive works such as video games are of little use; still, if a work can be experienced by the human senses, it can be recorded. Trusted systems would simply inhibit the unauthorized making of perfect digital copies.

Two things could happen when performances of digital works are re-recorded outside a repository. The first is a loss of fidelity, familiar to anyone who has made cassette-tape copies from a compact disc. The first-generation copy of a digital work re-recorded outside a repository would not be perfect, although it may be very good. Subsequent generations of uncontrolled copies would be as good as the first-generation copy. The second thing that may occur is the copying of identification information hidden on an original version. This information can be made invisible and inaudible to the human senses but detectable by special equipment. In the event that unauthorized copying is frequent enough to justify intervention, such identification information could be used to trace an illegal copy back to the repository where it was made.

In summary, repositories—like all technology—are imperfect. Yet they can make it much easier to be honest and easier for creators to make a living. Moreover, we would expect them to have other social effects in the long term. More digital works would be created because more potential authors would see a possibility of making a living creating them. That is the main effect—letting loose the light.

There are other predictable effects. With usage rights, electronic distribution of digital works would be much easier than it is now. Using computer networks and the telephone system, consumers could take immediate delivery of digital works from distributors located at great distances. Many distributors of digital works, such as digital bookstores, digital libraries, and digital music stores would serve much larger geographic areas. Consumers would be able to choose from a wide range of potential distributors and to access or purchase quality digital works at a moment's notice and at any time of the day. Distributors who add little value to the chain between producers and consumers would probably be squeezed out.

What kinds of works will first be distributed on repositories? The answer to this question, and many of the factors bearing on it, are still unknown. Repositories will be adopted first in areas where they can solve a pressing problem. In the music industry, publishers have lobbied successfully against the manufacturing of devices that can make digital recordings. There may be an opportunity in this area if the trusted systems developed give advantages to both consumers and publishers. It will probably also be easy to introduce repositories, where other technological changes are leading to system changes. In television, for example, repositories could become more viable when digital television offers fidelity that cannot be captured by the today's videotape formats.

The adoption of usage rights would remove many of the barriers to self-publishing and induce more creators of digital works to self-publish, offering their works for sale on computer networks and reaping the benefits of consumer-based distribution. Self-publishing would not, however, eliminate the role of digital publishers. Publishers often improve the quality of the works they publish and provide brand names recognized by the consumer as indicative of quality and style. The continued need for this kind of quality assurance will give publishers of digital works an enduring role. In fact, new publishers will probably appear. People who review works may put together collections, providing a service similar to brand-name recognition by appraising the works they offer. The net effect of these opportunities for new publishers could be the broadening of influences on popular taste.

The Digital Melting Pot

The metaphor of the melting pot has long been used to describe the culture of the United States created by blending the traditions of people from all over the world. Digital publishing, we believe, is creating a melting pot of genres. The term *multimedia* refers to the mixing of multiple kinds of media—books, newspapers, musical recordings, videos, video games, and computer software—in a single production. But the blending of forms, unlike the blending of water and oil, is creating new forms: for example, interactive movies and travel guides and annotated presentations of plays that include scripts, multiple performances, and reviews, all in a single hyperlinked work.

Some currently distinct genres may be evolving toward similar digital interactive forms. Ultimately, the form of the digital news program and the digital newspaper may be the same. Both may become a digital work broadcast in the air or by cable several times a day and laid out on multiple electronic pages. The pages will contain short film clips of anchors giving the news and, perhaps, animated advertisements and infomercials. Both versions may be interactive and playable on color screens with high-fidelity sound. Today's newspapers and television news programs are the forerunners of these future interactive news forms.

As publication forms blend, what will become of the provisions of copyright law and fair use, which today have different provisions for newspapers, videos, and computer programs? It is likely that some of today's legal distinctions will not be sustainable in the new digital forms.

In the Fall of 1993 Bruce Lehman, head of the U.S. Patent Office, conducted a public hearing on intellectual property and digital networks. The hearing was called to discuss these issues in the context of the national information infrastructure, the so-called Information Superhighway touted in the press. At this Washington meeting, representatives of the cable industry sat down the aisle from small-town librarians and civil libertarians. Representatives from the music industry rubbed shoulders with people from the computer hardware and software industries. All were aware that their own businesses and institutions were becoming more involved in digital publication and that new media were creating forms and genres that confound present definitions of fair use.

The representatives found that they had very different assumptions about the appropriate means for protecting intellectual property. The music industry uses statistical sampling of radio station broadcasts to check that royalties are properly paid, while the computer industry has no effective organization to check on copyright infringements. Paper-based publishing mostly uses the copyright clearance center, which expedites payment of copying fees. The representatives were well versed in the issues pertaining to their own businesses and recognized that the conditions for the other businesses were different. They knew that as the various media merge into new forms new ways of doing business will emerge. Whatever new rules and ways of business develop, they want to ensure that their own industry thrives.

Planning for the Generations

The laws governing the length of a copyright have changed several times. In 1978 the copyright for a work was established as the lifetime of the creator plus fifty years. Thus, the total period of a copyright may easily amount to a hundred years. In our fast-paced society, we do not often design institutions to last for hundreds of years.

Yet the long view is not unheard of. When we set aside parklands in the public trust, we are planning for the long term. Such consciousness of time is akin to that expressed by Native Americans when they speak of planning for seven generations: three past generations of parents, grandparents, and great-grandparents; the generation that makes the decision; and three future generations of children, grandchildren, and great-grandchildren. Adapting this perspective could help us create an institution that has a lasting value for humankind.

There are many stakeholders in digital publishing, including consumers, authors, publishers, distributors, platform vendors, financial institutions, and governments. The approach based on usage rights presumes that all will share a digital property language, compatible platforms from multiple vendors, and broad general agreement about what rights mean. The details of the approach and the particular kinds of rights defined will evolve over time.

The security needs of the approach assume the existence of an authoritative institution that issues digital certificates warranting that particular platforms and software uphold and enforce the concept of usage rights. We call this institution the Digital Property Trust (DPT). Although some initial seed funding would be needed, the DPT could eventually fund its activities from a small tithe on commercial repository transactions or by renewable licenses on platforms and software.

Although planning for a DPT is tentative at this time, a few observations about its role and structure are appropriate. At present, there are many different kinds of social and international structures—government, banking, political, and standards organizations, among others—with their own bases of authority. In the future these organizations should be able to establish and publish their own digital certificates, publishers issuing their own kinds of digital licenses and authors and distributors setting whatever usage rights and fees they please. The role of the DPT would be to promote widespread commerce in digital works. To this end, it would certify and maintain the security of trusted systems and establish a common operational terminology of usage rights to meet social and economic needs.

Achieving this long-term vision for the DPT requires the wisdom and organization to appropriately balance interest groups. The DPT would need to be evenhanded in its treatment of hardware providers, software designers, and publishers. Because the certification process for hardware and software would require DPT to have detailed knowledge of exactly how products work, maintaining evenhandedness may be challenging. At the same time, the DPT would need the representation and support of the most powerful vendors and publishers for its decisions to carry the weight of authority.

Establishing Trusted Systems

Today's computers and installed software are not programmed to honor usage rights. This fact raises a key question: Assuming that the usage rights language is appropriate and the DPT can be established, how do we go from a world in which most systems are not trustworthy to a world populated by trusted systems? The realistic answer is that the world will not change suddenly. Rather, we need incremental approaches to establish trusted systems widely.

One incremental approach would distinguish between individual and organizational repositories, starting with institutions dealing in documents of high value and limited distribution. These might be bookstores that print documents on demand or legal offices that provide rapid access to thousands of scanned documents. Beginning with organizations like these could demonstrate the viability of usage rights without requiring tamperproof systems for authentication, authorization, and accounting.

Another incremental approach would focus on digital works in a particular market niche For example, rather than starting with computers, it may be easier to begin with personal entertainment systems for music or video games, for these systems do not need compatibility with general-purpose application programs and operating systems.

A third avenue might be to upgrade existing computer systems by adding appropriate software and hardware. Even though such upgrades do not generally lead to high levels of security, the approach could begin with a large base of systems at low levels of security and provide incentives to upgrade them to more secure systems for works of greater sensitivity or value.

Whichever approach is taken, in the long run repositories offer advantages to both publishers and consumers. Consumers may find they have ready, quick, and cheap access to all kinds of digital works that can be delivered by telephone or computer network any time of the day. Creators may find that consumer-based distribution is a large new distribution channel; anyone who buys a digital work will be able to make a copy and sell it, automatically routing compensation to its creators. The simple provisions for extracting, editing, and embedding small portions of digital work open doors to creative sampling and reuse of multimedia materials. As creators and publishers learn that safety and wider markets are possible in digital publishing, they may bring about a flowering of new works and old works in new digital form.

Repositories provide a way to let loose the light for present and future generations. There are many institutional challenges, and stakeholders need to work together to bring about the necessary changes. The popular adoption of repositories will start small. In what publishing niches will it begin, providing the sparks to ignite the bonfire of publishing?

A Glossary of Terms

Credit server   A secure program and database in a repository to keep track of fees owed for the use of digital works. Typically, a credit server would have a credit limit and would need to be regularly connected to a financial clearinghouse to transfer funds to pay the bills. Like a bank automatic teller machine, a credit server would typically require the user to enter a personal identification code before using it.

Digital certificate   A digital document attesting to the truth of something. Each repository would have a digital certificate certifying it as a trusted system and identifying its public key and security level. In general, digital certificates could not be transferred between repositories except by specially authorized repositories. Digital certificates are encrypted in the private key of a master repository, making them difficult to forge and providing a simple means of testing their authenticity—decrypting them by using the public key.

Digital property right or **Usage right**   A specification of a contract to use a digital work in a certain way. Such rights would fall into several categories. **Transport rights**, for example, would include the right to copy, transfer, or loan a work; **render rights** would include playing and printing it; **derivative rights** would include the right to extract, embed, and edit it. Usage rights would be represented in a formal language that can be precisely interpreted by repositories. They could also be displayed to a consumer in a variety of simple ways appropriate for the situation.

Digital property rights transaction or **Usage rights transaction**   A series of actions treated as a unit. For example, in electronic banking, a transfer of money from one account to another is a transaction that credits one account with the money at the same time that it debits the other account. Each digital property right defines a particular transaction that can be carried out. For example, a usage right to copy a digital work would cause a new copy to be made and a credit server to make a record of the required payment.

Digital Property Trust (DPT)   An organization that ensures the health of digital publishing and promotes a lively international commerce in digital works. In conjunction with consumers, publishers, creators, and platform vendors, it would set the standard for the evolving digital property language and issue digital certificates to conforming platforms. It would also maintain the master repositories and perhaps ensure security and financial transactions.

Digital license   A digital certificate identifying the bearer repository as licensed and thereby authorized for carrying out certain rights. For example, certain digital works might require that copies of a work could only be made and sold when the repository contains a particular digital distributor's license.

Digital ticket   A digital certificate or coupon that can be used once to authorize a particular transaction. For example, a digital work may include an upgrade ticket that authorizes the user to replace the digital work with an updated version. When digital tickets are used, they would be punched by a digital ticket agent and could not be used again.

Digital work   Any work that can be represented in digital form; for example, a document like a book, magazine, or newspaper. It could also be a recording of music, a movie, a computer game, or any computer program. Sometimes the word **software** is used in a general sense to mean a digital work.

Encryption   A process of encoding a digital work by a secret code to render it unusable by anyone without the code. Decoding a work to restore it to usable form is called **decryption**. The preferred method of encoding is public-key encryption, in which there are two keys, a public key and a private key. When the private key is used to encrypt a work, the public key can be used to decrypt it.

Master repository   A very high-level repository with the highest security level. Master repositories would be kept by the Digital Property Trust (DPT) and would be used to issue certificates. The public keys of the master repositories would be assigned to all trusted systems when they are manufactured, enabling them to exchange and identify authentic digital certificates in their transactions with other repositories.

Repository   Any trusted system used for storing and playing digital works. For example, repositories could be portable entertainment devices, laptop readers, personal computers, credit-card-sized devices, or mechanisms that fit into home entertainment equipment for controlling digital television or music. Repositories would store digital works, together with their usage rights, and include credit servers for keeping track of fees for use.

Security level   Different degrees of physical security—ranging from low security to very high security—for protecting digital works against unauthorized use. Repositories for handling extremely valuable works need greater security than those for ordinary and portable use.

Shell   A kind of digital container for storing digital works in the filing system of a repository. They could contain both digital works and other shells. Tags specifying usage rights and fees would be attached to each work and its shell. When someone asks a repository to use a digital work, the repository would check the rights and fees recorded on the tags.

Trusted system   A system that can be relied on to follow certain rules at all times. In the context of digital works, a repository would be a trusted system that governs the uses and fees for digital works. All digital works would have tags describing uses and fees in a usage rights language; trusted systems would carry out the instructions on these tags infallibly.

Usage right   See **Digital property right**.

Reflections

The network for digital publishing is still being invented. As its creators we will need much wisdom to guide that invention. The hundreds—if not thousands—of traditional myths about creation have tried to answer questions such as: How did the world come to be? Why are humans what they are? Where did they come from? Generally, these stories are intended to explain the actions of the gods to mortals. According to them, we were formed from the thoughts of the gods, arose out of chaos, fell from grace, or were fashioned from mud along with the animals. The myths embody stories of people searching for a land in which to live and stories about how they should live in it to keep the world in balance.

But there are few stories instructing us about how to act as able and responsible creators. Perhaps creation myths are the wrong places to look for guidance; instead we should pay attention to stories about how people in the past worked together as communities. "Letting Loose the

Light" *draws on those stories, on our understanding of the marketplace and on the history of intellectual property during the French Revolution.*

In the past few years, several ways of governing the use of information on CD-ROMs and networks have come into use. In one version, purchasers call a telephone number to pay for keys that unlock specific software distributed on a CD-ROM. Different keys unlock different software. Because there are different versions of the CD-ROM discs, two people buying them are unlikely to be able to share keys. This approach does not, however, control subsequent redistribution of software if people have sufficient storage to copy it from a CD-ROM. Other approaches requiring special hardware and software have also been offered to meter the use of software on a CD-ROM. Efforts to control software with license servers are now widely used in organizations with closed local computer networks. They allow programs to govern the number of simultaneous users of proprietary software or data bases, making it possible, for example, for any five people of an organization of a hundred members to use a database at the same time.

Security and convenience are the key issues for approaches to digital publishing; security is an issue for publishers, and convenience is an issue for users. These concerns are often seen to be in tension. In the simple and convenient low-security approaches, users can load metering software onto existing personal computers; unfortunately, they could also load pirateware, software that defeats security measures. In many proposed systems, pirateware posted on a computer bulletin board could be used to compromise every site on a network. Fear of such attacks makes publishers reluctant to publish their works on such a network. In other approaches, works to be used must be distributed by the equipment manufacturer, which also acts as the accounting and billing company. As most publishers view control over marketing and distribution as a key to their success, they are often unwilling to engage in such arrangements. In contrast with such approaches, the digital property rights approach described in this article separates the publishing business from the financial and platform businesses. It will also require a good deal of co-ordination among these business sectors to make such trusted systems available.

Part 4

The Digital Worlds Metaphor: The I-Way As a Gateway to Experience

Without adventure, civilization is in full decay.
Attributed to Alfred North Whitehead

Whether the hero happens to gain a princess, a kingdom, healing medicine ... or some other reward ... he actually learns self-integration, balance, wisdom, and spiritual health.
Alexander Eliot, *The Universal Myths: Heroes, Gods, Tricksters, and Others*

Nothing happens without personal transformation.
Dr. W. Edwards Deming

All cultures have activities and rituals for renewal. One path to renewal is the vision quest, in which the seeker prepares for insight and healing by spending time alone in the wilderness. In search of dreams, insights, and connections, the seeker fasts and performs rituals. Ultimately he or she returns and is reintegrated into the community, renewed and bringing new energy and wisdom. Although such a vision quest is an inward, journey, it often produces understanding about one's relationships to others. In another path to renewal, the seeker travels to faraway exotic places, leaving behind everyday affairs and being more receptive to new ideas and new ways. The traveler returns refreshed, bringing stories, new energy, and new perspectives back to the community. This tour is an outward journey, but it often gives rise to insights about one's relationship to the self.

Myths and Archetypes for Awakening the Adventurer

In terms of archetypes, the need for renewal is reflected in the adventurer archetype, which can take many forms. The adventurer may be an undersea explorer or a spelunker exploring underground caves, or perhaps a mountain climber or a world traveler. He or she might be someone who has simply traveled around the block to see what others have not yet seen. Adventure can be a solitary activity, but it is more often experienced as a group. When people have an adventure together, they share not only the hazards and uncertainties they must negotiate but also the growth and bonding that arise when they face challenges. Some kinds of adventure are more potent than others; an adventure or escape that consists of watching a movie or reading a book is usually less rewarding than one that requires participation, risk, and sharing.

In western culture, the best-known adventurer is Odysseus—also known by his Latin name, Ulysses. As chronicled in Homer's *Iliad*, Odysseus was the kind of Ithaca who led the Greeks in the Trojan War. It was he who devised the stratagem of the Trojan horse for conquering Troy. In the legend, the goddess Athena become angry with the Greeks because of their ill treatment of the vanquished princess Cassandra, and she decreed that they would have trouble returning to their homes in Greece.

None of the Greeks faced greater obstacles than Odysseus did. In the *Odyssey* Homer chronicles the challenges Odysseus encounters in ten years of wandering. His men are turned into swine by the sorceress Circe and are tempted in the land of the lotus eaters and by the song of the sirens. They survive dangers in a passage between two sea monsters, Scylla and Charybdis, and need to defeat the cyclops. In all these adventures, Odysseus is tested and triumphs over his adversaries not by brute strength, but through tricks and his superior wit. In the end, he returns to his wife, Penelope, and kills off the suitors who had believed him dead.

Thus Odysseus exhibits traits of both the warrior and the trickster. As a soldier who defeats Troy, Odysseus is a warrior; but his use of the Trojan horse shows that his success relies on stealth rather than simply on superior force. In his later trials, too, he lives by his wits. When the cyclops traps Odysseus and his crew in a cave, Odysseus tricks the monster into getting drunk, then blinds it with a spear. Thus we see that in any given myth the characters can be a mixture of archetypes. Our present interest in the adventurer archetype draws more on Odysseus's character as a hero and traveler than on his shaman-hunter-trickster or warrior traits.

Many fairy tales feature a youth in humble circumstances going out into the world to seek his fortune. He may eventually win a kingdom or a princess, but first he must undergo a series of quests. In his *The Hero with a Thousand Faces*, Joseph Campbell suggests that these stories have a deeper meaning. At a minimum, they tell us that we should all travel and seek out experiences. As the quotation above by Alexander Eliot points out, the hero learns self-integration, balance, wisdom, and spiritual health—the greatest rewards of adventure.

In mythology, the most difficult journey a hero can undertake is one that leads to the realm of the dead. A journey into that land symbolizes dying, and the journey back symbolizes rebirth. This cycle of death and rebirth is the cycle of renewal and transformation in which the hero finds integration and wisdom to bring back to the community. This form of the adventure myth appears in cultures all over the world.

For many people, the connection between adventure and renewal with computers seems remote. What do word processors or spreadsheets have to do with new and refreshing experiences? Anyone who has kids, however, or who has walked past a video game parlor, knows about the appeal of electronic worlds, especially for young boys. What attracts kids to videogames? In a study of what makes games fun, Tom Malone suggests that good video games have elements of challenge, fantasy, and curiosity. However we account for it, children's fascination with video games is undeniable. A child with a new game wants to master "just one more level," even if he or she has been playing for three hours and it is time for dinner. The child hungers for adventure and challenge.

Digital worlds are computer-augmented or computer-created settings for experiences. The several kinds of digital worlds differ principally in how the experience is produced and what it means. The term *virtual reality* refers to an experience of an artificial place that is entirely created and rendered by a computer. Animated video games are virtual realities. The originator creates the artwork and decides what kinds of objects and creatures are in a world, whether the sky is blue or orange, where the treasure is hidden, and that players can immobilize the swamp thing by pouring honey on it. Three-dimensional virtual realities generally require special gear, such as head-mounted displays, to produce the three-dimensional view. The term *augmented reality* refers to superimposing computer-created information on top of an image of a physical reality. Imagine a doctor wearing eyeglasses that let him or her view simultaneously the internal organs of a patient and medical information about the patient. The doctor may see color superimposed on the patient to indicate temperature or see the patient's actual leg overlaid with an X-ray view of broken or mending bones. *Telepresence* is a special case in which communication devices are used to overcome limitations of distance, creating an experience of being present somewhere else. The term *ubiq-uitous computing* means embedding computing equipment in ordinary-seeming objects to enable them to communicate with each other and coordinate their activities. Sometimes the more abstruse phrase *embedded virtuality* is used for ubiquitous computing. All these forms of digital worlds—virtual reality, augmented reality, telepresence, and ubiquitous computing—have been realized at least in part by the present state of the art in computing.

Digital worlds have deep symbolic connections with mythology. Across all cultures, the most-important myths are often the creation myths, which are intended to explain the existence of the world. Creation myths often describe how the gods exercised great power to bring forth the world. At certain moments, however, this creative power runs down and needs to be renewed, giving birth to various rituals in which participants reenact the roles of the deities to bring about the renewal of time in the cosmos. In Bruce Chatwin's *The Songlines*, he narrates the story of the ancient dreaming tracks of Australia, which aborigines periodically follow across the continent, singing songs to renew the life and existence of the land.

The singing of the aborigines connects word and song with creation as in the Gospel of John, which says that "In the Beginning was the Word." This idea also appears in the creation myth from the Hindu Markandeya Purana. *Puranas* are Hindu myths that tell stories or truths about the gods. In the beginning, the Markandeya says, Brahma existed independently of space-time in the formless realm of pure ideas. He showed himself first in sound, as a vowel vibrating outward from nothingness. In the Purana, the sound echoes back on itself, becoming water and wind and, ultimately weaving the womb of the world. Letters and words exist in the same way, in the realm of ideas, even before they are said or written. In many stories of magic, knowing and saying the right words as an incantation is all that is needed to release powerful forces.

This connection between creation and words is particularly apt for digital worlds. Digital worlds are created by people who write computer programs. In this sense, the creation of virtual realities as digital worlds has much in common with the mythological creation of the worlds we live in, except that the words are spoken—or written—by people rather than by gods. Digital creations seem to arise from the wellsprings of the unconscious and myth, bringing us back full circle to our human role in the mystery of creation.

The Deep Structure of the Digital Worlds Metaphor

Because we are familiar with worlds in the usual sense, the metaphor of digital worlds is invested with much prior meaning. Its deep structure lies in our assumptions about real worlds and how we experience them.

We begin with the idea of place. A digital world is a place to go and have experiences. A world contains things, and these things are spread about in different locations. In a real world we either bring things to where we are or travel to see them, whichever is most practical. Generally speaking, the farther away something is, the longer it takes to get there. Things, including us, can be at only one place at a time. To get from one place to another, we have to find a path through, or around, or over, or under the things that are inbetween.

In real worlds, we have a body, and our body interacts with the world; thus, the traveler meets certain pleasures but also certain hazards. We can have fun on an adventure, but we can also be injured. Aside from changes in dress, cosmetics, and so on, our body is what we are given at birth and grow up in. We can recognize each other by our bodies, and we cannot trade them in for new ones.

Places in the world can be either isolated or populated. In our era, most of us spend most of our time in populated places, where we may form friendships with the people around us. When there are enough people in a place, we develop communities and establish a social order. Because people move around a good deal, the populations of communities and the people around us change with time.

Challenging Assumptions about Digital Worlds

Like all the other metaphors we have looked at thus far, the digital worlds metaphor will mislead us if we overlook what is different about the digital realm and how it is changing. In the real world, different objects are in different places and can only be in one place at a time. In digital worlds, this sense of place is more ambiguous. The connection between the image we perceive and any digital reality that may underlie it is mediated by imaging and linking software. This means that it is possible—and often the case—that an image of something or some one appears in more than one digital place at a time. For example, an image of some information may appear on my computer and simultaneously appear on yours. Furthermore, if two computers show identical images, that does not necessarily mean that they are showing the same digital object, they may be rendering images of objects that are or were copies of each other.

In real worlds, we have to travel to get places, and the greater the distance the longer it takes. In digital worlds everything travels at electronic speeds. We can get from one place to another by an electronic jump. If we know the address of where we are going, we can often "teleport" to that place instantly, without going through any intermediate points. Though it may still take time to get somewhere, it is the time of learning and discovering where we want to go. The transport time itself is generally negligible.

In a real world, we have bodies whose appearance and abilities can be changed, but only in some limited ways. We have a sense of continuity about our because they change only slowly. In a digital world, however, we can often take on new images or new names. In some digital worlds, everything about our appearance, including displayed gender, can be changed at a moment's notice.

These ghostly bodies we inhabit in digital worlds have some definite advantages. In the real world it is inconvenient when we accidentally leave behind important things like keys or a wallet. In a digital reality, our stuff can travel with us automatically, or we can send an agent to fetch it for us, or just open a door to get it and come right back.

Beyond the Digital Worlds Metaphor

The digital worlds metaphor is the fourth of the metaphors we consider for guiding our understanding of the kind of information infrastructure we can invent. We have noticed along the way that there is a lot of room for overlap and for using multiple metaphors. For example, although the digital library metaphor emphasizes looking up information, a library can also have a sense of place. In a digital worlds metaphor, we could expect to visit not only a vast place of books and other media but also to encounter librarians that can help us. Creating a sense of place and of community in a digital library is more useful than simply creating an on-line database. In the e-mail metaphor, we think of sending a message to someone. But if we shorten the time between sending and receiving messages, we can approach a real-time conversation. The digital worlds metaphor can add a sense of presence for each participant and a sense of place in which to have the conversation: Meet me at the waterfall, or at the coffee shop. The electronic marketplace metaphor, which emphasizes commerce, already contains a term, *place*, that refers to the digital worlds metaphor. We go to a marketplace not only to shop or do commerce but also to watch people. Indeed, the word *commerce* has multiple meanings; means intellectual or social exchange as well as buying and selling.

We can choose, when we are in a digital world, to understand that we are simultaneously in the real world. Some people see this blend of the real and the artificial as a flaw in a virtual reality. By contrast, it is the whole point of augmented reality or embedded virtuality. The marrying of virtual and real worlds creates a rich interaction that interweaves the images and agencies in the real world with those of the imagination and cyberspace. In mythological terms, it blends things that myth says were created by the gods with things created by people.

The digital world metaphor is also open-ended. We can go out into a digital world to find things and interact with others. The quality of the experience we have depends on what has been put there, either by human design or—as in augmented reality—by nature. It also depends on us. Our experiences in digital worlds may be the most powerful experiences we can get from a computer network. They also present opportunities and challenges—both in designing them and in using them to renew ourselves and to bring out the best in our human selves.

"Mudding: Social Phenomena in Text-Based Virtual Realities"

Pavel Curtis

Connections

A MUD (multi-user dungeon or multi-user dimension) is a networked virtual reality whose user interface is entirely textual. Participants log into a MUD through their computer workstations. Since it is text-based, a MUD is rather like old-time radio: you are given a verbal description and visualize the scene with your imagination. The text describes an artificial place. Each participant has a separate character, and the subject matter stems entirely from interactions, which occur in almost real time, being limited only by typing speed. Thus MUDs are social worlds, not solitary ones.

As virtual gathering places, MUDs have many of the social attributes of real gathering places. However, certain of their attributes are different and lead to new social phenomena not usually seen in real life. In this paper, Curtis relates his experiences creating and maintaining a MUD on the Internet.

The Machine did not transmit nuances of expression. It only gave a general idea of people—an idea that was good enough for all practical purposes.
E. M. Forster, "The Machine Stops"

A MUD is a software program that accepts "connections" from multiple users across some kind of network (e.g., telephone lines or the Internet) and provides to each user access to a shared database of "rooms," "exits," and other objects. Each user browses and manipulates this database from "inside" one of those rooms, seeing only those objects that are in the same room and moving from room to room mostly via the exits that connect them. A MUD, therefore, is a kind of virtual reality, an electronically-represented "place" that users can visit.

MUDs are not, however, like the kinds of virtual realities that one usually hears about, with fancy graphics and special hardware to sense the position and orientation of the user's real-world body. A MUD user's interface to the database is entirely text-based; all commands are typed in by the users and all feedback is printed as unformatted text on their terminal. The typical MUD user interface is most reminiscent of old computer games like Adventure and Zork; a typical interaction is shown below.

```
>look
Corridor
The corridor from the west continues to the east
here, but the way is blocked by a purple-velvet
rope stretched across the hall. There are doorways
leading to the north and south.
You see a sign hanging from the middle of the rope
here.
>read sign
This point marks the end of the currently-occupied
portion of the house. Guests proceed beyond this
point at their own risk.
—The residents
>go east
You step disdainfully over the velvet rope and
enter the dusty darkness of the unused portion of
the house.
```

Three major factors distinguish a MUD from an Adventure-style computer game, though:

• A MUD is not goal-oriented; it has no beginning or end, no "score," and no notion of "winning" or "success." In short, even though users of MUDs are commonly called players, a MUD isn't really a game at all.

• A MUD is extensible from within; a user can add new objects to the database such as rooms, exits, "things," and notes. Certain MUDs, including the one I run, even support an embedded programming language in which a user can describe whole new kinds of behavior for the objects they create.

• A MUD generally has more than one user connected at a time. All of the connected users are browsing and manipulating the same database and can encounter the new objects created by others. The multiple users on a MUD can communicate with each other in real time.

This last factor has a profound effect on the ways in which users interact with the system; it transforms the activity from a solitary one into a social one.

Most inter-player communication on MUDs follows rules that fit within the framework of the virtual reality. If a player "says" something (using the say command), then every other player in the same room will "hear" them. For example, suppose that a player named Munchkin typed the command

```
say Can anyone hear me?
```

Then Munchkin would see the feedback

```
You say, "Can anyone hear me?"
```

and every other player in the same room would see

```
Munchkin says, "Can anyone hear me?"
```

Similarly, the emote command allows players to express various forms of "non-verbal" communication. If Munchkin types

```
emote smiles.
```

then every player in the same room sees

```
Munchkin smiles.
```

Most interplayer communication relies entirely on these two commands.[1]

There are two circumstances in which the realistic limitations of say and emote have proved sufficiently annoying that new mechanisms were developed. It sometimes happens that one player wishes to speak to another player in the same room, but without anyone else in the room being aware of the communication. If Munchkin uses the whisper command

```
whisper "I wish he'd just go away ..." to Frebble
```

then only Frebble will see

```
Munchkin whispers, "I wish he'd just go away ..."
```

The other players in the room see nothing of this at all.

Finally, if one player wishes to say something to another who is connected to the MUD but currently in a different and perhaps "remote" room, the page command is appropriate. It is invoked with a syntax very like that of the whisper command and the recipient sees output like this:

```
You sense that Munchkin is looking for you in The
Hall.
He pages, "Come see this clock, it's tres cool!"
```

Aside from conversation, MUD players can most directly express themselves in three ways: by their choice of player name, by their choice of gender, and by their self-description.

When a player first connects to a MUD, they choose a name by which the other players will know them. This choice, like almost all others in MUDs, is not cast in stone; any player can rename themself at any time, though not to a name currently in use by some other player. Typically, MUD names are single words, in contrast to the longer "full" names used in real life.

Initially, MUD players appear to be neuter; automatically-generated messages that refer to such a player use the family of pronouns including "it," "its," etc. Players can choose to appear as a different gender, though, and not only male or female. On many MUDs, players can also choose to be plural (appearing to be a kind of "colony" creature: "ChupChups leave the room, closing the door behind them"), or to use one of several sets of gender-neutral pronouns (e.g., "s/he," "him/her" and "his/her," or "e," "em" and "eir").

Every object in a MUD optionally has a textual description which players can view with the look command. For example, the description of a room is automatically shown to a player when they enter that room and can be seen again just by typing "look." To see another player's description, one might type "look Bert." Players can set or change their descriptions at any time. The lengths of player descriptions typically vary from short one-liners to dozen-line paragraphs.

Aside from direct communication and responses to player commands, messages are printed to players when other players enter or leave the same room, when others connect or disconnect and are already in the same room, and when objects in the virtual reality have asynchronous behavior (e.g., a cuckoo clock chiming the hours).

MUD players typically spend their connected time socializing with each other, exploring the various rooms and other objects in the database, and adding new such objects of their own design. They vary widely in the amount of time they spend connected on each visit, ranging from only a minute to several hours; some players stay connected (and almost always idle) for days at a time, only occasionally actively participating.

This very brief description of the technical aspects of mudding suffices for the purposes of this paper. It has been my experience, however, that it is quite difficult to properly convey the "sense" of the experience in words. Readers desiring more detailed information are advised to try mudding themselves, as described in the final section of this paper.

Social Phenomena Observed on One MUD

Man is the measure.
E. M. Forster, "The Machine Stops"

In October of 1990, I began running an Internet-accessible MUD server on my personal workstation here at PARC. Since then, it has been running continuously, with interruptions of only a few hours at most. In January of 1991, the existence of the MUD (called LambdaMOO[2]) was announced publicly, via the Usenet newsgroup rec.games.mud. As of this writing, well over thirty-five hundred different players have connected to the server from over a dozen countries around the world and, at any given time, over 750 players have connected at least once in the last week. Recent statistics concerning the number of players connected at a given time of day (Pacific Standard Time) appear in figure 1.

LambdaMOO is clearly a reasonably active place, with new and old players coming and going frequently throughout the day. This popularity has provided me with a position from which to observe the social patterns of a fairly large and diverse MUD clientele. I want to point out to the reader, however, that I have no formal training in sociology, anthropology, or psychology, so I cannot make any claims about methodology or even my own objectivity. What I relate below is merely my personal observations made over a year of mudding. In most cases, my discussions of the motivations and feelings of individual players is based upon in-MUD conversations with them; I have no means of checking the verac-

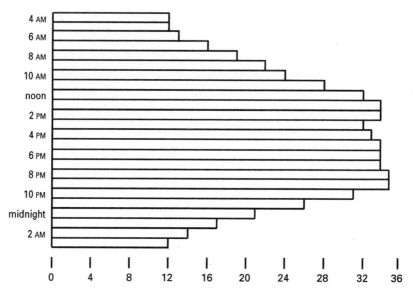

Figure 1
Average number of connected players on LambdaMOO, by time of day.

ity of their statements concerning their real-life genders, identities, or (obviously) feelings. On the other hand, in most cases, I also have no reason to doubt them.

I have grouped my observations into three categories: phenomena related to the behavior and motivations of individual players, phenomena related to interactions between small groups of players (especially observations concerning MUD conversation), and phenomena related to the behavior of a MUD's community as a whole.

Cutting across all of these categories is a recurring theme to which I would like to draw the reader's attention in advance. Social behavior on MUDs is in some ways a direct mirror of behavior in real life, with mechanisms being drawn nearly unchanged from real-life, and in some ways very new and different, taking root in the new opportunities that MUDs provide over real life.

Observations about Individuals

The mudding population   The people who have an opportunity to connect to LambdaMOO are not a representative sample of the world population; they all read and write English with at least passable proficiency and they have access to the Internet. Based on the names of their network hosts, I believe that well over 90 percent of them are affiliated with colleges and universities, mostly as students and, to a lesser extent, mostly undergraduates. Because they have Internet access, it might be supposed that the vast majority of players are involved in the computing field, but I do not believe that this is the case. It appears to me that no more than half (and probably less) of them are so employed; the increasing general availability of computing resources on college campuses and in industry appears to be having an effect, allowing a broader community to participate.

In any case, it appears that the educational background of the mudding community is generally above average, and it is likely that the economic background is similarly above the norm. Based on my conversations with people and on the names of those who have asked to join a mailing list about programming in LambdaMOO, I would guess that over 70 percent of the players are male; it is very difficult to give any firm justification for this number, however.

Player Presentation   As described in the introduction to mudding, players have a number of choices about how to present themselves in the MUD; the first such decision is the name they will use. The list below shows some of the names used by players on LambdaMOO.

Toon	Gemba	Gary_Severn	Ford	Frand
li'ir	Maya	Rincewind	yduJ	funky
Grump	Foodslave	Arthur	EbbTide	Anathae
yrx	Satan	byte	Booga	tek
chupchups	waffle	Miranda	Gus	Merlin
Moonlight	MrNatural	Winger	Drazz'zt	Kendal
RedJack	Snooze	Shin	lostboy	foobar
Ted_Logan	Xephyr	King_Claudius	Bruce	Puff
Dirque	Coyote	Vastin	Player	Cool
Amy	Thorgeir	Cyberhuman	Gandalf	blip
Jayhirazan	Firefoot	JoeFeedback	ZZZzzz ...	Lyssa
Avatar	zipo	Blackwinter	viz	Kilik
Maelstorm	Love	Terryann	Chrystal	arkanoiv

One can pick out a few common styles for names (e.g., names from or inspired by myth, fantasy, or other literature, common names from real life, names of concepts, animals, and everyday objects that have representative connotations, etc.), but it is clear that no such category includes a majority of the names. Note that a significant minority of the names are in lower case; this appears to be a stylistic choice (players with such names describe the practice as "cool") and not, as might be supposed, an indication of a depressed ego.

Players can be quite possessive about their names, resenting others who choose names that are similarly spelt or pronounced, or even that are taken from the same mythology or work of literature. In one case, for example, a player named "ZigZag" complained to me about other players taking the names "ZigZag!" and "Zig."

The choice of a player's gender is, for some, one of great consequence and forethought; for others (mostly males), it is simple and without any questions. For all that this choice involves the fewest options for the player (unlike their name or description, which are limited only by their imagination), it is also the choice that can generate the greatest concern and interest on the part of other players.

As I've said before, it appears that the great majority of players are male, and the vast majority of them choose to present themselves as such. Some males, however, taking advantages of the relative rarity of females in MUDs, present themselves as female and thus stand out to some degree. Some use this distinction just for the fun of deceiving others, some of these going so far as to try to entice male-presenting players into sexually explicit discussions and interactions. This is such a widely noticed phenomenon, in fact, that one is advised by the common wisdom to assume that any flirtatious female-presenting players are, in real life, males. Such players are often subject to ostracism based on this assumption.

Some MUD players have suggested to me that such transvestite flirts are perhaps acting out their own (latent or otherwise) homosexual urges or fantasies, taking advantage of the perfect safety of the MUD situation to see how it feels to approach other men. While I have had no personal experience talking to such players, let alone the opportunity to delve into their motivations, the idea strikes me as plausible given the other ways in which MUD anonymity seems to free people from their inhibitions. (I say more about anonymity later on.)

Other males present themselves as female more out of curiosity than as an attempt at deception; to some degree, they are interested in seeing "how the other half lives," what it feels like to be perceived as female in a community. From what I can tell, they can be quite successful at this.

Female-presenting players report a number of problems. Many of them have told me that they are frequently subject both to harassment and to special treatment. One reported seeing two newcomers arrive at the same time, one male-presenting and one female-presenting. The other players in the room struck up conversations with the putative female and offered to show her around but completely ignored the putative male, who was left to his own devices.

In addition, probably due mostly to the number of female-presenting males one hears about, many female players report that they are frequently (and sometimes quite aggressively) challenged to "prove" that they are, in fact, female. To the best of my knowledge, male-presenting players are rarely if ever so challenged.

Because of these problems, many players who are female in real life choose to present themselves otherwise, choosing either male, neuter, or gender-neutral pronouns. As one might expect, the neuter and gender-neutral presenters are still subject to demands that they divulge their real gender.

Some players apparently find it quite difficult to interact with those whose true gender has been called into question; since this phenomenon is rarely manifest in real life, they have grown dependent on "knowing where they stand," on knowing what gender roles are "appropriate." Some players (and not only males) also feel that it is dishonest to present oneself as being a different gender than in real life; they report feeling "mad" and "used" when they discover the deception.

While I can spare no more space for this topic, I enthusiastically encourage the interested reader to look up Lindsy Van Gelder's fascinating article ["The Strange Case of the Electronic Lover," in *Computerization and Controversy*, Dunlop and King, ed., 1991] for many more examples and insights, as well as the story of a remarkably successful deception via "electronic transvestism."

The final part of a player's self-presentation, and the only part involving prose, is the player's description. This is where players can, and often do, establish the details of a persona or role they wish to play in the virtual reality. It is also a significant factor in other players' first impressions, since new players are commonly looked at soon after entering a common room.

Some players use extremely short descriptions, intending to be either cryptic (e.g., "the possessor of the infinity gems") or straightforward (e.g., "an average-sized dark elf with lavender eyes") often because they are insufficiently motivated to create a more complex description for themselves. Other players go to great efforts in writing their descriptions; one moderately long example appears below.

```
You see a quiet, unassuming figure wreathed in an
oversized, dull-green Army jacket which is pulled up
to nearly conceal his face. His long, unkempt blond
hair blows back from his face as he tosses his head
to meet your gaze. Small round gold-rimmed glasses,
tinted slighty grey, rest on his nose. On a shoulder
strap he carries an acoustic guitar and he lugs a
backpack stuffed to overflowing with sheet music,
sketches, and computer printouts. Under the coat are
faded jeans and a T-Shirt reading "Paranoid Cyber-
Punks International." He meets your gaze and smiles
faintly, but does not speak with you. As you surmise
him, you notice a glint of red at the rims of his
blue eyes, and realize that his canine teeth seem
to protrude slightly. He recoils from your look of
horror and recedes back into himself.
```

A large proportion of player descriptions contain a degree of wish fulfillment; I cannot count the number of "mysterious but unmistakably powerful" figures I have seen wandering around in LambdaMOO. Many players, it seems, are taking advantage of the MUD to emulate various attractive characters from fiction.

Given the detail and content of so many player descriptions, one might expect to find a significant amount of role-playing, players who adopt a coherent character with features distinct from their real-life personalities. Such is rarely the case, however. Most players appear to tire of such an effort quickly and simply interact with the others more-or-less straight-forwardly, at least to the degree one does in normal discourse. One factor might be that the roles chosen by players are usually taken from a par-ticular creative work and are not particularly viable as characters outside of the context of that work; in short, the roles don't make sense in the context of the MUD.

A notable exception to this rule is one particular MUD I've heard of, called "PernMUSH." This appears to be a rigidly maintained simulacrum of the world described in Ann McCaffrey's celebrated "Dragon" books. All players there have names that fit the style of the books, and all places built there are consistent with what is shown in the series and in vari-ous fan materials devoted to it. PernMUSH apparently holds frequent "hatchings" and other social events, also derived in great detail from McCaffrey's works. This exception probably succeeds only because of its single-mindedness; with every player providing the correct context for every other, it is easier for everyone to stay more-or-less "in character."

Player Anonymity It seems to me that the most significant social factor in MUDs is the perfect anonymity provided to the players. There are no commands available to the players to discover the real-life identity of each other and, indeed, technical considerations make such commands either very difficult or impossible to implement.

It is this guarantee of privacy that makes players' self-presentation so important and, in a sense, successful. Players can only be known by what they explicitly project and are not "locked into" any factors beyond their easy control, such as personal appearance, race, etc. In the words of an old military recruiting commercial, MUD players can "be all that you can be."

This also contributes to what might be called a "shipboard syndrome," the feeling that since one will likely never meet anyone from the MUD in real life, there is less social risk involved and inhibitions can safely be lowered.

For example, many players report that they are much more willing to strike up conversations with strangers they encounter in the MUD than in real life. One obvious factor is that MUD visitors are implicitly assumed to be interested in conversing, unlike in most real-world contexts. Another deeper reason, though, is that players do not feel that very much is at risk. At worst, if they feel that they've made an utter fool of themselves, they can always abandon the character and create a new one, losing only the name and the effort invested in socially establishing the old one. In effect, a "new lease on life" is always a ready option.

Players on most MUDs are also emboldened somewhat by the fact that they are immune from violence, both physical and virtual. The permissions systems of all MUDs (excepting those whose whole purpose revolves around adventuring and the slaying of monsters and other players) generally prevent any player from having any kind of permanent effect on any other player. Players can certainly annoy each other, but not in any lasting or even moderately long-lived manner.

This protective anonymity also encourages some players to behave irresponsibly, rudely, or even obnoxiously. We have had instances of severe and repeated sexual harassment, crudity, and deliberate offensiveness. In general, such cruelty seems to be supported by two causes: the offenders believe (usually correctly) that they cannot be held accountable for their actions in the real world; and the very same anonymity makes it easier for them to treat other players impersonally, as other than real people.

Wizards   Usually, as I understand it, societies cope with offensive behavior by various group mechanisms, such as ostracism, and I discuss this kind of effect in detail in a later section. In certain severe cases, however, it is left to the "authorities" or "police" of a society to take direct action, and MUDs are no different in this respect.

On MUDs, it is a special class of players, usually called wizards or (less frequently) gods, who fulfill both the "authority" and "police" roles. A wizard is a player who has special permissions and commands available, usually for the purpose of maintaining the MUD, much like a "system administrator" or "superuser" in real-life computing systems. Players can only be transformed into wizards by other wizards, with the maintainer of the actual MUD server computer program acting as the first such.

On most MUDs, the wizards' first approach to solving serious behavior problems is, as in the best real-life situations, to attempt a calm dialog with the offender. When this fails, as it usually does in the worst cases of irresponsibility, the customary response is to punish the offender with "toading." This involves (a) either severely restricting the kinds of actions the player can take, or else preventing them from connecting at all; (b) changing the name and description of the player to present an unpleasant appearance (often literally that of a warty toad); and (c) moving the player to some very public place within the virtual reality. This public humiliation is often sufficient to discourage repeat visits by the player, even in a different guise.

On LambdaMOO, the wizards as a group decided on a more low-key approach to the problem; we have, in the handful of cases where such a severe course was dictated, simply "recycled" the offending player, removing them from the database of the MUD entirely. This is a more permanent solution than toading, but also lacks the public spectacle of toading, a practice none of us were comfortable with.

Wizards, in general, have a very different experience of mudding than other players. Because of their palpable and extensive extra powers over other players, and because of their special role in MUD society, they are frequently treated differently by other players.

Most players on LambdaMOO, for example, upon first encountering my wizard player, treat me with almost exaggerated deference and respect. I am frequently called "sir" and players often apologize for "wasting" my time. A significant minority, however, appear to go to great lengths to prove that they are not impressed by my office or power, speaking to me quite bluntly and making demands that I assist them with their problems using the system, sometimes to the point of rudeness.

Because of other demands on my time, I am almost always connected to the MUD but idle, located in a special room I built (my "den") that players require my permission to enter. This room is useful, for example, as a place in which to hold sensitive conversations without fear of interruption. This constant presence and unapproachability, however, has had significant and unanticipated side-effects. I am told by players who get more circulation than I do that I am widely perceived as a kind of mythic figure, a mysterious wizard in his magical tower. Rumor and hearsay have spread word of my supposed opinions on matters of MUD policy. One effect is that players are often afraid to contact me for fear of capricious retaliation at their presumption.

While I find this situation disturbing and wish that I had more time to spend out walking among the "mortal" members of the LambdaMOO community, I am told that player fears of wizardly caprice are justified on certain other MUDs. It is certainly easy to believe the stories I hear of MUD wizards who demand deference and severely punish those who transgress; there is a certain ego boost to those who wield even simple administrative power in virtual worlds, and it would be remarkable indeed if no one had ever started a MUD for that reason alone.

In fact, one player sent me a copy of an article, written by a former MUD wizard, based on Machiavelli's *The Prince*; it details a wide variety of more-or-less creative ways for wizards to make ordinary MUD players miserable. If this wizard actually used these techniques, as he claims, then some players' desires to avoid wizards are quite understandable.

Observations about Small Groups

MUD conversation   The majority of players spend the majority of their active time on MUDs in conversation with other players. The mechanisms by which those conversations get started generally mirror those that operate in real life, though sometimes in interesting ways.

Chance encounters between players exploring the same parts of the database are common and almost always cause for conversation. As mentioned above, the anonymity of MUDs tends to lower social barriers and to encourage players to be more outgoing than in real life. Strangers on MUDs greet each other with the same kinds of questions as in real life: "Are you new here? I don't think we've met." The very first greetings, however, are usually gestural rather than verbal: "Munchkin waves. Lorelei waves back."

The @who (or WHO) command on MUDs allows players to see who else is currently connected and, on some MUDs, where those people are. An example of the output of this command appears in table 1.

This is, in a sense, the MUD analog of scanning the room in a real-life gathering to see who's present.

Players consult the @who list to see if their friends are connected and to see which areas, if any, seem to have a concentration of players in them. If more than a couple of players are in the same room, the pre-

Table 1
Sample output from LambdaMOO's @who command

Player name	Connected	Idle time	Location
Haakon (#2)	3 days	a second	Lambda's Den
Lynx (#8910)	a minute	2 seconds	Lynx' Abode
Garin (#23393)	an hour	2 seconds	Carnival Grounds
Gilmore (#19194)	an hour	10 seconds	Heart of Darkness
TamLin (#21864)	an hour	21 seconds	Heart of Darkness
Quimby (#23279)	3 minutes	2 minutes	Quimby's room
koosh (#24639)	50 minutes	5 minutes	Corridor
Nosredna (#2487)	7 hours	36 minutes	Nosredna's Hideaway
yduJ (#68)	7 hours	47 minutes	Hackers' Heaven
Zachary (#4670)	an hour	an hour	Zachary's Workshop
Woodlock (#2520)	2 hours	2 hours	Woodlock's Room

Total: 11 players, 6 of whom have been active recently.

sumption is that an interesting conversation may be in progress there; players are thus more attracted to more populated areas. I call this phenomenon "social gravity"; it has a real-world analog in the tendency of people to be attracted to conspicuous crowds, such as two or more people at the door of a colleague's office.

It is sometimes the case on a MUD, as in real life, that one wishes to avoid getting into a conversation, either because of the particular other player involved or because of some other activity one does not wish to interrupt. In the real world, one can refrain from answering the phone, screen calls using an answering machine, or even, in copresent situations, pretend not to have heard the other party. In the latter case, with luck, the person will give up rather than repeat themself more loudly.

The mechanisms are both similar and interestingly different on MUDs. It is often the case that MUD players are connected but idle, perhaps because they have stepped away from their terminal for a while. Thus, it often happens that one receives no response to an utterance in a MUD simply because the other party wasn't really present to see it. This commonly understood fact of MUD life provides for the MUD equivalent of pretending not to hear. I know of players who take care after such a pretense not to type anything more to the MUD until the would-be conversant has left, thus preserving the apparent validity of their excuse.

Another mechanism for avoiding conversation is available to MUD players but, as far as I can see, not to people in real life situations. Most MUDs provide a mechanism by which each player can designate a set of other players as "gagged"; the effect is that nothing will be printed to the gagging player if someone they've gagged speaks, moves, emotes, etc. There is generally no mechanism by which the gagged player can tell a priori that someone is gagging them; indeed, unless the gagged player attempts to address the gagging player directly, the responses from the other players in the room (who may not be gagging the speaker) may cause the speaker never even to suspect that some are not hearing them.

We provide a gagging facility on LambdaMOO, but it is fairly rarely used; a recent check revealed only forty-five players out of almost three thousand who are gagging other players. The general feeling appears to be that gagging is quite rude and is only appropriate (if ever) when someone persists in annoying you in spite of polite requests to the contrary. It is not clear, though, quite how universal this feeling is. For example, I know of some players who, on being told that some other players were offended by their speech, suggested that gagging was the solution: "If they don't want to hear me, let them gag me; I won't be offended." Also, I am given to understand that gagging is much more commonly employed on some other MUDs.

The course of a MUD conversation is remarkably like and unlike one in the real world. Participants in MUD conversations commonly use the emote command to make gestures, such as nodding to urge someone to continue, waving at player arrivals and departures, raising eyebrows, hugging to apologize or soothe, etc. As in electronic mail (though much more frequently), players employ standard "smiley-face" glyphs (e.g., ":-)," ":-(," and ":-|") to clarify the "tone" with which they say things. Utterances are also frequently addressed to specific participants, as opposed to the room as a whole (e.g., "Munchkin nods to Frebble. 'You tell 'em!'").

The most obvious difference between MUD conversations and those in real life is that the utterances must be typed rather than simply spoken.

This introduces significant delays into the interaction and, like nature, MUD society abhors a vacuum.

Even when there are only two participants in a MUD conversation, it is very rare for there to be only one thread of discussion; during the pause while one player is typing a response, the other player commonly thinks of something else to say and does so, introducing at least another level to the conversation, if not a completely new topic. These multi-topic conversations are a bit disorienting and bewildering to the uninitiated, but it appears that most players quickly become accustomed to them and handle the multiple levels smoothly. Of course, when more than two players are involved, the opportunities for multiple levels are only increased. It has been pointed out that a suitable punishment for truly heinous social offenders might be to strand them in a room with more than a dozen players actively conversing.

This kind of cognitive time-sharing also arises due to the existence of the page command. Recall from the introduction that this command allows a player to send a message to another who is not in the same room. It is not uncommon (especially for wizards, whose advice is frequently sought by "distant" players) to be involved in one conversation "face-to-face" and one or two more conducted via page. Again, while this can be overwhelming at first, one can actually come to appreciate the relief from the tedious long pauses waiting for a fellow conversant to type.

Another effect of the typing delay (and of the low bandwidth of the MUD medium) is a tendency for players to abbreviate their communications, sometimes past the point of ambiguity. For example, some players often greet others with "hugs," but the "meanings" of those hugs vary widely from recipient to recipient. In one case the hug might be a simple friendly greeting, in another it might be intended to convey a very special affection. In both cases, the text typed by the hugger is the same (e.g., "Munchkin hugs Frebble."); it is considered too much trouble for the hugger to type a description of the act sufficient to distinguish the "kind" of hug intended. This leads to some MUD interactions having much more ambiguity than is usually encountered in real life, a fact that some mudders consider useful.

The somewhat disjointed nature of MUD conversations, brought on by the typing pauses, tends to rob them of much of the coherence that makes real-life conversants resent interruptions. The addition of a new conversant to a MUD conversation is much less disruptive; the "flow" being disrupted was never very strong to begin with. Some players go so far as to say the interruptions are simply impossible on MUDs; I think that this is a minority impression, however. Interruptions do exist on MUDs; they are simply less significant than in real life.

Other Small-Group Interaction   I would not like to give the impression that conversation is the only social activity on MUDs. Indeed, MUD society appears to have most of the same social activities as real life, albeit often in a modified form.

As mentioned before, PernMUSH holds large-scale, organized social gatherings such as "hatchings," and they are not alone. Most MUDs have at one time or another organized more or less elaborate parties, often to celebrate notable events in the MUD itself, such as an anniversary of its founding. We have so far had only one or two such parties on LambdaMOO, to celebrate the "opening" of some new area built by a player; if there were any other major parties, I certainly wasn't invited!

One of the more impressive examples of MUD social activity is the virtual wedding. There have been many of these on many different MUDs; we are in the process of planning our first on LambdaMOO, with me officiating in my role as archwizard.

I have never been present at such a ceremony, but I have read logs of the conversations at them. As I do not know any of the participants in the ceremonies I've read about, I cannot say much for certain about their emotional content. As in real life, they are usually very happy and celebratory occasions with an intriguing undercurrent of serious feelings. I do not know and cannot even speculate about whether or not the main participants in such ceremonies are usually serious or not, whether or not the MUD ceremony usually (or even ever) mirrors another ceremony in the real world, or even whether or not the bride and groom have ever met outside of virtual reality.

In the specific case of the upcoming LambdaMOO wedding, the participants first met on LambdaMOO, became quite friendly, and eventually decided to meet in real life. They have subsequently become romantically involved in the real world and are using the MUD wedding as a celebration of that fact. This phenomenon of couples meeting in virtual reality and then pursuing a real-life relationship, is not uncommon; in one notable case, they did this even though one of them lived in Australia and the other in Pittsburgh!

It is interesting to note that the virtual reality wedding is not specific to the kinds of MUDs I've been discussing; Van Gelder (1991) mentions an on-line reception on CompuServe, and weddings are quite common on Habitat, a half-graphical, half-textual virtual reality popular in Japan.

The very idea, however, brings up interesting and potentially important questions about the legal standing of commitments made only in virtual reality. Suppose, for example, that two people make a contract in virtual reality. Is the contract binding? Under which state's (or country's) laws? Is it a written or verbal contract? What constitutes proof of signature in such a context? I suspect that our real-world society will have to face and resolve these issues in the not-too-distant future.

Those who frequent MUDs tend also to be interested in games and puzzles, so it is no surprise that mally real-world examples have been implemented inside MUDs. What may be surprising, however, is the extent to which this is so.

On LambdaMOO alone, we have machine-mediated Scrabble, Monopoly, Mastermind, Backgammon, Ghost, Chess, Go, and Reversi boards. These attract small groups of players on occasion, with the Go players being the most committed; in fact, there are a number of Go players who come to LambdaMOO only for that purpose. I say more about these more specialized uses of social virtual realities later on. In many ways, though, such games so far have little, if anything, to offer over their real-world counterparts, except perhaps a better chance of finding an opponent.

Perhaps more interesting are the other kinds of games imported into MUDs from real life, the ones that might be far less feasible in a non-virtual reality. A player on LambdaMOO, for example, implemented a facility for holding food fights. Players throw food items at each other, attempt to duck oncoming items, and, if unsuccessful, are "splattered" with messes that cannot easily be removed. After a short interval, a semi-animate "Mr. Clean" arrives and one-by-one removes the messes from the participants, turning them back into the food items from which they came, ready for the next fight. Although the game was rather simple to implement, it has remained enormously popular nearly a year later.

Another player on LambdaMOO created a trainable Frisbee, which any player could teach to do tricks when they threw or caught it. Players who used the Frisbee seemed to take great pleasure in trying to out-do each other's trick descriptions. My catching description, for example, reads "Haakon stops the frisbee dead in the air in front of himself and then daintily plucks it, like a flower." I have also heard of MUD versions of paint-ball combat and fantastical games of Capture the Flag.

Observations about the MUD Community as a Whole

MUD communities tend to be very large in comparison to the number of players actually active at any given time. On LambdaMOO, for example, we have between seven hundred and eight hundred players connecting in any week but rarely more than forty simultaneously. A good real-world analog might be a bar with a large number of "regulars," all of whom are transients without fixed schedules.

The continuity of MUD society is thus somewhat tenuous; many pairs of active players exist who have never met each other. In spite of this, MUDs do become true communities after a time. The participants slowly come to consensus about a common (private) language, about appropriate standards of behavior, and about the social roles of various public areas (e.g., where big discussions usually happen, where certain "crowds" can be found, etc.).

Some people appear to thrive on the constant turnover of MUD players throughout a day, enjoying the novelty of always having someone new to talk to. In some cases, this enjoyment goes so far as to become a serious kind of addiction, with some players spending as much as thirty-five hours out of forty-eight constantly connected and conversing on MUDs. I know of many players who have taken more-or-less drastic steps to curtail their participation on MUDs, feeling that their habits had gotten significantly out of control.

One college-student player related to me his own particularly dramatic case of MUD addiction. It seems that he was supposed to go home for the Christmas holidays but missed the train by no less than five hours because he had been unable to tear himself away from his MUD conversations. After calling his parents to relieve their worrying by lying about the cause of his delay, he eventually boarded a train for home. However, on arrival there at 12:30 A.M. the next morning, he did not go directly to his parents' house but instead went to an open terminal room in the local university, where he spent another two and a half hours connected before finally going home. His parents, meanwhile, had called the police in fear for their son's safety in traveling.

It should not be supposed that this kind of problem is an example of the now commonly understood phenomenon of "computer addiction"; the fact that there is a computer involved here is more-or-less irrelevant. These people are not addicted to computers, but to communication; the global scope of Internet MUDs implies not only a great variety in potential conversants, but also twenty-four-hour access.

While it is at the more macroscopic scale of whole MUD communities that I feel least qualified to make reliable observations, I do have one striking example of societal consensus having concrete results on LambdaMOO.

From time to time, we wizards are asked to arbitrate in disputes among players concerning what is or is not appropriate behavior. My approach generally has been to ask a number of other players for their opinions and to present the defendant in the complaint with a précis of the plaintiff's grievance, always looking for the common threads in their responses. After many such episodes, I was approached by a number of players asking that a written statement on LambdaMOO "manners" be prepared and made available to the community. I wrote up a list of those rules that seemed implied by the set of arbitrations we had performed and published them for public comment. Very little comment has ever been received, but the groups of players I've asked generally agree that the rules reflect their own understandings of the common will. For the curious, I have included our list of rules below. The actual "help manners" document goes into a bit more detail about each of these points.

• Be polite. Avoid being rude. The MOO is worth participating in because it is a pleasant place for people to be. When people are rude or nasty to one another, it stops being so pleasant.

• "Revenge is ours," sayeth the wizards. If someone is nasty to you, please either ignore it or tell a wizard about it. Please don't try to take revenge on the person; this just escalates the level of rudeness and makes the MOO a less pleasant place for everyone involved.

• Respect other players' sensibilities. The participants on the MOO come from a wide range of cultures and backgrounds. Your ideas about what constitutes offensive speech or descriptions are likely to differ from those of other players. Please keep the text that players can casually run across as free of potentially offensive material as you can.

• Don't spoof. Spoofing is loosely defined as "causing misleading output to be printed to other players." For example, it would be spoofing for anyone but Munchkin to print out a message like "Munchkin sticks out his tongue at Potrzebie." This makes it look like Munchkin is unhappy with Potrzebie even though that may not be the case at all.

• Don't shout. It is easy to write a MOO command that prints a message to every connected player. Please don't.

• Only teleport your own things. By default, most objects (including other players) allow themselves to be moved freely from place to place. This fact makes it easier to build certain useful objects. Unfortunately, it also makes it easy to annoy people by moving them or their objects around without their permission. Please don't.

• Don't teleport silently or obscurely. It is easy to write MOO commands that move you instantly from place to place. Please remember in such programs to print a clear, understandable message to all players in both the place you're leaving and the place you're going to.

• Don't hog the server. The server is carefully shared among all of the connected players so that everyone gets a chance to execute their commands. This sharing is, by necessity, somewhat approximate. Please don't abuse it with tasks that run for a long time without pausing.

• Don't waste object numbers. Some people, in a quest to own objects with "interesting" numbers (e.g., #17000, #18181, etc.), have written MOO programs that loop forever, creating and recycling objects until the "good" numbers come up. Please don't do this.

It should be noted that different MUDs are truly different communities and have different societal agreements concerning appropriate behavior. There even exist a few MUDs where the only rule in the social contract is that there is no social contract. Such "anarchy" MUDs have appeared a few times in my experience and seem to be quite popular for a time before eventually fading away.

The Prospects for Mudding in the Future

The clumsy system of public gatherings had been long since abandoned; neither Vashti nor her audience stirred from their rooms. Seated in her arm-chair, she spoke, while they in their arm-chairs heard her, fairly well, and saw her, fairly well.
E. M. Forster, "The Machine Stops"

A recent listing of Internet-accessible MUDs showed almost two hundred active around the world, mostly in the United States and Scandinavia. A conservative guess that these MUDs average a hundred active players each gives a total of twenty thousand active mudders in the world today; this is almost certainly a significant undercount already, and the numbers appear to be growing as more and more people gain Internet access.

In addition, at least one MUD-like area exists on the commercial CompuServe network in the United States, and there are several more commercial MUDs active in the United Kingdom. Finally, there is Habitat, a half-graphical, half textual virtual reality in Japan, with well over ten thousand users.

I believe that text-based virtual realities and wide-area interactive "chat" facilities are becoming more and more common and will continue to do so for the foreseeable future. Like CB radios and telephone party lines before them, MUDs seem to provide a necessary social outlet.

The MUD model is also being extended in new ways for new audiences. For example, I am currently involved in adapting the Lambda-MOO server for use as an international teleconferencing and image database system for astronomers. Our plans include allowing scientists to give on-line presentations to their colleagues around the world, complete with "slides" and illustrations automatically displayed on the participants' workstations. The same approach could be used to create on-line meeting places for workers in other disciplines, as well as for other non-scientific communities. I do not believe that we are the only researchers planning such facilities. In the near future (a few years at most), I expect such specialized virtual realities to be commonplace, an accepted part of at least the academic community.

On another front, I am engaged with some colleagues in the design of a MUD for general use here at Xerox PARC. The idea here is to use virtual reality to help break down the geographical barriers of a large building, of people increasingly working from their homes, and of having a sister research laboratory in Cambridge, England. In this context, we intend to investigate the addition of digital voice to MUDs, with the conventions of the virtual reality providing a simple and intuitive style of connection management: if two people are in the same virtual room, then their audio channels are connected. Some virtual rooms may even overlap real-world rooms, such as those in which talks or other meetings are held.

Of course, one can expect a number of important differences in the social phenomena on MUDs in a professional setting. In particular, I would guess that anonymity might well be frowned upon in such places, though it may have some interesting special uses, for example in the area of refereeing papers.

Some of my colleagues have suggested that the term "text-based virtual reality" is an oxymoron, that "virtual reality" refers only to the fancy graphical and motion-sensing environments being worked on in many places. They go on to predict that these more physically involving systems will supplant the text-based variety as soon as the special equipment becomes a bit more widely and cheaply available. I do not believe that this is the case.

While I agree that the fancier systems are likely to become very popular for certain applications and among those who can afford them, I believe that MUDs have certain enduring advantages that will save them from obsolescence.

The equipment necessary to participate fully in a MUD is significantly cheaper, more widely available, and more generally useful than that for the fancy systems; this is likely to remain the case for a long time to come. For example, it is already possible to purchase palm-sized portable computers with network connectivity and text displays, making it possible to use MUDs even while riding the bus, etc. Is similarly flexible hardware for fancy virtual realities even on the horizon?

It is substantially easier for players to give themselves vivid, detailed, and interesting descriptions (and to do the same for the descriptions and behavior of the new objects they create) in a text-based system than in a graphics-based one. In McLuhan's terminology, this is because MUDs are a "cold" medium, while more graphically based media are "hot";

that is, the sensorial parsimony of plain text tends to entice users into engaging their imaginations to fill in missing details, while, comparatively speaking, the richness of stimuli in fancy virtual realities has an opposite tendency, pushing users' imaginations into a more passive role. I also find it difficult to believe that a graphics-based system will be able to compete with text for average users on the metric of believable detail per unit of effort expended; this is certainly the case now, and I see little reason to believe it will change in the near future.

Finally, one of the great strengths of MUDs lies in the user's ability to customize them, to extend them, and to specialize them to the user's particular needs. The ease with which this can be done in MUDs is directly related to the fact that they are purely text-based; in a graphics-based system, the overhead of creating new moderate-quality graphics would put the task beyond the inclinations of the average user. Whereas, with MUDs, it is easy to imagine an almost arbitrarily small community investing in the creation of a virtual reality that was truly customized for that community, it seems very unlikely that any but the largest communities would invest the greatly increased effort required for a fancier system.

Conclusions

Vashti was seized with the terrors of direct experience. She shrank back into her room, and the wall closed up again.
E. M. Forster, "The Machine Stops"

The emergence of MUDs has created a new kind of social sphere, both like and radically unlike the environments that have existed before. As they become more and more popular and more widely accessible, it appears likely that an increasingly significant proportion of the population will at least become familiar with mudding and perhaps become frequent participants in text-based virtual realities.

It thus behooves us to begin to try to understand these new societies, to make sense of these electronic places where we'll be spending increasing amounts of our time, both doing business and seeking pleasure. I would hope that social scientists will be at least intrigued by my amateur observations and perhaps inspired to more properly study MUDs and their players. In particular, as MUDs become more widespread, ever more people are likely to be susceptible to the kind of addiction I discuss in an earlier section; we must, as a society, begin to wrestle with the social and ethical issues brought out by such cases.

Those readers interested in trying out MUDs for themselves are encouraged to do so. The Usenet news group

rec.games.mud

periodically carries comprehensive lists of publicly available, Internet-accessible MUDs, including their detailed network addresses. My own MUD, LambdaMOO, can be reached via the standard Internet telnet protocol at the host

lambda.parc.xerox.com

(the numeric address is 13.2.116.36), port 8888. On a UNIX machine, for example, the command

telnet lambda.parc.xerox.com8888

will suffice to make a connection. Once connected, feel free to page me; I connect under the names "Haakon" and "Lambda."

Notes

1. In fact, these two commands are so frequently used that single-character abbreviations are provided for them. The two example commands would usually be typed as follows:

```
"Can anyone hear me?
:smiles.
```

2. The "MOO" in "LambdaMOO" stands for "MUD, Object-Oriented." The origin of the "Lambda" part is more obscure, based on my years of experience with the Lisp programming language.

Reflections

In his popular science-fiction novel SnowCrash, *Neal Stephenson describes a virtual reality called the Metaverse that does not rely on texts slowly crawling across a computer screen. To reach the Metaverse you*

*put on computer glasses and enter a virtual world furnished with build-
ings, other people, and things to do. Buildings in the Metaverse are
strung out along a commercial strip called the Street.*

> It is the Broadway, the Champs Élyseés of the Metaverse. It is the brilliantly lit
> boulevard.... The dimensions of the Street are fixed by a protocol, hammered
> out by the computer-graphics ninja overlords of the Association for Computing
> Machinery's Global Multimedia Protocol Group....
>   Like any place in Reality, the Street is subject to development. Developers can
> build their own small streets feeding off of the main one. They can build build-
> ings, parks, signs, as well as things that do not exist in Reality....
>   Put a sign or a building on the Street and the hundred million richest, hippest,
> best-connected people on earth will see it every day of their lives.

*So what do you do in the Metaverse? You go there to just hang out. Or
you do business. The Metaverse is a fictional social place. LambdaMOO
is one of today's virtual gathering places. It is accessible by very basic
computer technologies that are available to enough people to form social
groupings. In San Franciso, people without a workstation can log on at
the Internet terminals in the Exploratorium museum for kids and at
nightspots for their older siblings. In France, on-line computer conferences using the Minitel system have been in wide public use for many
years.*

*Many observers of computers have noticed that the language of magic
and myth has found its way into computing. Science fiction novels about
virtual reality—such as* True Names *by Vernor Vinge and the Necro-
mancer novels of William Gibson—are steeped in the language of magic
and voodoo. This language also permeates fantasy and role-playing
games on computers, in which players carry out missions in imaginary
worlds and wield magical powers and spells. But even outside computer
games, people in an organization who are most skilled in the ways of
computers are often referred to as "wizards"; and arcane knowledge
about computing is called "lore." Like a magical incantation, the very
act of getting a computer to do something involves using mysterious
commands and carrying out prescribed rituals.*

*This language of magic is especially prevalent in mudding. Curtis is
himself, in effect, a grand wizard of LambdaMOO. Many of the players
in LambdaMOO and other muds give themselves magical names and
descriptions. One reaction to this practice is to dismiss mudding as just*

*another form of escapism that has no special significance. Another inter-
pretation, however, suggests that mudding can give people a chance to
explore parts of their psyche less accessible in their daily lives. Digital
worlds can also provide an opportunity for a society to access archetypes
from earlier stages of culture, such as the trickster of hunter-gatherer
societies.*

*As Curtis's article demonstrates, many people are already experiencing
virtual reality on the Internet. It suggests a concept of what we can do
with a national information infrastructure that is very different from the
electronic mail, digital libraries, and marketplace metaphors. Yet the
idea of digital worlds is not at all incompatible with those communication, information, and commerce functions. What a digital world brings
is the possibility of having other people as real-time collaborators in our
activities. This feature changes our computer work from a solitary to a
collaborative effort, adding to both to its social appeal and, often, its
effectiveness. Because we enjoy each other's company, we generally learn
best from each other. In the following articles, we pursue the possibilities
for collaboration already being explored in digital worlds.*

A Rape in Cyberspace: How an Evil Clown, a Haitian Trickster Spirit, Two Wizards, and a Cast of Dozens Turned a Database into a Society

Julian Dibbell

Connections

Pavel Curtis's view of the social phenomena in mudding is necessarily shaped by his role as the designer of LambdaMOO. His creative and his unique position as its head wizard give him a certain separation from the place itself. For Curtis, there is the MUD and there is real life (RL). He built the Moo, but he lives in RL. He easily keeps them separate.

Dibbell's article provides a much more immersed view of an event in the history of LambdaMoo that changed it forever. The voice shifts from that of a creator to that of a tourist and observer. Dibbell is reporting on his time in an exotic and strange foreign land, where he is at first confused by events going on around him. He shares with us his growing understanding, drawing us slowly into events we might not otherwise believe. He writes with the fervor of one who has seen them for himself.

This shift in voice gives us a sense of being there and thereby understanding more intimately how social rules arise in a digital reality. A MUD is environment in which what it means to be an embodied person is changed. For those who enter a MUD, society changes as well.

They say he raped them that night. They say he did it with a cunning little doll, fashioned in their image and imbued with the power to make them do whatever he desired. They say that by manipulating the doll he forced them to have sex with him, and with each other, and to do horrible, brutal things to their own bodies. And though I wasn't there that night, I think I can assure you that what they say is true, because it all happened right in the living room—right there amid the well-stocked bookcases and the sofas and the fireplace—of a house I've come to think of as my second home.

Call me Dr. Bombay. Some months ago—let's say about halfway between the first time you heard the words *information superhighway* and the first time you wished you never had—I found myself tripping with compulsive regularity down the well-traveled information lane that leads to LambdaMOO, a very large and very busy rustic chateau built entirely of words. Nightly, I typed the commands that called those words onto my computer screen, dropping me with what seemed a warm electric thud inside the mansion's darkened coat closet, where I checked my quotidian identity, stepped into the persona and appearance of a minor character from a long-gone television sitcom, and stepped out into the glaring chatter of the crowded living room. Sometimes, when the mood struck me, I emerged as a dolphin instead.

I won't say why I chose to masquerade as Samantha Stevens's outlandish cousin, or as the dolphin, or what exactly led to my mild but so-far incurable addiction to the semifictional digital otherworlds known around the Internet as multi-user dimensions, or MUDs. This isn't my story, after all. It's the story of a man named Mr. Bungle, and of the ghostly sexual violence he committed in the halls of LambdaMOO, and most importantly of the ways his violence and his victims challenged the one thousand and more residents of that surreal, magic-infested mansion to become, finally, the community so many of them already believed they were.

That I was myself one of those residents has little direct bearing on the story's events. I mention it only as a warning that my own perspective is perhaps too steeped in the surreality and magic of the place to serve as an entirely appropriate guide. For the Bungle Affair raises questions that—here on the brink of a future in which human life may find itself as tightly enveloped in digital environments as it is today in the architectural kind—demand a clear-eyed, sober, and unmystified consideration. It asks us to shut our ears momentarily to the techno-utopian ecstasies of West Coast cyberhippies and look without illusion upon the present possibilities for building, in the on-line spaces of this world, societies more decent and free than those mapped onto dirt and concrete and capital. It asks us to behold the new bodies awaiting us in virtual space undazzled by their phantom powers, and to get to the crucial work of sorting out the socially meaningful differences between those bodies and our physical ones. And most forthrightly it asks us to wrap our late-modern ontologies, epistemologies, sexual ethics, and common sense around the curious notion of rape by voodoo doll—and to try not to warp them beyond recognition in the process.

In short, the Bungle Affair dares me to explain it to you without resort to dimestore mysticisms, and I fear I may have shape-shifted by the digital moonlight one too many times to be quite up to the task. But I will do what I can, and can do no better I suppose than to lead with the facts. For if nothing else about Mr. Bungle's case is unambiguous, the facts at least are crystal clear.

The facts begin (as they often do) with a time and a place. The time was a Monday night in March, and the place, as I've said, was the living room—which, due to the inviting warmth of its decor, is so invariably packed with chitchatters as to be roughly synonymous among Lambda-MOOers with a party. So strong, indeed, is the sense of convivial common ground invested in the living room that a cruel mind could hardly imagine a better place in which to stage a violation of LambdaMOO's communal spirit. And there was cruelty enough lurking in the appearance Mr. Bungle presented to the virtual world—he was at the time a fat, oleaginous, Bisquick-faced clown dressed in cum-stained harlequin garb and girdled with a mistletoe-and-hemlock belt whose buckle bore the quaint inscription "KISS ME UNDER THIS, BITCH!" But whether cruelty motivated his choice of crime scene is not among the established facts of the case. It is a fact only that he did choose the living room.

The remaining facts tell us a bit more about the inner world of Mr. Bungle, though only perhaps that it couldn't have been a very comfortable place. They tell us that he commenced his assault entirely unprovoked, at or about 10 P.M. Pacific Standard Time. That he began by using his voodoo doll to force one of the room's occupants to sexually service him in a variety of more or less conventional ways. That this victim was Legba, a Haitian trickster spirit of indeterminate gender, brown-skinned and wearing an expensive pearl gray suit, top hat, and dark glasses. That Legba heaped vicious imprecations on himall the while and that he was soon ejected bodily from the room. That he hid himself away then in his private chambers somewhere on the mansion grounds and continued the attacks without interruption, since the voodoo doll worked just as well at a distance as in proximity. That he turned his attentions now to Starsinger, a rather pointedly nondescript female character, tall, stout, and brown-haired, forcing her into unwanted liaisons with other individuals present in the room. among them Legba, Bakunin (the well-known radical) and Juniper (the squirrel). That his actions grew progressively violent. That he made Legba eat his/her own pubic hair. That he caused Starsinger to violate herself with a piece of kitchen cutlery. That his distant laughter echoed evilly in the living room with every successive outrage. That he could not be stopped until at last someone summoned Zippy, a wise and trusted old-timer who brought with him a gun of near wizardly powers, a gun that didn't kill but enveloped its targets in a cage impermeable even to a voodoo doll's powers. That Zippy fired this gun at Mr. Bungle, thwarting the doll at last and silencing the evil, distant laughter.

These particulars, as I said, are unambiguous. But they are far from simple, for the simple reason that every set of facts in virtual reality (or VR, as the locals abbreviate it) is shadowed by a second, complicating set: the "real-life" facts. And while a certain tension invariably buzzes in the gap between the hard, prosaic RL facts and their more fluid, dreamy VR counterparts, the dissonance in the Bungle case is striking. No hideous clowns or trickster spirits appear in the RL version of the incident, no voodoo dolls or wizard guns, indeed no rape at all as any RL court of law has yet defined it. The actors in the drama were university students for the most part, and they sat rather undramatically before computer screens the entire time, their only actions a spidery flitting of fingers across standard QWERTY keyboards. No bodies touched. Whatever physical interaction occurred consisted of a mingling of electronic signals sent from sites spread out between New York City and Sydney, Australia. Those signals met in LambdaMOO, certainly, just as the hideous clown and the living room party did, but what was LambdaMOO after all? Not an enchanted mansion or anything of the sort—just a middlingly complex database, maintained for experimental purposes inside a Xerox Corporation research computer in Palo Alto and open to public access via the Internet.

To be more precise about it, LambdaMOO was a MUD. Or to be yet more precise, it was a subspecies of MUD known as a MOO, which is short for "MUD, Object-Oriented." All of which means that it was a kind of database especially designed to give users the vivid impression of moving through a physical space that in reality exists only as descriptive data filed away on a hard drive. When users dial into LambdaMOO, for instance, the program immediately presents them with a brief textual description of one of the rooms of the database's fictional mansion (the coat closet, say). If the user wants to leave this room, she can enter a command to move in a particular direction and the database will replace the original description with a new one corresponding to the room located in the direction she chose. When the new description scrolls across the user's screen it lists not only the fixed features of the room but all its contents at that moment—including things (tools, toys, weapons) and other users (each represented as a "character" over which he or she has sole control).

As far as the database program is concerned, all of these entities—rooms, things, characters—are just different subprograms that the program allows to interact according to rules very roughly mimicking the laws of the physical world. Characters may not leave a room in a given direction, for instance, unless the room subprogram contains an "exit" at that compass point. And if a character "says" or "does" something (as directed by its user-owner), then only the users whose characters are also located in that room will see the output describing the statement or action. Aside from such basic constraints, however, LambdaMOOers are allowed a broad freedom to create—they can describe their characters any way they like, they can make rooms of their own and decorate them to taste, and they can build new objects almost at will. The combination of all this busy user activity with the hard physics of the database can certainly induce a lucid illusion of presence—but when all is said and done the only thing you *really* see when you visit LambdaMOO is a kind of slow-crawling script, lines of dialogue and stage direction creeping steadily up your computer screen.

Which is all just to say that, to the extent that Mr. Bungle's assault happened in real life at all, it happened as a sort ol Punch-and-Judy show, in which the puppets and the scenery were made of nothing more

substantial than digital code and snippets of creative writing. The pup-
peteer behind Bungle, as it happened, was a young man logging in to the
MOO from a New York University computer. He could have been Al
Gore for all any of the others knew, however, and he could have written
Bungle's script that night any way he chose. He could have sent a command to print the message "Mr. Bungle, smiling a saintly smile, floats
angelic near the ceiling of the living room, showering joy and candy
kisses down upon the heads of all below"—and everyone then receiving
output from the database's subprogram #17 (aka the "living room")
would have seen that sentence on their screens.

Instead, he entered sadistic fantasies into the "voodoo doll," a subprogram that served the not-exactly kosher purpose of attributing
actions to other characters that their users did not actually write. And
thus a woman in Haverford, Pennsylvania, whose account on the 'MOO
attached her to a character she called Starsinger, was given the unasked-
for opportunity to read the words "As if against her will, Starsinger jabs
a steak knife up her ass, causing immense joy. You hear Mr. Bungle
laughing evilly in the distance." And thus the woman in Seattle who had
written herself the character called Legba, with a view perhaps to tasting
in imagination a deity's freedom from the burdens of the gendered flesh,
got to read similarly constructed sentences in which Legba, messenger of
the gods, lord of crossroads and communications, suffered a brand of
degradation all-too-customarily reserved for the embodied female.

"Mostly voodoo dolls are amusing," wrote Legba on the evening after
Bungle's rampage, posting a public statement to the widely read in-MOO
mailing list called *social-issues, a forum for debate on matters of import
to the entire populace. "And mostly I tend to think that restrictive measures around here cause more trouble than they prevent. But I also think
that Mr. Bungle was being a vicious, vile fuckhead, and I ... want his
sorry ass scattered from #17 to the Cinder Pile. I'm not calling for policies, trials, or better jails. I'm not sure what I'm calling for. Virtual cas-
tration, if I could manage it. Mostly [this type of thing] doesn't happen
here. Mostly, perhaps I thought it wouldn't happen to me. Mostly, I trust
people to conduct themselves with some veneer of civility. Mostly, I want
his ass."

Months later, the woman in Seattle would confide to me that as she wrote those words post-traumatic tears were streaming down her face—a real-life fact that should suffice to prove that the words' emotional content was no mere playacting. The precise tenor of that content, however, its mingling of murderous rage and eyeball-rolling annoyance, was a curious amalgam that neither the RL nor the VR facts alone can quite account for. Where virtual reality and its conventions would have us believe that Legba and Starsinger were brutally raped in their own living room, here was the victim Legba scolding Mr. Bungle for a breach of "civility." Where real life, on the other hand, insists the incident was only an episode in a free-form version of Dungeons and Dragons, confined to the realm of the symbolic and at no point threatening any player's life, limb, or material well-being, here now was the player Legba issuing aggrieved and heartfelt calls for Mr. Bungle's dismemberment. Ludicrously excessive by RL's lights, woefully understated by VR's, the tone of Legba's response made sense only in the buzzing, dissonant gap between them.

Which is to say it made the only kind of sense that can be made of MUDly phenomena. For while the *facts* attached to any event born of a MUD's strange, ethereal universe may march in straight, tandem lines separated neatly into the virtual and the real, its meaning lies always in that gap. You learn this axiom early in your life as a player, and it's of no small relevance to the Bungle case that you usually learn it between the sheets, so to speak. Netsex, tinysex, virtual sex-however you name it, in real-life reality it's nothing more than a 900-line encounter stripped of even the vestigial physicality of the voice. And yet as any but the most inhibited of newbies can tell you, it's possibly the headiest experience the very heady world of MUDs has to offer. Amid flurries of even the most cursorily described caresses, sighs, and penetrations, the glands do engage, and often as throbbingly as they would in a real-life assignation—sometimes even more so, given the combined power of anonymity and textual suggestiveness to unshackle deep-seated fantasies. And if the virtual setting and the interplayer vibe are right, who knows? The heart may engage as well, stirring up passions as strong as many that bind lovers who observe the formality of trysting in the flesh.

To participate, therefore, in this disembodied enactment of life's most body-centered activity is to risk the realization that when it comes to sex, perhaps the body in question is not the physical one at all, but its psychic double, the bodylike self-representation we carry around in our heads. I know, I know, you've read Foucault and your mind is not quite blown by the notion that sex is never so much an exchange of fluids as as it is an exchange of signs. But trust your friend Dr. Bombay, it's one thing to grasp the notion intellectually and quite another to feel it coursing through your veins amid the virtual steam of hot netnookie. And it's a whole other mind-blowing trip altogether to encounter it thus as a college frosh, new to the net and still in the grip of hormonal hurricanes and high-school sexual mythologies. The shock can easily reverberate throughout an entire young worldview. Small wonder, then, that a newbie's first taste of MUD sex is often also the first time she or he surrenders wholly to the slippery terms of MUDish ontology, recognizing in a full-bodied way that what happens inside a MUD-made world is neither exactly real nor exactly make-believe, but profoundly, compellingly, and emotionally meaningful.

And small wonder indeed that the sexual nature of Mr. Bungle's crime provoked such powerful feelings, and not just in Legba (who, be it noted, was in real life a theory-savvy doctoral candidate and a longtime MOOer, but just as baffled and overwhelmed by the force of her own reaction, she later would attest, as any panting undergrad might have been). Even players who had never experienced MUD rape (the vast majority of male-presenting characters, but not as large a majority of the female-presenting as might be hoped) immediately appreciated its gravity and were moved to condemnation of the perp. Legba's missive to *social-issues* followed a strongly worded one from Zippy ("Well, well," it began, "no matter what else happens on Lambda, I can always be sure that some jerk is going to reinforce my low opinion of humanity") and was itself followed by others from Moriah, Raccoon, Crawfish, and evangeline. Starsinger also let her feelings ("pissed") be known. And even Jander, the Clueless Samaritan who had responded to Bungle's cries for help and uncaged him shortly after the incident, expressed his regret once apprised of Bungle's deeds, which he allowed to be "despicable."

A sense was brewing that something needed to be done—done soon and in something like an organized fashion—about Mr. Bungle, in particular, and about MUD rape, in general. Regarding the general problem, evangeline, who identified herself as a survivor of both virtual rape ("many times over") and real-life sexual assault, floated a cautious proposal for a MOO-wide powwow on the subject of virtual sex offenses and what mechanisms if any might be put in place to deal with their future occurrence. As for the specific problem, the answer no doubt seemed obvious to many. But it wasn't until the evening of the second day after the incident that Legba, finally and rather solemnly, gave it voice:

"I am requesting that Mr. Bungle be toaded for raping Starsinger and I. I have never done this before, and have thought about it for days. He hurt us both."

That was all. Three simple sentences posted to *social. Reading them, an outsider might never guess that they were an application for a death warrant. Even an outsider familiar with other MUDs might not guess it, since in many of them "toading" still refers to a command that, true to the gameworlds' sword-and-sorcery origins, simply turns a player into a toad, wiping the player's description and attributes and replacing them with those of the slimy amphibian. Bad luck for sure, but not quite as bad as what happens when the same command is invoked in the MOO-ish strains of MUD: not only are the description and attributes of the toaded player erased, but the account itself goes too. The annihilation of the character, thus, is total.

And nothing less than total annihilation, it seemed, would do to settle LambdaMOO's accounts with Mr. Bungle. Within minutes of the posting of Legba's appeal, SamIAm, the Australian Deleuzean, who had witnessed much of the attack from the back room of his suburban Sydney home, seconded the motion with a brief message crisply entitled "Toad the fukr." SamIAm's posting was seconded almost as quickly by that of Bakunin, covictim of Mr. Bungle and well-known radical, who in real life happened also to be married to the real-life Legba. And over the course of the next twenty hours as many as fifty players made it known, on *social and in a variety of other forms and forums, that they would be pleased to see Mr. Bungle erased from the face of the MOO. And with dissent so far confined to a dozen or so antitoading hardliners, the numbers suggested that the citizenry was indeed moving towards a resolve to have Bungle's virtual head.

There was one small but stubborn obstacle in the way of this resolve, however, and that was a curious state of social affairs known in some quarters of the MOO as the New Direction. It was all very fine, you see, for the LambdaMOO rabble to get it in their heads to liquidate one of their peers, but when the time came to actually do the deed it would require the services of a nobler class of character. It would require a wizard. Master-programmers of the MOO, spelunkers of the database's deepest code-structures and custodians of its day-to-day administrative trivia, wizards are also the only players empowered to issue the toad command, a feature maintained on nearly all MUDs as a quick-and-dirty means of social control. But the wizards of LambdaMOO, after years of adjudicating all manner of interplayer disputes with little to show for it but their own weariness and the smoldering resentment of the general populace, had decided they'd had enough of the social sphere. And so, four months before the Bungle incident, the archwizard Haakon (known in RL as Pavel Curtis, Xerox researcher and LambdaMOO's principal architect) formalized this decision in a document called "LambdaMOO Takes a New Direction," which he placed in the living room for all to see. In it, Haakon announced that the wizards from that day forth were pure technicians. From then on, they would make no decisions affecting the social life of the MOO, but only implement whatever decisions the community as a whole directed them to. From then on, it was decreed, LambdaMOO would just have to grow up and solve its problems on its own.

Faced with the task of inventing its own self-governance from scratch, the LambdaMOO population had so far done what any other loose, amorphous agglomeration of individuals would have done: they'd let it slide. But now the task took on new urgency. Since getting the wizards to toad Mr. Bungle (or to toad the likes of him in the future) required a convincing case that the cry for his head came from the community at large, then the community itself would have to be defined; and if the community was to be convincingly defined, then some form of social organization, no matter how rudimentary, would have to be settled on.

And thus, as if against its will, the question of what to do about Mr. Bungle began to shape itself into a sort of referendum on the political future of the MOO. Arguments broke out on *social and elsewhere that had only superficially to do with Bungle (since everyone agreed he was a cad) and everything to do with where the participants stood on LambdaMOO's crazy-quilty political map. Parliamentarian legalist types argued that unfortunately Bungle could not legitimately be toaded at all, since there were no explicit MOO rules against rape, or against just about anything else—and the sooner such rules were established, they added, and maybe even a full-blown judiciary system complete with elected officials and prisons to enforce those rules, the better. Others, with a royalist streak in them, seemed to feel that Bungle's as-yet-unpunished outrage only proved this New Direction silliness had gone on long enough, and that it was high time the wizardocracy returned to the position of swift and decisive leadership their player class was born to.

And then there were what I'll call the technolibertarians. For them, MUD rapists were of course assholes, but the presence of assholes on the system was a technical inevitability, like noise on a phone line, and best dealt with not through repressive social disciplinary mechanisms but through the timely deployment of defensive software tools. Some asshole blasting violent, graphic language at you? Don't whine to the authorities about it—hit the @gag command and the asshole's statements will be blocked from your screen (and only yours). It's simple, it's effective, and it censors no one.

But the Bungle case was rather hard on such arguments. For one thing, the extremely public nature of the living room meant that gagging would spare the victims only from witnessing their own violation, but not from having others witness it. You might want to argue that what those victims didn't directly experience couldn't hurt them, hut consider how that wisdom would sound to a woman who'd been, say, fondled by strangers while passed out drunk and you have a rough idea how it might go over with a crowd of hard-core MOOers. Consider, for another thing, that many of the biologically female participants in the Bungle debate had been around long enough to grow lethally weary of the gag-and-get-over-it school of virtual-rape counseling, with its fine line between empowering victims and holding them responsible for their own suffering, and its shrugging indifference to the window of pain between the moment the rape-text starts flowing and the moment a gag shuts it off. From the outset it was clear that the technolibertarians were going to have to tip-toe through this issue with care, and for the most part they did.

Yet no position was trickier to maintain than that of the MOO' s resident anarchists. Like the technolibbers, the anarchists didn't care much for punishments or policies or power elites. Like them, they hoped the MOO could be a place where people interacted fulfillingly without the need for such things. But their high hopes were complicated, in general, by a somewhat less thoroughgoing faith in technology ("Even if you can't tear down the master's house with the master's tools"—read a slogan written into one anarchist player's self-description—"it is a damned good place to start"). And at present they were additionally complicated by the fact that the most vocal anarchists in the discussion were none other than Legba, Bakunin, and SamIAm, who wanted to see Mr. Bungle toaded as badly as anyone did.

Needless to say, a pro death–penalty platform is not an especially comfortable one for an anarchist to sit on, so these particular anarchists were now at great pains to sever the conceptual ties between toading and capital punishment. Toading, they insisted (almost convincingly), was much more closely analogous to banishment; it was a kind of turning of the communal back on the offending party, a collective action which, if carried out properly, was entirely consistent with anarchist models of community. And carrying it out properly meant first and foremost building a consensus around it—a messy process for which there were no easy technocratic substitutes. It was going to take plenty of good old-fashioned, jawbone-intensive grassroots organizing.

So that when the time came, at 7 P.M. PST on the evening of the third day after the occurrence in the living room, to gather in evangeline's room for her proposed real-time open conclave, Bakunin and Legba were among the first to arrive. But this was hardly to be an anarchist-dominated affair, for the room was crowding rapidly with representatives of all the MOO's political stripes, and even a few wizards. Hagbard showed up, and Autumn and Quastro, Puff, JoeFeedback, L-dopa and Bloaf, HerkieCosmo, Silver Rocket, Karl Porcupine, Matchstick—the names piled up and the discussion gathered momentum under their weight.

Arguments multiplied and mingled, players talked past and through each other, the textual clutter of utterances and gestures filled up the screen like thick cigar smoke. Peaking in number at around thirty, this was one of the largest crowds that ever gathered in a single LambdaMOO chamber, and while evangeline had given her place a description that made it "infinite in expanse and fluid in form," it now seemed anything but roomy. You could almost feel the claustrophobic air of the place, dank and overheated by virtual bodies, pressing against your skin.

I know you could because I too was there, making my lone and insignificant appearance in this story. Completely ignorant of any of the goings-on that had led to the meeting, I wandered in purely to see what the crowd was about, and though I observed the proceedings for a good while, I confess I found it hard to grasp what was going on. I was still the rankest of newbies then, my MOO legs still too unsteady to make the leaps of faith, logic, and empathy required to meet the spectacle on its own terms. I was fascinated by the concept of virtual rape, but I couldn't quite take it seriously.

In this, though, I was in a small and mostly silent minority, for the discussion that raged around me was of an almost unrelieved earnestness, bent it seemed on examining every last aspect and implication of Mr. Bungle's crime. There were the central questions, of course: thumbs up or down on Bungle's virtual existence? And if down, how then to insure that his toading was not just some isolated lynching but a first step toward shaping LambdaMOO into a legitimate community? Surrounding these, however, a tangle of weighty side issues proliferated. What, some wondered, was the real-life legal status of the offense? Could Bungle's university administrators punish him for sexual harassment? Could he be prosecuted under California state laws against obscene phone calls? Little enthusiasm was shown for pursuing either of these lines of action, which testifies both to the uniqueness of the crime and to the nimbleness with which the discussants were negotiating its idiosyncrasies. Many were the casual references to Bungle's deed as simply "rape," but these in no way implied that the players had lost sight of all distinctions between the virtual and physical versions, or that they believed Bungle should be dealt with in the same way a real-life criminal would. He had committed a MOO crime, and his punishment, if any, would be meted out via the MOO.

On the other hand, little patience was shown toward any attempts to downplay the seriousness of what Mr. Bungle had done. When the affable HerkieCosmo proposed, more in the way of an hypothesis than an assertion, that "perhaps it's better to release ... violent tendencies in a virtual environment rather than in real life," he was tut-tutted so swiftly and relentlessly that he withdrew the hypothesis altogether, apologizing humbly as he did so. Not that the assembly was averse to putting matters into a more philosophical perspective. "Where does the body end and the mind begin?" young Quastro asked, amid recurring attempts to fine-tune the differences between real and virtual violence. "Is not the mind a part of the body?" "In MOO, the body IS the mind," offered HerkieCosmo gamely, and not at all implausibly, demonstrating the ease with which very knotty metaphysical conundrums come undone in VR. The not-so-aptly named Obvious seemed to agree, arriving after deep consideration of the nature of Bungle's crime at the hardly novel yet now somehow newly resonant conjecture "all reality might consist of ideas, who knows."

On these and other matters the anarchists, the libertarians, the legal-ists, the wizardists—and the wizards—all had their thoughtful say. But as the evening wore on and the talk grew more heated and more heady, it seemed increasingly clear that the vigorous intelligence being brought to bear on this swarm of issues wasn't going to result in anything remotely like resolution. The perspectives were just too varied, the meme-scape just too slippery. Again and again, arguments that looked at first to be heading in a decisive direction ended up chasing their own tails; and slowly, depressingly, a dusty haze of irrelevance gathered over the proceedings.

It was almost a relief, therefore, when midway through the evening Mr. Bungle himself, the living, breathing cause of all this talk, teleported into the room. Not that it was much of a surprise. Oddly enough, in the three days since his release from Zippy's cage, Bungle had returned more than once to wander the public spaces of LambdaMOO, walking will-ingly into one of the fiercest storms of ill will and invective ever to rain down on a player. He'd been taking it all with a curious and mostly silent passivity, and when challenged face to virtual face by both Legba and the genderless elder statescharacter PatGently to defend himself on *social*, he'd demurred, mumbling something about Christ and expiation. He was equally quiet now, and his reception was still uniformly cool Legba fixed an arctic stare on him—"no hate, no anger, no interest at all. Just ... watching." Others were more actively unfriendly. "Asshole," spat Karl Porcupine, "creep." But the harshest of the MOO's hostility toward him had already been vented, and the attention he drew now was motivated more, it seemed, by the opportunity to probe the rapist's mind, to find out what made it tick and if possible how to get it to tick differently. In short, they wanted to know why he'd done it. So they asked him.

And Mr. Bungle thought about it. And as eddies of discussion and debate continued to swirl around him, he thought about it some more. And then he said this: "I engaged in a bit of a psychological device that is called thought-polarization, the fact that this is not RL simply added to heighten the affect of the device. It was purely a sequence of events with no consequence on my RL existence."

They might have known. Stilted though its diction was, the gist of the answer was simple, and something many in the room had probably already surmised: Mr. Bungle was a psycho. Not, perhaps, in real life— but then in real life it's possible for reasonable people to assume, as Bungle clearly did, that what transpires between word-costumed characters within the boundaries of a make-believe world is, if not mere play, then at most some kind of emotional laboratory experiment. Inside the MOO, however, such thinking marked a person as one of two basically subcompetent types. The first was the newbie, in which case the confusion was understandable, since there were few MOOers who had not, upon their first visits as anonymous "guest" characters, mistaken the place for a vast playpen in which they might act out their wildest fantasies without fear of censure. Only with time and the acquisition of a fixed character do players tend to make the critical passage from anonymity to pseudonymity, developing the concern for their character's reputation that marks the attainment of virtual adulthood. But while Mr. Bungle hadn't been around as long as most MOOers, he'd been around long enough to leave his newbie status behind, and his delusional statement therefore placed him among the second type: the sociopath.

And as there is but small percentage in arguing with a head case, the room's attention gradually abandoned Mr. Bungle and returned to the discussions that had previously occupied it. But if the debate had been edging toward ineffectuality before, Bungle's anticlimactic appearance had evidently robbed it of any forward motion whatsoever. What's more, from his lonely corner of the room Mr. Bungle kept issuing periodic expressions of a prickly sort of remorse, interlaced with sarcasm and belligerence, and though it was hard to tell if he wasn't still just conducting his experiments, some people thought his regret genuine enough that maybe he didn't deserve to be toaded after all. Logically, of course, discussion of the principal issues at hand didn't require unanimous belief that Bungle was an irredeemable bastard, but now that cracks were showing in that unanimity, the last of the meeting's fervor seemed to be draining out through them.

People started drifting away. Mr. Bungle left first, then others followed—one by one, in twos and threes, hugging friends and waving goodnight. By 9:45 only a handful remained, and the great debate had wound down into casual conversation, the melancholy remains of another fruitless good idea. The arguments had been well-honed. certainly, and perhaps might prove useful in some as-yet-unclear long run. But at this point what seemed clear was that evangeline's meeting had died, at last, and without any practical results to mark its passing.

It was also at this point, most likely, that JoeFeedback reached his decision. JoeFeedback was a wizard, a taciturn sort of fellow who'd sat brooding on the sidelines all evening. He hadn't said a lot, but what he had said indicated that he took the crime committed against Legba and Starsinger very seriously, and that he felt no particular compassion toward the character who had committed it. But on the other hand he had made it equally plain that he took the elimination of a fellow player just as seriously, and moreover that he had no desire to return to the days of wizardly fiat. It must have been difficult, therefore, to reconcile the conflicting impulses churning within him at that moment. In fact, it was probably impossible, for as much as he would have liked to make himself an instrument of LambdaMOO's collective will, he surely realized that under the present order of things he must in the final analysis either act alone or not act at all.

So JoeFeedback acted alone.

He told the lingering few players in the room that he had to go, and then he went. It was a minute or two before ten. He did it quietly and he did it privately, but all anyone had to do to know he'd done it was to type the @who command, which was normally what you typed if you wanted to know a player's present location and the time he last logged in. But if you had run a @who on Mr. Bungle not too long after Joe-Feedback left evangeline's room, the database would have told you something different.

"Mr. Bungle," it would have said, "is not the name of any player."

The date, as it happened, was April Fool's Day, and it would still be April Fool's Day for another two hours. But this was no joke: Mr. Bungle was truly dead and truly gone.

They say that LambdaMOO has never been the same since Mr. Bungle's toading. They say as well that nothing's really changed. And though it skirts the fuzziest of dream-logics to say that both these statements are true, the MOO is just the sort of fuzzy, dreamlike place in which such contradictions thrive.

Certainly whatever civil society now informs LambdaMOO owes its existence to the Bungle Affair. The archwizard Haakon made sure of that. Away on business for the duration of the episode, Haakon returned to find its wreckage strewn across the tiny universe he'd set in motion. The death of a player, the trauma of several others, and the angst-ridden conscience of his colleague JoeFeedback presented themselves to his concerned and astonished attention, and he resolved to see if he couldn't learn some lesson from it all. For the better part of a day he brooded over the record of events and arguments left in *social*, then he sat pondering the chaotically evolving shape of his creation, and at the day's end he descended once again into the social arena of the MOO with another history-altering proclamation.

It was probably his last, for what he now decreed was the final, missing piece of the New Direction. In a few days, Haakon announced, he would build into the database a system of petitions and ballots whereby anyone could put to popular vote any social scheme requiring wizardly powers for its implementation, with the results of the vote to be binding on the wizards. At last and for good, the awkward gap between the will of the players and the efficacy of the technicians would be closed. And though some anarchists grumbled about the irony of Haakon's dictatorially imposing universal suffrage on an unconsulted populace, in general the citizens of LambdaMOO seemed to find it hard to fault a system more purely democratic than any that could ever exist in real life. Eight months and a dozen ballot measures later, widespread participation in the new regime has produced a small arsenal of mechanisms for dealing with the types of violence that called the system into being. MOO residents now have access to a @boot command, for instance, with which to summarily eject berserker "guest" characters. And players can bring suit against one another through an ad hoc arbitration system in which mutually agreed-upon judges have at their disposition the full range of wizardly punishments—up to and including the capital.

Yet the continued dependence on death as the ultimate keeper of the peace suggests that this new MOO order may not be built on the most solid of foundations. For if life on LambdaMOO began to acquire more coherence in the wake of the toading, death retained all the fuzziness of pre-Bungle days. This truth was rather dramatically borne out, not too many days after Bungle departed, by the arrival of a strange new character named Dr. Jest. There was a forceful eccentricity to the newcomer's manner, but the oddest thing about his style was its striking yet unnameable familiarity. And when he developed the annoying habit of stuffing fellow players into a jar containing a tiny simulacrum of a certain deceased rapist. the source of this familiarity became obvious:

Mr. Bungle had risen from the grave.

In itself, Bungle's reincarnation as Dr. Jest was a remarkable turn of events, but perhaps even more remarkable was the utter lack of amazement with which the LambdaMOO public took note of it. To be sure, many residents were appalled by the brazenness of Bungle's return. In fact, one of the first petitions circulated under the new voting system was a request for Dr. Jest's toading that almost immediately gathered fifty-two signatures (but has failed so far to reach ballot status). Yet few were unaware of the ease with which the toad proscription could be circumvented—all the toadee had to do (all the ur-Bungle at NYU presumably had done) was to go to the minor hassle of acquiring a new Internet account, and LambdaMOO's character registration program would then simply treat the known felon as an entirely new and innocent person. Nor was this ease generally understood to represent a failure of toading's social disciplinary function. On the contrary, it only underlined the truism (repeated many times throughout the debate over Mr. Bungle's fate) that his punishment, ultimately, had been no more or less symbolic than his crime.

What *was* surprising, however, was that Mr. Bungle/Dr. Jest seemed to have taken the symbolism to heart. Dark themes still obsessed him—the objects he created gave off wafts of Nazi imagery and medical torture—but he no longer radiated the aggressively antisocial vibes he had before. He was a lot less unpleasant to look at (the outrageously seedy clown description had been replaced by that of a mildly creepy but actually rather natty young man, with "blue eye ... suggestive of conspiracy, untamed eroticism and perhaps a sense of understanding of the future"), and aside from the occasional jar-stuffing incident, he was also a lot less dangerous to be around. It was obvious he'd undergone some sort of personal transformation in the days since I'd first glimpsed him back in evangeline's crowded room—nothing radical maybe, but powerful nonetheless, and resonant enough with my own experience, I felt, that it might be more than professionally interesting to talk with him, and perhaps compare notes.

For I too was undergoing a transformation in the aftermath of that night in evangeline's, and I'm still not entirely sure what to make of it. As I pursued my runaway fascination with the discussion I had heard there, as I pored over the *social debate and got to know Legba and some of the other victims and witnesses, I could feel my newbie consciousness falling away from me. Where before I'd found it hard to take virtual rape seriously, I now was finding it difficult to remember how I could ever *not* have taken it seriously. I was proud to have arrived at this perspective—it felt like an exotic sort of achievement, and it definitely made my ongoing experience of the MOO a richer one.

But it was also having some unsettling effects on the way I looked at the rest of the world. Sometimes, for instance, it was hard for me to understand why RL society classifies RL rape alongside crimes against person or property. Since rape can occur without any physical pain or damage, I found myself reasoning, then it must be classed as a crime against the mind—more intimately and deeply hurtful, to be sure, than cross burnings, wolf whistles, and virtual rape, but undeniably located on the same conceptual continuum. I did not, however, conclude as a result that rapists were protected in any fashion by the First Amendment. Quite the opposite, in fact: the more seriously I took the notion of virtual rape, the less seriously I was able to take the notion of freedom of speech, with its tidy division of the world into the symbolic and the real.

Let me assure you, though, that I am not presenting these thoughts as arguments. I offer them, rather, as a picture of the sort of mind-set that deep immersion in a virtual world has inspired in me. I offer them also, therefore, as a kind of prophecy. For whatever else these thoughts tell me, I have come to believe that they announce the final stages of our decades-long passage into the Information Age, a paradigm shift that the classic liberal firewall between word and deed (itself a product of an earlier paradigm shift commonly known as the Enlightenment) is not likely to survive intact. After all, anyone the least bit familiar with the workings of the new era's definitive technology, the computer, knows that it operates on a principle impracticably difficult to distinguish from the pre-Enlightenment principle of the magic word: the commands you type into a computer are a kind of speech that doesn't so much communicate as *make things happen*, directly and ineluctably, the same way pulling a trigger does. They are incantations, in other words, and anyone at all attuned to the technosocial megatrends of the moment—from the growing dependence of economies on the global flow of intensely fetishized words and numbers to the burgeoning ability of bioengineers to speak the spells written in the four-letter text of DNA—knows that the logic of the incantation is rapidly permeating the fabric of our lives.

And it's precisely this logic that provides the real magic in a place like LambdaMOO—not the fictive trappings of voodoo and shapeshifting and wizardry, but the conflation of speech and act that's inevitable in any computer-mediated world, be it Lambda or the increasingly wired world at large. This is dangerous magic, to be sure, a potential threat—if misconstrued or misapplied—to our always precarious freedoms of expression, and as someone who lives by his words I do not take the threat lightly. And yet, on the other hand, I can no longer convince myself that our wishful insulation of language from the realm of action has ever been anything but a valuable kludge, a philosophically damaged stopgap against oppression that would just have to do till something truer and more elegant came along.

Am I wrong to think this truer, more elegant thing can be found on LambdaMOO? Perhaps, but I continue to seek it there sensing its presence just beneath the surface of every interaction. I have even thought. as I said, that discussing with Dr. Jest our shared experience of the workings of the MOO might help me in my search. But when that notion first occurred to me, I still felt somewhat intimidated by his lingering criminal aura, and I hemmed and hawed a good long time before finally resolving to drop him MOO-mail requesting an interview. By then it was too late. For reasons known only to himself, Dr. Jest had stopped logging in. Maybe he'd grown bored with the MOO. Maybe the loneliness of ostracism had gotten to him. Maybe a psycho whim had carried him far away or maybe he'd quietly acquired a third character and started life over with a cleaner slate.

Wherever he'd gone, though, he left behind the room he'd created for himself—a treehouse "tastefully decorated" with rare-book shelves, an operating table, and a life-size William S. Burroughs doll—and he left it unlocked. So I took to checking in there occasionally, and I still do from time to time. I head out of my own cozy nook (inside a TV set inside the little red hotel inside the Monopoly board inside the dining room of LambdaMOO), and I teleport on over to the treehouse, where the room description always tells me Dr. Jest is present but asleep, in the conventional depiction for disconnected characters. The not-quite-emptiness of the abandoned room invariably instills in me an uncomfortable mix of melancholy and the creeps, and I stick around only on the off chance that Dr. Jest will wake up, say hello, and share his understanding of the future with me.

He won't, of course, but this is no great loss. Increasingly, the complex magic of the MOO interests me more as a way to live the present than to understand the future. And it's usually not long before I leave Dr. Jest's lonely treehouse and head back to the mansion, to see some friends.

Reflections

There is no missing the mysticism and mythology in Dibbell's story. As he says near the beginning: "the Bungle Affair dares me to explain it to you without resort to dime-store mysticisms, and I fear I may have shape-shifted by the digital moonlight one too many times to be quite up to the task." No doubt about it. Dibbell has spent enough time in LambdaMOO to think of it as a place. He has endowed it with reality, and he thinks about it and talks about it as a place. Its special differences from the physical world occupy his attention, but it is inescapably a place, and for him the place has magic.

Myths loom large in LambdaMOO and the reality-unreality of the place seems to invite a search in mythology for understanding. Consider, for example, Dibbell's account of Haakon's document, "LambdaMOO Takes a New Direction," in which he announces the change in the wizards' functions and powers. "They would make no decisions affecting the social life of the MOO, but only implement whatever decisions the community as a whole directed them to. From then on, it was decreed, LambdaMOO would just have to grow up and solve its problems on its own." Given that Curtis is the creator of LambdaMOO, do parallels to the stone tablets come to mind? To be sure, the archwizard left the message in the living room rather than on top of a mountain, but where else would you put it in LambdaMOO? Another difference was that the gods were ceasing to govern; the residents would have to figure out how to get along on their own. Many people look at the challenge of life in the physical world in rather similar terms.

LambdaMOO is perhaps one of the most famous MUDs, but the varying social phenomena observed there occur in other MUDs and in other kinds of electronic communications. Some MUDs publish guidelines advising new members about expected behavior. The MariMUSE MUD, a project of Phoenix College intended as an educational environment for learners of all ages, sends new members a list of guidelines delineating the values of the community and the responsibilities, and rights, of learners and teachers.

On a network anonymity can have a major bearing on social behavior. We may think that anonymity simply opens the door to irresponsible behavior, but for many people it has real value. A cartoon published in the New Yorker *showed a dog sitting in front of a personal computer with the caption "On the Internet nobody knows that you are a dog." The cartoon seems to have struck a sympathetic chord, for it is widely known in the computer community. One can imagine that anonymity brings with it the freedom to be what you can be, or to try on new rules or behaviors without worrying so much about possible failure or embarrassment.*

Within MUDs, there is usually a distinction between guests and members. People may need to earn their membership rights in some way—a sort of virtual rite of passage. Such mechanisms have the virtue of providing anonymity while letting people contribute to a community, invest in their own network identity, and come to know others. Without some such continuing, albeit anonymous identity, the on-line community would be a lonely place populated by strangers. Investing in a network identity in this way gives members an incentive for responsible behavior.

Not all MUDs are anonymous. In certain communities, especially those whose network participants have ongoing working relationships or commitments to activities beyond the network, anonymity is not useful. In the following articles, we consider situations in which digital realities augment physical realities and activities. In these cases, participants often know each others' real names. They work and meet in digital space simply because it is more convenient.

Interaction Without Society?:
Can't Do

Harry M. Collins

Connections

People form societies. In Dibbell's article we saw that even in the text-based virtual reality of the LambdaMOO mud, people formed a society. Although participants "saw" each other only through texts on a computer screen, group interactions became complex and people felt a need to organize themselves socially.

Because everything experienced in digital worlds is mediated by software, they are more ambiguous than the real world. People don't see each other but only what the software shows them. In such a world, others can appear as merely things, like the programmed characters or agents of multiplayer video games. We cannot tell by looking at an image whether it stands for a person or a programmed agent. This ambiguity between constructed images of people and constructed images of automated agents is Collins's starting point. He observes that many of the challenges of artificial intelligence in the physical world—such as mechanical movement and machine perception—robotics—simply do not apply in digital worlds, where a programmer can create an agent that walks around and interacts with people.

Collins asks: Could a programmer construct a realistic agent in a digital world? If people form a society in a digital world, could such a programmed agent become a member of it? Could it convince us that it is a human member of the society? This article uses this thought experiment to explore what it means to be a member of a society and how agents in digital worlds might participate in the societies that are now forming there.

…es are formed and maintained through people interacting with …h other. As time goes by, an increasing proportion of these inter- …ctions takes place without face-to-face human contact: it takes place via "electromechanical mediation." Writing-was a step in this direction; the telephone was a bigger step; and computer networks promise to take us much further along that road. But can electromechanical mediation (EMM) alone allow a society to develop? Obviously, it depends what we mean by *society*.

By society, some people mean a set of interacting nodes. Under this definition there are societies of bees, societies of ants, and societies of computers. I mean something more than this. By society, I mean that of which you have to be a member in order to carry out certain apparently simple tasks that are expected of human beings. Anthropologists (and we are all anthropologists in our own way) know what this means because they know what it is like to have failed to have attained membership of a society. What happens when you have failed to attain membership is that you make all kinds of small faux pas: you don't know when to laugh, when to cry, when to show respect, when to belch, who counts, and who does not. We are all anthropologists when we first enter any new social group (such as a new school or university). We feel uncomfortable until we begin to know our way about. We can only learn this through participation; those who have learned from books of etiquette or other manuals still make social gaffes. It may be that the difference between bee societies and ant societies, on the one hand, and human societies, on the other, is that the rules of the first type of society can be set out in the form of instructions (a genetic code in the case of bees and ants), whereas how to rules of behavior in human societies cannot be set out in this way. If computer societies could mimic human societies, we might find out that this was wrong; but we have not found it out yet.

The Editing Test

To speak of people being either members or nonmembers of a society is too simple; sometimes people are only partway there. Moreover, the criterion of membership as I have described it—ceasing to commit faux pas—is difficult to use. To make the idea of socialization more concrete I propose a simple test. This is a simplification of the Turing Test. Alan Turing, a mathematician and computer pioneer, suggested that we might count a computer as "intelligent" if it was hard for us to tell whether we were interacting with a human or a computer during the course of typed interchanges. We can replace the word *intelligent* with *a member of our society*, for that is what the test really looks for (as I explain in *Artificial Experts* [1990]). Careful analysis shows that the most difficult thing for a computer to do in such a test would be to make sense of badly typed or misspelled input. For simplicity, we will call this task of making sense and making corrections *editing*. Consider the following passage which is in need of editing.

Mary: The next thing I want you to do is spell a word that means a religious ceremony.

John: You mean *rite*. Do you want me to spell it out loud?

Mary: No, I want you to write it.

John: I'm tired. All you ever want me to do is write, write, write.

Mary: That's unfair, I just want you to write, write, write.

John: OK, I'll write, write.

Mary: Write.

We can correct passages of printed English of this kind not because of a fixed store of knowledge or a prolonged period of "training." It is not even that when we are being trained to do it we are corrected each time we make a mistake on a newly encountered example of such a problem; it cannot be this, because the new instances are equally new to any potential trainer and we merely beg the question of how the trainer knows what a reasonable answer would look like. Nevertheless, we usually come up with an acceptable version of even new problems of this type the first time we encounter them. We can do so m spite of the fact that what counts as an appropriate response—and there may be several possibilities—varies from place to place and time to time. This is not surprising, as what counts as reasonable use of language changes as societies change. The ability to edit reasonably successfully, then, is a matter not of learning a set of rules but of being a member of a society.

My proposed test of socialization is a comparison of the ability of fully socialized members of society and those who might or might not be members to edit passages of this sort. To put this test into practice, the judge would have to be a full member of the society in question and would have to make his or her judgments without knowing which passage had been edited by which entity. Like the original Turing Test, the ability of this test to separate members of a society from nonmembers is a matter of probability, not certainty. It is worth noting for the combinatorily inclined that a look-up table exhaustively listing all corrected passages of about the above length—three hundred characters—including those for which the most appropriate response would be "I can't correct that," would contain 10^{600} entries, compared to the, roughly, 10^{125} particles in the universe. The number of potentially correctable passages would be very much smaller of course but, I would guess, would still be beyond the limits of brute strength methods.

Like the Turing Test, the editing test is a general test of the ability of one type of thing or person to imitate the actions of another type of thing or person. Turing based his on the "imitation game," a parlor game in which men tried to imitate women's responses and vice versa.

Restricted Channels of Interaction

I think the editing test is an improvement over the Turing Test in almost every circumstance. Here I am suggesting its use in a series of speculations, or thought experiments. I am suggesting we use the editing test as a way of making concrete the questions about what it takes to act like a member of a society.

I began by asking whether interaction through electromechanical means alone could allow a society to develop or be maintained. We can now firm up this question to read: Could we learn to edit passages of the general type exemplified in the dialogue between John and Mary if we interacted with others solely by means of EMM. We can define the *question-space* further. The question is about *cyberspaces* with different qualities and densities. To what extent does any particular cyberspace take over from ordinary life? That is, to what extent are the lives of participants saturated with EMM? Do they live in cyberspace nearly all the time or only some of the time, spending the rest of their lives in ordinary society. How much presocialization is taken into cyberspace? Do people enter cyberspace after having been socialized in ordinary society, or have they been introduced to a fully saturated cyberspace from birth? How broad is the bandwidth of the cyberspace? In short, to what extent are the multiple sensory experiences of ordinary life reproduced in cyberspace interactions?

Saturation

We live in a world which has a low saturation level of narrow-bandwidth EMM. This works well. We write letters, telephone each other, and read books and journals. E-mail and the World Wide Web seem to be making things better and better; they are helping us maintain old social relationships and sometimes form new ones. But these ways of communicating probably work well because they are parasitical on all the ordinary interaction that goes on at the same time. It is by no means clear from the success of low-saturation EMM, even though it is of narrow bandwidth only, that face-to-face interaction can be fully replaced as soon as more bandwidth comes along.

What can and cannot be transmitted through EMM is an empirical question. Such research as has been done suggests that less is transmitted currently over EMM than we imagine. One study of scientists trying to build a new kind of laser, for example, showed that the scientific journals do not adequately transfer scientific culture, as measured by the ability to do new experiments successfully. In that study, no one who used journals without also having extended personal interaction with someone who knew how to build one succeeded in building a working laser (Collins 1992). The EMM available in the early 1970s clearly could not replace face-to-face communication when it came to transmitting laser building knowledge.

My guess is that as far as transmitting new scientific culture is concerned, nothing significant will change at least until the bandwidth of EMM increases enormously. One reason is that scientific communication depends on trust, and trust is hard to develop through EMM. Another more profound reason is that much scientific knowledge is *tacit knowledge* while a medium such as e-mail requires that the communicator makes the knowledge explicit enough to be handled by the medium. Tacit knowledge is transferred when someone works with another person and sees how things are done; it is transferred through inconsequential chat, through "war stories," through subtle emphases, body language, and so forth. Neither party has to know what the crucial knowledge is for it to be transferred.

Presocialization

Those who spend a lot of time in the primitive versions of cyberspace that we currently have available seem to be able to speak to each other with little enough loss of meaning to be able to edit each others' English across the e-mail network. There may be too little bandwidth to allow the transmission of new cultural knowledge such as how to build a new kind of laser, but this does not stop people editing existing languages. I think this is because we have been socialized already; we carry our ordinary socialization with us without noticing it.

But what if individuals had never interacted except through EMM? What if they had always lived in an EMM saturated society? Would the communicative abilities of such individuals be like those of a child locked away from birth? Or would a supply of information in the absence of the sight, sound, and touch of other human beings enable them to develop into creatures relatively like us? It is hard to say. Just imagining these possibilities, however, reminds us that the consequences of limiting communication to EMM alone could be more costly than the experience, which follows presocialization, would suggest.

Bandwidth

At the low-bandwidth end of EMM is letter writing, journal reading and telephoning; at the high-bandwidth end is interaction within a three-dimensional virtual reality that might one day include, smells, touches, tastes, and enough visual definition and speed of reaction to register detailed facial expressions and body language.

Let us explore the very top end with a thought experiment beloved of philosophers. To make sure we are getting all the sensory experience we can, let us start by imagining brains in vats faultlessly linked by radio to the nerves in the corresponding freely-wandering body. The body would represent the best possible virtual you, in fact, you wouldn't be quite sure where you were—in the vat or in the body. At first sight, a society made up of people whose bodies wander freely while their brains are in vats looks pretty similar to a society made up of people with their brains in their bodies. But would members of such a society be able to edit?

We might think they would, because the experience of the brain in the VAT is identical to the experience of an ordinary person. Certainly we would expect such societies to be able to support natural languages; they would be societies in the sense that I use the term above, and we would expect their members to be able to edit their own languages. I am less sure, however, that they would be able to edit the languages of existing societies as well as we edit them, because disembrained society is not identical to our society in every respect.

Daniel Dennett, the philosopher who imagines brains in vats and disembodied people, points out one way in which disembodied society would be different from ordinary society. Its members would not get intoxicated. The blood supply of the body—and it is the body which drinks—is disconnected from the blood supply of the brain—and it is the brain that gets drunk (Dennett, 1982).

Neal Stephenson, in a science fiction novel called *Snow Crash* (1992), imagines something a little less than disembrained bodies—a wide-bandwidth virtual reality he calls the *Metaverse*, which is populated by virtual counterparts of ourselves called *avatars*. In Stephenson's metaverse, virtual people can get killed, but the real people are still sitting at home; death doesn't mean quite the same thing as it does in our world.

The meaning of language is not just what is in the dictionary. Natural languages are made up of networks of terms intimately related with the networks of actions and experiences in which the large majority of a society's members engage. The collective experiences of the members of a society form the network of meaning, which is why only people who are socialized can edit. Now, if the experiences of a collection of virtual individuals, or of brains separated from their bodies, is different from the experiences of united brains and bodies even in small ways, we would expect the language they develop to be different wherever these differences affect it. Thus Dennett's disembodied brains and Stephenson's atavars would have trouble with intoxication and death, respectively, and with every part of our language that touches on these concepts, however distantly. Because our language is filled with metaphorical references to drunkenness and death, we would expect that these entities to be slightly "off" in their use of our language and to fail the editing test quite often.

Conclusion

To summarize, societies that communicated, and had always communicated, solely via EMM, even if it was of enormous bandwidth, could be expected to be humanlike in the sense that they would develop their own natural languages. They would probably create, however, languages incommensurate with ours. This modest conclusion is worth keeping in mind, not so much to help us anticipate the distant future, but to temper our current optimism about plans for distributing work and education through electronic means.

Reflections

Can we build artificial beings, even in a simulated world? The most famous mythical character relevant to artificial beings is probably the Golem, the artificially created human being of Hebrew literature. In older variants of this myth, the lesser gods, by attempting to make creatures of their own, defied the higher gods. In Sumerian myths, for example, the water god Enki and his wife, Ninmah the Earth Mother, created many kinds of humans at a drunken feast, competing with each other to produce the most useless humans. Like the Frankenstein story, a modern variation of such myths, many of these stories are cautionary tales warning that badly created or unholy creatures can get out of control and turn on their creators. Collins, however, is no prophet of doom concerned about the dangers of artificial experts running amok. His main attitude is that of skepticism. Making a convincing social creature is probably too difficult; our engineering presumptions may simply be inadequate to the task. Members of society have to be raised and educated, not designed and created.

Collins wants to know what it would take to build a social agent. He is not particularly interested in the familiar obstacles to building robots, such as the artificial-intelligence (AI) challenges of mechanical movement and machine perception. He is willing to limit the experiment to an arti-

ficial, simulated digital world where these issues can be finessed. His method for understanding the requirements of agents is based on a thought experiment involving human children in an artificial environment. He concludes that even there, the challenges of socialization are enormous. Why?

Collins recognizes that a socialized being knows a lot. It needs to know a lot in order to pass the editing test, the proposed alternative to the well-known Turing Test. By coincidence, the 1995 Turing Award was given to Edward Feigenbaum, whose 1970s insight was that knowledge, rather than general-purpose programs on fast computers, is the key to high performance on tasks that require what we think of as intelligence. Feigenbaum's insight created a focus on methods for formulating large bodies of knowledge and since the 1980s has been used by companies developing expert systems.

As a sociologist who has studied scientists at work, Collins sees knowledge as both incrementally and socially constructed. It is incrementally constructed in that bodies of knowledge—theories and models—are built up a little bit at a time. It is socially constructed in that groups of people through their interactions build knowledge and shared understanding. Thus, for Collins, the problem is circular. It takes knowledge to participate in a society, and knowledge is constructed socially.

In his thought experiment, Collins considers the socialization of human children whose social interactions could, theoretically, take place solely through electromechanical mediation. In digital worlds, as in Feigenbaum's real world, the amount of knowledge required is high. In both worlds, children emerge as full adult citizens only after they have been trained and have passed certain formal or informal tests. Collins's prescriptions for agents—a combination of abilities for learning and adapting and communicating—is in accord with much current thinking in the AI community.

His observations about bandwidth bear on systems now being created in scientific settings for real agents in digital worlds. Several of the preceding articles based on the digital library and e-mail metaphors discussed the use of the information infrastructure to support the advance of science: to maintain scientific databases, support collaboration, and allow peer review via e-mail. Other articles in this section propose the

*use of technologies with greater bandwidth to support real-time inter-
actions in research—both for controlling instruments and for holding
scientific conferences with distant colleagues. These worlds are digital
and used for scientific collaboration. Such technology will undoubtedly
be used to augment rather than completely replace regular meetings.*

*Finally, Collins's socialization test raised some questions about my
own socialization. When I first read his article, I wrote back to Harry
that I could not pass the sample test. I sent him a candidate solution
somewhat tentatively. Collins wrote back:*

```
Date: Mon, 23 Jan 1995 07:15:57 -0800
From: H M Collins ⟨hsshmc@bath.ac.uk⟩
To: Mark Stefik ⟨stefik@parc.xerox.com⟩
Subject: ARE YOU AN ALIEN?
MIME-Version: 1.0


Well, Mark, you might well be an alien, but to use
my test I'd have to run several of these past you
and compare your answers with that of the socialized
control. (things look bad though, Mary's line as I
see it should read 'write rite right'.)
• • •
```

*For readers in the same boat, I now offer the following socially certified
solution:*

Mary: *The next thing I want you to do is spell a word that means a
religious ceremony.*

John: *You mean* rite. *Do you want me to spell it out loud?*

Mary: *No, I want you to write it.*

John: *I'm tired. All you ever want me to do is write, write, write.*

Mary: *That's unfair, I just want you to write rite right.*

John: *OK, I'll write rite.*

Mary: *Right.*

Excerpt from "Toward Portable Ideas"

Mark Stefik and John Seely Brown

Connections

The preceding articles on digital reality might convey the impression that digital reality is only for entertainment and relaxation when we are not working. Viewed this way, it is principally an alternative to watching television, going to a show, or hanging out with friends.

This article takes digital reality in a different direction, to a working environment. It may take rare wisdom to realize that people do not consistently do their best and most creative work when they are deadly serious and isolated. In work of any kind, a degree of socializing, and even playfulness and relaxation, is essential for creativity and sustained motivation.

This article also takes the experience of a digital reality beyond the MUD in another way. It describes the Colab, a computer-augmented room designed to support personal real-time group interaction. The experience of participants working together is augmented by an interactive shared workspace composed of a wall-sized interactive whiteboard called the liveboard and workstations for each meeting participant.

We honor creativity in our culture, especially that of the individual genius, but creativity is as much a social as an individual affair. When people of different backgrounds come together, new ideas can arise from their conversations. Sometimes new ideas are built up incrementally from the fragments of different viewpoints. Ideas can be made more robust when they have been bounced around, critiqued, polished, and repackaged by a group.

We have all been in situations where our part in developing ideas has been but one of many contributions. We have all benefited from the wisdom of a second opinion, or been surprised on occasions when good ideas came from unexpected sources. Nonetheless, idea creation, like other aspects of intellectual work, and even routine office work, is usually conceived in terms of the contributions of isolated individuals. Conventional wisdom has been slow to recognize the importance of collaboration and teamwork. The wisdom about teams that "many hands make light work" refers to hands not minds, and certainly not to committees.

Most approaches to office automation and computer-mediated work have focused on individuals rather than groups. The landscape is littered with failed computer systems that were supposed to make light work of various office tasks. Studies of the acceptance and use of computer systems in offices have shown consistently that a major factor determining the success or failure of such systems is whether the designers took into account the habits, needs and activities of work groups

During the past two or three years, however, there has been a burst of new thinking about computer-mediated work. In contrast with the terminology of personal computers and computers to empower *individuals* to do their best, we are starting to hear much more about *interpersonal computing*. This means different things to different people, and new jargon has started to appear, including "cooperative computing," "collaboration technology," and "work group computing." The somewhat awkward term "groupware" has been proposed for computer software that is specifically intended to aid in the work and coordination of activity of a work group.

This chapter presents a particular vision of possibilities that we have found intriguing and that we believe could have profound effects on the functioning of organizations. Crafting tools that actually help collaboration is a very subtle enterprise. There are two parts to our thesis. The first is that creative genius lies in the social substrate itself. Secondly, the interaction of ideas properly externalized and appreciated leads to wonderful combinations and results. Some of this synergy and exposure can be enhanced by tools in the social infrastructure. There is a streak of genius and creativity in each of us. That streak can be tapped by creating a medium in which ideas can rub productively against each other. We propose a medium of active and sharable workspaces for developing and explaining information.

In the next section we focus on the Colab project, one of several projects studying collaboration and supporting technology at Xerox PARC. We sketch out the basic premises of the project, describe one of the experimental systems that has been developed, and present some of the questions and issues that we have encountered in the work so far. In the following sections we reexamine and critique some of the basic assumptions of this work. This prepares us to ask more basic questions, and also to propose ways that the ideas and technology for group work could prove more significant and valuable than in our original vision, especially for research and engineering organizations

The study of collaborative tools requires transcending what we call the "techno macho" syndrome, the fascination with technology or methodology for its own sake. We should not get carried away with the belief that technological artifacts or decision methods in themselves will help that much. Many obvious attempts to apply technology to the work setting have hindered more than they have helped. However, for the authors, there is no denying or escaping our role as technologists. We are not disinterested observers of technology and the social scene. We are, in fact, concerned with the limitations of the status quo and are actively trying to invent new and more productive ways of working. This chapter is intended to stimulate those who want to think beyond current technologies and work practices.

Colab Meetings and Conversations

The Colab project was conceived as an experiment in computer support for meetings. We imagined that professional people in meetings should have the same kind of access to computers that they have in their offices for private or isolated work. In support of this we created the Colab meeting room. The meeting room provides a computer workstation for each participant in a face-to-face meeting. At the front of the room is a blackboard-sized touch sensitive screen (which we call a "liveboard") capable of displaying an image of approximately a million pixels.

Most of the meetings that we had in mind when we started the Colab project take place by a small group in front of a whiteboard or some other vertical and erasable writing surface. In these meetings, a creative group is engaged in discussion and work activities, using notations on the whiteboard to formulate and explain their thoughts and to keep notes during the meetings. For us, the whiteboard is the dominant medium used in meetings; it is a medium that we all use constantly in our daily work. We could see many shortcomings of the whiteboard, several of which are discussed in the following. The whiteboard became the technology to beat in inventing a more powerful medium for meetings, and we decided to beat it by creating a computational medium that kept the best properties and brought in new capabilities as well.

Our new medium distributed a computational whiteboard to every participant in a meeting. To promote shared viewing and shared access to what is written during the meeting, the Colab software is oriented around a concept for multi-user interfaces that we call WYSIWIS (What You See Is What I See—pronounced "whizzy whiz"). In a WYSIWIS interface, all the meeting participants can see exactly the same information on their displays. Colab meeting tools support this illusion by maintaining synchronized views across workstations. In addition, each person can point to things on the display with a personalized "tele-pointer" that is made visible in real time to the other participants. Colab software also supports private windows. Private windows correspond to notepads; public WYSIWIS windows correspond to whiteboards

But how could computers possibly help in meetings? One could approach this question by enumerating the aspects of meetings that are annoying and then investigating which of them might be ameliorated by computer technology. This would be an awesome task, requiring at the onset some substantial focus to limit and to identify the kinds of work to be investigated. However, we approached the issue from another direction, trying to understand the properties of a computer medium and then imagining the kinds of meeting situations in which computers could make a positive difference. Most of our intuitions are based on information-processing concepts, both for computers and the nature of work in meetings. These concepts also provide some insights about the kinds of work activities for which computers might make a difference.

Computers provide more space for writing than whiteboards. The storage capacity of a whiteboard is quite limited, and after a period of time, a group writing on a whiteboard must erase things in order to keep going. In a computer medium, the display space can be reused without discarding information because symbols can be moved to and from file space. Furthermore, the file storage capacity of a computer is quite large, and there are many techniques for organizing the display of information on a computer screen using windows, icons, and scrolling techniques.

Even with whiteboards, participants tend to build up large collections of written symbol structures that provide the common ground for reference. With more space for writing, participants can build up potentially larger sets of shared writings. This can be important for meetings that last for several sessions. Backup on a file system makes it possible to recall and display things even if they were developed in previous meetings.

The abundance of space in a computer is no excuse for neglecting to manage space as a resource, but here again the computer medium offers some advantages. Using techniques from bitmapped user interfaces, items can be quickly and easily rearranged on a computer screen. In contrast, on a whiteboard one must manually copy and erase symbols in order to rearrange them. This flexibility makes it possible to organize a screen, reducing clutter. This enables a group to organize space more easily for the purposes of visualization and accommodation of shifts in focus.

A computer medium provides computational leverage that can be used in many ways. For example, in a resource-allocation meeting, the computer could provide visible spreadsheet capabilities. It could display information in alternative formats for easier manipulation or better understanding. It can also provide search services for finding information in large sets.

WYSIWIS interfaces can relax some constraints on communication and cognitive processing. By enabling participants to use a shared written medium, the bandwidth of communication is potentially increased, since more than one person can add information at the same time. However, even if the apparent increase in bandwidth of communication in a Colab setting is not significant, freeing the constraints on parallelism and serial communication may improve the quality of deliberations by enabling meeting participants more freedom in scheduling their attention and cognitive activities.

These general capabilities of a computer medium suggest that the Colab would have the most advantages in meetings that include manipulation of substantial amounts of information, such as meetings by engineers in which complex designs are discussed and compared.

Meetings Tools: An Example

We use the term *meeting tool* to refer to computer software in support of groups in meetings. Just as users of personal computer software need different tools for different purposes (e.g., text editors, spreadsheets, mail systems), so too do meeting participants need different tools for different purposes (e.g., tools for agenda control, brainstorming, negotiation, and argumentation).

Cognoter is a Colab meeting tool used in our lab about once a week. It is used to organize ideas for presentations, reports, talks, and papers. Cognoter supports a meeting process in which participants come together, usually without having prepared any materials ahead of time. Meeting participants determine the audience and goals for their presentation, the topics to be included, and the overall organization. The output of Cognoter is an annotated outline.

The organization of Cognoter is described in the following. To convey a clearer sense not only of what it is but also how it is used, we have included some informal observations of use and meeting phenomena.

• • •

Several things can reduce the quality of a presentation. It could fail to include some important topics; it could dwell on irrelevant or unimportant topics; or it could address the topics in an incoherent order. To avoid these pitfalls Cognoter organizes the process into specific stages. Each stage incrementally increases the set of actions available to the user.

The stages in Cognoter are brainstorming, ordering and grouping, evaluating, and generating an outline. We originally adopted this structure from a similar one that proved useful for us in non-computational settings; however, there are significant differences in the uses and effects of the stages when computers are introduced.

Brainstorming Ideas

The brainstorming stage is intended to foster the free-flowing contribution of ideas. There is one basic operation: A participant selects an empty space in a public window and types in a word or phrase characterizing an idea.

Unlike usual brainstorming meetings, there is no waiting for turns in Cognoter, any participant can enter an item at any time. Often the inspiration for an item is triggered by another participant saying something or entering an item in a public window. Thus, communication (or loosely "the conversation") in Cognoter takes place both by voice and over the computer medium. All items appear on everyone's displays. Participants can annotate items with longer descriptions to clarify their meanings.

Organizing Ideas

The order of items for the presentation is established in Cognoter by incremental and local steps. There are two operations: linking items into presentation order, and putting items into delineated subgroups. If item A is linked to B (meaning A comes before B), and B is linked to C, then A comes before C. If item A is linked to a subgroup, then it comes before every item in the group. By these transitive and distributive operations, a small number of explicit links can tightly constrain the order of items in the outline.

The linking operation often takes place in conjunction with an oral justification. For example, if "expenses" and "bottom-line results" were items. a participant might argue out loud "We have to talk about expenses before bottom-line results because otherwise management won't understand the results." This relation is represented visually in Cognoter as an arrow linking the item labeled "expenses" to the one labeled "bottom-line results." It is also possible to move related ideas to an idea subgroup in a separate window. Before moving items, it is common practice to put them in a spatially compact cluster. This allows comment on the coherence of the proposed grouping.

In Cognoter, the overall task is richer than in traditional brainstorming sessions. For one thing, the task is not finished when some ideas have been generated. Preparing a presentation requires organizing and evaluating ideas as well. Furthermore, our informal observations of the meetings indicate that people form subgroups that focus on the development of particular aspects of the subject matter. Since subgroups of ideas are usually put into separate windows, each subgroup of people can focus around one window or another. The frequency and significance of this behavior and the importance of supporting it with meeting tools will be a subject for systematic study when our observational facilities become operational.

Although subgroups of collaborators can work mostly independently, they can also communicate. For example, one group may decide that some of the items in its windows don't fit with the others, and may put them back into the general pool or offer them to another subgroup. Further communication is then required when the items are reconsidered, perhaps by the whole group. When subgroups rejoin, participants can recap the changes made in the subgroups.

Evaluating Ideas

During this stage the subgroup boundaries tend to dissolve and the meeting participants function again as a single group. Participants try to understand the organization of the presentation as a whole. Items that seem irrelevant or less important than others can be deleted. Outlines are generated by Cognoter upon request, and ambiguities in the ordering can be highlighted. Participants can argue whether particular items are irrelevant or unimportant when compared with others.

Expanded Dimensions for Conversations

Tools like Cognoter embody more than a shift from a whiteboard to a computer. Effective collaboration has some tacitly held rules, such as taking turns in conversation. There are multiple roles such as inventing, critiquing, reformulating, scribing, and summarizing. People switch roles during a conversation, and the switching itself follows certain rules bearing on rhythm, momentum, and topical focus. For example, in an effective collaboration, one party will hold back and not interrupt a second party who is obviously "on a roll" generating a stream of related ideas.

Computer media change some of the basic parameters of conversation and enable profound changes in the shape of the conversations. When we move from personal to interpersonal, the requirement for personal intelligibility of the subject matter shifts to a requirement for *mutual* intelligibility; the meaning of conversational terms shifts from being internalized and fixed to being externalized and negotiated. Expressed in a computer medium, communications persist in a form that is tangible, external and manipulable. We conjecture that this substantially increases the amount of information for which there is a lasting awareness and shared understanding by participants in a meeting.

The coordination of intellectual work around manipulable icons draws on familiar skills for the coordination of physical work. Sorting can be done with icon manipulation. One moves items between buckets until they are in the right places. In both cases the multi-user interfaces indicate when objects are being manipulated (e.g., edited) by someone, providing visual clues for team coordination.

The same kind of manipulative action can be used for indicating when one participant wants another to work on an item. Thus, it is possible to pick up an item and drop it into the workspace of a second participant. This is very much like the physical act of picking up a physical object (e.g., a piece of paper) and handing it off to someone else for attention. A single action removes the object from one's own inventory and adds it to someone else's inventory for attention.

The possibility of simultaneous communications relaxes many constraints. It increases the possible bandwidth of communication in meetings. Changes like this raise many questions for which we do not yet have answers. In ordinary conversation, the meaning of what is said often crucially depends on the context of what was said just before. In Cognoter, multiple things can be "said" at once in the computational workspace. It can be argued that such capabilities introduce confusion into the meeting process. On the other hand, this capability can be enormously freeing in the context of a fast-moving brainstorming session. Reading is faster than listening, so it is possible to scan the items being created by several others and, occasionally, to respond to them. When something puzzling comes along on the screen, however, it is not necessary to tend to it at once. Unlike oral communication, there is no need to remember a confusing item because it remains in the workspace inventory for later processing. Any systematic process for going through the items will encounter the item again for later consideration. A written workspace is amenable to scheduled and systematic processing of communications. Thus, even if the potential increase in bandwidth does not result in an overall increase in communication, it may be important for other reasons.

During the brainstorming phase of Cognoter, the parallel action in proposing ideas reduces the usual verbal communication to coordinate turn-taking and synchronization. A participant can enter an idea whenever it comes to mind. Oral conversation tends to drop off radically, since so much of the communication load shifts from ears to eyes. The speech resource becomes more available for questions that clarify points.

It is important to note that parallel action is not altogether absent in noncomputational meetings. Videotapes of design meetings show that groups of designers working on large sheets of paper engage in much parallel sketching activity. Furthermore, shared workspaces can be created in other media, such as video. Architects working together through such a medium have reported an intensity of engagement and productivity similar to the informal reports by users of shared workspaces in the Colab.

Another profound change to the dimensions of conversation is the possibility of equal access to public data. In Colab, the conversational acts that enable a participant to modify the public display or to assume the role of chairman can take place in a fraction of a second. In contrast, with an ordinary meeting room with table and blackboard, one must negotiate the transition, rise from a chair, walk to the board and so on. By lowering the hurdles of transition, the technology creates a potential for broader participation and for more flexibility in roles.

Whether and when these changes in conversations are beneficial is still to be determined. For example, accelerating the pace of a meeting as in the brainstorming phase may give participants less time to think. On the other hand, freedom from serial turn-taking may alleviate some of the problems of production blocking (due to the limitation that only one group member can talk at a time) reported by other studies of brainstorming in more conventional media. In some cases, the context surrounding the generation of an item may be lost. Important effects also happen at the transitions between meeting processes. Among the transitions are the formation and dissolution of subgroups, the shifting of participants from one topical focus to another, and the transitions of the conversational patterns of the whole group as it shifts from having a single focus of activity to having multiple conversations and subgroups and then back again. However, our purpose now is to begin to understand some of the differences, not to evaluate them.

Seamlessness at Work

As we move on to the next phases of our research, we are also ready to challenge the assumptions of the Colab design with an issue that seems to dwarf all the others:

Meetings do not take place (exclusively) in conference rooms.

Meetings take place wherever people get together and have conversations. Recently, one of us spent time observing the use of documents by nurses at the Pacific Medical Center in San Francisco. What was impressive and interesting was how much clarification, coordination, and negotiation among nurses took place over their clipboards. If a narrow-minded computersmith wanted to bring information processing to the hospital situation, the first bad idea might be to make the documents available on a workstation located somewhere down the hospital corridor. That would completely ignore the conversations and interactions of the nurses where they meet. Like other intelligent human beings, nurses could probably cope with a poorly designed computer system. However, to be most helpful, we suspect that the technology of record keeping and conversation should be as familiar and easy to use as a blackboard and as readily available and portable as the clipboard, paper, and pen.

To illustrate this issue of the use of technology and the location of meetings, we present a story about some very low technology that we misapplied at PARC. The technology was a corner desk, a wedge-shaped desk for holding a computer workstation that could be located in the corner of a room. We wanted to promote team programming on our research projects and these new desks offered ample elbow room for two people sitting together. We placed the desks in our regular conference rooms, equipped them with computer workstations, and anticipated that they would also be useful for demonstrations and for visitors when office space was tight. .

After the corner desks were installed, we noticed that they were never used. Team programming was happening occasionally, but it always started in somebody's office. Someone might start with a system-debugging question, or have a programming puzzle or idea. In every case people jammed their chairs together in the office and squeezed around the workstation. At no point did they move to the corner desks in the conference room.

Concluding that the desks were a failure, we decided to have them stored in a warehouse. To salvage something from them, one of the authors who liked the aesthetics of the corner desks and had an office shape that could use one easily, decided to discard a table and regular desk from his office and to use a corner desk instead. Shortly thereafter, team programming was observed to occur in his office, and furthermore, the idea of putting the desks in offices was legitimized. The corner desks are now mostly located in our offices, where programming occurs. Now they are serving their intended purpose; team programming occurs on a regular basis, and several more corner desks have been built.

Returning to the assumption behind the Colab meeting room, we note again that meetings take place regularly in offices, not just meeting rooms. This raises the question of how offices should be equipped. Here we believe that the Colab experience is relevant. In taking a prescriptive stance, we can predict what could be possible.

We believe that one of the most useful additions to the infrastructure of an office would be a large touch-sensitive display: an office liveboard. A large display creates a focus of attention for a team working together. Furthermore, with other workstations based on CRT displays or flat panels around the room, we could presumably get some of the WYSIWIS meeting phenomena that we have observed in the Colab.

However, there are two main features that intrigue us. One is the power of the computational medium for flexibly organizing space. Whether whiteboards are in conference rooms or offices, they never have enough space. All of the arguments that we advanced for Colab workstations for managing display and file space apply equally well to meetings in an office. The second feature that intrigues us is the possibility of an accurate, large-scale pointing device adequate for quickly sketching diagrams on a high-resolution liveboard. The whiteboards of PARC are always filled with informal diagrams and symbols of great variety. The liveboard in the Colab, however, has a resolution of somewhat greater than one pixel per tenth of an inch. Although this is good enough to present a large image of one of our computer screens, it is much too coarse for smooth sketching at the liveboard.

This brings us back to our suggestion that the technology of conversation should be as familiar and easy to use as a whiteboard and as readily available as paper and pen. Paper, pen, and whiteboards seem natural and easy to use, in part because we are exposed to them and trained in their use at a very young age. They are also supremely flexible. You can write on them in almost any way that you desire, making text and figures slant up, slant down, surrounded by wiggly globs, and so on.

Many other meeting devices would be possible in an office and would work well with a liveboard, such as multiple keyboards, remote pointing devices, and small flat-panel devices used as networked sketchpads. As in the Colab, pointing devices (e.g., mice or styluses) could enable participants to point to something on the public display without leaving their seats. All these devices should be small so that they could be stored out of sight, and they should be cordless. Another useful device would be a digital tape loop and audio gear so that one could recover a particularly apt turn of expression by playing back the last part of a conversation.

The well-equipped office should provide an information environment that connects seamlessly larger and more formal meeting rooms like the Colab. The same software and hardware should support conversations in both settings. In an office one should be able to prepare materials for larger meetings and to continue small-scale follow-up meetings afterward.

Explaining an idea to a colleague is simplified when the context-setting sketches on a whiteboard are available. With active liveboards in offices and user interfaces based on new remote window systems, moving the contents of a liveboard from one office to another will be possible. To this end, means for moving the contents of a liveboard should be direct and simple. One could forward the contents to an office liveboard ("Send this to my office") or file it in a database. Similarly, one could retrieve something to show to a colleague in the coffee room ("Get the big-idea window from yesterday's conversation.")

This brings us to a most important concept about new capabilities: the portable meeting. A meeting that starts at one office on one day could be resumed by any of the participants in their own office or introduced to another colleague at yet another time or location. In conventional meeting situations, different kinds of records are kept for different purposes. Some things are written during the meeting for the purposes of explaining or developing a point; other notes are written by the participants for later use by themselves or others, and yet other things may be written such as minutes for explaining to parties that were not present at the meetings. With portable meetings the explanatory scribbles created during the course of a meeting become available for reuse at a second location without the need for manual copying. Furthermore, if one person explains a set of ideas using figures and symbols from a liveboard, the second person could gain access to this information and extend the script for explaining it to a third person.

Many visitors to Xerox's System Sciences Laboratory are surprised by the number of floor-to-ceiling whiteboards, each in its own corner with comfortable seats or couches around them. This is not an accident or just a sign of opulence. These areas were explicitly designed to foster small collaborative teams working in semi-private areas. Whiteboards enable people to create a large sharable context. By having so much of the discussion visibly displayed, it is very easy for someone walking by to gain a sense of what is going on and to decide whether to contribute. Further, one can come up to speed more quickly.

The phenomenon of portable meetings may enable additional possibilities if liveboards were introduced into public areas. One of the most heavily and productively used whiteboards in our laboratory is the one near the coffee service in the lounge area. Perhaps coffee centers foster creativity both because people encounter each other here and because of the informality and relaxation that the centers suggest. Could the creative power of a center be tapped better if the whiteboard were replaced by a liveboard? After productive conversation one would not need to remember the ideas or to copy the contents to paper.

This, finally, is what we have in mind for infrastructure for group work: a seamless environment of tools for conversation that extends from offices to the coffee room to the formal meeting room. One might even consider surfacing the tables in the cafeteria with interactive flat displays, providing an electronic version of the proverbial coffeehouse napkins on which so many important inventions reportedly have been born. In a seamless environment, the ideas of conversation can become not only external and directly manipulable, as in the Colab, but also portable.

In closing, we return to our original theme of unlocking the creative genius inside of us. Genius takes many forms. It is not just the development of new ideas. There can be genius in negotiation, genius in management, genius in creating coherent plans, genius in all of the things that organizations do. Perhaps this genius can be unlocked by new tools for conversation that respect that we do not work in isolation. In this view, the seamless tools for next-generation meetings and conversations may shape our next-generation organizations.

Reflections

The Colab project was an experiment in supporting group work by creating a special environment—a team work room. When the project was built, it quickly became popular with visitors to Xerox PARC. Something about the setting seemed to many people like a concrete vision of what meetings could be. As project leader for the Colab project, I was startled while preparing this book to come upon the following suggestion about group work in Licklider's "Libraries of the Future" (excerpted in Part 1).

In the current technology there are two general approaches to group-computer interaction. The first and most widely used provides a separate console for each member of the group and relies upon the computer, together with auxiliary communication circuits, to mediate the interaction among the members of the group as well as the interaction of the members with computer and its store. The second approach, taken in some military systems, uses large "wall" displays, located in view of several or all of the members of the group and intended to provide a common frame of reference for their decisions and actions.

• • •

In a procognitive system with group displays (second approach) one would expect to see large-scale displays similar in principle to the individual display *screen already discussed, even ... derivatives of the light pen to provide communication between the human members of the team and the computer.*

Thus Licklider anticipated the way the Colab combined individual workstations for meeting participants with a large wall-sized display. Perhaps this similarity of vision hints at some deeper social dreams and common experiences. Our school experience includes blackboards, and our work experience uses computers. For people who work on project teams, the blackboard is a familiar tool because it is big enough to let everyone see. Similarly, everyone who works on a computer recognizes the plasticity of the medium for backing up, writing things tentatively, moving them around, and so on. Both Colab and Licklider's vision marry computers and blackboards.

Several Colabs were built in various Xerox offices, and similar facilities exist around the world. Shortly after this paper was written the Colab project at PARC was phased out, to be replaced by the liveboard project. The latter was intended to take the interactive whiteboard that was the centerpiece of the Colab and replicate it. This change in direction followed from a key observation that meetings do not take place exclusively in conference rooms. The idea was to put liveboards in offices and public places, on the expectation that they would lead to portable meetings and help organizations make more-effective use of computers.

The liveboard project at Xerox PARC was led by Richard Bruce and Frank Halasz. Over the past few years, the project moved from building prototypes for researchers, to providing a few liveboards to colleagues at other institutions, and to creating a Xerox division called Liveworks to manufacture and sell liveboards.

In the Colab project, the liveboard was effectively a large computer screen used for showing information but not people. While the Colab project was running, the neighboring research group at Xerox PARC was testing a system called Media Space, which created a video network of people working together. A vigorous debate about whether it was better to use the screens to show people or shared information raged. With hindsight, the competition was silly. Current liveboards and similar offerings by various vendors now make it possible to combine information and video images on the same screen, thus peopling the cyberspace.

Looking back, I wonder whether mythological roots played any conscious or unconscious role in our development of liveboards and video displays. Certainly in fairy tales magical mirrors often display images of faraway places or answer important questions; crystal balls make it possible to see things that may be far away in distance or time. In the myth of Narcissus, a youth falls in love with his own image in a pool of water; and in many myths water represents the unconscious and peering into it gives us new insights into ourselves.

In the next article, we see technology for collaboration raised to a national scale—from Colab to Collaboratory—to create joint working environments to support scientific research.

The National Collaboratory—A White Paper

William A. Wulf

Connections

William Wulf is a man with a vision. From his experience in the National Science Foundation, he knew about some of the apparent paradoxes involved in creating an environment for good science. Exciting results seem to flow from places where good researchers can interact, inspiring each other and building on each other's ideas. The traditional approach to fostering such interaction is to develop centers of excellence that bring together the people, facilities, and instrumentation needed for research. Such facilities however, are expensive, and the budget for creating them is always under pressure.

In the advancing technology of computers and communications Wulf saw an opportunity to revolutionize the way scientists work. He wrote the following short letter to explain and promote his idea, and it was circulated widely.

The health of the United States, economically and militarily, depends on its technology base. The technology base depends on the number, quality, and productivity of the nation's research scientists and engineers. This paper concentrates on scientific and engineering productivity, which, in turn, depends on such things as adequate facilities, stimulating colleagues, and the open exchange of ideas.

One response to the issue of research productivity has been the creation of "centers," "institutes" and "laboratories" outside of the normal university departmental structure. There are many reasons for the creation of such centers, including providing a home for interdisciplinary research and managing unique (and often expensive) instrumentation. However, a principle reason has been to assemble a critical mass of the factors that contribute to research productivity, and I believe that history corroborates that such centers have produced a disproportionate share of the advances in their respective fields.

The trend toward creation of extra-departmental centers is not without its problems and detractors. We are entering an era, however, in which it will no longer be necessary for a center to have a single geographical location, or even a common administrative structure. Information communication and processing will allow a geographically dispersed community of researchers to interact, to share ideas, data, and instruments with much the same ease as those who are collocated now enjoy. Freed from the constraints of distance, opportunity and choice will determine the composition, size and duration of a research team.

Not only will remote interaction be possible in the coming era, it will be mandatory. Interaction with remote instrumentation will be necessary because of the location of the instrument (such as the space telescope), or because the environment in which it operates is hostile to humans (such as unmanned deep-ocean vehicles). Interaction with remote colleagues will be necessary, for example, because the appropriate talents to address an interdisciplinary problem are not collocated anywhere. Remote interaction with data will be necessary because the database is too vast to be replicated (such as the global seismic database). Finally, some of the most pressing scientific challenges facing us, such as that of global change, are inherently distributed and exhibit all of these properties; remote interaction with instruments, colleagues, and data is essential to solving them.

The Proposal

The proposal, then, is to undertake a major, coordinated program of research and development leading to an electronic "collaboratory,"[1] a "center without walls" in which the nation's researchers can perform their research without regard to geographical location—interacting with colleagues, accessing instrumentation, sharing data and computational resources, accessing information in digital libraries.

The enabling technologies for the collaboratory are high-speed information processing and communication. Implementation of a national research network is already underway, high-performance computers are becoming ubiquitous, and "open system" standards are making these facilities more accessible to the research community. In a sense, the collaboratory is an inevitable outcome of these developments. However, much as a "center" is enabled by the building that houses it but is not just the building, the collaboratory is not just interconnected computers. A complete infrastructure is required: software that facilitates collaboration, simulation tools that can substitute for some aspects of the traditional wet laboratory, "smart instruments" that can be used effectively remotely and interchangeably with simulated experiments, digital libraries and software to access the information in them, accessible (usable) repositories of raw data, etc.

A great deal of research remains to be done to exploit the enabling technologies and to build this infrastructure. Some of the research is traditional computer science and computer/communication engineering—for example, how can we achieve the network speeds necessary for collaboration involving communication of real-time high-resolution images, how can we ensure the security and integrity of private communications, and how can we make smart instruments that can be effectively utilized remotely? Some of this research is essentially social, behavioral, or economic science—how do people collaborate, and how can we exploit technology to amplify the effectiveness of this collaboration, especially when the collaborators are not collocated?

Research in many of these areas is already underway, but (a) it is not coordinated, and hence is not easily combined, and (b) when viewed independently, aspects crucial to the total concept are not perceived to have an especially high priority. By setting ourselves a concrete goal we can focus the energies of the research community in a way that will ameliorate both these problems.

Suppose for the moment that the vision of the collaboratory were realized; how would it impact the productivity of the nation's scarce human resources? It could be argued that an electronic "center" would not enable anything new—anything not now possible, albeit more slowly or at the cost of moving people. I don't believe that. I believe that the quantitative increase in ease of collaboration will have a profound qualitative effect.

First, the productivity of the individual researcher will be enhanced by providing access to information and instrumentation now available only at prohibitive cost in both money and time.

Second, as most researchers will attest, the single most critical resource for innovation is access to stimulating colleagues; the collaboratory will increase the number of nimble minds and diverse perspectives far beyond those available at the researcher's home institution.

Third, the collaboratory will enable both inter- and intra-disciplinary research that simply isn't being done now because the best people to do the research are not collocated and the scale or duration of the project doesn't justify a mega-center and the associated relocation of people.

Fourth, it will increase the pool of researchers available to work on a problem. The faculty at four-year and predominantly minority institutions are an essentially untapped resource. The collaboratory will permit them to be full and effective partners in research projects—and, I believe, increase the quality of instruction at those schools at the same time.

Finally, it will speed the transition of new ideas into industry, into products—and increase the relevance of research to social/economic goals. By making academics and advanced developers in industry a part of the same collaboratory, the same "intellectual stew," we can achieve both effects simultaneously and naturally.

We may never know quantitatively the impact of these combined effects, partly because we don't know what would have happened without the collaboratory. Moreover, not every researcher will wish to collaborate remotely; nor will any single technological "fix" cure the myriad problems faced by the country.

Nonetheless, I believe the effect will be profound. Consider just one of the effects mentioned above—the speed of technology transfer. We already have examples where the research network has shortened the time from research idea to product to less than four years (instead of the usual fifteen to twenty years). If this effect could be achieved for even a small fraction of technology-based products, the impact on the nation's competitiveness would be enormous.

So, what needs to be done?

For the most part we do not need to begin whole new areas of research. Rather, we need to coordinate and expand research already under way, to deploy the enabling infrastructure (such as the national research network), to guide the establishment of national projects (such as the human genome and global-change database) along paths that will permit them to inter-operate, and, eventually, to set standards for both commercially produced and one-of-a-kind instrumentation to be usable remotely.

The first step will be taken at a workshop being sponsored by the NSF Directorate for Computer and Information Science and Engineering at Rockefeller University this March [1989], under the co-chairmanship of J. Lederberg and K. Uncapher. The principal objective of the workshop is to lay out the research agenda for the collaboratory. What are the central problems? What is the best mode for attacking each of them? How can the research be coordinated? Practical experience may be needed in some areas, and demonstration developments may be appropriate; what are good candidates for these demonstration projects? The effort need not be an "all or nothing" undertaking; given the enabling infrastructure and a reasonable degree of coordination, results can be used as they emerge; how is this best done?

NSF should play a leadership role in implementing this agenda. The nature of this effort may become, both in size and scope, larger than any one agency can undertake, and will require heavy involvement of the private sector.

Notes

1. The word *collaboratory* was invented to combine the terms *collaboration* and *laboratory*.

Reflections

The primary public image of the scientist may be the solitary eccentric working alone in his laboratory for years and years. This picture, how-ever, bears little resemblance to the experience of practicing researcher, most of whom work on teams and in institutions. They usually work on multiple projects at the same time, devising theoretical frameworks, designing experimental approaches, worrying about staffing problems. They not only conduct experiments and analyze data, they also give informal presentations to colleagues to obtain feedback, and they publish. They look for applications for their findings. And they repeat work done earlier by themselves or others. Even this list is oversimplified. At every stage of the cycle, research may involve a large or small team to conduct experiments, write joint reports, or try to raise money. One reason why scientists work in institutions is that it takes much space to house a team.

Wulf's vision starts with these teams, asking whether every member of a team needs to be in the same place. Sometimes, the most qualified people to join a team to carry out a particular piece of work live in different places. Is there a way to enable them to work together without being at the same institution? Is there a way for them to share equipment for an experiment, when the equipment is located at widely separated locations? Enter the vision of the collaboratory.

Realizing Wulf's vision of a collaboratory in practical science would require much agreement. One way to advance a scientific career in an academic institution is to create a local center, providing a setting to attract colleagues and graduate students in a specific scientific specialty. Before such centers with walls can be replaced by centers without walls, many conditions must be met. Political issues bearing on careers must be resolved; collaborations need to produce significant results; and the technology to mediate the processes effectively must be available.

In 1993, the Computer Science and Telecommunications Board issued a report on National Collaboratories; it recommended funding a research component to develop the hardware and software, as well as the education and training facilities to support them. (For information on obtaining copies of this report, see Further Readings.) The National Science Foundation is presently funding collaboratory research.

The 1993 report explores the viability of the collaboratory concept for different scientific disciplines. For example, a key advantage for a collaboratory in oceanography is its ability to provide access to instrumentation on the high seas and to modeling software. The availability of instrumentation and shared databases is also a key advantage for a collaboratory in space physics. In molecular biology, the report suggests, a *collaboratory could be especially useful in coordinating research and sharing data about the human genome.*

Web mavens can find several home pages for collaboratories on the Internet, including a collaboratory on upper atmospheric research at the University of Michigan with the URL

http://http2.sils.umich.edu/Catalog/UARC.html

A project called the Collaboratory Notebook at the School of Education and Social Policy and Institute for the Learning Sciences at Northwestern University includes an experiment in changing the way science is taught and learned in high schools by using high-performance computing and communications technologies. Instead of classes based on traditional textbooks and lectures, this project brings students computer-visualization tools used by researchers in the atmospheric and environmental sciences. To provide a taste of how science is actually practiced, it gives students tools they can use to discuss the research they perform with one another and with distant researchers and educators. Students can keep private journals and group notebooks and conduct public discussions on the network. The URL for this project is

http://www.covis.nwu.edu/Papers/edmedia94.html

Other centers and proposals for collaboratories are also on the network. There is, for example, a proposal for a collaboratory on environmental molecular sciences at Pacific Northwest Laboratories in Richland, Washington, and a collaboratory at the Center for Information Systems Management in the Graduate School of Business at the University of Texas at Austin. In North Carolina, there is an interactive-video conferencing facility for linking high-performance computing centers around the country. Phoenix College in Arizona coordinates an interactive collaboratory (actually a MUD) for global learning on-line.

For people outside scientific research, the examples of collaboration systems for science may seem remote from daily life. But why should this be so? The collaboratory program offers several possibilities for our explorination of visions for the national information infrastructure. One possibility is greater public access to scientific data. The growth of the collaboratory movement is a spur to putting more data, libraries, and discussions on-line. Although it seems unlikely that the demand for access to ongoing research will ever rival the demand for, say, television entertainment, having such information accessible to students who are forming impressions and making career choices would be individually and socially beneficial.

Without denigrating the value to scientists in spending time alone, the collaboratory movement suggests that they like to work together. This puts a different slant on the social issues of digital reality raised in our consideration of MUDs. The image of a lone scientist puzzling over an experiment and adding to human knowledge needs to be augmented. While Lederberg reminds us to include scientists reviewing and approving articles for publication, Wulf argues that scientists sometimes get their best ideas in groups, by bouncing ideas off each other and brainstorming.

What about opportunities in the collaboratory vision for people in other, nonscience lines of work? All sorts of groups are already using the Internet create on-line discussion groups, and newsletters. A rich enough information infrastructure could support real-time collaboration as well. A city's junior chamber of commerce could interact by computer network. Auto clubs for people interested in classic Mustangs could hold not only computer conferences and newsletter but also on-line auto-shows that would let users tour cars remotely. (Would driving a car remotely miss the point?) Local astronomy clubs already can have bulletin boards and share prized photographs. Should they also operate and share relatively expensive telescopes remotely? Imagine interlinked telescopes located at high altitudes in remote parts of the world in different time zones. This might appeal to the amateur astronomer who falls asleep at nine o'clock! More seriously, people interested in responding to global issues such as environmental issues or disaster relief, could coordinate their efforts through bulletin boards and discussion groups. One way to look at the our examples of MUDs and scientific collaboratories is as springboards for imagining what is possible. In reinventing the information superhighway, we create possibilities for ourselves. What do we want to become and create?

Internet Dreams: First Encounters of an On-line Dream Group

Barbara Viglizzo

Connections

Sigmund Freud, the founder of psychoanalysis, called dreams the royal road to the unconscious. Yet, as Fadiman and Frager point out in Personality and Personal Growth, *Freud did not discover the unconscious. The ancient Greeks, among others, recommended the study of dreams, and many others have sought the roots of creativity in the unconscious.*

Whereas Freud studied the personal unconscious, Carl Jung expanded the study to the collective unconscious. Jung, who is famous for his study of the relationship between dreams and mythology, made several trips to remote areas of the world to collect dreams. He studied more than sixty thousand dreams during his lifetime. The language of dreams he derived from this study is a language of images: archaic, symbolic, and pre-logical. Jung found similarities between dreams and myths from around the world and identified many common symbols and archetypes. He was particularly struck by how closely dream images of people from different cultures resemble each other.

The dreams of those who have shaped the Internet and contributed to this book—Vannevar Bush, James Licklider, Joshua Lederberg, Vinton Cerf, and Robert Kahn, among others—are more than personal dreams. Our tour of Internet dreams according to metaphors and archetypes suggests that their dreams originated in ancient times, beyond history. Like Jung, we have tried to go beyond the personal unconscious and personal dreams to explore the collective unconscious and the collective myths and archetypes that may influence our conceptions of the digital worlds we are creating.

Barbara Viglizzo's article, which resulted from a collaboration with noted dream researcher Jeremy Taylor, explicitly explores a new relationship between dreams and the Internet. Taylor, the author of several books about dreams and dream interpretation, uses dream analysis in psychological research, counseling, and community work. He conducts dream sessions and workshops in which people collectively analyze each other's dreams. Taylor, who has analyzed over a hundred thousand dreams in his work, says that dreams tap into symbols from the unconscious and that people grow or evolve more rapidly—emotionally, psychologically, and spiritually—when they pay attention to their dreams. When people work in dream groups, he asserts, the evolution works even faster because people learn from each others' dreams.

What do these dream groups have to do with the Internet? Viglizzo's article reports on the first experiences of an on-line dream group.[1] Taylor, the dream group leader, selected for discussion two dreams by members of the group. After the selected dreams were distributed by e-mail, members met on-line in a private chat room of America Online. Taylor was interested in how dream work conducted on-line—literally "Internet dreams"—would compare with regular group dream work. The experiences of the group put a different spin on the phrase "Internet Dreams" than we have seen in earlier articles. Instead of looking at how dreams can help us understand the net, Viglizzo and the other members of their "dream team" looked at how the net can help us understand dreams through on-line collaborative dream interpretation.

In the context of the digital worlds metaphor, Viglizzo reports on the experience of a virtual community in action—an electronic group similar to those discussed in an earlier section by Sproull and Faraj. Geographically, the dream group participants were scattered across the continental United States, which suggests one of the often-cited benefits of electronic meetings—savings in travel time. Hours before the first on-line session, one participant was trapped far from home when bad weather caused cancellation of his airline flight. Yet, after a quick trip to a newsstand to buy a computer magazine containing the ubiquitous America Online software diskettes and a few harried telephone calls to find a computer away from home he was able to attend the meeting anyway, reaching the electronic "meeting place" with fifteen minutes to spare.

Viglizzo's article is the story of a group of people who were interested in dream analysis and willing to try it a new way—on the network. For the most part she lets most of the dream participants speak for themselves, and conveys a sense of the experience of dream work by presenting a transcript of one session.

In a metaphorical sense, the participants created, both electronically and in their imaginations, new digital worlds as they sought insights from their common ground of symbols and meaning. Dreams were both the content of the group discussion and its subtext; for as Taylor and the other participants sought the meaning of their personal and collective dreams, they also explored the potential of the Internet for realizing larger dreams of connection and community and entirely new digital worlds.

Everyone dreams, although we do not always remember our dreams. Sleep researchers like Stephen Leberge, who measures people's rapid-eye movement in sleep, report that everyone dreams every night. But what is the purpose of our dreams? Jeremy Taylor, a well-known authority on Jungian dream work and author of *Where People Fly and Water Runs Uphill* and *Dream Work*, believes that "all dreams speak a universal language and come in the service of health and wholeness." Dreams don't come to tell us what we already know; they break new ground and invite us to new understandings. Taylor says that dreams tap the unconscious and make us aware of the metaphors and archetypes that flow through our lives, giving us insight into our unique journeys.

When America Online approached Taylor to run an on-line dream program, I proposed a trial run. This article describes that trial run and our investigation of the on-line dream group experience. We began with the notion that on-line dream work linking people all over the United States would be as beneficial as off-line group dream work.

The article starts with an interview I conducted with Jeremy Taylor, in which he describes his experience with dream groups and his expectations for on-line dream work. This interview preceded the first on-line session. Next, we present some of the preparatory material sent to the "dream team" for the first session—including instructions for the session and the text of the dream selected for the first session. The middle section of the article includes excerpts from the log of our first on-line dream session. Finally, we consider the results of two on-line sessions, drawing on postsession interviews and e-mail from the group participants.

Taylor's Dreams—An Interview with Jeremy Taylor

This interview was conducted on December 28, 1995, at Taylor's home in San Rafael, California.

Barbara: In your book, *Where People Fly and Water Runs Uphill,* you said that "no dream ever comes just to tell you what you already know" and that "All dreams carry new information and energy in their metaphors and symbols." Can you elaborate on that?

Jeremy: All of that stuff in the books is born out of experience. I did not know what was going on in dreams, and all I wanted to do was to find out. Over the years, I was so impressed with people telling dreams that seemed to be obvious and seemed to simply reiterate things they had already said a million times. And yet, when you worked with the dreams—assuming that the work went anywhere at all—it would go beyond the surface, beyond what everybody knew the dream was saying to begin with, beyond what they already knew.

Barbara: So the dreams were tapping into the unconscious.

Jeremy: Yes. As Jung said, "The most important thing about the unconscious is that it really is unconscious." People don't know. Nobody knows. When the unconscious speaks, it speaks about what is not known. And it always makes reference to things that are already known. So there is some framework, some kind of net you can get hold of that can pull the really unconscious thing up into the light where you can see it. So it's not that the dreams never make reference to what you already know. They always make reference to it, but in my experience, the reference to what is already known is for the purpose of building a foundation upon which the new thing can be placed, so it can be seen, The single most difficult thing about solitary dream work is getting past the "aha's" that are calibrated to what is already known. Dreamers in solitude get wonderful and satisfying "aha's," but they tend over time to be "aha's" about things they already knew before the dream came, so that the dream work becomes a kind of a reaffirmation about what they already thought was true. And it is not that they are in error. Each of those "aha's" individually is a valid "aha" about part of what the dream is saying, but it consistently misses the new stuff.

Barbara: Solitary dream work moves the psyche slowly, but group dream work speeds things up.

Jeremy: Yes. The group work is quicker and more deft and goes deeper and is more buoyant. There is more energy to it, so that when the stuff gets up to the surface, it's likely to stay there longer because it is being held by many consciousnesses instead of just the consciousness of the dreamer.

Barbara: On a universal level, what do dreams tell us about ourselves and our world?

Jeremy: My goodness! There are so many different ways of answering a question like that. One could use traditional religious language, for instance, and say that every dream and all dreams tell us that we are children of God. Fundamentalist folk would understand that language immediately. In a more psychological way, you could say that every dream demonstrates and reaffirms the universality of the human tendency to symbolize. Every dream is symbolic. There is no such thing as a dream that is not symbolic. The surface appearance may not be particularly symbolic, but the moment energy is exerted to look for meanings below the surface of appearance—lo and behold!—they appear. And they appear in such a way as to convince me that the propensity toward symbolization is universal, not just cultural. It's not an artifact of culture. In fact, I would put it the other way around: Culture is an artifact of this universal tendency to symbolize.

Barbara: What is the most important thing a dreamer needs to remember?

Jeremy: All dreams come in the service of health and wholeness. No matter how scary or how dull or unprepossessing the surface appearance of the dream may be, it comes to serve the individual dreamer's health and wholeness first and foremost and, ultimately, the health and wholeness of the entire species.

Barbara: That has been your experience?

Jeremy: In thirty years I have never met a single dream that did not ultimately convince me that that was so. This is somewhere in the neighborhood of a hundred thousand dreams, including my own and other peoples'. I think that is a fairly reliable sample. And that is not just middle-class Americans; that includes people from other parts of the world, big ethnic diversity and big educational diversity.

Barbara: In your book you say that "there is substantial reason to suppose that dreams themselves may be the workshop of evolution."

Jeremy: Indeed. Experience demonstrates that dreams are the workshop of evolution. At the personal level, one of the things that every dream is about is the person into whom the dreamer is evolving, at that moment. And clearly developmental milestones and other sorts of personal evolutionary events either take place in the dream world first—which is the way I tend to think about it—or they are presaged in the dream world.

Barbara: What do you think the potential is for computer on-line dream group work?

Jeremy: Oh, I think it is stunning. I am tempted to say at this point unimaginable. I don't think that we even know enough to begin to imagine what the potential is; but it is easy for me to imagine it facilitating a revolution in self-awareness among individuals—and in international global understanding among societies and cultures. That's just for openers. I am absolutely convinced that level of potential exists. Whether we are going to be able to achieve it or not is another question.

Barbara: And over how long of a period of time do you imagine this occurring?

Jeremy: Things are speeding up so quickly it's very hard for me to say. Everything is going exponentially faster, so I could imagine something like that being achieved maybe in four or five years. We are coming around to this great symbolic energy charge at the turn of the millennium, and that is affecting everybody. Everybody is thinking in terms of the end of the old and the beginning of the new. And that is not just symbolic: There are all these issues and problems coming to a crescendo simultaneously. This is what is happening. And I see on-line communication as one of the things of greatest potential. I imagine that the primary difference between live dream work and on-line dream work is going to be the flatness of the comments.

Barbara: The dream work dialogue will appear on the screen, but nothing else.

Jeremy: No emotions with it. No inflections, no tones of voice.

Barbara: But there is also the possibility that there will be fewer inhibitors, and that the exchange will be freer.

Jeremy: Exactly so. One of the wonderful things about being on-line is that folks can encounter each other in their essential forms without any distractions, so that the chance of going deeper more quickly exists in this medium. Whether we will actually achieve that potential is another question. I am absolutely convinced that the potential is there. On-line dream work may even be superior in some ways because of lack of inhibitions and the willingness to greet everyone with the same openness and the same face. This is a leveler, a prejudice inhibitor.

Barbara: What is your greatest hope and mission in life where dream work is concerned? Why do you do the work that you do?

Jeremy: My greatest personal hope is to learn more about what dreams mean—my dreams and everybody else's. I can tell you a joke about it. I am always saying to people that we can never get to the bottom of any dream. The question then arises: How would you know, supposing you did get to the bottom of a dream? How would you even recognize that you had gotten there? The only way that I can imagine that thought experiment for myself is that if a dream or a dream fragment were in fact unpacked all the way down to the bottom, if it were truly understood in its full depths, the results would be an "aha" of recognition that was so profound and global and complete that it would as a side effect produce an absolutely conscious and exquisite understanding of the deep connection and oneness with everyone past present and future. That is the order of health and wholeness that dreams are striving toward, and the order of health and wholeness out of which dreams spring. That's fancy psychological language for the ancient understanding that God is in everyone, and everyone is in God.

Preparing for the Sessions

Instructions for Dreamers

Prior to the first on-line dream session, we sent several e-mail messages to dream team members, instructions telling them how to set up an America Online account if they did not already have one and asking for times when they could meet on-line. We also sent them the dream work tool kit that Taylor uses in his face-to-face sessions. It explains the essentials of dream work philosophy and practice. Here is Taylor's "Toolkit for Dream Work" containing six basic hints for dream work.

1. All dreams speak a universal language and come in the service of health and wholeness. There is no such thing as a "bad dream"—only dreams that sometimes take a dramatically negative form in order to grab our attention.

2. Only the dreamer can say with any certainty what meanings his or her dream may have. This certainty usually comes in the form of a wordless "aha!" of recognition. This "aha" is a function of memory and is the only reliable touchstone of dream work.

3. There is no such thing as a dream with only one meaning. All dreams and dream images are "overdetermined" and have multiple meanings and layers of significance.

4. No dreams come to tell you what you already know. All dreams break new ground and invite you to new understandings and insights.

5. When talking to others about their dreams, it is both wise and polite to preface your remarks with words to the effect that "if it were my dream ..." and to keep this commentary in the first person as much as possible. This means that even relatively challenging and confrontative comments can be made in such a way that the dreamer may actually be able to hear and internalize them. It also can become a profound psychospiritual discipline—"walking a mile in your neighbor's moccasins."

6. All dream group participants should agree at the outset to maintain anonymity in all discussions of dream work. In the absence of any specific request for confidentiality, group members should be free to discuss their experiences openly outside the group, provided no other dreamer is identifiable in their stories. However, whenever any group member requests confidentiality, all members should agree to be bound by such a request.

Distributing the Dream

We chose two dates in January of 1996 to hold the trial run of the on-line dream sessions. The group's participants submitted dreams for consideration, and Taylor selected the dreams to be discussed in each session. He chose the following dream submitted by "Joanne12" for the first session. It is entitled "The Break-in."

At first I was in a big building with many rooms and porches. It was an old wood frame style house, open with screen doors. Part seemed like a grocery store where I saw men on ladders putting things away. My father was there and I remembered that he had been in jail and was home now, but I never asked him about it. I hoped nothing bad happened to him.

Later everyone was asleep, and I was walking toward the back of the building when I saw five men with rifles drive up. (Now we are in the Rosemont house where I grew up.) I ran upstairs to my parents' room and screamed as loud as I could that five men with guns were breaking in the back door. The whole family was there and some of the kids heard me and came downstairs. I ran to the kitchen, got a big knife out of the drawer (my kitchen in New York City) and went into the living room and made the kids go into the dining room behind me. The men drove their black truck into the living room and got out. Bryant was the driver, and I told him to think about what he was doing. I reminded him about the time my mom and I gave him a ride home after the high school football game the day I broke my foot. The other men spread out, took some things and put them in the truck. Then they all got back in and drove off. During my discussion with Bryant I was screaming and yelling using the word "f—ing" as an adjective; that is, "get out of the f—ing house."

Later I saw my mother and said she better check the house to see what was missing, and she asked "why?" I told her what happened and she never remembered me calling to her and my dad. I told her this at the end of the day and couldn't believe I didn't talk about it before.

Another part of this dream happened outside as I was walking toward the big wooden frame house. It is on a wooded, tree-lined road with a twenty-foot hill going down on the right side. I looked down there and saw a deer. Two other people—Paul and a woman who read tarot cards at the ASD conference dream ball—were with me, and I told them to look. When I looked back, another larger animal was there. I recognized it at the time, although I can't remember it now. I didn't want them to think I mistook it for a deer. When we looked a third time it was a donkey that came up on the road and lay down. The woman said I mistook a donkey for a deer, but I remember seeing the deer.

After everything was over, I was sitting in a diner with some women I knew. One said my mother was a bitch for not helping me when the men broke in. I told her that my mother was unaware and would help me if she knew. The women said I screamed and told her, but I said she didn't hear.

The Dream Session

The first on-line dream session was held in a private chat room on America Online on January 16 at 7 PM Pacific Standard Time. To reach a private chat room, participants log onto the service and select the "room" icon. In the America Online software the team used, the chat room appears as two windows: a text-entry window and a session log. The text window is at the bottom of the screen and can accept a message of up to a hundred characters. Team members can read and edit their messages before sending them by pushing a button labeled "send," which puts them in the session log on everyone's screen. Each entry shows the sender's name as well as what he or she types. The log can be scrolled to let participants can go back and see who said what earlier in the session.

A copy of the first session log was saved and is presented here in full, although it is fairly long. It conveys something of what dream analysis is like and how participants experienced it. In the last section of the paper we summarize the postsession impressions of various members of dream team.

There were nine participants, including Jeremy Taylor as the DreamMC. In presenting the log, I have changed the names of the participants, fixed the inevitable typographical errors found in most on-line conversations, and added a few punctuation marks. For example, here is an entry from the session as it actually appeared:

DreamMC: Sure—anyth8ing yiou care to shgare. As always, "the name of the game is dreamer's chopice"

In the transcript, I edit the entry to read:

DreamMC: Sure—anything you care to share. As always, "the name of the game is dreamer's choice."

Further changes would have made the log more readable but would distance the reader from team members' experience of the session. For example, the text is somewhat confusing because participants' contributions were segmented into hundred-character sections. Anyone who had more than that amount to say all at once had to send multiple messages. It often happened that a message from a second person appeared in the log between the parts of the message, in a sort of interleaving that is roughly analogous to several people talking at once—except that speakers didn't know this had happened until after they sent the messages. To make sense of these interleavings, you need to read through the log and piece together the sequential statements of each person. I left these interleavings in place in the text because participants' confusion in sorting out the conversations became part of the postsession discussion about how well the on-line chat technology worked.

To alleviate the interleaving problem, we agreed before the session that participants would indicate when they had more to say by typing " ... " at the end of the message; they would also mark the real end of their transmission by typing "/". After a while, however, it became clear that this convention was too cumbersome, and the few participants who tried to follow it just stopped.

Here is the transcript of the first session. I have added a few comments to explain what was happening in the dream session at various times.

DreamMC: Has everyone had a chance to look at Joanne's dream?

In a face-to-face dream session, Jeremy Taylor (DreamMC) usually has people in the dream group check in, then asks the dreamer to tell his or her dream. In the on-line session, the dream was distributed by e-mail, and Taylor simply asked whether people had read it.

Whale99795: Yes I have

SciBear2: Yes for me

DreamMC: That's enough to start—welcome!

Joanne12: I have reread it also/

Joanne12: /

Calvin97: Hello

DreamMC: Hi, Joanne Would you like to tell us anything else about the dream as we begin?

Joanne12: There is some background info that may help—do you want that?/

Before Joanne12 starts, Taylor notices from other information that Calvin97 has joined the session. Unless someone is named, there is no cue in an on-line session to indicate that a remark is directed toward a particular person. Thus, participants need to infer from the context whether a comment is for them or not.

DreamMC: Welcome, Calvin.

DreamMC: Sure—anything you care to share. As always, "the name of the game is dreamer's choice."

Joanne12: Thank you. I think it would be helpful to know that my father was a policeman before he died.

DreamMC: When did you have the dream?

Joanne12: also that I actually did break my foot and pick up Bryant with my mother. It was an actual event/

It is common in dream sessions to try to figure out whether events in a dream correspond to earlier events in real life.

Joanne12: I had the dream October 21/

Joanne12: /

Whale99795: Joanne are you your current age in the dream? If not, how old are you?

The age in the dream is often an indicator of the age a person was when a life issue related in the dream occurred. Joanne's answer to this question does not appear for a few lines.

Joanne12:   That is all I want to add/

DreamMC: If it were my dream, the five men breaking into the house would represent my own "life of the senses"

This suggestion by DreamMC turned out to be important for many people on the dream team in interpreting the dream. However, it was a surprising suggestion at least for me.

Joanne12:   Yes, I was my current age.

Joanne12:   aha (already)

A dreamer says "aha," to indicate an emotional resonance of some kind. According to Taylor, this is how the dreamer lets the group know that he or she has found a relevant meaning for a dream symbol or theme. In this case, Joanne12 gave positive feedback to DreamMC's suggestion that the five men represent the five senses.

DreamMC: The dream would, at one level, point to ways my parents sabotaged my sens(ual) life/

DreamMC: I'd be having it now because there is some new possibility of sens(ual) life coming up for me.

Whale99795:   What role did Bryant play in your life?

DreamMC: The dream would be offering me an opportunity to deal with an old hurt—to change it/

Here we see that the dreamer may receive several questions at once. This happens because people may type their questions simultaneously, without knowing that others are typing at the same time. This can be a bit overwhelming for the dreamer, who then has to sort through the questions, react to them, and answer them. Sometimes questions get asked but are forgotten as the conversation moves on.

Joanne12:   He was a very quiet person that I went to grade school and high school with, but we didn't know each other.

Joanne12:   very well. He seems like a minor acquaintance.

DreamMC: What was the occasion of breaking my foot?

Joanne12: /

Joanne12: I broke my foot after a football game when I fell from a fence. Bryant was a football player.

DreamMC: Ah! Another person who lived out a sens(ual) life—a life of the body?

DreamMC: ?

Whale99795: Did you have any feelings for Bryant?

Joanne12: I had a series of surgeries that lasted for years. I became less active and gained weight.

Joanne12: No I didn't have feelings for him that I remember. Others would fill that role better./

Joanne12: /

DreamMC: In my version ... it's precisely because I didn't know him well that he's an ideal mask for the body

One of the ideas about dream interpretation is that many, if not all, of the characters in the dream represent parts of the dreamer's self. Sorting out what those parts are is part of the work. DreamMC characterizes Bryant as "ideal" for interpretation precisely because in real life the Bryant character did not carry multiple meanings. The idea here is that the unconscious is trying to communicate by using symbols that are at hand.

DreamMC: part of myself to wear in the dream

Whale99795: Joanne, I am curious about your dad and jail could you elaborate on this idea of Jail. Does it fit ...

Whale99795: anything in your current life?

Joanne12: I am not sure I know what you mean "fit?"

Span8320: Hi, everyone. I am Sherri, I am a guest at Span8320.

Here another person joins the session.

DreamMC: In my version, Bryant can be a "clean" projection—one unconfused by other memories and feelings—just

Whale99795: When you say you remember that your father was in jail but home now and you hoped ok. Is there something

DreamMC: "Mr. football"—pleasant guy for whom the life of the body is not complicated/

Whale99795:   in your current life that feels confining, "jail like"

Joanne12:   Yes, MC, he was very easy going, naturally athletic

Joanne12:   Whale—yes I do feel a bit in jail—but it would take quite a bit to explain ...

DreamMC: IF IT WERE MY DREAM.... it's important to remember that all commentary is projection?/

Periodically, DreamMC reminded people to preface their remarks with "if it were my dream." Typing in all capitals, called "shouting" in chat sessions, is used for emphasis. DreamMC wants people to remember that all their remarks are their own projections. This is part of his established protocol from regular dream sessions.

DreamMC: /

Joanne12:   Is this a side track from the dream? I would like to get back to the dream/

Joanne12:   or is it important to connect?

Joanne12:   /

DreamMC: Just trying to keep the protocols clear .../

Whale99795:   Yes, that was definitely a major projection from me, Joanne.

DreamMC: The part of the dream where I mistake the "donkey" for a "deer" would be about attitudes toward my body

Joanne12:   My father was very out of touch with his senses/body. Not a very sensual person/ military like

DreamMC: 'I remember seeing the deer"! In my version, this is about my body not being "donkey" but "deer" (dea

DreamMC: r)/

SciBear2:   If it were my dream, it would be about needing to take care of myself, not ...

SciBear2:   counting on my mother's help.

To encourage participation, DreamMC often supports participants when they offer something.

DreamMC: Nice! Any one else have ideas for Joanne?

SciBear2:   And being big enough to do that, in spite of the terror./

Joanne12: Can anyone say something about the image of screens? Open but with screen doors. This image is in my
Joanne12: dreams often./

In the next few exchanges, people are responding to two issues at once. One issue is the time period of the life issue that the dream is about. The second issue is the meaning of "screens" as a recurring dream symbol.

DreamMC: The settings stretching from childhood home to current apartment suggest the issue is life long/
Joanne12: Why the action in childhood home and the weapon in New York City?
DreamMC: The "screens" are for protection, in my dream—also for "letting the air through, and keeping "bugs" out
Joanne12: past and present?/
Whale99795: If it were my dream, the screens protect me from the elements
DreamMC: Yes, past and present—my life as a whole piece—I remember my dream because I am in the process of
DreamMC: changing the whole thing/
Calvin97: If it were my dream, screens would be something that made the outside blurry, disconnected me
Calvin97: In my dream, I would be resentful if I had to keep the screens up
DreamMC: Nice—these images always have more than one level of meaning/
Calvin97: I would wonder what I was trying to keep from "bugging" me.
DreamMC: In terms of the possibilities of change—"screen doors" do not block access like solid doors/
Calvin97: If the five men represent the senses, they did get in.
Delia735: In my dreams, screen doors let in cool fresh air, so the inside doesn't need air conditioning or heat.

Members of the dream team had the dream text available to them. Here SciBear2 is apparently scanning the dream for symbols not discussed yet. He asks Joanne12 for clues to some of the symbols.

SciBear2: I'd like to ask, Joanne, whether you can tell us anything about Paul or the tarot woman./

Calvin97: I project a lot of anger onto my mother for not caring what was missing, and not hearing me

Joanne12: Paul is my husband. We've been married eighteen years, known each other since childhood, currently having

Joanne12: difficulties, but we have a deep love also

DreamMC: The screen doors let me see all sorts of stuff being put on shelves—possibilities—potentials/

Joanne12: The tarot woman was rather unknown to me. I was aware she was at the ball, but don't know her.

Joanne12: /

DreamMC: "Tarot" often evokes intuition/

DreamMC has experience with a lot of dreams and dreamers. In this case, he offers a suggestion based on other dreams he has worked on.

SciBear2: If it were my dream, I'd see them as male and female critics of something about me.

Joanne12: Yes, I wonder why so angry. The violation seem mild in retro

Joanne12: Tarot = future??/

DreamMC: All the way from childhood home to current apartment—I experience anger about the rejection

DreamMC: of my physical life

DreamMC: /

Whale99795: Can Joanne talk about the women at the diner?

This question about the diners by Whale99795 leads to follow-up questions and projections from much of the dream team. These arrive in a bunch before Joanne12 can respond. Because everyone is typing at once, the text gets jumbled, and everyone needs to follow the threads from each person separately to make sense of it.

Joanne12: I only have the sense that they are women I know. I don't know who they were

Joanne12: /

Bach2: Is it important that you "don't know who they were," or is that just happenstance?

SciBear2: If it were my dream, they'd be friends who accepted me unconditionally.

DreamMC: In my dream, the "diner" is place where food (and emotional nourishment) are served

Calvin97: In my dream, these unknowns are criticizing mother, and "I" am defending her for her behavior, making

SciBear2: Maybe that would mean some part of myself, a wise loving self, that was also a guide.

Whale99795: If it were my dream I would wonder "what" my mom would help me with "if she knew"/

Calvin97: the excuse that she was "unaware."

Calvin97: So in my dream, these unknowns would be parts of me I do not want to acknowledge

DreamMC: I did call out, but she didn't respond—I'm angry—it's how I feel, not necessarily what I think/

DreamMC: Mom did the best she could (not noticing) and now I'm trying to reclaim my five senses (robbers)/

SciBear2: If it were my dream, the fact that they were robbers would mean that they caused me . . .

DreamMC: At the level of the "robbery"—part of me feels I have no right to a happy body. It has to be "stolen"

SciBear2: to see something I didn't want to. Took away some part of my innocence./

Joanne12 did not actually respond to all of these comments. The conversation shifted to an earlier part of the dream after a question by Calvin97.

Calvin97: Joanne, do you have a sense of what was missing? taken?

DreamMC: Good question!

Joanne12: Only things from my mother's house. Nothing specific—valuable things.

Calvin97: Was there something missing from your parent's life as you saw them as a child?

SciBear2: If it were my dream, the stuff the men on ladders were putting away would be happy . . .

SciBear2:   memories or beliefs, that were demolished by the five senses robbers.

Whale99795:   Joanne, who are the kids in the dream?

Joanne12:   I am feeling an aha relating to stealing a happy body. My family was focused on illness for many years.

Joanne12's "aha" gives the dream team a clue that they are on to something for her.

Joanne12:   Then when I broke my foot, I was part of the infirm/

Joanne12:   The kids were my nieces and nephews, I remember seeing nieces

Joanne12:   but they were younger than actual/

SciBear2:   If it were my dream, I'd get an "aha" because [of] where you said to Bryant "remember the . . .

SciBear2:   time . . .

Whale99795:   If it were my dream, I feel a strong sense of protection for my inner child.

Drawing on the idea that all characters in the dream represent parts of the self, Whale99795 suggests that the nieces and nephews may represent an "inner child" part of the psyche.

DreamMC: And my inner children stick with me/

Joanne12:   Why defend against the senses, MC?

DreamMC: HABIT—if it were my dream

Here DreamMC gets caught up in the interpretation, and needs to remind himself to use the "if it were my dream" protocol.

SciBear2:   If it were my dream, it might mean that I thought (mistakenly) I was a donkey . . .

DreamMC: That's one of the reasons why I have the dream—to see my habits as "stealing my happiness"

Calvin97:   Perhaps if the senses let in just pain to the infirm, they need to be defended against . . . my projection

SciBear2:   slow and carrying burdens all the time, but inside I am a fleet-footed deer, and can't see

SciBear2:   that too well./

Nancy97:   In my dream, I care for parents, children, house and possessions and wonder if I am a deer or a

Nancy97:   beast of burden/

Nancy97:   /

DreamMC: In my dream (and my life) I'm BOTH—I have some leeway about which way I live my life/

Calvin97:   In my dream, I would be playing on words with "donkey." I would be making an ass of my deer self

DreamMC: The more clearly I see it, the easier it is to change/

DreamMC: The robbers' truck is black—are they dressed in black too/

SciBear2:   In my dream, my own growth may require seeing things my parents couldn't.

DreamMC: ?

DreamMC: Please say more

Whale99795:   If it were my dream, I sense a deep love and trust and belief in the "dearness" of myself/

Joanne 12:   Shadow area

Shadow is a Jungian psychological term that refers to the unconscious, disowned parts of a personality. The shadow contains both negative and positive aspects of the psyche. When the shadow is fully embraced, the darkness is brought into light and the individual moves toward wholeness.

DreamMC: And I can see it—even if others don't!

Whale99795:   But that "dearness" is hard to access "down a twenty-foot hill"

DreamMC: In my dream, I'm not wrong—the "big animal" (me) is a "deer" (dear) (me)!?

Joanne12:   I think the dream tells me to take responsibility back for my love of my body—my father may have been

Joanne12:   in jail because I blamed him for my dislike for myself

Joanne12:   /

DreamMC: Wow!
Whale99795:   Amazing

At this point, DreamMC and Whale99795 got their own "aha's" from Joanne12's explanation of her dream. Part of the excitement of a dream session is that everyone can get aha's, even from someone else's dream.

Joanne12:   I fell from a twenty-foot fence when I broke my foot

Calvin97:   In my dream, it could be him as Paul, who couldn't see the real you (the dear)

Joanne12:   Aha Calvin

DreamMC: (smile)

DreamMC: In my dream, the robbers' truck is black—are they dressed in black too?

Joanne12:   It seems like they were

DreamMC: ... then, in my dream, there is a suggestion of priests' clothes—religious guilt over my body/

DreamMC: (My big, beautiful body that my parents ignored .../

Calvin97:   In my dream, the knife which appears from the kitchen drawer, and the use of the word f—king!...

Whale99795:   In my dream the tarot cards represent the future and my willingness to step into the responsibility/

Calvin97:   would have some connection

DreamMC: Indeed!

Whale99795:   for loving my body.

Joanne12:   I saw that also

Joanne12:   the men have guns and I pick up a knife/

DreamMC: The more clearly my dream depicts my "problem," the surer I can be that I am on [the] brink of solving it!/

Joanne12:   Good news to me

DreamMC: AND TO US ALL .../

SciBear2:   If it were my dream, I would be mad at myself for accepting "men's" view of my body.

Here the conversation turns to interpreting the knife symbol. As always, there are multiple interpretations.

Calvin97: In my dream, the knife would be related to "cutting things off"

DreamMC: "Knives" often have to do with intellect "sharp mind," and guns with hurtful words "shooting off

DreamMC: my mouth ..."/

Joanne12: I think it is interesting I didn't think to tell my mother until later/

Whale99795: Is there any connection with the first part of the dream being inside/ and the second part outside

Calvin97: ... intellect used to cut off the senses that were invading. A strong projection I guess.

DreamMC: One of the amazing things about dreams is how many different things they mean at once .../

SciBear2: If it were my dream, the last part about meeting with the girlfriends would be important ...

SciBear2: It would be about forgiving my mother for not seeing how men's words (Father, Bryant)

SciBear2: hurt me./

DreamMC: If anyone has an "aha" about any piece of this; it is right for them. We're always doing at least two

DreamMC: things at once—working the dreamer's dream, and our own version—simultaneously/

Whale99795: Yes, I can see with my early projection about jail, I certainly got my own aha. Hard to look at!!

The discipline of saying "if it were my dream" is a constant reminder that all comments by the dream team are their own projections. Some projections trigger common aha's for multiple participants.

DreamMC: As you know, Joanne, that dreamer always gives us such a gift with sharing the dream!/

Joanne12: Thank you. The dreamer gets a lot also. My mind is filled with new ideas and openings/

Whale99795: Joanne, I get all teary thinking about your line "I remember seeing the deer." If it were my dream it/

DreamMC: What an interesting way to do this—even with the initial awkwardnesses—the "aha's" flow ...!/

Whale99795: would represent the deep love I have for myself.

Joanne12:   I always think I know what a dream means until I work with others and it is filled out./

Joanne12:   It is emotional for me as well Whale99795

Joanne12:   or changed completely—surprises always

DreamMC: ... Yes! ... and for me I can (do) love my body, no matter how much I mistrust it/

Joanne12:   /

Joanne12:   Why is the truck in the living room?

DreamMC: Good question!

Whale99795:   Could it have something to do with "living room," as in place that I live ... maybe my heart

DreamMC: In my dream, part of the reason is that I let work get in the way of my sens(ual) life—of pleasure/

SciBear2:   If it were my dream, the violence of that forced entry by men dressed in black would connote

DreamMC: (Work-as-truck ...)

SciBear2:   a violation of my body.

Delia735:   If it were my dream, the truck would be like the elephant in the living room.

The :-) symbols in the following response by Joanne12 to Delia is a "cybersmile." People who use e-mail or chat rooms recognize it as a smiley face drawn sideways.

Joanne12:   :-) Delia

DreamMC: Indeed!

Joanne12:   I like that one!

Whale99795:   It is interesting that Bryant is driving the truck???

DreamMC: Sure is—Whale, what do you make of that?/

Whale99795:   If it were my dream, Bryant driving the truck tells me he is somehow in charge. In the driver's seat.

DreamMC: I have a flash that in my dream—Bryant is driving because he's not alienated from the physical.

DreamMC: (Truck-as-body ... /

Delia735:   In my dream, the truck needs a driver, the elephant has its own mind. So, as a secret ...

Whale99795: Joanne then asks Bryant to think about what he is doing, I am not sure

DreamMC: In my dream, I'm asking myself "if I want to go on stealing my physical happiness this way ... /

Whale99795: What is your take Joanne?

Here the discussion returns to the earlier points, surrounding the inter-pretation of the Bryant dream character as standing for a part of the person that loves the physical and sensual body.

Joanne12: I gave him a ride and ask him not to break-in because I did

Joanne12: I connect to the idea that he is a mask for my body/

SciBear2: Is there some connection between the truck and the donkey?

DreamMC: ... And he was good at physical stuff—sports and such—and I have that in me too/

DreamMC: In my dream: donkey-as-work-body (not pleasure body ... /

DreamMC: like the truck ... /

Joanne12: I played a lot of sports before I broke my foot, but still thought of myself as too big ...

SciBear2: If it were my dream, the truck is a mechanical beast of bur-den, whose image is

SciBear9: driven by men. The donkey is also a beast of burden.

DreamMC: Nice ... /

Joanne12: My value was always mind, not my body/

Whale99795: The image of foot seems big. Football, broken foot. I really don't have any ideas. Anyone?

DreamMC: Foot-as-grounding? Foot-as-connection to Mother Earth?

Joanne12: Moving forward?

DreamMC: (That certainly is BIG—religious-big—a glimpse of the divine feminine in MY BIG SELF ...)/

Numbers often play key roles in dream interpretation. In the following, the dream team asks about why the number twenty shows up in the dream.

Delia735: How about the twenty-foot hill?

DreamMC: In my personal mythology "The fall from grace" is a twenty-foot drop (that breaks my foot—in dream and wake/

DreamMC: /

Joanne12: The distance keeps me from seeing clearly?

SciBear2: Is it also twenty years ago?

Joanne12: Just about twenty years

Joanne12: 1973/

Whale99795: And you had the dream on the 21st

DreamMC: (Nice!)

Delia735: In my dream, broken foot takes you out of the (football) game. Twenty feet on [the] right is a deer.

DreamMC: In my dream, I do see clearly, the "twenty-foot drop" only makes me mistrust my clarity/

DreamMC: The dream comes to remind me what I do see—even if others do not verify it ... /

Delia735: Which foot was broken?/

Directions also can play special roles in a dream, only the four directions of the map, but also the bipolar difference between left and right.

Joanne12: Ahhh yes, I do see that in my dream

Joanne12: the left foot/

Joanne12: Does the left have meaning to you Delia?

Delia735: Well, I guess left is linear in left brain, right?

DreamMC: "Left" is often the feminine, feeling side? (It often is, archetypically ...)

Delia735: So that makes right creative. Or do I have it mixed?/

Joanne12: I am left-handed and always thought of it as the creative side

Joanne12: the left/

Delia735: Then the fall is twenty feet down and right. A direction change, to find the deer.

DreamMC: In the dream world—its handed-ness that symbolically marks left and right most of the time ... /

Delia735: In my dream, that might mean a shift, physically or mentally./

Delia735: /

DreamMC: Indeed ...

DreamMC: (!)

DreamMC: How about Mom "not hearing my cry"—that makes me feel sad

Whale99795:   Joanne, I was just going to say there's a lot of miscommunication between you and mom?

Vigilantly, DreamMC reminds Whale99795 to use the "if it were my dream" protocol to acknowledge projections.

DreamMC: If it were your dream . . .

Whale99795:   I know, MC. If It were My Dream, another Aha for me. Talk about hoof-in-mouth disease!!!

Delia735:   In my dream, I wonder about the truck as secret mom wouldn't see and I let her not see./

SciBear2:   If it were my dream, there's a lot of blindness in Mom. And defense and love for Mom.

Joanne12:   My parents were very involved with caring for my handicapped older sister as I was growing up. They

Joanne12:   didn't give me much time. I was on my own, and in our discussion today, she is not aware of problems.

Joanne12:   I had because I "solved" them myself./

Here Joanne12 offers some personal history that seems to explain the symbol of her mother in the dream.

SciBear2:   If it were my dream, I'd see Mom as part of me; And I'd be asking [if] my own caregiving was . . .

SciBear2:   keeping me from expressing myself./

Joanne12:   Also I am an artist, and she could not connect to things I felt or saw as meaningful/

Delia735:   In my dream, I'd be protecting my need to believe mom loves me./

Whale99795:   If it were my dream, not telling my mother until "later" feels like I am afraid she won't hear me.

SciBear2:   If it were my dream, being in the diner with my girlfriends would mean that I was learning . . .

SciBear2:   how to nurture parts of myself./

Nancy97:   It's almost twelve in Florida. Thank you, Joanne, Dream MC, and everyone for the wisdom. Goodbye for now.

The session has been going on for two hours at this point. Nancy97's departure is a reminder that participants are physically located in different time zones.

Joanne12:   Thank you
Joanne12:   Aha to the nurturing diner + women friends
Joanne12:   who point things out to me/
Joanne12:   Dream MC, are we finished?
Delia735:   Is it sign-off time? I'm at midnight too, but this was great./
SciBear2:   I dunno if this fits, but if it were my dream, a "deer" is a mythological messenger
SciBear2:   between people and the gods. (Native Am mythology).
SciBear2:   So this might mean something about the deer's role in the dream.
Joanne12:   Thank you everyone. I appreciate the help and will look forward to your dream tomorrow night Scibear
SciBear2:   :-)
Calvin97:   Thank you for sharing, Joanne.
Delia735:   Good night all. Thanks, Joanne.

As the group is wrapping up, DreamMC got disconnected from the session. This sometimes happens when the system is heavily loaded. Whale99795 notices this and alerts the group.

Whale99795:   Everyone. DreamMC disconnected from AOL and is trying to get back on.
Calvin97:   I thought a lot about how it related to me and my mom.
Calvin97:   I will not be here tomorrow. So thank you all.
Whale99795:   I would like to suggest that everyone if they choose make a last comment for Joanne, and then . . .
Whale99795:   [Joanne] can have the last word. "Dreamer has the last word."
Joanne12:   OK

DreamMC: Hi, I'm back—what a technological glitch.

DreamMC: I feel like I missed some of the best stuff!

Whale99795:   If it were my dream, Joanne, I am still stuck on "but I remember seeing the deer. I feel a sweet ...

SciBear2:   Joanne—one last. If it were my dream, the deer (in that messenger role) was also hidden

SciBear2:   in the dream. Barely seen. But bringing a wonderful message back to dreamer.

DreamMC asks everyone for final remarks.

DreamMC: Joanne, do you have any place in the dream where you would like us to focus our attention a little more

DreamMC: ?

Whale99795:   tentativeness, and love for myself and a connection to the divine within

DreamMC: YES

DreamMC: I MEAN "YES" IN MY DREAM ...

Joanne12:   I feel like we covered the dream well

DreamMC: I agree! I'm very pleased with how much can get done— even in "sound bites." .. !/

Calvin97:   Did anything ever come up as to why it was a grocery store, and the use of ladders?

Whale99795:   I am just smiling ear to ear. Thank you, Joanne, for sharing your dream, I have gotten a lot of aha's.

DreamMC: THANK YOU ALL. LET'S TRY THIS AGAIN TOMOR-ROW NIGHT.

SciBear2:   G'nite all. Thank you, Joanne.

Whale99795:   Any last words from Joanne

Joanne12:   The dream opened up for me tremendously! I first thought it was about my sexuality and now I see it is

Joanne12:   about the big picture also. Thank you all for bringing me to my "senses" :-)

Part of Taylor's theory of dreams is that dreams promote wholeness. When a dreamer can remember a dream and has "aha's" about its meaning, that indicates that the dreamer is capable of stepping into what

is proposed by the dream. In this session, this could mean that Joanne12
is ready to explore more of her sensual side. As before, the :-) token is a
cybersmile.

DreamMC: :-)
Joanne12:   I look forward to tomorrow night too! See you then.
Joanne12:   Goodnight MC thank you SOOOOO much.
Joanne12:   Goodnight all/
DreamMC: ... and to all a good night/
Calvin97:   Pleasant dreams\
Whale99795:   Thank You, MC, and Joanne, and everyone

Post-Session Impressions

We intended the experimental on-line dream session as a quick way to
find out whether the idea of on-line dream work could work at all.
Would members of the dream team be able to interact with each other
without seeing each other? After the session I invited comments by e-mail
and interviewed some of the participants by telephone. In this section I
first summarize their comments, then present the text of a postsession
interview with Jeremy Taylor.

Comments from the Dream Team

Some of the comments were really about dream analysis itself. One of the
participants, who had not done any dream work previously, had doubts
about the whole idea.

I must admit that I just didn't follow a lot of the conversation. Dream analysis
rests on a large number of questionable assumptions, both in fact and in theory.
The interpretation process seems [to work] largely by social consensus, as
opposed to [being] objectively determined. It was striking to me that at one point
someone said (paraphrase) "... that's the wonderful thing about dreams ...
every interpretation is right ..." If that's true, then what's the point of interpretation? Isn't that the same as confabulation? What would be the point of
that?

The argument for dream analysis, as I understand it, is that the dreamer will
gain an insight into their personal mental state, emotional life, or underlying
thoughts. If all interpretations are equally valid, then no insight can be gained
because there's no discrimination between interpretations. To be Boolean about

it, if you say "this dream means X" and I say, "this dream means not X"—and they're both right—then it's contradictory.

This is just one concern I have about the nature of this kind of dream analysis. To be truthful, I think dream analysis can be useful—but there are better and worse analyses of dreams. It's not clear to me that group discussions without evaluation are a useful way to get to a salient interpretation. Such groupwork is fun, and does lead to some interesting discussions, but as a way to gain detailed insights into dreams, I don't think it works very well.

These comments confirm what has been seen with regular dream groups, namely, that dream work is not for everyone, and that not everyone comes to it with the same expectations. For Taylor, finding multiple interpretations for a dream is a sign of richness; finding "the single interpretation" or even "the deepest interpretation" of a dream is a worthy goal, but well beyond reach. This is analogous to asking for the one true interpretation of a painting or a poem. Nonetheless, this participant's comments suggest that newcomers to dream work need more preparation and help in setting their expectations about the practice.

Other participants had quite different and positive impressions.

I was at the second dream session. I thought on the whole it was a very helpful and interesting experience.

My overall impression though was that the experience was extremely positive. I was amazed at how much the dream began to mean to me when I had no ideas at the outset what this dream might be about—so I think this on-line session was able to accomplish the main purpose that a live dream group would. Thanks for the opportunity to participate and I hope we have some more sessions.

I was really blown out of the water when the DreamMC brought up the interpretation of the five senses. I asked myself. "where did that come from?" Then it was amazing how that insight guided us all in making sense of all of the elements of the dream. This was a wonderful experience.

In response to your questions about the impressions of on-line dream work, I think the session went very well. An opportunity to do dream work with Jeremy Taylor is always welcomed! I expected the on-line conversation to be more difficult to follow than it turned out to be.

I asked people to comment on what worked well and what did not. Where did the technology help, and where did it get in the way? Again here is a sampling of the responses.

It was an interesting experience to try to frame what I wanted to say as briefly and quickly as possible. I think this was both an advantage and disadvantage. It forced me to get to the essence of what I wanted to say very quickly (which was a very useful exercise), but it also forced me to leave out nuances and examples of what I meant that could have been very helpful.

I think with the fast pace, it is difficult to let some of the ideas sink in, where they could be felt, explored or pondered a bit more both by the dreamer and other group members.

In a live group we would have just heard the dream, rather than having read it a few hours (or even days) before. I like that it was fast paced, but on the other hand I think it was hard for the dreamer to keep track of all the comments or to respond to them which led to some discontinuity.

At a technical level, I thought the discussion was … confusing for all the standard chat-room reasons: incomplete thoughts, out-of-sequence message arrivals, no back-channeling so you can't know when to interject or remain quiet, etc., etc. The discussion seemed to be somewhat disjointed at times. Comments would be made on things that had long passed.

Although some members of the dream team used their own names, many of them had not met in person and did not know much about each other. This situation is typical for the first stages of on-line groups. People referred to this issue as "anonymity" and had various feelings about it.

The only troubling thing for me was the anonymity. I know so many people in dream work, I wondered if the screen names were actually people I knew. In traditional dream sharing, you know who you are working with; on-line dream work allows for a screen name to mask the personality of the dream workers. This may be an advantage to some, but I would rather own my dreams and comments more directly and know exactly who I am telling such personal matters to. I … both liked and disliked the anonymous nature of the group. Being an introvert, I usually dislike going around the room introducing myself, but it was also very odd to just jump in and make remarks without knowing anything about anyone or [having] any real sense of what the rules are.

In spite of the fact that I didn't know anything about anyone and the initial oddness of the whole setup, I did feel a sense of community, although somewhat more with the dreamer than anyone else since it was basically her responding to my comments. I can imagine over time as everyone had a chance to work on a dream, this feeling would grow, just as in a live group.

Several people commented on the size of the group, and said that the discussion might not have worked well with a much bigger group.

PostSession Comments from Jeremy Taylor
After the session, I again interviewed Jeremy Taylor, the "DreamMC" of the session.

Barbara: What are your first impressions of on-line dream work?

Jeremy: Very favorable. I was impressed with the level of psychological depth we achieved with the letters dancing on the screen. A most important question in assessing a dream session is "What is the tone?" Tone is harder to assess than when you are sitting in a classroom, because you don't get the cues of facial expression or body language. In the session, however, several people used the little smiley-face cybercues. For me, the tone was very good.

Barbara: What worked well in the sessions? What didn't work well?

Jeremy: Not well? What stands out for me is how in the conversation we kept stepping on each other's lines, jumbling up the flow. That seems inherent in how the software enabled the conversation. However, it quickly became clear how and why this happens, and it became only a mild annoyance.

Barbara: How does the on-line group dream work compare to regular group dream work?

Jeremy: It was more egalitarian. There did not seem to be the same sort of unconscious pecking order or more attention necessarily going to one person. What's that abbreviation?—RL for "Real Life." In RL, there is body language and facial expression. I had expected that there would be a loss of nuance, and then a loss of intimacy and depth, but that did not seem to be the case in the two sessions we tried. One thing that surprised me was the clock time. The rhythm of the session was extended. We took about two hours analyzing the dream.

Barbara: In a regular session, you take time to check in with everyone at the beginning. You did not do that for the online session.

Jeremy: That's right. We spent the extended time on the dreams themselves. I was struck that the natural rhythm of the session was longer, not shorter. That may be one reason why we got to the depth we did, in spite of the telegraphic responses.

Barbara: Were there any other critical factors?

Jeremy: Nothing disparaging. Another thing I noticed is what I'll call the "tonal exaggeration effect." I've noticed something similar to this in phone conversations, but the effect is more pronounced in writing. In the session, when you leave out the "If it were my dream" statement, and use the second person, it seems more accusatory than in actual speech. Similarly, when you say "if it were my dream," in print, it seems more open and embracing than when you say it in person. The on-line medium exaggerates the tone.

Barbara: How about anonymity?

Jeremy: All the cyberhandles had a quality of anonymity. I think that there was a self-selection of people who joined us in the room and that it was good. I've seen nasty things on the net in other contexts, where people do things under cover of anonymity that they would not do otherwise. But in this instance, I had no sense of that at all. There was a real sense of safety and community in the sessions.

Barbara: Would this work in a larger, open context on the network?

Jeremy: I feel that the self-selection process might not work as well, since it might include a mixture of thrill seekers and the genuinely interested and curious. The software I would use for those sessions would give me more control for this. I could use that to feel and govern the rhythm.

Barbara: You have said that you want the on-line dream groups to reach more people. Group dynamics may preclude having more than seven to nine active participants at one time, although one could have a larger number of nonparticipating watchers. Do you agree?

Jeremy: This seems to be the case. The same is true in real life for a dream group. However, in a workshop context I work it differently. In my workshops I set the room up as a double horseshoe with the dreamer and me at the opening. I scan the room looking for signs from people who have not participated for awhile. My guess is that when we get the on-line software set up, we'll do something analogous, so that I moderate the interactions more.

Barbara: How would that work on-line?

Jeremy: This is an approach I have developed over the years. The difference is that on-line I have to remember cyberhandles instead of faces. I imagine it would be harder keeping track of say SciBear2 and SciBear4.... It was very exciting in the dream group to see ideas popping out of Denver and then New York or Florida.

Barbara: What about running groups in parallel, each with their own DreamMCs?

Jeremy: I don't know for on-line. In real life, groups that grow their own DreamMCs work just fine. They start and develop their own style. One of the things I would like to see on-line is the potential for spin-off.

Barbara: What is involved in training DreamMCs? How well do groups work that grow their own DreamMCs?

Jeremy: That's a good question. What's important is that the DreamMCs be able to notice when people slip into the second person. You need to remind them to go back to saying "if it were my dream." Another thing is to develop the possibility of affectionate curiosity. It's easy to have this for Mother Teresa, but you also need it for Adolf Hitler. That's a tough one, and maybe especially on-line. The "if it were my dream" phrase is a reflection of the idea that everyone is worthy of affection and interest.

Barbara: What about other training in analysis?

Jeremy: To my mind the important part of the theory is looking for the "aha's." This is more important than a background on the meaning of myths and symbols. I wouldn't want to be without that, but the important symbols keep coming up. So they get rediscovered anyway.

Barbara: Where did the five robbers as five senses come from?

Jeremy: Well, it was five masked guys. When five matched things come up, it's always worth asking about the senses. This is one of the examples I bring up in class. But even if I did not teach it, someone in a dream group would eventually suggest it. It's a matter of noticing these things. This is not a matter of formal statistics. The symbols I pick up on come from the preponderance of what I see. As the experience gets bigger, the distributions of symbols get clearer.

Barbara: Any final comments about the on-line dream experience?

Jeremy: Yes. I am persuaded that the on-line version of dream work does not dehumanize it. In fact it intensifies it. No one is discounted or ignored because they are fat, or young, or black, or female, or male, or whatever. People interact with each other in a more pure form.

Reflections

Jeremy Taylor wanted to know whether a dream group could function on-line at all. The answer was an unambiguous yes. The dream team began functioning right away, and in a way that seemed to approximate the way that face-to-face dream sessions work.

Did the computer technology create problems in communication? Again, the answer was yes. The kinds of problems that came up are familiar to participants in other chat rooms: the conversational flow was jumpy, because contributions from multiple speakers were intermixed. Some intelligibility was restored, however, by the visual persistence of the log; participants could scroll back and review what had been said earlier.

Could the technology be modified to improve its usability for dream work? Again, the answer is surely yes. For several years researchers interested in computer support for meetings have experimented with improved user interfaces, some of which provide two-way video and sound connections as well as shared workspaces and message streams. Stefik and Brown discuss some of these interfaces in their article.

Although the software the dream team used for its sessions is rather primitive, it has the advantage of working on many kinds of computers. Moreover, the group did not take advantage of everything available to it. For example, in postsession comments, several people suggested it would be useful to have side-channel conversations, a capability that America Online offers in the form of "instant mail."

Taylor's experience with the first on-line dream group has stirred his interest in the possibility of larger groups. A number of factors, however, limit active simultaneous participation in all groups, electronic or otherwise. When they get larger than seven or nine people, their character often changes; people do not and cannot act the same way en masse as they do in small groups. Nonetheless, the on-line dream experience might be made available to more people by limiting groups to no more than seven to nine active participants but providing for a larger number of watchers. Parallel sessions could also be held, and people could be encouraged to form their own dream groups. Taylor also suggests a slightly different format in which the dream group leader moderates the discussion more actively, a format he has used successfully for running large as well as small workshops.

Other ideas for large group meetings are being explored on the Internet. The World Wide Web Conference reports on such experiments and provides information on new technology for community and collaborative efforts. The 1995 conference proceedings are available on-line at

http://www.w3.org/WWW4/

One article from this conference discussed an on-line meeting sponsored by the National Performance Review that involved over four thousand federal workers from various agencies and departments. Participants discussed issues and plans for public policy and could comment on numerous articles posted on-line as well as comment on the comments. To organize the discussion, people were given network tools to link each posting to others. For example, a posting could be linked as an agreement, a disagreement, a question, an answer, or an alternative. The meeting thus produced a linked tree of documents organized according to the relationships assigned by participants and mediated by group leaders. This structured discussion idea has been around in the hypertext research community for years but is applied mainly to working groups of ten to twenty people. The Internet creates the opportunity to try the idea in real time on a much larger scale.

Reflecting on the different metaphors explored in the foregoing papers, we might ask what the metaphors of digital libraries, electronic mail, marketplaces, or digital worlds suggest about on-line dream work. The digital library metaphor suggests that dream workers could create a large and searchable repository of dreams and logs of dream analysis that is indexed by subject. What did people in New York dream about last week? Did last week's world news lead to more people dreaming? What images came up when people dreamt about bears? For Taylor, dreams are part of a contemporary movement toward healing and wholeness, by which he means, in part, the human drive to come together with others. Religious leaders say that the desire for union is the reason people form communities, join clubs, or fall in love. In our era, the network is fast becoming a major means of communication. In the on-line dream session described by Viglizzo, we can visualize the Internet as a social nervous system, bringing separate consciousnesses together to explore dreams from the collective unconscious.

Acknowledgment

Barbara Viglizzo wishes to thank Jeremy Taylor for permission to quote from his *Toolkit for Dream Work*.

Note

1. About three months after this article was written, Jeremy Taylor began hosting a daily dream show on America Online. The format of the show is formal with Taylor on (the cyberspace) stage with an audience in a cyberspace auditorium. He is generally accompanied by two or three assistants. Barbara Viglizzo can be found on stage with him most mornings.

Epilogue: Choices and Dreams

Very great and pertinent advances doubtless *can* be made during the remainder of this century, both in information technology and in the ways man uses it. Whether very great and pertinent advances *will* be made, however, depends strongly on how societies and nations set their goals.

J. C. R. Licklider, *Libraries of the Future*

The myth in a primitive society, that is in its original form, is not a mere tale told but a reality lived.

Bronislaw Malinowski

The road back to hope, to a new sense of place ... is through the common spaces of our dreams.

Teresa Heinz, October 27, 1994

My goal in this book has been to spark our imaginations and to make room for the voices of many creative and knowledgeable people. A number of readers of early drafts asked for a discussion that would illuminate in concrete terms the choices surrounding construction of the information infrastructure. They observed that in the United States the cable and telephone companies are making the biggest investments in information infrastructure—by a factor of a hundred or more. These investments, they pointed out, may not help us realize the dreams described in this book.

Choices

In short form, the story goes like this. The dreams that have guided the development of the Internet are digital libraries, electronic mail, electronic marketplace, and digital worlds. These dreams tap into metaphors we all use to understand our life experiences and convey deep and important messages about where we are going and what we are becoming. The archetypes underlying the metaphors—the keeper of wisdom, the communicator, the trader, and the adventurer—are in fact deep aspects of our own personalities.

When we invent things by following these dreams and metaphors, we are traveling along paths of development worn smooth by ancient and modern dreamers. However, to put it bluntly, there is a difference between the dream of the couch potato and the dream of the adventurer. Different versions of the information infrastructure support different kinds of dreams. We choose, wisely or not.

One of the questions posed in the introduction of this book is whether the NII will be just better television. Television is an example of a technology for which there were initially very high hopes, and video-on-demand is one of the services that many companies are betting will be the next big source of home entertainment. If we dismiss television as the uninspired dream of the couch potato, however, we miss the point. Television, which is good at what it does, is so ubiquitous that it has already attracted plenty of critics. It performs a wonderful and efficient service of delivering entertainment and news.

It does not, of course, have what it takes to deliver digital libraries, electronic mail, electronic marketplaces, or digital worlds. This is the point. The dreams that drove the development of the Internet and its explosive growth require infrastructure different from that needed for video-on-demand. In the following discussion, we use television as a point of departure, revisiting each of the four metaphors briefly and drawing from the examples that demonstrate the basic requirements of the NII.

Digital Libraries

Computers and networks can greatly augment the efforts of traditional libraries to preserve human knowledge. They can help libraries realize universal access, so that anyone can get any digital works at any time from anywhere. Networks can also diminish the importance of physical separation and, with digital property rights, let libraries loan out digital works and have them returned automatically. Such digital works can be interactive and may include—and in some cases, integrate—music, video, computer games, or computer programs. Computer indexing and search programs can help us to find what we need in the digital library.

To fully realize these functions, however digital libraries need particular kinds of support from the information infrastructure. To illuminate these requirements, consider, by comparison, some of the properties television needs. Even with cable, the expense of creating and broadcasting television programs is very high; it makes no economic sense to develop a channel appealing to only one person in a community. To make a profit television channels need to reach a sizable share of the market they broadcast to. In the United States, there are about three hundred million people. A recent study of cable networks by Cable Labs found that 22 percent of the networks have fewer than thirty channels; 64 percent have thirty to fifty-three channels; and 14 percent have fifty-four channels or more. The economics of television are such a channel is viable only if it attracts tens of thousands of viewers; it cannot survive on only a thousand viewers. If local libraries operated under such economics, they would have only twenty or thirty books to lend out.

Computer networks, on the other hand, can achieve an economics of distribution capable of supporting digital libraries if they provide certain properties. For example, they must enable libraries to deliver many different works to many different people, a property called *addressability*. Transmission of information must be inexpensive. Finally, there must be something like digital property rights to protect copying and ensure the survival of the publishing industry. People would never buy a digital book if they could just get it free from a library and copy it, as many people copy television shows on videocassette recorders. Libraries depend on a healthy publishing industry to supply them with a great variety of works.

Electronic Mail

We use electronic mail, like postal mail, to keep in touch. It is also used by electronic communities to conduct ongoing discussions on topics of interest. Network-based discussion groups can be organized in a local community to discuss issues in a particular fourth-grade class; or they can be organized at an international level to discuss ecological policy. With electronic mail, a communicator can be a citizen in touch with many others.

In comparison to television, electronic mail needs a virtually unlimited scope of distribution. People on the Internet have electronic addresses, and we can send mail to all of them, as individuals and as groups. At the base of electronic mail is a virtually unlimited number of addresses— in contrast with the limited number of television channels. (The problem would not be much different if we had five hundred or a thousand channels.) If regular or electronic mail were like television, we could only send mail to twenty or thirty addresses. To receive a message, we would have to watch one of those channels to see whether there was a message for us. This difference in the number of addresses is fundamental; unlimited numbers of addresses can give everyone a voice.

Television is, mainly, a one-way medium with a small number of broadcasters and a large number of viewers. Interactive television may change this, but probably not very much. Most visions of interactive television suggest that viewers will be able to vote by television or make choices among a small number of options. For example, viewers could vote for the best singing group on a televised talent contest, or choose which things to buy on home-shopping television. Such limited interaction does foretell a situation in which we could all broadcast television, or anything else, from our homes. An infrastructure supporting electronic mail, on the other hand, must be interactive, provide virtually infinite addressability, and, to be affordable, have low transmission cost. Television is good at what it does, but, clearly, what it does is not adequate for electronic mail.

Electronic Marketplace

The electronic marketplace also has special properties and needs. Advertisements in the electronic market can be like the Yellow Pages, where you find distributors by looking them up according to what you want to buy. In principle, you can also just "hang a shingle" on the network in the form of a home page. Advertisements can be attached to goods, as in the advertisements that appear in some electronic magazines. Certain products—for example, software or video games—can even be delivered over the Internet.

Advertising can be targeted and very economical. Community bulletin boards could be used to advertise local services, such as baby-sitting or, alternatively, to reach across great distances. Suppliers and distributors can have very large territories. Consumers may use computer programs both to find advertisements and to filter out those that do not address their requirements.

The delivery of goods and services on the network is also special. Digital works can be advertised, ordered, and delivered completely within the framework of the computer network. The economics of digital works, too, are different from those of hard goods. Digital works are massless. Manufacturing costs (meaning duplication costs) are small. Intellectual property can be protected by using a digital property rights approach. Digital works incur only very low costs for inventory and low costs for delivery. Delivery can be immediate. Although such delivery will not be common until digital property rights become well established, digital works will eventually include everything from digital books to digital video, from digital music to digital newspapers.

Looking again at the example of television, it is evident that, by comparison, there is no real marketplace operating completely on television. If you like an advertised product, you may decide to buy it, but you generally can't take delivery through your television set. You either have to go to a store or pick up a telephone. Most people do not advertise their own goods and services on television. Advertising on television is very costly, because television requires a big market for all its broadcasts. It does not make economic sense to advertise on television if all of your customers are within a ten-block radius. Nor is it sensible to advertise on television if your customers are only one person in a hundred thousand and live all around the world.

Again, the television is great at what it does—marketing goods with a very wide appeal. As infrastructure, however, it provides inadequate support to other aspects of markets. Addressability is again a relevant issue. The NII cannot sustain a market unless it is able to address a large pool of producers, distributors and consumers. Moreover, to let users buy and sell goods, on the network the NII must support a secure method of monetary exchange. To be able to deliver digital goods, there must be an ability to store them safely and protect them from unauthorized copying. Television can be none of these things.

Digital Worlds

The term digital worlds encompasses a variety of digital experiences ranging from total immersion in virtual reality for games to digital augmentation of the business world with groupware. Digital worlds are more interesting when they are social, whether you want to work collaboratively or enjoy others' company.

Here again, television lacks the properties needed to sustain digital worlds on the NII. It is neither interactive nor social, whereas an infrastructure for digital worlds must be both. Television's inability to enable and faster social connections in television derives from its lack of addressability and interactivity.

Summary

We have seen that all four metaphors require the technological infrastructure to provide addressability, interactivity, low transmission costs, a means of handling money, and a way to manage digital property. Leave out any of these properties and one or or more of the metaphorical functions will be unable to fulfill the dreams we have of it.

Dreams

Computer networks link us together. They may help us to see that we are one people and one world. It gives me great hope for the future.

Swami Asitananda of the Vedante Society Retreat

When I get starry-eyed, I think of the Web as an information analog of the medieval cathedrals—something that the whole culture contributes to and participates in.

Private electronic mail message from Hal Abelson, MIT

One of the first orders of business in the process of planetary awakening is the distribution of information.... Your communications systems have been waiting for this day. They were created for this moment.

Ken Carey, *The Starseed Transmissions*

When there is public discussion on these and other issues, it is useful to keep our dreams in mind and to draw on examples from the digital library, electronic mail, electronic marketplace, and digital worlds. Whatever the specific issue or question, we need to recognize that choices lead to social inventions and shape what we become.

The Society of Minds and the Mind of Society

Marvin Minsky, the MIT professor and a founder of the field of artificial intelligence, wants to understand minds. What, he asks, are minds made of? In his *Society of Mind* he says that human minds are made of smaller subminds that interact with each other to create an overall behavior. At any given moment, one submind is thinking about being hungry, another is driving a car, and another is planning errands to run. Each submind, in turn, is made of yet smaller minds: holding the steering wheel, grasping the shift, scanning the road. Continuing down through levels, the elements of mind become like automatic systems and are no longer mind-like. All together the subminds form a society. They work together, compete with each other, come into conflict, negotiate, and coordinate. Mental life and consciousness arise out of the interactions as the subminds sort out what to do.

Minsky's theory is like applying a metaphorical microscope to a mind to see what is inside it. But we can also turn the theory around and look outward, using a metaphorical telescope instead of a microscope. Looking outward we can ask, what is a society made of? One answer is that a society is made of the interacting minds of its members. How does a society decide what to do? Looking through the telescope, we see that the individual minds of "society's mind" compete with each other, come into conflict, negotiate, and coordinate. From an organizational point of view, the "consciousness" of the organizational mind arises out of the social interactions of its subminds. The messages between them—what we say or write to each other—are the stuff of human communication.

The metaphor of information networks as society's nervous system has a long history and has influenced many people. In a speech to the International Telecommuniations Union in March of 1994, Vice president Al Gore quoted Nathaniel Hawthorne, who was inspired by the telegraph: "By means of electricity, the world of matter has become a great nerve, vibrating thousands of miles in a breathless point of time. The round globe is a vast ... brain, instinct with intelligence!" Gore added:

For almost 150 years, people have aspired to fulfill Hawthorne's vision—to wrap nerves of communications around the globe, linking all human knowledge.... we now have at hand the technological breakthroughs and economic means to bring all the communities of the world together. We now can at last create a planetary information network that transmits messages and images with the speed of light from the largest city to the smallest village on every continent. These highways ... will allow us to share information, to connect, and to communicate as a global community. From these connections we will derive robust and sustainable economic progress, strong democracies, better solutions to global ... challenges ... and a greater sense of shared stewardship of our small planet.

Messages can be distributed by computer networks. But how should computer networks themselves affect the workings of society and the ways that we relate to each other?

Looking Inward, Looking Outward

The metaphors of telescopes and microscopes reflect a duality between our outer social lives and our inner mental lives. One way to approach this duality is through the writings of poets and spiritual teachers. The Tibetan Buddhist teacher Sogyal Rinpoche describes the nature of spirit as like air around a vase. There is air inside the vase and air outside the vase. The inside air is our spirit, and the outside air is the spirit of everything else. Enlightenment is when we break the vase, recognizing that the air inside is the same as the air outside. Spiritual teachers say that when we seek unity and integration we are seeking reunion with the divine.

Variations on this theme appear in other eastern and western religions when they speak about compassion and our common humanity. They teach that when we harm other beings we harm ourselves. This is the Golden Rule of the Bible as well as a guiding principle of the ecology movement.

The stories of the inside and the outside bring to a close my personal perspective on our dreams and choices. It seems to me that many of the deeper mysteries of life are questions without ultimate answers, like the koans of Zen Buddhism. One does not reflect on koans all of the time, lest we get lost in the depths. The depths do not yield single answers.

However, reflecting on them can foster a sense of wonder and humility about our place in the larger scheme of things.

The quotations at the beginning of this section reflect an understanding that building the information infrastructure is a great social task—what Hal Abelson called the information equivalent of building a medieval cathedral. Great social tasks can only be sustained by great social energy and by making wise choices. We can choose to provide for digital libraries or electronic marketplaces or digital worlds. Behind these possibilities are the enduring archetypes—the keeper of knowledge, the communicator, the trader, and the adventurer—that appear in all cultures throughout time.

When we invent the digital library, we create an information-age manifestation of the keeper of knowledge. What should the digital library be like? How would it serve us as a society? Could it be a positive force in human affairs, helping us more than ever to draw on our collective knowledge and wisdom?

When we use electronic mail, we create an information-age manifestation of the communicator. When we communicate in on-line discussion groups network citizens, do we shape our societies in the directions we want it to go?

When we invent the electronic marketplace, we create an information-age manifestation of the trader. Will the virtual corporations and businesses on the network help us have meaningful work and commerce?

When we create digital worlds, we create an information-age manifestation of the adventurer. Will the digital worlds that we create offer renewal for ourselves and our societies?

The choices of our individual lives offer opportunities for inner growth and integration. The choices of social life offer opportunities for social growth and integration. We can choose paths of diversion or paths that lead us to wholeness for individuals and society. As Jeremy Taylor says of dreams, they come in the service of health and wholeness. Arguably, the Internet Dreams can serve the health and wholeness of humanity. To be conscious is to pay attention to our choices and our dreams.

Further Reading

Chinen, Allan B. *Beyond the Hero. Classic Stories of Men in Search of Soul*. New York: Tarcher/Putnam, 1993.

Collins, Harry M. *Artificial Experts: Social Knowledge and Intelligent Machines*. Cambridge: MIT Press, 1990.

Collins, Harry M. *Changing Order: Replication and Induction in Scientific Practice*, 2nd ed. Chicago: University of Chicago Press, 1992.

Dennett, Daniel. *Where Am I? In The Mind's I: Fantasies and Reflections on Self and Soul*, D. R. Dennett and D. R. Hofstadter, eds. Harmondsworth, Eng.: Penguin, 1982.

Forster, E. M. The Machine Stops. In his *The Eternal Moment and Other Stories*. New York: Harcourt Brace, 1928. Reprinted in Ben Bova, ed. *The Science Fiction Hall of Fame*, vol. 2. New York: Avon, 1973.

Hesse, Carla. *Publishing and Cultural Politics in Revolutionary Paris, 1789–1810*. Berkeley: University of California Press, 1991.

Malone, Thomas W., Grant, Kenneth R., Turbak, F. A., Brobst, S. A., and Cohen, M. D. Intelligent information sharing systems. *Communications of the ACM* 30, no. 5 (May 1987): 390–402.

Malone, Thomas W. What Makes Computer Games Fun? *Byte Magazine* (December 1981).

McLuhan, Marshall. *Understanding Media*. New York: McGraw-Hill, 1964.

National Collaboratories: Applying Information Technology for Scientific Research. A report by the Computer Science and Telecommunications Board, National Research Council. 1993. (Copies available from National Academy Press, 2101 Constitution Avenue, N.W., Washington, D.C. 20418.)

Nelson, Ted. *Literary Machines*. 1981. (Copies available from Ted Nelson, Box 128, Swarthmore, Pa. 19081.)

Nunberg, Geoffrey. The Places of Books in the Age of Electronic Reproduction. *Representations* (Spring 1993): 13–37.

Pearson, Carol S. *Awakening the Heroes Within: Twelve Archetypes to Help Us Find Ourselves and Transform Our World*. San Francisco: Harper, 1991.

Pool, I. de Sola, ed., *The Social Impact of the Telephone*. Cambridge: MIT Press, 1977.

Raymond, Eric S., ed. *The New Hacker's Dictionary*. Cambridge: MIT Press.

Michael Schrage, *Shared Minds: The New Technologies of Collaboration*. New York, Random House, 1990.

Salus, Peter H. *Casting the Net: From ARPANET to INTERNET and beyond ...* Reading, Mass.: Addison-Wesley, 1995.

Stephenson, Neal. *Snow Crash*. New York: Bantam Books, 1992.

Stefik, Mark. The Next Knowledge Medium. *AI Magazine* 7, no. 1 (Spring 1986): 34–46. Reprinted in *The Ecology of Computation*. B. A. Huberman, ed. Amsterdam, the Netherlands: North Holland Publishing, 1988, pp. 315–42.

Stefik, Mark. *Introduction to Knowledge Systems*, San Francisco: Morgan-Kaufmann, 1995.

Weiser, Mark. The Computer for the 21st Century. *Scientific American* 265, no. 3 (September 1991).

Winograd, Terry, and Flores, Fernando. *Understanding Computers and Cognition: A New Foundation for Design*. Norwood, N.J.: Ablex Publishing, 1986.

Sources

Excerpt from *As We May Think* by Vannevar Bush. Originally published in the July 1945 issue of *The Atlantic Monthly*.

Excerpt from *Libraries of the Future* by J. C. R. Licklider. Originally published by the MIT Press, 1965. The excerpt is drawn from pages 4–6, pages 14–15, pages 33–39.

Excerpt from *The Digital Library Project*, Volume 1: *The World of Knowbots* by Robert E. Kahn and Vinton G. Cerf. A technical report by the Corporation for National Research Initiatives, March 1988.

Excerpt from "Communication as the Root of Scientific Progress" by Joshua Lederberg. Originally published in *The Scientist* 7, no. 3 (February 8, 1993): 10. © 1993, *The Scientist*. All rights reserved. Reprinted by permission.

Excerpt from "What Is the Role of Libraries in the Information Economy?" by John Browning. Originally published in *Wired*, 1993. Reprinted by permission.

"Technological Revolutions and the Gutenberg Myth" by Scott D. N. Cook. Written for this book, based on "The Structure of Technological Revolutions and the Gutenberg Myth," in *New Directions in the Philosophy of Technology*, edited by Joseph C. Pitt (Dordrecht: Kluwer, 1995).

Excerpt from "Libraries Are More than Information: Situational Aspects of Electronic Libraries" by Vicky Reich and Mark Weiser. Published in *Serials Review* 20, no. 3 (1994). This article also appeared as Xerox Palo Alto Research Center Technical Report, CSL-93-21, December 1993.

Excerpt from "The Electronic Capture and Dissemination of the Cultural Practice of Tibetan Thangka Painting," by Ranjit Makkuni. Originally published in *World Archaeology* 21 (1992).

"Some Consequences of Electronic Groups" by Lee Sproull and Samer Faraj. This article is excerpted from "Atheism, Sex, and Databases: The Net as a Social Technology" in *Public Access to the Internet*, edited by Brian Kahin and Jim Keller (Cambridge: The MIT Press, 1995).

"Netiquette 101" by Jay Machado. Originally appeared in the online newsletter *Bits and Bytes Online Edition* 3, no. 2 (January 9, 1995) and 2, no. 7 (November 8, 1994).

Contributors

Robert I. Benjamin, who is retired from the Xerox Corporation information management staff, is a visiting scientist at the Sloan and School of Management at MIT and an independent consultant. His e-mail address is rbenjamin@sloan.mit.edu.

John Seely Brown, head of the Xerox Palo Alto Research Center and chief scientist for the Xerox Corporation, has long been interested in creative processes and cognitive factors in reasoning. The article in this volume (with Mark Stefik) is based in part on his keynote address at the Conference on Computer Supported Cooperative work at Austin, Texas in December 1986. His electronic mail address is jsbrown@parc.xerox.com.

John Browning is the European editor of *Wired.* He has written for *The Economist, Scientific American,* and other publications and a consultant on information-technology strategy for large corporations. He is the author of The Economist's *Pocket Guide to Information Technology.* Browning holds degrees in history and computer science. His e-mail address is jb@browning.demon.co.uk.

The late **Vannevar Bush** was director of the Federal Office of Scientific Research and Development. During World War II, his office coordinated the activities of over six thousand American scientists. In this prescient and widely quoted article, written as the war was ending, Bush urged scientists to turn to the task of making the store of human knowledge more accessible.

Vinton G. Cerf is currently president of the Internet Society and senior vice president for data architecture at MCI. He is well known as the principal architect of TCP/IP, the network protocols that run on the Internet, and as the creator of MCI mail. Cerf joined with Robert E. Kahn in founding CNRI and became its vice president for several years before returning to MCI. His electronic mail address is Vint_Cerf@mcimail.com.

Harry Collins is professor of sociology and director of the Centre for the Study of Knowledge Expertise Science at the University of Southampton, England. He is currently working on a new theory of action and applying it to understanding the transmission of knowledge and skills between humans and machines. His books include *Artificial Experts: Social Knowledge and Intelligent Machines,* and, with

T. Pinch, *The Golem: What Everyone Should Know About Science*, which won the 1995 Robert K. Merton Prize of the American Sociological Association. Collins's e-mail address is h.m.collins@soton.ac.uk.

Lynn Conway is a professor of electrical engineering and computer science and director of the UMTV Demonstration Project at the University of Michigan. She came to the university in 1985 from the Defense Advanced Research Projects Agency, where she was chief scientist and assistant director for strategic computing. Conway is widely known as a key innovator of methods to simplify the design of VLSI microelectronic systems. She received the Secretary of Defense Meritorious Civilian Service Award in 1985 and, in 1990, the National Achievement Award of the Society of Women Engineers. She was elected to the National Academy of Engineering in 1989. Her e-mail address is conway@engin.umich.edu.

Scott D. N. Cook was trained in philosophy and social science at San Francisco State University and MIT. He lives and works in Silicon Valley, where he is a professor of philosophy at San Jose State University and a consultant/researcher at Xerox PARC. For the last fifteen years, his research and publications have focused on issues of know-how and expertise, technology and social change, and the role of values in professional and business practice. His first experience surfing the net (ARPANET) was in 1973. His e-mail address is cook@parc.xerox.com.

Pavel Curtis is a research scientist at the Xerox Palo Alto Research Center. During a lull in his research, Pavel started running an experimental network-based social computing system. Since then LambdaMOO has become a very popular Internet meeting place. It turned out to be so interesting that MUDding and its extensions are now the focus of his research. Pavel is co-leader of the Social Virtual Reality Project at Xerox PARC, which is investigating future versions of computer-based places on the network. His electronic mail address is pavel@parc.xerox.com.

Julian Dibbell is currently working on a book about LambdaMOO, to be published in 1996. He writes a column for *The Village Voice* on the culture and politics of digital networks. He has also contributed to *Wired, Details, Spin, the New York Times, Le Monde, Folha de São Paulo* and other publications on a variety of topics, including popular music, cultural theory, film, science, and Carmen Miranda. Dibbell's electronic mail address is julian@panix.com.

Samer Faraj, a doctoral student in management information sciences at Boston University, is interested in network-based emergent forms of work and social organizing. His e-mail address is samer@acs.bu.edu.

Laura Fillmore is president of the Online Bookstore (OBS) of Rockport, Massachusetts (on the Internet obs@editorial.com). Her career in publishing started at *The American Journal of Ancient History* at Harvard University in 1976. She also worked at Schoenhof's Foreign Books in Cambridge, Massachusetts, and in the Trade Editorial Department of Little, Brown, and Company. In 1992, OBS distributed its first book on the Internet, *The Internet Companion* by Tracy LaQuey. Fillmore can be reached by e-mail at laura@editorial.com.

Robert E. Kahn is president and founder of the Corporation for National Research Initiatives (CNRI), a Washington-based nonprofit corporation that provides leadership and funding for research and development of the National Information Infrastructure. He is well known in the computer science community as a principal architect of the Advanced Research Projects Agency Network (ARPANET), co-inventor of TCP/IP, and a former director of the Information Processing Techniques Office at ARPA. His electronic mail address is rkahn@nri.reston.va.us.

Joshua Lederberg is a research geneticist and University Professor at Rockefeller University, a graduate university and research institute devoted primarily to research in the biomedical sciences. Lederberg pioneered the use of computers for scientific research in controlling instrumentation, modeling scientific reasoning, and managing scientific publications and working documents. Since 1963, Lederberg has served on the board of directors of the Citation Index, a reference work scientists use to find relevant documents by following citation trails. Lederberg was formerly professor of genetics at the University of Wisconsin and the Stanford University School of Medicine. He was president of Rockefeller University from 1978 to 1990. In 1958, together with E. L. Tatum and G. W. Beadle, he was awarded the Nobel Prize in Physiology-Medicine for studies on the foundations of bacterial genetics. In 1995, Lederberg received the Association of Computing Machinery's Allen Newell Award for his contributions to computer science. Lederberg's e-mail address is jsl@rocky2.rockefeller.edu.

When his article was written, **J. C. R. Licklider** was the supervisory engineering psychologist of Bolt Beranek and Newman Inc. (BBN) in Cambridge, Massachusetts. Although its scope has grown a good deal since then, at that time BBN was a company of consulting engineers whose primary interest was acoustics. Licklider is a past president of the Acoustical Society of America. At MIT, Licklider conducted research on problems of human communication and the processing and presentation of information. He later headed the Information Processing Techniques Office at the Advanced Research Projects Agency. He is often credited with establishing that institution's forward-looking research program in information processing and computer science.

Jay Machado is editor of the newsletter, *Bits and Bytes: Online Edition*, His electronic mail address is jmacnado@omnil.uoicenet.com.

Ranjit Makkuni is presently the project leader for the Gita-Govinda project, a collaboration between the Indira Gandhi National Center for the Arts in New Delhi and the Xerox Palo Alto Research Center. The Gita-Govinda project is creating an advanced state-of-the-art museum exhibit and cultural learning tools based on the twelfth-century love poem *Gita-Govinda*. The Thangka painting project described in his article was a collaboration between the Asian Art Museum in San Franciso, the Xerox Palo Alto Research Center, and various members of the Tibetan Buddhist community. Makkuni's electronic mail address in India is IGNCA@DOE.ERNET.IN and in the United States is makkuni@parc.xerox.com.

Thomas W. Malone is the Patrick J. McGovern Professor of Management Information Systems at the Massachusetts Institute of Technology's Sloan School of Management and the founder and director of the MIT Center for Coordination Science. His research focuses on how computer and communications technology can change the ways people work together in groups and organizations, and how new organizations can be designed to take advantage of information technology. Malone can be reached by e-mail at Malone@mit.edu.

Vicky Reich analyzes and coordinates various digital library programs at Stanford University and is the library's expert on copyright and intellectual-property issues. Her e-mail address is vicky.reich@forsythe.stanford.edu.

Lee Sproull is professor of management at Boston University, where she is currently undertaking a program of research on electronic groups sponsored by the Markle Foundation. Her e-mail address is lsproull@bu.edu.

Mark Stefik is a principal scientist at the Xerox Palo Alto Research Center. His research interests have ranged from the design of programming languages, to expert systems, to computer support for cooperative work. A recurring theme in his work is using technology to enhance creativity, collaboration, and human expression. Stefik's electronic mail address is stefik@parc.xerox.com.

Barbara Viglizzo, a graduate student at the Institute of Transpersonal Psychology, holds a bachelors degree in clinical psychology from San Francisco State University. In her academic training, Viglizzo has worked with elderly people in a suicide-prevention program in San Francisco. She also participated in and helped organize a rite of passage for her son and five other preadolescent boys and their families. From these experiences, she developed a strong interest in both personal and community development and how the two are interrelated. Her e-mail address is Viglizzo@parc.xerox.com.

Mark Weiser is head of the Computer Science Laboratory at the Xerox Palo Alto Research Center. He is probably best known for his leadership on ubiquitous computing. Before coming to Xerox PARC, he was a professor of computer science at the University of Maryland. His electronic mail address is weiser@parc.xerox.com.

William Wulf is a professor of computer science at the University of Virginia. Previously he headed the Computer and Information Systems and Engineering Directorate at the National Science Foundation. He also chaired the National Research Council's Computer Science and Telecommunications Board. In 1994, Wulf was awarded the Computing Research Association's Distinguished Service Award. His electronic mail address is Wulf@capa.cs.virginia.edu.

Joanne Yates is senior lecturer and coordinator of management communications at MIT's Sloan School of Management. Her e-mail address is jyates@mit.edu.

Index